FORT WORTH

THE CIVILIZED WEST

By Caleb Pirtle III

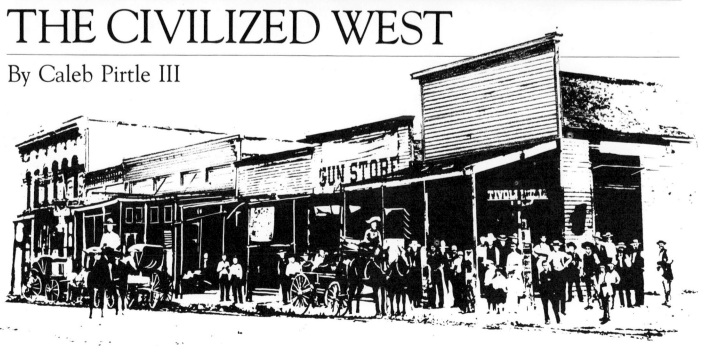

Fort Worth: The Civilized West

a pictorial and entertaining commentary on the growth and development of Fort Worth, Texas

by Caleb Pirtle III

To Linda and Joshua who let me
write this spring instead of
mowing the grass.

Publishers:
Larry P. Silvey
Douglas S. Drown

Editor:
Ellen Sue Blakey

Associate editor:
Peggi Ridgway

Art director:
Rusty Johnson

Assistant art director:
James Michael Martin

Project director:
Douglass Hoyt

Fort Worth: The Civilized West is sponsored by the Fort Worth Chamber of Commerce.

Copyright 1980 by Continental Heritage Press, Inc., P.O. Box 1620, Tulsa, Oklahoma 74101. All rights reserved.
Library of Congress Catalogue Card Number: 80–66340.
ISBN: 0–932986–13–7.

Fort Worth: The Civilized West is one of The American Portrait Series published by Continental Heritage Press. Others include:

Charlotte: Spirit of the New South
Cleveland: Prodigy of the Western Reserve
Columbus: America's Crossroads
Des Moines: Capital City
Detroit: American Urban Renaissance
Houston: A History of a Giant
Los Angeles Two Hundred
The San Antonio Story
San Diego: California's Cornerstone
San Jose: California's First City
The Saint Louis Portrait
The Tulsa Spirit

West Texas visit: Prominent citizens of west Texas visit Fort Worth in 1903 and gather around the Hayne monument, erected in 1893 by the Women's Humane Society. The Texas and Pacific Railroad station is in the background.

3

Prologue

It was nothing but a dusty, erratic river—
cursed, some called it—
that marked the jumping-off place of civilization.
Beyond it, the land stretched under a warm sun,
and those that basked in it were horny-toads,
buffalo and small bands of roaming Indians.
When you got right down to it, it didn't have that much to offer.

And yet, it was free land—
and those in the east and the south and the north
were cramping with the pangs of hunger
for land, for money, for space, for a new life,
for an empire they could carve and call their own.
To them, the land stretched
limitless as the possibilities they dreamed.
And so they came to the Texas prairie.

It wasn't easy in the beginning.
The Indians had first claim.
But that had never really held back the flow of people across the continent.
The sporadic clashes of cultures brought the military,
and the fort they built eventually became a village—Fort Worth.
By 1859, the townspeople were talking of courthouses and elections.
The trappings of civilization had found their way into the southwest.

In some ways, it was a harsh land.
But if it had its drawbacks, it also had an advantage.
For the mild climate was kind to the prairies.
Vast numbers of cattle—leftovers from the herds
of the Spanish conquistadores—lived off the land.
The rangy critters were a ready cash crop.
America's taste for beef had grown,
and up north, in Kansas, the railroads waited to haul
the longhorns to those whose tastes matched their money.

The cattle drives moved north through Fort Worth,
the last supply center before Indian Territory.
Though the drives lasted only a few decades,
Fort Worth was tagged with a title it still retains—Cowtown.

But the drives did something more.
They brought banks and services and businesses.
They spread the city beyond its first reliance on the land.
By the 1880s, there was even a railroad.
The town was actually beginning to be civilized.
That early frontier spirit still existed—
but teas and cake walks, churches, schools and skyscrapers
lived alongside city bootleggers and marshals and Hell's Half Acre.
Then came oil—
Texas-black and thick, gushing out of the land—
at Ranger and Burkburnett and Desdemona.
The oil poured out of the west Texas boomtowns
into Fort Worth where railroads and transportation sat waiting,
where banks and businessmen could make deals
across drinks and across country.
The excitement fit right into the spirit of the frontier town.

The boom did more than turn over a fast buck and a few fortunes.
It gave impetus to the city itself.
Airports sprouted where cattle had grazed, paved streets
where the cowboys had whistled the dogies along.
Fort Worth had become an honest-to-god city,
launched into the twentieth century
but carved from a backbone of hide and horn.

PERSPECTIVE MAP OF.

FORT WORTH, TEX.

1891

Benefactors and Sponsors

The following Fort Worth area firms, organizations and individuals have invested toward the quality production of this historic book and have thereby expressed their commitment to the future of this great city and to the support of the book's principal sponsor, The Fort Worth Chamber of Commerce.

*The AMF Ben Hogan Company
A.R.B., Inc.
Charles F. Adams
Lillie K. Adams
The Advantage Co.
Aeroprocess, Inc.
Alamo Machine Works, Inc.
Alcon Laboratories, Inc.
Allied Auto Stores
Allied-Binyon-O'Keefe Moving & Storage, Inc.
Allied Iron Works, Inc.
*American Airlines, Inc.
American Flight Center Inc.
*American Manufacturing Company
American National Mortgage Company, Inc.
*American Quasar Petroleum Co.
Americana Hotel/Tandy Center
Amsco Steel Co.
John A. Andrews
Appraisal Services, Inc.
Atco Rubber Products, Inc.

Babich & Associates, Inc.
*Bank of Fort Worth
*Bell Helicopter Textron
Blackburn Electric Co., Inc.
Boise Cascade Corp.
Borden's Florist Inc.
*Gordon Boswell Flowers
A. Brandt Company, Inc.
Brants Realtors, Inc.
Buffalo Sound Studios
Thos. S. Byrne, Inc.
W. W. Cannon Co., Inc.
*Cantey, Hanger, Gooch, Munn & Collins
Carter Foundation Production Company
Capitol County Mutual Fire Insurance Company
*Central Bank & Trust
*Champlin Petroleum Company
City of Fort Worth
Clampitt Paper Company
Clark Nowlin Company
Clarklift of Ft. Worth Inc.
Mr. & Mrs. Heywood C. Clemons

Colonial-Jetton's, Inc.
*Color Tile, Inc.
Comcast Music Network, Inc.
Community Public Service Company
Container Corporation of America
*Continental National Bank
Cordy Tire and Auto Service
Corpening Enterprises
Cozart Nurse Placement Service, Inc.
Crouch Supply Co., Inc.
Cummins Supply Company
Cushman & Wakefield of Texas, Inc.
Daniel Drug, Inc.
Davidson-Kernan Corporation
Day Realty of Texas, Inc.
Mr. & Mrs. John Henry Dean, Jr.
Deep Flex Plastic Molds, Inc.
Deloitte Haskins & Sells
Dietz Opticians
Dike Company

*Dillard's Department Stores, Inc.
Doogs & Co.
The Drummond Company, Realtors
Dun & Bradstreet
*The Dunlap Company
Electronic Data Systems Corporation
*Equitable General Insurance Group
*Ernst & Whinney
Essner Metal Works, Inc.
Farris Cash Register Sales, Inc.
Fasteners Et Al, Inc.
First Land Title Company
*The First National Bank of Fort Worth
*Fort Worth & Denver Railway
Fort Worth Bank and Trust
Fort Worth Lawn Sprinkler Co., Inc.
*The Fort Worth National Bank
*Fort Worth Star-Telegram
Ft. Worth Stock Yards
Fort Worth Truck Center Inc.
Foster Financial Corporation
*Freese & Nichols, Inc.

6

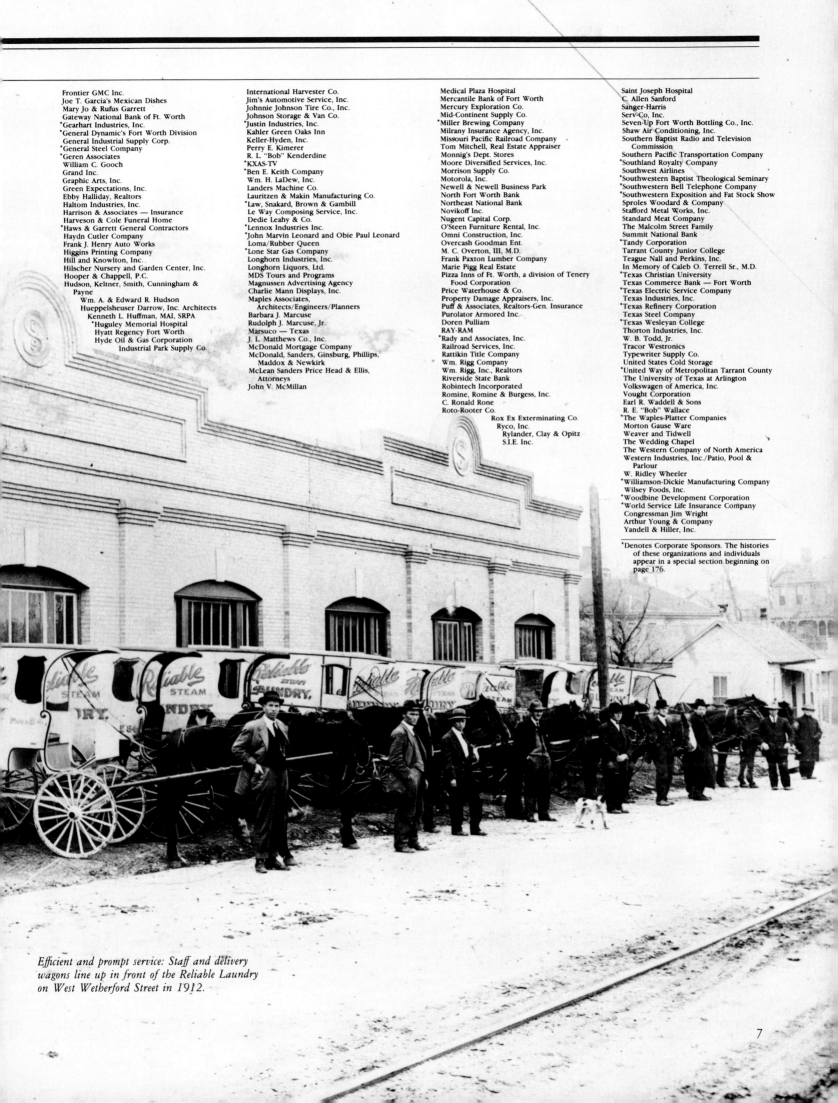

Frontier GMC Inc.
Joe T. Garcia's Mexican Dishes
Mary Jo & Rufus Garrett
Gateway National Bank of Ft. Worth
*Gearhart Industries, Inc.
*General Dynamic's Fort Worth Division
General Industrial Supply Corp.
*General Steel Company
*Geren Associates
William C. Gooch
Grand Inc.
Graphic Arts, Inc.
Green Expectations, Inc.
Ebby Halliday, Realtors
Haltom Industries, Inc.
Harrison & Associates — Insurance
Harveson & Cole Funeral Home
*Haws & Garrett General Contractors
Haydn Cutler Company
Frank J. Henry Auto Works
Higgins Printing Company
Hill and Knowlton, Inc.
Hilscher Nursery and Garden Center, Inc.
Hooper & Chappell, P.C.
Hudson, Keltner, Smith, Cunningham &
Payne
Wm. A. & Edward R. Hudson
Hueppelsheuser Darrow, Inc. Architects
Kenneth L. Huffman, MAI, SRPA
*Huguley Memorial Hospital
Hyatt Regency Fort Worth
Hyde Oil & Gas Corporation
Industrial Park Supply Co.

International Harvester Co.
Jim's Automotive Service, Inc.
Johnnie Johnson Tire Co., Inc.
Johnson Storage & Van Co.
*Justin Industries, Inc.
Kahler Green Oaks Inn
Keller-Hyden, Inc.
Perry E. Kimerer
R. L. "Bob" Kenderdine
*KXAS-TV
*Ben E. Keith Company
Wm. H. LaDew, Inc.
Landers Machine Co.
Lauritzen & Makin Manufacturing Co.
*Law, Snakard, Brown & Gambill
Le Way Composing Service, Inc.
Dedie Leahy & Co.
*Lennox Industries Inc.
*John Marvin Leonard and Obie Paul Leonard
Loma/Rubber Queen
*Lone Star Gas Company
Longhorn Industries, Inc.
Longhorn Liquors, Ltd.
MDS Tours and Programs
Magnussen Advertising Agency
Charlie Mann Displays, Inc.
Maples Associates,
Architects/Engineers/Planners
Barbara J. Marcuse
Rudolph J. Marcuse, Jr.
Marsuco — Texas
J. L. Matthews Co., Inc.
McDonald Mortgage Company
McDonald, Sanders, Ginsburg, Phillips,
Maddox & Newkirk
McLean Sanders Price Head & Ellis,
Attorneys
John V. McMillan

Medical Plaza Hospital
Mercantile Bank of Fort Worth
Mercury Exploration Co.
Mid-Continent Supply Co.
*Miller Brewing Company
Milrany Insurance Agency, Inc.
Missouri Pacific Railroad Company
Tom Mitchell, Real Estate Appraiser
Monnig's Dept. Stores
Moore Diversified Services, Inc.
Morrison Supply Co.
Motorola, Inc.
Newell & Newell Business Park
North Fort Worth Bank
Northeast National Bank
Novikoff Inc.
Nugent Capital Corp.
O'Steen Furniture Rental, Inc.
Omni Construction, Inc.
Overcash Goodman Ent.
M. C. Overton, III, M.D.
Frank Paxton Lumber Company
Marie Pigg Real Estate
Pizza Inns of Ft. Worth, a division of Tenery
Food Corporation
Price Waterhouse & Co.
Property Damage Appraisers, Inc.
Puff & Associates, Realtors-Gen. Insurance
Purolator Armored Inc.
Doren Pulliam
RAY-RAM
*Rady and Associates, Inc.
Railroad Services, Inc.
Rattikin Title Company
Wm. Rigg Company
Wm. Rigg, Inc., Realtors
Riverside State Bank
Robintech Incorporated
Romine, Romine & Burgess, Inc.
C. Ronald Rone
Roto-Rooter Co.
Rox Ex Exterminating Co.
Ryco, Inc.
Rylander, Clay & Opitz
S.I.E. Inc.

Saint Joseph Hospital
C. Allen Sanford
Sanger-Harris
Serv-Co, Inc.
Seven-Up Fort Worth Bottling Co., Inc.
Shaw Air Conditioning, Inc.
Southern Baptist Radio and Television
Commission
Southern Pacific Transportation Company
*Southland Royalty Company
Southwest Airlines
*Southwestern Baptist Theological Seminary
*Southwestern Bell Telephone Company
*Southwestern Exposition and Fat Stock Show
Sproles Woodard & Company
Stafford Metal Works, Inc.
Standard Meat Company
The Malcolm Street Family
Summit National Bank
*Tandy Corporation
Tarrant County Junior College
Teague Nall and Perkins, Inc.
In Memory of Caleb O. Terrell Sr., M.D.
*Texas Christian University
Texas Commerce Bank — Fort Worth
*Texas Electric Service Company
Texas Industries, Inc.
*Texas Refinery Corporation
Texas Steel Company
*Texas Wesleyan College
Thorton Industries, Inc.
W. B. Todd, Jr.
Tracor Westronics
Typewriter Supply Co.
United States Cold Storage
*United Way of Metropolitan Tarrant County
The University of Texas at Arlington
Volkswagen of America, Inc.
Vought Corporation
Earl R. Waddell & Sons
R. E. "Bob" Wallace
*The Waples-Platter Companies
Morton Gause Ware
Weaver and Tidwell
The Wedding Chapel
The Western Company of North America
Western Industries, Inc./Patio, Pool &
Parlour
W. Ridley Wheeler
*Williamson-Dickie Manufacturing Company
Wilsey Foods, Inc.
*Woodbine Development Corporation
*World Service Life Insurance Company
Congressman Jim Wright
Arthur Young & Company
Yandell & Hiller, Inc.

*Denotes Corporate Sponsors. The histories
of these organizations and individuals
appear in a special section beginning on
page 176.

*Efficient and prompt service: Staff and delivery
wagons line up in front of the Reliable Laundry
on West Wetherford Street in 1912.*

7

Contents

*Fort Worth skyline, 1980, from Oakwood
cemetery.*

Chapter 1

The taming of an untamed land

Comanche Indian group: Their tribe caused strife with the white settlers on the plains of Texas.

The river with no name never quite knew what to do with the land that sprawled away from its minnows and mud, whether to punish it or baptize it. So the river did a little of both, depending entirely on its mood, the particular curse of the season and how hard the last rainfall had been, if there had been any rain at all.

The river damned the land—and nourished it.

The river was cantankerous, a tyrant whose angry floodwaters never knew their own strength or when they might strike out next. Yet, during the thirsty days of summer, it could be docile, even indolent, hardly moving and in no hurry to ever leave those oak thickets that crowded down around its troubled shoreline. It had no temper at all.

The river with no name tempted. It taught and its lessons were hard. It always beckoned, praised for the life it gave, blasphemed for the life it took away. The land, for better or for worse, found itself relying on a waterway it could never trust. It had no choice.

The river was boss.

It clawed its way for 600 hard-rock miles across the backbone of Texas, sometimes clear and sparkling, sometimes thick with the color and texture of mud and blood, until it emptied, at last, into the Gulf of Mexico.

And its banks would be scarred by great herds of buffalo, the solitary footsteps of man, wagon wheels searching for a road west and making one, the wooden stakes of villages that became the settlements that, in time, became the rawhide and log-notched foundation for cities.

One, on a high bluff overlooking the twin forks of the river with no name, would be called Fort Worth.

Its eastern shoulder was the Grand Prairie, flat and rich and ideal for anyone who might want to plant his roots in an unknown land with a plow—and oxen strong enough to pull it. Its western arm reached past the broad expanse of Cross Timbers, on toward the breaks, the rolling caliche hills, the burden of mesquite trees and creek beds that promised nothing and, too often, kept its promise.

The man who journeyed first to drink from the river-with-no-name left behind neither tradition nor identity nor even his bones.

He came stalking out of the final days of the Pleistocene epoch, walking upright and carrying primitive tools for survival, the conqueror who explored new lands simply because he was hungry. He had no desire to own the ground beneath him. He did not need it. As far as he was concerned, the whole world—or at least as far as he could see—belonged to him anyway. Its only boundaries were hunger and thirst.

He left his footprints on the prairie for a time, while closely pursuing those of the elephant and mastodon and camel. He would leave but not before his belly was full. That was perhaps the only law, the only commitment, his instincts fully understood.

His traces are few.

His legacy is nothing more than those fourteen hearths uncovered in the floor of a barrow pit—and the mystery of the three stone heads, roughly carved, discovered in the ancient gravels of the river with no name. They have little to tell, and their secrets are safe within them.

In the hearths, (found during the excavation for the Garza-Little Elm Dam in Denton County) were shells, hackberry seeds and the scorched remains of extinct Pleistocene animals, along with one Clovis-fluted point used to hunt them. Radiocarbon tests say they've all been around, for at least, 37,000 years, probably much longer.

The stone heads are a puzzle with most of the pieces missing. Were they carved in the honor and image of men or animals or gods? No one can be sure. It is only known that the oblong heads—each weighing from 60 to 135 pounds—lay for centuries amidst the Pleistocene fossils of elephants, mastodons, horses, camels and ground sloths, all vanished from the earth that holds their

The man who journeyed first to drink from the river-with-no-name left behind neither tradition nor identity nor even his bones.

Traces of an early man: Earliest residents date to the Pleistocene era. The Clovis-fluted point was used in the region for hunting. The projectile point is characterized by fluting along the mid-line, parallel to slightly convex sides and a concave base. The point was named for the archaeological dig near Clovis, New Mexico, where it was first categorized.

scattered bones, gone from the river that quenched their thirst.

For generations the prairie was a dying ground. Most blamed the river with no name.

The buffalo came for water. The Indian, the savage hunter, was never very far behind. As far as the Indian was concerned, the buffalo was a gift from the gods themselves, sent to the tall grass of the prairie solely for the preservation of the tribal way of life.

From the great shaggy-necked bison came food—bones and horns for weapons, tools, glue and even cosmetics—and a tough hide that could be worn for clothes, stretched for shelter and woven for ropes.

Buffalo died beside the river.

But old frontiersmen swore they were not slaughtered until the white hunters brought their repeating rifles and indulged themselves in a sport that was as easy as shooting fish in a rain barrel and just about as dangerous.

Indians built their camps and villages beside the river with no name, harvesting crops from the grand eastern prairie and hunting the dry arroyos, the endless western sweep of the plains, always aware that, sooner or later, the buffalo, the nomadic symbol of survival, would be returning to the water that flowed at their feet.

They waited beside the place of two forks.

They never waited long.

In 1542, the buffalo did not come alone. A village of Caddo Indians watched as a ragged remnant of Hernando de Soto's expedition, led by Moscoso de Alvarado, splashed into the unpredictable river, promptly chalking up another major discovery for Spain. They ignored altogether that the Caddos were already feeling very much at home when the Spanish ponies stumbled into the water. The Indians did not count.

The Indians never counted, not until they grew tired of losing the land that nobody owned to settlers who were dead set on claiming it. Then they were feared but never respected. And the river with no name washed over a trail of toil and trouble soaked with greed and blood and more determination than good sense. The land would never be quite so peaceful again.

Too many wanted it.

The land would hold their cabins, hear their prayers, soak their sweat and be their graves.

Frontiersman fought the Indian for the right to live beside the place of two forks. Soldiers added firepower behind the protection of a camp called Worth. Farmers battled the cattlemen. Cities feuded, politicians squared off against each other with words and weapons, gunmen stalked the shadows, hell-raisers found a half acre all their own, and preachers dueled the devil in his own den of iniquity.

It all began because once there was a river.

And the Spanish, at last, gave it a name.

In 1690 Alfonso de Leon was making his way diligently toward east Texas for the righteous duty of founding a Spanish mission. He rode to the mud-spackled banks of the river and—perhaps feeling the religious weight of his errand—christened it on his map as "Rio de la Santisima Trinidad"—the sacred Trinity.

A historian in the late nineteenth-century, Judge C.C. Cummings, felt called upon to interpret Alfonso's reasoning behind his choice of names. He wrote: "Fort Worth sits on the high bluff at the junction of the first two prongs of the Trinity River, known as the Clear Fork and the West Fork of the Trinity River. The third prong, the Elm Fork, flows thirty miles below, just above the city of Dallas. These make the trine of the Trinity. . . . The Spaniards saw the clear pure waters of the Clear Fork and idealized it as the spirit, the red waters of the West Fork the impurities, representing the soul; thus they thought that the river is a symbol of the body, soul, and spirit."

Perhaps so.

But when Father Juan Augustín de Morfi came along almost a century later, he scribbled in his diary that the Rio de la Santisima Trinidad "is subject to

Living on the land: The Indian's tribal way of life centered around plentiful game, such as wild turkey, buffalo and antelope.

Many Spanish missions: When a ragged remnant of Hernando de Soto's expedition splashed into an unpredictable Texas river, they chalked up another discovery for Spain. This river was later a campsite for Spanish explorers sent by King Charles (above) to search for gold. In 1690, the Spanish led by Alfonso de Leon, who was diligently headed for east Texas to found a Spanish mission, gave the river a name—"Rio la Santisima Trinidad."

terrible floods in the rainy season, or when the snow melts."

It would forever be called Trinity.

It would never really be considered sacred again.

The explorers found what the Indians already knew. The land was rich, though untamed and virtually untapped. Wild flax, rye and hemp spread across the fields, edging back into the shelter of the woodlands where vines hung in season thick and heavy with grapes, where the thickets themselves offered protection, a hiding place for both beast and man.

The beast got there first.

Wild chickens and turkeys ran rampant. At times, the sky could be dark with the arrowhead flight of geese. Partridges scampered in the tightly-woven grasses. Great herds of deer and antelope dotted the prairie.

But the buffalo—massive and clumsy and slow-footed—was king. He was food. He was life. He was the easy victim. On the great plains, herds were seen that covered 50 square miles, numbering as many as 12 million animals. The buffalo, it seemed, would last forever. No one need ever to worry about hunger.

No one did.

Men merely came west, to the banks of the Trinity, expecting to live off whatever the land and its beasts could offer them. They were as stubborn as they were foolish.

By 1756, a Spanish mission—Nuestra Senora de la Luz—and the presidio San Augustin had been nailed down near the mouth of the river, bringing faith and Christianity to Indians while making sure French traders had no luck trespassing on Spain's untrodden soil.

Almost two decades later, a Spanish cattle baron, Ybaro, established a second settlement on the Trinity. He proclaimed it Nuestra Senora del Pilar de Bucareli in honor of the viceroy of New Spain. He should have saved himself the trouble.

Indian raids ripped the village apart. Floods took what was left, which was not much. The cursed Trinity had made it a habit of beating down anyone who tried to hitch his hopes to its restless water. But still men came, still they hoped.

Raw, fertile land was awaiting them.

So were the Indians.

Comanches

Lipanes.

Plains people: Indian tribes living on the Texas plains included the Comanches and the Lipen Apaches.

A great wall of woods—the Cross Timbers—cut directly past the western shores of the Trinity and headed north toward the Red River. It was a tangled, knotted landmark of hardwood and bramblebush that rose up unexpectedly from the prairie. This series of forests is a curiosity, so remarkably straight in appearance that some swear it is a work of art, fashioned by that unknown race of men who built the mounds and fortifications of the Mississippi Valley, then vanished without a trace. One old timer swore he was told that the Cross Timbers did not exist until after the flight of the pigeons. It was a day the sky was blotted out by huge flocks of passenger pigeons, moving across a broad expanse that held no trees in its soil. The droppings of the birds contained seeds. The seeds took root and from them came the oak, elm, hickory and holly wall of Cross Timbers.

They provided shelter upon a prairie that had little. They became the one eye-catching landmark for Indians and hunters alike. And—according to Colonel Randolph B. Marcy who helped calm (if not tame) the country—Cross Timbers for years roughly marked the dividing line that separated civilized man from the savage.

For a time, the entire span of North Central Texas was ruled by the empire of the Wichita Confederacy. They were agricultural and industrious Indians, content to hunt while their women harvested maize, watermelons, beans and pumpkins; made tents and clothes of buffalo hides and hauled back saline chunks from the salt flats to preserve their deer meat. The Wichita men were well dressed—even dignified—carrying leather shields and wearing helmets adorned with buffalo horns and tails, all dyed with resplendent colors. And they made sure they always had a good supply of tallow, lard and hides (bear, deer and buffalo) on hand when the white traders came riding by.

The traders were not much of a threat.

The Comanches were.

They took what they wanted and what they wanted most were horses. Colonel Dodge, a veteran of the plains wars, once noted about the Indians:

"All are such magnificent thieves, it is difficult to decide which of the plains tribes deserves the palm for stealing. The Indians themselves give it to the Comanches, whose designation in sign language of the plains is a forward, wriggling motion of the forefinger, signifying a snake, and indicating the silent stealth of that tribe. This is true of the Comanches, who for crawling into a camp, cutting hobbles and lariat ropes, and getting off with animals undiscovered, are unsurpassed and unsurpassable. . . . I have known a Comanche to crawl into a bivouac where a dozen men were sleeping, each with his horse tied to his wrist by the lariat, cut a rope within six feet of a sleeper's person, and get off with the horse without waking a soul."

The horse changed the Comanche's way of life, gave him speed and mobility and the power to strike quickly, then be gone just as quickly. The tribe no longer had to chase down buffalo herds on foot, living off the meat of stragglers they could run down in desperation. The horse gave them strength and dignity. The buffalo—and almost every other living creature—was now at the tribe's mercy. The mustang—tough and swift and durable—and the Comanche formed the perfect union to govern the prairies. As the frontiersmen pointed out: "A white man will ride the mustang until he is played out. A Mexican will take him and ride him another day until he thinks he is played out. A Comanche will mount him, and ride him to where he is going."

The Comanche could not be trusted. Even the Wichita did not particularly like him, but the Wichita needed him—the tribal confederacy had gone to war and was ready to depend on any ally it could get, even unscrupulous horse thieves.

By 1837, the Wichita tribes—the Keechi, Tawakoni, Waco and Pawnee—had looked around and witnessed too many cabins being hammered down upon their hunting lands, too many wagon wheel ruts scarring the prairie. They struck back with anger and with vengeance. After all, the settlements had all sorts of good supplies that seemed to be theirs for the taking.

That year the Standing Committee on Indian Affairs reported that the Indians

Táncahues.

Táncahues: *peuplade misérable des côtes du Texas.*

Cados.

Cados ou Caddoquis: *Indiens des environs de Nacogdoches.*

Changing the frontier: Tonkawas (above) and Caddos (below) threatened the white man's attempts to remold the Texas frontier. General William Jenkins Worth directed that a line of forts to protect white settlers be established just west of San Antonio, Austin, Waco Village and Dallas.

of the prairie "hunt altogether for a living, travel altogether on horseback armed mostly with the Bow and Lance, what fire arms they have are smooth bores or traders guns of little value and seldom used. They run from place to place, move with great celerity, and are but little dependent on civilized man for necessary articles. They are now at war with this Republick [sic]. Their number is about 500 warriors despicable soldiers but formidable rogues, and for 5 years past have greatly annoyed our frontier during which time they have occasionally found opportunities to commit most horrible outrages and to carry off children and females as prisoners. The latter of whom your Committee are justified in saying are forced to subserve to purpouses [sic] that any beings other than fiends would blush to think of. These Indians reside mostly on the Head waters of the Trinity. . . ." These Wichita did cause trouble. But it was the Comanches—the Panatekas or Honey-Eaters—who caused alarm. They were 8,000 strong, and the mustang had changed them from a poor, weak bunch of scavengers to a mighty military force, one with which to be reckoned.

The Comanche dress was drab, but war made the braves dashing, colorful and deadly. Warriors dabbed red paint on their faces and wore headdresses of buffalo horns or deer antlers. Long lances also bore splashes of red, and their tanned buffalo hide shields carried bright, even gaudy, colors, as well as a circle of feathers that fluttered wildly in the wind to ruin an enemy's aim. At times, they tied red ribbons in their horses' tails and bedecked themselves with the spoils from a past raid. John Jenkins, at the Battle of Plum Creek in 1840, watched one warrior who wore "a stovepipe hat" and another who had dressed himself royally in a "fine pigeon-tailed cloth coat, buttoned up behind."

They would never give up their land until the buffalo were gone. But the buffalo were passing.

The Comanche's life blood, too, would soak into the sun-blistered earth along the Trinity before he ran. The Plains Indian had a strange creed for battle—retreat or fight but die before falling into an enemy's hands. Noah Smithwick, an Indian fighter, wrote that he never knew a warrior to submit to capture. "They fought to the death," he said. And twice, Smithwick would watch as a wounded brave would lie "flat on his back and fight till dead."

Such was the threat facing the settler who drove his wagons across the Trinity River and left behind the long, weary tracks for civilization to follow. Men believed it was a chance worth taking. They believed they were as stubborn and as tough as the land that dared them to stay. They feared the Indian, but they came anyway. The strong held onto their farms and kept them or were buried in them. The weak never bothered to come. It was just as well. The land had no use for them. The survivors inherited it all.

Many—like Louis and Cristena Finger—made the long journey to the grand prairie region near the Trinity after reading newspaper advertisments offering free land in Texas to any and all who would establish a headright and cultivate the property.

Those same newspapers carried stories of Indian atrocities. But Louis Finger, like most, was too eager to get his hands on free land to worry much about being scalped. After all, by 1845 Texas was a state and could not be too dangerous and uncivilized.

That kind of thinking got a lot of men killed.

Louis and Cristena Finger, joining 40 other families, left the home fires of Indiana and headed for Texas, hauling their hopes, dreams and furniture in a horse-drawn wagon. Six weeks later, Finger had reached Johnson's Station and staked his 640 acres. The section was his as long as he built a shelter, tilled the land and raised enough crops and livestock to support his family.

A year later, Louis Finger was on the frontier fighting Indians. It was sometimes difficult to be a farmer during the 1840s in Texas. Cristena had it all to herself. She grabbed an axe and cut down trees, then split the wood. She looked after four children and took in washing, earning enough money to hire someone to do the heavy plowing. But Cristena nailed the fence herself—

Existence on the Texas frontier was at best precarious for those who chose to travel or settle there.

putting up enough posts and wire to keep in the hogs and cattle.

Such were the survivors. Sturdy stock. No one left because there was never time to quit.

Not far down the road there lived and preached the good Reverend John Allen Freeman. He had trekked to the twin forks of the Trinity in 1844, coming because the entire congregation of his small Baptist Church in Missouri had up and voted to head for Texas. In time, he and a dozen of his faithful members established the Lonesome Dove Baptist Church. It was aptly named. It was lonely indeed, being known for years as the only Baptist Church between Tarrant County and the Pacific Ocean. In April of 1850, Reverend Freeman was asked by a major to hold Sunday services within a new fort. It was the first sermon ever heard in Fort Worth.

When George (Press) Farmer and his wife arrived on the Grand Prairie, they found—Jane Farmer later recalled—"no sign of life anywhere and nature was undisturbed." It was a hard land but a good land. "At the time we settled here, game of all kinds and honey and wild grapes were plentiful. Grapes, however, were the only fruit we had, and there were no vegetables whatever. Ten years elapsed before I had a mess of Irish potatoes. Groceries and provisions of all kinds had to be hauled from Houston, and sometimes during the rainy season it took two or three months to make the trip."

The Farmers buit a home.

The Indians burned it down.

The northern frontier of Texas (as Sam Houston said) was bleeding "at every pore with Indian depredations and treachery." Its population was also growing. As early as 1840, Captain Jonathan Bird put together a company of Rangers to stand guard along the Trinity. He established a military post to encourage settlers looking for homesteads and discourage the Comanches who were hell bent on discouraging any kind of settlement.

The Rangers rode about 21 miles south of the Clear and West Fork junction of the river, then traded their rifles for axes and chopped enough logs to construct Bird's Fort on the edge of a lake. Beyond the clearing, they were shielded by a growing wall of oaks. The fortress was quite safe.

The frontier was not. Families looking for land came all right, just as the Rangers knew they would. They cast their lot beside the river that counted

Scattered law and struggling peoples: Before statehood in 1845, the northern plains were left to the defense of those who struggled to build and to the mercy of those who wanted them out. There were too few Texas Rangers to provide adequate control.

But too often the Indian attacks came after the Rangers had left or before they got to where the trouble was brewing.

on Bird's Fort for refuge and protection during times of calamity, times as certain as the sunrise. The Indians were not far behind. The prairie was just too immense, the Ranger company far too small, for the Comanches to be whipped on their own chosen land. Besides, the Comanches were not spreading death and havoc alone.

As Mark R. Roberts, one captain of the Rangers, reported:

"In the month of Feby there was seven persons murdered by the Indians near Journeys Camp and the indians made their retreat across Red River we then believed them to be Caddo or Kickapoo, but lately we have been visited by a band of Cherokee Indians from Arkansas which stole 20 head of horses they were pursued to the nation and the horses found, and also one of the horses of the murdered men in February last seen amongst them which is a convincing proof that the murder was done by the same indians. I was ranging on the waters of the Trinity when the murders were committed. . . ."

The Rangers roamed far and wide. But too often the Indian attacks came after the Rangers had left or before they got to where the trouble was brewing.

The impoverished Republic, since 1836, had few keepers of the peace. Most of them patrolled the southern border, still smouldering from the War of Independence with Mexico. Those northern plains—until after statehood in 1845—were pretty much left to the defense of those who took homes there and to the mercy of those who wanted them out.

Sam Houston had tried to bring peace to the Grand Prairie. He knew and understood the Indian, and he wrote to the chiefs of the Border Tribes: "My Friends: The path between us has been red, and the blood of our people remains on the ground. Trouble has been upon us. . . . I learn that our red friends want peace; and our hand is now white, and shall not be stained with blood. Let our red brothers say this, and we will smoke the pipe of peace.. . . Let the tomahawk be buried. . . ." His commission delivered the letter and rode home, confident that war and bloodshed would no longer taint the land around them.

Perhaps the Indian had grown tired of battle, of killing and being killed. But it was not to be.

On a May 24 mid-morning in 1841, General Edward H. Tarrant had done his best to take all the glory out of dying for the Indian braves. He waited beside the mud of Village Creek while Henry Stout and the six scouts told him of the sprawling Indian camp that lay three miles beyond the thickets.

Their search was at an end. Quietly, patiently, Tarrant moved his 69 militia men into the thickets only 400 yards from the warriors who would have no warning that death was upon them. The general's voice was muffled as he calmly told his troops: "There is great confusion ahead. Never will all of us meet again on this earth. I shall expect every man to fill his place and do his duty. Are you ready?"

It was an unnecessary question.

Tarrant glanced back toward the thickets. The memory of burning cabins, of fallen men and women, lay heavy on his mind. Revenge was at hand. The general watched as the men threw aside their blankets and packs then remounted.

The time had come. Tarrant turned to his bugler. His words were grim but steady: "Sound Charge." The thicket echoed with wild yells and gunfire. The Fourth Brigade of the Texas Militia stormed down upon the village, thundering across those 400 yards with speed and rage. Bullets ripped through the camp. Warriors died in their single moment of surprise. Some tried to fight. Others ran. The village fell swiftly, lying in a curious silence as the clamor of battle marched madly down the creek bank. A second village was captured, then a third, with huts stretching for a mile and a half along a shoreline now smudged with the agony of dying.

Tarrant regrouped his men, their faces streaked with sweat and dust and

The earliest businessmen: Even as peace was attempted on the plains, traders—only intent on out-trading the Indians—moved in. Trader Edward Terrell, one of the first white men to camp on land that is now Fort Worth, barely escaped death at the hands of Comanches.

gunpowder. They drank from the creek and filled their empty bellies with dried buffalo meat found in the abandoned huts. Only ten were wounded. None would die until Stout and John B. Denton turned their backs on caution and chased the fleeing warriors, riding fast into an ambush from which Denton would not return. Those Indians who escaped did so because Tarrant had no desire to be burdened down with prisoners.

The militia left the carnage of Village Creek, carrying with them the spoils of battle—six cattle, 37 horses, 300 pounds of lead, 30 pounds of powder, 20 brass kettles, 21 axes, 73 buffalo robes, fifteen guns and three swords and shovels.

Houston hoped that Tarrant's swift victory would crush the Indian threat on the prairie. He was heartened when tribal delegates told him, "We are willing to make a line with you, beyond which our people will not hunt. Then in red man's land beyond the treaty line unmolested by white men, the hunter can kill the buffalo and the squaws can make corn."

A treaty was to be agreed upon at Bird's Fort. The Delaware, Chickasaw, Waco, Tiwocano, Keechi, Caddo, Anadah-kah, Ionie, Biloxi and Cherokee tribes were all on hand for the signing. As Ke-chi-ka-roqua, the Tawakoni Chief, said, "I am strong for making a firm peace. War is like an arrow sticking in the side; I have plucked it out and now I am for peace. Such are my thoughts and they are like Houston's. I want to make a big white path so that no man can be lost. . . . when we make a white path we do not want it to get bloody, yet by stealing and killing it will be so."

It was. Peace was at hand inside Bird's Fort.

But the Comanches did not come. They were not yet ready to pluck out that arrow of war. They had watched surveyors and locators (sent out by the land office of the Texas Republic) mark trees far beyond the settlements of the Brazos and Trinity valleys. And they had listened intently as Mexican agents told them, "The buffalo and deer are the Indian's cattle, the turkey and geese his poultry. When white men come to the prairie, they not only will take the Indian's cattle and poultry, but also will drive him from his prairie hunting ground."

The Comanches saw that it was so. They struck back with a frenzy. The treaty was soon ignored by white man and Indian alike, trounced in the dust of violence. For a time the hope of peace was shattered. Men such as Edward Terrell and William Lusk shouldered the consequences.

Terrell and Lusk had become intoxicated by the get-rich-in-a-hurry prospect of out-trading the Indians. So they loaded down a couple of burros and ambled out of Fort Smith, Arkansas, striking out for those promising grasslands that lay beyond the Red River. A buffalo stampede hurried them along; the banks of the Trinity reached out and stopped them. Terrell remembered: "In those days, this country was infested with Indians and herds of buffalo were all around us. There were more panthers in these parts than I have ever seen before or since; antelopes without number, wild turkeys in every tree—in fact, in those days this was God's own country."

Along the river, the traders found the well-worn tracks of mankind heading west. That was all right. They saw signs of Comanches, and that was better. That was what they were looking for. Terrell and Lusk were ready to start trading.

What they did not know was that hanging on to their lives would be the best deal they made.

It was not easy.

Beside a cold spring, beneath a grove of trees on the West Fork of the Trinity, Terrell and Lusk became the first known civilians to camp upon the exact spot that one day would be Fort Worth.

They did not tarry long. They should have. On the south bank of the river, the two Arkansas traders stumbled across a small Comanche camp. They hauled their trinkets out of the packsaddles and quickly dazzled the women and old men who sat around tanning buffalo hides. But Terrell and Lusk made their mistake by not leaving before the chief and his warriors returned from a hunt.

They were striken with greed.

The chief was not dazzled. He promptly ordered the traders placed in custody, and refused to let them out of his sight. At last Terrell saw his chance to escape, and he hit the prairie running, scrambling back to the shelter of Bird's Fort. The Rangers wasted no time. They mounted up, rode down hard on the scattered Comanche tepees and freed Lusk from the grasp of the suspicious chieftain.

Terrell, just before his death in 1905, recalled: "We then lost no time in leaving this section, and I did not return until 1849, when the troops were stationed here. . . . It was either a case of leaving Tarrant County—or what is now Tarrant County—or losing our scalps, and when a man lost his hair in those days he generally lost something else."

It would take troops—many of them—to ultimately bring some fashion of order to the Trinity and that northern piece of Texas, badly scarred by the wounds of the long lance. The vanguard was led by Brevet Major Ripley A. Arnold, U.S.A. He had fought under the command of William Jenkins Worth and distinguished himself at the battles of both Monterrey and Buena Vista when Mexico again went to war against an old foe that had achieved statehood—Texas.

And now he rode north through Texas, carrying General Worth's orders in his pocket—orders that would forever change the face and the future of the Trinity. They read: "Company F and I, 2nd Dragoons . . . will be concentrated as soon as practicable and establish a military post at a point near Towash Village on the Brazos River." Worth had decided to establish a whole series of forts in the state, stretching from San Antonio to Dallas. Arnold would build them.

He quickly laid the foundation for Fort Graham at Towash just west of Waco Village, then turned his men toward the Trinity. The column of 41 tired, blue-jacketed men halted finally at Johnson's Station on a hot June day in 1849. Colonel Middleton Tate Johnson, commander of the Mounted Texas Volunteers, was waiting for them, along with a couple of tobacco-chewing Texas Rangers who knew the land as well as an old friend, who distrusted it as though that old friend had betrayed them.

Two years earlier the colonel had built a home and a mill beside the Ranger headquarters. He was delighted to see the prospects of reinforcements riding his way.

Johnson met Arnold and wasted no words. "Major," he said, "we have been in need of you. Our homes have been burned; our women and children kidnapped and held for ransom; and our livestock stolen by the Indians from reservations north of the Red River. We have sent protest upon protest to Governor George T. Wood but to no avail. Thank heaven the President has heard and answered our plea."

It was Johnson and the Rangers who escorted Major Arnold and his troops through the eastern Cross Timbers and into the Trinity River Valley. Simon Farrar, one of the Rangers, later wrote: "We passed through and across timbers, crossing the different creeks as best we could, through a wild, beautiful country inhabited only by Indians, wild mustang horses, innumerable deer, wolves and wild turkey.

"About three o'clock in the evening we halted in the valley east of where Fort Worth now stands and killed a deer for supper. We could have killed many more but did not wish to be encumbered with them. We passed our first night under Terry Springs . . . later to be known as Cold Springs where we enjoyed ourselves with jokes, etc., indifferent to Indians, wolves, and all the wild enemies of white men."

The next morning, Arnold, Johnson and the Rangers climbed the bluff that overlooked the valley to choose the site for the fort. They decided on a stretch of flat land in a bend of the river, one that offered a plentiful supply of good water. Farrar remembered: "I thought it the most beautiful and grand country that the sun ever shone on and while we were at that place in view of all advantages of a natural point of defense, and our late experience in Monterrey,

It was either a case of leaving Tarrant County—or what is now Tarrant County—or losing our scalps, and when a man lost his hair in those days he generally lost something else.

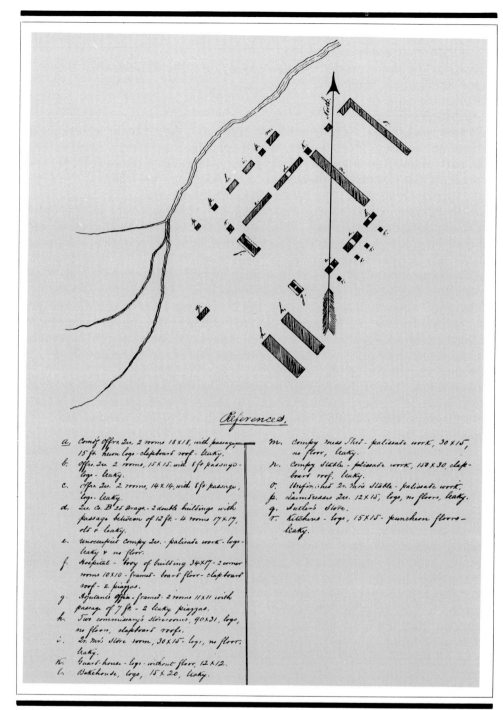

References.

a. Comdg Offrs. 2u. 2 rooms 18×18, with passage, 15 ft. hewn logs - clapboard roof - leaky.

b. Offrs. 2u. 2 rooms, 15×15. with 8 ft passage - logs - leaky.

c. Offrs. 2u. 2 rooms, 14×14, with 8 ft passage, logs - leaky.

d. 2u. Co. B 2d Drags - 2 double buildings with passage between of 12 ft - 4 rooms 17×17, etc + leaky.

e. Unoccupied Compy 2u. - palisade work - logs - leaky + no floor.

f. Hospital - body of building 34×17 - 2 corner rooms 10×10 - framed - board floor - clapboard roof - 2 piazzas.

g. Adjutant's Offce - framed - 2 rooms 11×11 with passage of 7 ft - 2 leaky piazzas.

h. Two commissary's Storerooms, 90×31, logs, no floor, clapboard roof.

i. 2r. Mr's Store room, 30×15 - logs, no floor, leaky.

k. Guard-house - logs - without floor, 12×12.

l. Bakehouse, logs, 15×20, leaky.

m. Compy mess Shed - palisade work, 30×15, no floor, leaky.

n. Compy Stable - palisade work, 150×30, clapboard roof, leaky.

o. Unfinished 2r. Mr's Stable - palisade work.

p. Laundresses 2u. 12×15, logs, no floors, leaky.

q. Sutler's Store.

r. Kitchens - logs, 15×15 - puncheon floors - leaky.

A new name: "We there, in honor of that grand old hero, named the point Fort Worth." That was June 1849. Four years later, the flat land at the bend in the river took on the appearance of a military fort.

wherein the strategic action of General Worth had so terribly defeated the Mexicans, we there, in honor of that grand old hero, named the point Fort Worth."

The property already had an owner—Colonel Johnson himself and his partner Archibald Robinson. But Johnson made the government a deal. He gave them the land, taking it back only after the fort had been abandoned.

Major Arnold rode back to Fort Graham where he received word that Worth had died of cholera, never learning of the outpost that bore his name. Arnold left behind half of his command—Company I—and returned to Camp Worth, bringing with him a horse-powered saw mill that would turn the cottonwoods on the river bank into the buildings of the fort.

Arnold faced a lonely, isolated life and he knew it. He even left the message for his mail to be forwarded to Dallas, Dallas County, Texas, "a town about thirty-five miles east of me."

Log buildings were patched together beneath the bluff, all neatly whitewashed. The quadrangle was enclosed by a rope fence that also served as a cattle guard. The officers (as was to be expected) had the finest view of the countryside, looking out across Blue Mound, so named (the soldiers said) because those cold blue northers of winter always seemed to bunch up behind it before blasting out across the prairie.

The order had been issued in San Antonio to fortify Camp Worth with "one mountain howitzer, proper equipment, and well-broken mules."

But what Arnold needed most was men—good ones. When he looked around him, he realized just how risky his position really was. His duty was to protect the frontier. He was not even sure he could protect himself.

On June 15, 1849, the major wrote his commanding officer, General William S. Harney, and explained, "I am building a new post at this place (the extreme northern frontier yet occupied) and my company is so small that I cannot keep up my scouting parties."

He pointed out that a company such as his was authorized three officers and 86 enlisted men. His Company F, however, only had three sergeants, four corporals and 25 privates fit for duty. Major Arnold was the only commissioned officer hanging around the fort. In reality, Arnold's predicament was even worse than it seemed. He needed men, to be sure. But what he wanted were "drilled recruits." The major wrote: "Those assigned me . . . in November last with one exception had not even been drilled in the Carbine Manual or Saber Exercises or at least knew nothing of them."

On the full roster of his men sent to the adjutant general in Washington,

An untimely death: General William Jenkins Worth, who had directed that a fort be placed west of Dallas, died of cholera before he could learn that his name would live forever along the banks of the Trinity.

Texas was well pleased with the protection provided by the small band of untrained, undrilled soldiers.

Arnold listed one of them as nothing more than a "saddler, and always at work at old equipment." Another was written off as "perfectly worthless. Can't trust him with horse or equipment."

Keeping the peace on the frontier was going to be tougher than Brevet Major Arnold had imagined.

He had few men.

He had fewer rations.

So two weeks later, Arnold sat down and wrote the adjutant general again. He was not bashful. "Now permit me to say, that this being a Frontier Post, near sixty miles from any other Post; and a considerable distance from settlements that all entertainment necessarily falls upon the officers of the Post. Many Citizen Gentlemen are traveling through this Country, who cannot always provide themselves with all that they need; and whose gentility and necessities call loudly for our Hospitality. I think that I may safely assert that the Comdt. Officer of this Post will be obliged to entertain more Persons, than the Comdt. Officer of any Atlantic Station."

Arnold had a point. Double rations were immediately granted Camp Worth by the War Department—eight dollars worth.

The good major had his problems, but none took a heavy toll. In late July, the Trinity—forever the menace—flooded and sent the soldiers scrambling for higher ground. And before the long, hot days of summer ended, mosquitoes and an outbreak of malaria chased the troops out of the river bottom and up onto the clear air of the bluff.

Arnold had chosen that particular site for the fort because of its access to water. Now he realized that had been a mistake. The water was deadly when the rains came and unhealthy since it served as a breeding ground for mosquitoes.

The fort had to be moved. Again axes attacked the forests, and horses began dragging felled trees—but this time up a steep, winding trail that led to the crest of the bluff.

By mid-winter, the new outpost—with three sets of officers quarters, an earthen-floor log barracks to house 120 men, a hospital and dispensary, a commissary store, guard house, quartermaster storehouse and stables—had been officially nailed into place.

Major Arnold was satisfied. Lieutenant William H.C. Whiting, an engineer, was appalled. He visited the fort and hastily sent off a critical report, pointing out, "The fort has been laid out on a scale rather contracted—probably as designed but for one company. And the arrangement of the stables I cannot commend: they are much too near the quarters of both officers and men, and, however thorough the police may be, cannot but be offensive in summer." He found that "fever and ague prevailed through the whole year," a sickness blamed on the "heavy growth of trees and underwood" in the valley, and on "the great mass of half-rotted vegetable matter and half-dried mud" left untended on the riverbanks. On the bluff, the outpost exposed the men "all winter to the northers and sleets of the country and in summer to the scorching heat."

It was not ideal. It took a tough, perhaps unordinary, breed of man to survive it all. Whiting may have been critical during his inspection tour, but Texas was well pleased with the protection provided by the small band of untrained, undrilled soldiers.

An editorial in the Marshall *Texas Republican* applauded the work of Major Arnold and his troops:

"We are gratified to learn that the Dragoons stationed between the Brazos and Trinity, under the command of Captain [sic] Arnold, have proven themselves to be fully as efficient as the Rangers that proceeded them. During the period that they have been stationed on the Brazos, the settlers have enjoyed a complete immunity from Indian depredations. . . . These treacherous savages have their haunts in the Wichita Mountains of Arkansas, and have been in the habit of making forays into the settlements between the Trinity and the Brazos. Nothing but the fear

that the Dragoons would carry fire and sword through the villages could have induced them to sue for peace."

Arnold had been known as a fighter. He was tough yet compassionate. And he was decisive. No one misinterpreted his actions. He made sure of it. The Indians learned quickly that Major Arnold was not the kind to back down, and he paid little attention to the odds, especially if they were against him.

He and his men stood within the fort and watched as a mounted band of 300 Comanches and Caddos, led by Chief Towash, attacked a ragged group of Tonkawahs in a live oak grove. Hunger had turned the Indians against each other. A drought had chased the animals away.

The battle was swift. The Tonks fell back, fled to the fort and begged for a sanctuary. They were doomed and they knew it. Arnold let them in. And an angry Towash demanded that the Army return them. Sergeant Abe Harris remembered:

"They were yelling out there like red devils. The Major ordered us into line and said if fight was what they wanted fight it was. Sergeant Dan McCauly, who had charge of the big gun, our only howitzer, brought it out and unlimbered it (at the northwest corner of the square at the head of Houston Street.) The major told the rag messenger (an Indian who rode up waving a flag of truce) that he was not in the habit of serving up his guests for breakfast, at least to strangers, and they might as well be prepared for a fight.

"The Indians were about 300 strong, and let me tell you we fellows in blue were but a squad in comparison to them but we had the gun and were sure they had never heard her bellow, so while the Indians were scattered around over the bottom there over the bluff, looking northwest, the major said to McCauly, 'Sergeant, touch her off and graze the heads of the big bucks over there in the valley if you can without hitting them, but if you should hit one, mind you, there will be no love lost, even if you take his head smooth smack off.' So the sergeant he pulled the lanyard, and shrapnel rang over the heads of the bucks and the Indians clattered hither and thither, scared out of their wits.

". . . their belligerent attitude vanished, and Indian like, the next instant they were begging for something to eat. Major Arnold told them he would just as soon fight them as feed them, but nevertheless had three beeves driven out to them. Those savages were certainly more

Aesthetics of military life on the prairie: An officer and his lady share the front seat while an enlisted man holds the horse steady for the photographer.

The Indians were not foolish. They rode clear of the fort. Isolated homesteads were easier prey.

hungry than hostile, for the next morning there was neither hide, nor hair nor hoof of those devoted cattle to be seen. And this was the peaceful outcome of the only hostilities Fort Worth ever experienced."

The Indians were not foolish. They rode clear of the fort. Isolated homesteads were easier prey. Finally 44 men petitioned the governor of Texas, asking that the officers at Fort Graham and Fort Worth remove the Caddo, Ioni Anadarko and Delaware tribes from the area and prevent their return for any reason. The petition pointed out that "freequent and greevious Complaints are made by our Citizens against said Indians on account of their steeling our horses Killing our Cattle and hogs burning the prairies woods and etc."

Arnold did what he could. He really had little choice. From the north, Comanche Chief Jim Ned, backed by 100 warriors, was moving quietly toward the fort. He had one aim—destroy it. The military outpost, he had decided, was much too close to his hunting grounds. Besides, an army scout had gotten away with one of the Comanche's stolen horses. Chief Jim Ned would take no more humiliation from the white men. They must die.

Not far away, Chief Feathertail, with another 100 warriors, was also slowly descending on the fort. Together, the two Indian armies planned to squeeze Arnold and his Dragoons between them, crush the soldiers and wipe them from the prairie. And perhaps they would have.

But fate had another idea. A fur trader, returning from his trap lines, stumbled across the camping warriors of Jim Ned in the darkness when he overheard muffled voices down in the valley below him. The trader grabbed his horse and raced madly to the fort. Within an hour, Major Arnold with 40 men and that deadly six-pound howitzer were riding cautiously toward the bluff that overlooked the sleeping Indians.

The Comanches—wearing trinkets carved from human bones and carrying the blood-dried scalps of fallen settlers—had no warning, no chance at all.

The troops attacked from three directions, galloping down on the dazed, bewildered warriors who lay in the draw, illuminated by the moonlight. The soldiers could not miss. Chief Jim Ned, with as many men as he could rally, fled to fight another day, meeting up with Chief Feathertail and retreating back into the timbered hills of Palo Pinto.

In the brief clash the Comanches lost 37 braves, with another 15 wounded too badly to escape. Not a soldier was scratched. The warriors had run into the night. But Arnold was not satisfied. He refused to let them go.

The troops caught up with the Comanches two days later in the canyons and wind-carved grottos of Palo Pinto (Spanish for painted wood). Jim Ned and Feathertail chose to make their stand on the ground they knew best.

Feathertail died there. Howard Peak, the first Anglo born in Fort Worth, heard his father's tales of the battle, and he wrote:

"The battle call sounded and the three columns moved forward, dismounted, horses tethered, guns in hand, eyes alert. For a brief moment silence reigned supreme, and then there burst on the air of that spring morning the tumultous roar of savage war whoops that echoed through the canyon as though a thousand devils of hell were loose. From every boulder poured a shower of swift arrows . . ."

The fight lasted for hours. When Feathertail fell, so did the hopes of the Comanches. Beaten and dying, the warriors melted away in the confusion, withdrawing into a secret cut in the canyon that hid them.

Never again would the Grand Prairie of Texas confront the serious threat of an Indian war. Horses would be stolen and petty raids were always annoying. But the blood shed would dry up in the rich soil and wash away. The time for dying was behind the settlers. The time for building had begun.

An editorial in the *Texas Republic* forecast a prediction for the Trinity River Valley, now patrolled by the guns of Fort Worth. "The country around the spring is exceedingly fertile and abounds in excellent pasturage. It will doubtless become the seat of extensive and flourishing settlements."

Such was the prophecy. It would not take long.

Dallas—to the far east—numbered 350 residents. John A. Hust—only a

No surreys on this trip. Dragoons as they cross a north Texas stream in the late 1800s.

Prowling panther: A Texas leopard cat, as captured by J.W. Audubon, often vexed homesteaders.

dozen miles away from the outpost—worried more about panthers prowling in his front yard than he did about Indians. He raised the first wheat grown in that part of the country, cutting it by hand and thrashing it with sticks. Twenty-three other families scattered their homesteads over the prairie. About 50 hardy souls took over the ruins of Bird's Fort, renaming it Birdville and developing the first thriving community in the area.

Even Fort Worth had its first civilian.

Press Farmer, his wife and daughter had the good fortune of living in a tent on the land where Major Arnold chose to construct his new fort. Since the army had no reason to kick the Farmers off the property, the major allowed him to open the Sutler's Store and stay on. Press Farmer traded away 22 acres of dirt that one day would become downtown Fort Worth. All he received in return was a powerful team of mules. It was (they all said) a helluva good deal for Farmer. It was to be his last one.

Growth and prosperity, it seemed, were just around the corner. Fort Worth had not even been completed, and already people were clamoring for self-imposed (perhaps self-inflicted) government. During the midst of a cholera epidemic, a few of them rounded up 100 electors who signed a petition calling for the creation of a new county.

General Edward Tarrant, a crusty-voiced attorney and Indian fighter who had claimed victory at Village Creek back in '41, led the fight. He constantly debated his cause during the Third Legislature, predicting a massive wave of immigration, and urging the establishment of Texas' 80th county.

His argument did not fall on deaf ears. On December 20, 1849, the Legislature gave him the county, taking the necessary land from a portion of the old Peters Land Grant. The county was appropriately named Tarrant.

Fort Worth was barely more than a watering station in 1839 when the chief concerns of most Texas settlers were to find food and avoid Indian attacks. It was a particularly bitter winter as well; the ice and sleet storms were terrible. In the midst of one such storm, a young settler named Ben McCulloch proved himself an outstanding military leader. McCulloch, a few white men and several members of the friendly Toncahua Indian tribe set out to battle other Indians who had ravaged several new settlements.

The fighting dragged on through several cold nights, the enemy having taken shelter in the dry Texas thicket. Finally McCulloch's patience ran out, and he and three of his men crawled through the thicket, attacked and killed the Indians one by one.

McCulloch was rewarded with a position as a Texas ranger and later served in the Texas military. He entered the Civil War as the first Confederate colonel from Texas and left the war as a brigadier general.

Times were hard but bearable.

In an election held within the log cabin of Ed Terrell, (the trader who almost lost it all to the Comanches in '45), Birdville was easily chosen as county seat. It obviously had the largest and only bloc vote in the area.

At the fort itself, prosperity had not moved in at all. The Army's quartermaster general had sent a letter to all the frontier forts asking about their food supply and their ability to live off the land. At Fort Worth, Lieutenant Sam Starr, the commissary officer, answered,

"Flour cannot be had except in small parcels of very inferior quality. There are no flouring mills . . .

"Beans cannot be procured at any price. As a substitute, Cow Peas can be had.

"Tallow, in small quantities can be procured if the trouble be taken to collect it at the scattered farm houses.

"Candles are not procurable.

"Hard soap is not procurable. Soft soap as a substitute has been offered to me at eight cents per pound; three-fourths of it being water, at that price it is equivalent to thirty-two cents a pound.

"Cattle are grazed on the prairies attended with no other expense in summer than branding them. In winter, if intended for beef, it will be nice and easy to find them."

Times were hard but bearable.

Major Arnold was much more disturbed about the newspaper reports that his men were losing too many horses to the Indians. That went against his grain. He had fought too hard for his reputation to be slandered in print. Arnold angrily sat down and wrote a letter, addressing it "To all newspapers:"

"I have the honor to contradict such a report and to state that the two companies of dragoons under my command have not had a horse stolen nor have I heard of any Indian depredations committed in this part of the country for several months.

"About 100 Indians of different tribes are now visiting me. They brought down and delivered up some 35 horses which they had taken from the Wichitas—horses stolen within the last year from citizens. Three Wichita Chiefs are here and have given me their pledges. All is peace and quiet on this frontier."

But it would not stay that way.

All the settlers had to fear now was themselves, and the hard-talking, hard-drinking, hard-nosed business of bringing civilization to a primitive, sometimes barbaric, place. That was a two-fisted challenge if there ever was one. That would be the roughest fight of all.

Chapter 2

Nailing a village to the prairie

Pioneers all: Six of Fort Worth's earliest settlers take time to let history be recorded. Standing (from left) and dates when they arrived: Howard W. Peak (1856), Captain J.C. Terrell (1857), Dan Parker (1858); seated, Captain Sam Woody (1850), Captain Ed Terrell (1843) and Richard King (1854).

It was to be a God-fearing land, plowed by the hands of men who feared nothing and went out of their way to prove it.

The Reverend John Allen Freeman knew that his mission was to pack the word of God in his saddlebags and carry it to the uncleansed ear of the Texas frontier. And along the twin forks of the Trinity, he found the men whom he believed needed to hear it most.

He wrote, "At that time they were a wild, rough-looking set of men, some of them dressed in buckskin, and some of them wore coonskin caps; some of them were drinking bad whiskey and some of them were playing cards. In this way they spent their time when not in pursuit of Indians, who came in now and then to commit depredations on the settlers."

Yet it was the determination of these men, their strength, their roots, that gave Fort Worth the chance to become a viable community, then a city. Reverend Freeman made sure they did so with the threat of brimstone and damnation hanging heavy over their heads.

It was to be a God-fearing land, plowed by the hands of men who feared nothing and went out of their way to prove it.

Reverend John Allen Freeman called congregations together in log cabins, using I Peter 3:12 as his text: "For the eyes of the Lord are over the righteous, and His ears are open unto their prayers." It was definitely a time for praying, though the righteous numbered few. He and eleven of the good and faithful even amened the Lonesome Dove Baptist Church into existence on the banks of Denton Creek, establishing a pulpit with a steadfast warning: "If any Brother being hurt with another and not applying to him for satisfaction nor the church but proceeds to make remarks before the world and the Brethern he shall be deemed in disorder and shall be dealt with accordingly."

Preachers knew how to deal with sinners.

Over in the fort, Major Ripley Arnold had just about as much intolerance when dealing with law breakers. His particular brand of justice left lasting impressions and few repeat violations—if any at all. One soldier stole a pig and would have gotten away with the crime if guards had not uncovered the porkchops and ham tucked away in the trooper's quarters.

The Army records reported, "Arnold had the pork swung around the culprit's neck, and with his hands uplifted and tied above his head, he was made to stand for hours in the broiling sun where all passersbys could view him."

The major had a fort to run. His wife did her best to bring a touch of culture to an uncultured place where men had the habit of worrying more about their scalp than their breeding. She moved a piano into the fort—the first heard on the banks of the Trinity. The Indians were haunted by its range of sounds, fearing that those ivory keys, at best, were the teeth of wild animals that spoke out with strange, ominous noises.

In his Sutler's Store, Press Farmer kept the soldiers supplied with tobacco, crackers and brass polish. By law, his only customers wore military blue. Henry Daggett and Archibald F. Leonard took care of the settlers, peddling (they advertised) "general merchandise" from a cabin beneath a live oak tree a good mile from the fort. That, by law, was as close as they could get.

And the Daggett-Leonard store knew all about law. After all, within its walls was held the first term of District Court ever convened in Tarrant County, with Oran M. Roberts calling for order on the morning of November 4, 1850.

It only took the judge two days to rule on the six indictments that had been handed down by the grand jury. There is little crime, it seems, when the population is so sparse and widespread. Besides, those days, men usually handed down their own justice before a magistrate ever got wind of a foul deed. Judge Roberts, an east Texan who one day would be governor, remembered the weather long after he had forgotten the three assault and battery cases, the two prairie burnings and one house burning that had been presented him.

"We were invited to dine with Major Arnold who was then quartered with his wife in a hewed log cedar house upon the hill," he later wrote. "Just before sitting down to dinner it was discovered that a norther was coming up. We all ran out of the house, mounted our horses, and with rapid speed

"Old Scout's Tale": Fort Town was a magnet for anyone hoping to build a new way of life.

crossed the river with a chilling wind blowing furiously, and in about a mile reached the house of a Mr. Robertson where we were boarding, nearly frozen, where we remained shut up two days, sheltered from the worst norther that I was ever in. There was only one house west of us this side of the Rio Grande."

Major Arnold and his undrilled dragoons had marched upon the Grand Prairie and knocked a sense of respectability into a country that had respect only for those obstinate enough to endure. By August 13, 1852, they were no longer needed. Thirteen months later, the brevet major lay dead, shot down at Fort Graham during a quarrel with the post surgeon, Dr. Josephus M. Steiner. (He attempted to arrest the doctor for "drunkeness and falsifying." He fired twice but missed. The doctor did not.)

His days at Fort Worth had been both satisfying and tragic; he had two children die there beside the Trinity. Arnold's tenure had been risky and stormy and generally dull, interrupted only by the wild antics of soldiers who could either fight, curse or drink the bad times and boredom away.

Arnold's replacement, Brevet Major Hamilton W. Merrill, had men who were more interested in planting and caring for an eight-acre garden, the righteous kind who had an ear always ready for their prayers.

A lieutenant colonel who inspected the outpost in September of 1853, William Freeman, reported: "The company had only fatigue clothing of the old pattern, but some of the men wore sky blue, instead of dark blue jackets. They were armed . . . with musketoons, sabres, and Colt's revolving pistols. . . . The horses (60) are all serviceable, and in finer condition than those of any mounted troops in Texas. . . . I was gratified to find it was the solitary exception throughout my tour . . . the guardhouse . . . without a prisoner. But Major Merrill informs me that most of his men belong to the temperance society and that he has rarely occasion to confine any one of them."

The Reverend John Allen Freeman must have been just as pleased.

Eleven days after Major Ripley Arnold drew his last breath, Fort Worth was abandoned. It, too, was no longer needed.

The buildings did not stay empty long. They were crude. They were not attractive at all. They became downtown Fort Town. Daggett and Leonard wasted no time moving their mercantile store into the roomy old barracks, then they sat back and waited for that rampant immigration that General Tarrant had so urgently predicted.

It came. Fort Town was a magnet for anyone hoping to build a business or even a new way of life. It was opportunity with a roof. The stores were already completed. All they needed was someone to move in and hang a shingle outside.

Wagons were pointed toward Fort Town. Horses raced for its well-beaten streets. Steamboats wheezed out of Galveston and trudged up the Trinity. And many turned their backs on Birdville, even Dallas, and headed for the old outpost in dugout canoes.

Rugged Indian-fighting, card-playing, buckskin-clad reprobates—along with the good and faithful few—had gambled their lives on the Grand Prairie. A more refined class of gentlemen pioneers would inherit what the tough-breed had won. "The immigrants are generally men of wealth, their families traveling

One of the first: Charles Turner was among the original party that helped locate the site on which Fort Worth was located. He later opened a grocery with E.M. Daggett.

in carriages," one newspaper reported. "They are chiefly from Tennessee, Kentucky and Missouri, and bring their Negroes with them. The amount of immigrants is considerably more than last year. Lands are rapidly appreciating in value. Unimproved lands now sell at from $2 to $5 per acre; while lands under some improvements bring from $8 to $10 per acre."

They came crossing that 525-foot-long cedar log bridge that spanned the Trinity at Dallas. It was the largest bridge in Texas, and, by 1855, an average of 10 to 15 wagons were rumbling across those logs every day.

Dallas was not at all pleased to see them come and go the way they did. It was looking for settlers also and even tried to recruit families who had ideas about rolling on past.

One promoter eased up to Kentuckian Stephen Terry, sure that a man with such fine holdings and fine wagons would be cautious, even suspicious, of the unknown land that sprawled before him. The promoter spoke of hardships, even the threat of death, that awaited beyond the Trinity. Dallas was safe, he reasoned. But "Indians will scalp you if you go to Fort Worth," he warned. Mrs. Francis Caroline Terry merely lifted her aristocratic chin and snapped, "I'd just as soon be scalped by Indians as stay here and be eaten up by mosquitoes. Besides, if wild Indians were thirty miles away you wouldn't be here."

The Terrys bounced on off for Fort Town.

Daggett and Leonard by now had competition, a reliable sign of growth. Captain Julian B. Feild, however, only thought of himself as a trader when he moved into one of the officers' quarters and promptly began selling hammers, picks, oxen yokes, huge chunks of solidified sugar for children, coffee grinders, thread and bolts of cloth for the women who knew the art of sewing homespun clothes (and they all did). Ox wagons, lumbering along a rough road, kept bringing coffee and sugar from Shreveport and salt from Grand Saline.

Francis Knaar and Louis Westmore, two soldiers whose enlistments had ended, stayed behind when Major Merrill marched his troops on to Fort Balknap. Knaar became the village blacksmith. And Westmore, using a drag stone made of limestone, carved Fort Town's first street, plowing through waist-high grass.

John Peter Smith had walked most of the way from Kentucky before grabbing a ride on a wagon train to Dallas, then striking out on foot again toward old Fort Worth. He was bright, a graduate of Bethany College in Virginia, and so John Peter Smith felt called upon to establish the community's first school, teaching twelve students in one of the garrison buildings. He lasted three months before retiring as an educator, announcing that he would rather work outdoors in the open air because he dreaded the possibility of being stricken with consumption. Smith traded his ruler for a surveyor's rod.

C.B. and Captain Eph Daggett saw that brother Henry was doing quite well in Fort Town and realized that the growing community sorely lacked anything resembling a hotel. They corrected that oversight in a hurry, putting one into the dirt-floor cavalry stables up on the bluff. It was not much to look at or even live in, but Captain Eph was the perfect host. He was somewhat of a celebrity, remembered for his daring exploits in the Mexican War. And within the hotel, the captain proudly displayed Santa Anna's personal silver washbasin that he himself had captured on a day he almost nabbed Santa Anna as well.

B.F. Bamberg became the town butcher, slaughtering his beef out on the farm, then bringing it to a ramshackle little shop downtown to let it hang and drip. His place was never locked, but no one stole from him. They would rather pay that penny a pound for good meat. Noel Burton established Tarrant County's first liquor store but devoutly prohibited any drinking on the premises and sold only one pint to the customer. He would have the whiskey trade all to himself until 1859 when Ed Terrell finally got around to opening the First and Last Chance Saloon, stocking his bar with whiskey, gin, bitters and peach brandy, along with a bucket of water for anyone weak enough to need a chaser.

The good life: It was not all back-breaking labor on the prairie. There were rare hours for candy pullings, parties and, of course, dancing the harvest home in Texas (far right).

And they all depended on the fortitude and hard-driving skills of John White, whose lot in life was to take that ox-drawn wagon of his 600 roundabout miles to Houston for a new supply of sugar, salt, coffee, dried fruit, fish, flour, shoes, cloth and, even garden seeds. A crowd would see him off, hearing John White call, "I guarantee you—no bad luck—I'll make the voyage inside of six weeks." And men gave him those full 35 days before gathering again to wait and watch for his return, straining to catch a glimpse of the teamster by the time he hit Captain Daggett's farm.

Families quickly flocked to the streets. It was a time for sales and celebration. Uncle Jack Durrett, the self-appointed court musician of Tarrant County, would cut loose on such popular tunes as "Billy in the Low Ground," "Dilcey Hawkins," or "Cotton-Eyed Joe," fiddling away the hated whiskey famine. And strong men fought and shoved and feuded to purchase salt, the saving grace for those smokehouses that would preserve the meat for months to come.

Home life on the farmsteads, clustering closer than ever to the village, was simple. Families worked hard and they worked together, living primarily in chinked single-room log cabins. Women cooked in fireplaces, spreading those roughhewn tables with cornbread, beef, bacon, butter and coffee. Gingerbread was for Sundays, if at all. Men tended to the soil by day, patched their harnesses by the light of the fireplace at night, longing for hog-killing time when the smokehouse emptied and the first chill of autumn swept the countryside. Wives carded wool, wove it into fabric, then colored it with dyes homemade from roots and herbs and the bark of the bois d'arc tree.

When Captain Julian Feild, at long last, put in his mill in 1856, farmers no longer had to make that trek to Dallas to have their corn and wheat ground into meal and flour.

It was not all back-breaking labor on the prairie. Women still found those rare hours for singing bees, quilting parties, corn shuckings and candy pullings. Money sometimes ran low, then out. So families loaded up eggs and butter and chickens to barter for the luxuries of life, for snuff and sugar and a yard or two of calico.

And those who fell ill either recovered from healthy home remedy doses of quinine, sassafras, castor oil, or blue mass, or their next of kin went riding to the carpenter's shop for a coffin.

Dr. Carrol M. Peak changed their odds.

It was a wonder he came at all. He had not intended to come. But in 1853 Captain Feild fell seriously ill, worn out from his struggle to get established on the frontier. A friend rode hard to Three Forks, just outside of Dallas, in search of medical aid. All he found was Dr. Peak. It was more than enough. The young physician pushed pills and tonic down Feild and listened while the Captain bragged about the future of Fort Town. It would not be just an abandoned fort forever, Feild said. Someday it'll be a city. It's got everything going for it except a doctor.

Peak liked what he heard. He had always said that his area of medical practice was "bounded on the west by the setting sun." He simply decided to move a little farther west, just 30 miles closer to that sunset. Peak returned to Three Forks, packed up his wife and became the sole medical sage of a town desperately in need of one.

He was also the proprietor of the Maitland Peak Drug Store, pulling teeth for $1 a tooth, setting broken bones, peddling beef for three cents a pound, selling cologne, soap, brandy, tobacco, mustang liniment and making house calls for $2 a visit. Peak's prescriptions may have been bitter and hard to take, but they were, at least, a shade better than dying. His favorite pain killer was a concoction of alcohol, pepper, mustard, sassafras root, ammonia and camphor gum. If he thought an individual needed to "sweat out a cold or ache," Peak would put together a compound of quinine, camphor gum, opium and nitrate of silver. He got rid of "the summer complaints" by prescribing a mixture of charcoal, rhubarb and ipecac. And during winter, the good doctor recommended that age-old scientific discovery—wearing a lump of asafetida in a sack around the neck, guaranteed to scare away all

And those who fell ill either recovered from healthy home remedy doses of quinine, sassafras, castor oil, or blue mass, or their next of kin went riding to the carpenter's shop for a coffin.

The first one burned: The second Tarrant County courthouse in Fort Worth was started in 1876, the year the first one was destroyed by fire. It was completed the following year.

sorts of diseases.

Peak did not have the entire county to himself. Over in Birdville, Dr. B.F. Barkley from Kentucky was settling down to cure the political—as well as physical—ills of a community that was quickly watching Fort Town usurp its power as well as its population.

Birdville was worried. It had a right to be. It began to view the growth at the fort through a jaundiced eye, one that ultimately would tear the county apart with ridicule, distrust and, finally, a funeral or two.

By 1856, Fort Town began to feel more and more comfortable with the old name, Fort Worth. Julian Feild had been appointed as the first postmaster by President Franklin Pierce, but he did not keep the job long. The pay was little and the hours were terrible. No one ever knew just when the mail-toting stagecoach would hit town, but the postmaster had to be there to meet it. He had a schedule all right, but the stagecoach might be anywhere from a day to a week late, depending entirely on how many bridges had been washed out along its journey. During the next three years, three others would hold the title as postmaster, always eager to give it up when the year passed.

Lawrence Steele shut down the merchandise business and built a two-story concrete hotel, called it a tavern and provided one room for the stagecoach office. Out front, Steele hung a bell, cast in London, England in 1782. He rang it loudly to celebrate weddings, announce dinner time, say goodbye to the dearly departed and signal for help when fire struck.

Tarrant County also had a jail. Captain Daggett paid for it. Colonel Johnson donated the land. There was reasoning behind their sudden outburst of extravagance. Birdville proudly hailed itself as the county seat. For men like Daggett and Johnson, that was inconvenient, out of the way and downright galling. Birdville might have the court. But Fort Worth had the jail. And it wanted the whole shooting match.

Daggett feared that Fort Worth might dry up and wither away without the prestige of a courthouse standing sentinel over its dirt streets. And besides, Court Mondays meant big business. Everyone was in town on Court Mondays, the day when justice was handed down and long lines of buggies and wagons wound into the heart of a town's merchandising district. It was a time for trading, haggling, bartering and spreading money around, a place to pick up a new dress or an old hound dog. Dollars in the street were (perhaps) more important than decisions in the courtroom. They were, at least, to Fort Worth.

So Daggett led a delegation to the capital in Austin.

Fort Worth had long planned for the day when it finally got what Birdville already had. As early as 1850, every male newcomer who settled near the fort was asked for his vote come election day. Election day was six years in the making.

Down in Austin, Birdville's Isaac Parker—an Indian fighter who had served with Andrew Jackson during the Creek Wars—authored a bill that gave Texas counties the right to relocate their county seats by a majority vote rather than a two-thirds vote.

That was all Daggett needed to know. For him, the waiting was over.

Isaac Parker had made the change feasible. Fort Worth leaders believed they probably owned a majority of the population in the county. All they had to do was make sure all the proper voters showed up to cast their ballot the right way. Fort Worth's campaign was simple—hard work and hard whiskey. On the frontier, nothing could beat it.

Birdville tried. But Birdville was the victim of theft.

By election day morning in November of 1856, Fort Worth politicos had dutifully set up two large barrels of whiskey out front of its two mercantile stores, being careful to stash a bucket of sugar beside each in case any voter happened to prefer his liquor sweetened.

And an Irishman, it is told, stumbled around the square, chanting, "Fort Worth water tastes like whiskey; Fort Worth salt tastes like sugar. Hurrah for Fort Worth." He spoke for most of the population who marched into town to sip a little and perform its civic duty.

Birdville had a similar plan.

It went awry. Birdville, too, had purchased a barrel of whiskey to comfort and attract its share of voters. But the county seat did not trust Fort Worth. Its leaders carried the barrel out into an oak grove and hid it. On election eve Fort Worth stole the whiskey, siphoning the liquor into its own barrels. Birdville came up with too many dry mouths and too few votes.

All day, voters rode into the county's polling places. Fort Worth delegates, on horseback, kept up with the tally, racing back into town as the day dimmed and reporting that votes were becoming as scarce as hen's teeth. M.J. Brinson, a member of the board of trustees for the town's Male and Female School, leaped up on a box and eloquently yelled, "Something has to happen damn quick!"

It did. Julian Feild and Max Dunn, without a debate, mounted up and headed for the open country, dashing madly out to those scattered farms in hopes of digging up a few more votes before sundown shut the polls. At dusk, a pair of hard-charging riders stormed into the Fort Worth Square, yelling, "Hell's afloat and no pitch hot. Fort Worth has won."

Some say the victory margin was 13 votes; some remember it as seven.

It makes little difference. Birdville was on the short end, and Birdville was angry, claiming that Fort Worth had voted every man as far west as the Rio Grande. It wasn't just the idle accusation of a sore loser. As Sam Woody was to say, "They (Birdville) were not able to find as many citizens in the entire county as . . . had recorded their ballots at the three polling places."

Sam Woody should know. He was indeed the king maker that day.

Missionary of the plains: "The Circuit Rider," as painted by O.C. Seltzer, laid the cornerstone for as many denominations as Fort Worth could harbor.

"I had until a short time prior been a citizen of Tarrant County, but when the election came off I was living in Wise County," Woody later recalled. "Around me were fourteen other settlers, and on the day of the election I got them together and started down to Fort Worth to help my former fellow citizens get what they wanted. . . .

I corralled my lads, and said to them: 'Boys, we've got to stay sober til this election is over. I must vote every one of you, so we must hold it til we get home. It is a penitentiary offense, and if they find us defrauding the ballot we will have to leave home for several years. . . .'

"The Birdville people never once suspected that I did not belong to Tarrant County, and supposed that my fourteen companions were neighbors from over in the western part of the county. . . .

"I led the way to the polls, followed by my supporters, and pretending to be in a great hurry, I pushed forward to the judges, saying, 'Come on boys, let's vote, for we've got a long way to go, and must get home before dark.' They never challenged one of us, and there were fifteen votes for Fort Worth that came from Wise County."

Those were the votes Fort Worth needed.

For the new county seat it was a night of wild celebration. Saloon keepers rolled kegs of whiskey out into the street and opened them. Speakers were carried around on the shoulders of the crowd, and everyone, it seemed, wanted to speak. Trees were chopped down and thrown into a huge bonfire on the square. Uncle Jack fiddled "Money Musk" and "Dog in the Rye Straw." And a torchlight parade headed out for Birdville. Before morning, the record books, yellowed law books, well-worn desks and cane-bottom chairs were loaded into a wagon and hauled back to Fort Worth.

Birdville never forgave nor forgot until it finally died away and was forgotten. But Birdville did not go without a fight.

Angry words fueled the feud, along with gunfire. Jack Brinson, George Slaughter and Tom Johnson quarreled with a Birdville man named Tucker. Tucker was killed. The three Fort Worth men—tried in the court they had helped relocate in their hometown—were promptly acquitted.

In Birdville, the two newspapers carried on a hot, even caustic, debate on the editorial pages. John J. Courtney, editor of the *Birdville Western Express,* was in favor of moving the county seat to Fort Worth. A.G. Walker, who founded the *Birdville Union,* was violently opposed.

The county seat controversy, however, was not the only difference of opinion between the editors. It was merely the skirmish before the battle. Courtney firmly believed that slavery should be preserved even if it took full-fledged secession to do it. Walker was a devout Union man.

He was also quicker on the trigger.

The editors traded their acrimonious pens for pistols, and Courtney wound up in the obituary column. Walker returned to his editorial page in order to take wicked potshots at Fort Worth, even taking the new county seat into court, charging fraud. The Texas Supreme Court—still not too sure of itself—merely ruled that lawmakers had not provided for such an emergency. Fort Worth was the winner in spite of the evidence.

Neither Walker nor Dr. Barkley gave up. They kept complaining. The Legislature had no other choice but to listen. And, in 1860, they ordered another election. For Birdville, it came too late.

From the beginning, Daggett had realized that Fort Worth was in dire need of a tangible, legal, honest-to-God courthouse to go along with its new title.

But the new three-room courthouse served its purpose and became a late-night sanctuary for sleeping drunks and stray dogs. The doors never closed.

On the morning after the '56 election, he dispatched men with wagons and ox teams to Cherokee County to buy lumber from the Rough and Ready Mill. Enough was brought back to construct a small three-room building with a wide hallway through the middle. It was not much. But it served its purpose and became a late-night sanctuary for sleeping drunks and stray dogs. The doors never closed.

By 1859, Fort Worth decided it needed a new stone and brick courthouse, anchored in rock, strong enough to withstand the unexpected threat posed by Birdville and the new election order. City leaders immediately got together in a closed room, and 41 of them subscribed $2,700 to erect a two-story, eight-room courthouse. The money would come from their own pockets, but they were convinced the county seat would be worth the investment.

The feud between Fort Worth and Birdville and the resulting election was said to have cost the state of Texas $30,000.

It cost Birdville its life. Fort Worth grabbed 548 votes. Even a non-existent point at the center of the county outpolled Birdville. The center received 301 votes. Birdville counted four.

Fort Worth now had a solid foundation upon which to grow. The $2,700 courthouse was built for $10,000, but that graceful dome on top made folks overlook the added expenditure. Popular subscription, not taxation, still paid for it all.

Religion, perhaps, was the first law ever staked into the conscience of the Grand Prairie. And it expanded as quickly as the community. Circuit-riding preachers—missionaries of the plains—laid the cornerstone for as many denominations as Fort Worth could harbor. The Reverend A.M. Dean—his Bible and hymnal in his saddlebags, his pistol on his hip—arrived by horseback to help Colonel Terry harvest wheat. He stayed around long enough to establish the First Christian Church at the home of Carrol Peak. The Baptists—those who couldn't make it to Lonesome Dove Church—gathered in the home of Press Farmer to listen to the fiery words of Noah T. Byars. Reverends Lewis J. Wright and William Bates came to town often enough to satisfy the Methodists. The Right Reverend Alexander Gregg, bishop of Texas, held service for Episcopalians, a strong sect that would have itinerant priests say mass for a dozen years before they finally got one of their own.

Most services, however, were irregular and usually quite infrequent. They were, at all times, honored and revered, a rare moment to worship instead of work. As Captain Joseph C. Terrell said, "Two crimes were never condoned—theft of horses and disturbance of religious worship." And he said of his neighbors, "As a rule they were pious people, for I cannot recall an irreligious family."

For Howard Peak, whose father had been Fort Worth's doctor, recalled the religion that stirred him most came from those old-fashioned camp meetings. He recalled, "There as the religious brethren and sisters, regardless of faiths, assembled under brush arbors and sitting on crude benches, with their feet in the straw listening intently to the earnest and heartfelt exhortations from the zealous preachers. . . . one could feel the moving of the Spirit. . . . and the Spirit took hold of the contrite sinner, the body gave way to the nervous strain and culminated in shouts of joy."

Captain Terrell, however, had other reasons for following after the ways of the church. He and Dabney C. Dade were young attorneys who were having a difficult time (Terrell said) in "breaking the social ice." So they created the "Disciples of the Christian Order" and founded Fort Worth's first official Sunday School. And it worked. Terrell remembered, "I was unattached, but gave valuable service teaching the Bible class; was well up in faiths, baptisms and was specially versed in Revelations. . . . We had a prosperous and profitable time, broke the ice and got acquainted with the girls." Prayers were answered.

In the late 1850s Fort Worth found itself with another physician, Dr. William P. Burts who immediately launched a campaign to improve the city's water supply. He favored the digging of deep cisterns, saying cleanliness was the

best prescription he could think of for good health. Fort Worth agreed and dug cisterns, sixteen in all. Now horses could be easily watered, streets could be properly drained, and the bucket brigades never had to go for water when fire broke out.

It behooved Fort Worth to remain in as good a health as possible, especially when depending upon Doctor Burts to come running everytime sickness crept in. The doctor had one severe weakness. He was superstitious—devoutly so. If a jackrabbit crossed his path while enroute to treat an illness, without hesitation Burts turned and rode home before beginning his journey again. Neither miles nor the severity of the affliction bothered him. The doctor did not trust the bad luck of the jackrabbit. Only the patient knew how bad the luck really was.

William T. Ferguson opened the doors to a new drugstore, featuring "staple drugs, peewee marbles, candy lozenges, and some notions." And the Fort Worth-Jacksboro Stage Line kept bringing travelers—bound for the dreams of California—to Steele's Tavern for a few days rest, while Fort Worth promoters diligently escorted them to the edge of the bluff, urged them to gaze out on the beauty of the Trinity Valley and suggested they forget all about California. More than a few did. The rest rolled away for Jacksboro and that connection with the Butterfield Overland Stage, determined to reach the Pacific regardless of the bone-jarring miles they suffered. But it was not a stagecoach that brought Sam Houston to Fort Worth.

It was a heated campaign for governor. In Birdville, he had debated Louis T. Wigfall—a supporter of Democratic candidate Hardin R. Runnels—then agreed to accompany Captain Daggett back home. The political fight was a bitter one, especially painful for Houston who watched Texas slowly turning away from him simply because he was pro-Union. Houston could not condone slavery. Fort Worth, as a whole, found little wrong with it.

Slaves were quite an investment. And Fort Worth had plenty of them.

The Marshall *Texas Republican* had reported: "Negroes were sold at what we consider to be very high prices. Ordinary Negro men sold for from fifteen to eighteen hundred dollars; Negro women from a thousand to twelve hundred. Negro men (ordinary field hands) hired from $235 to $312 [per year]. Women at from $140 to $170; in these cases the hirer paying for clothing. The natural inference would be that a country must be very productive when people can afford to pay such prices for labor."

Fort Worth was productive. Slave labor made it profitable. Houston saw the storm clouds, and he did not like them. Even Eph Daggett, in spite of his friendship with the old warrior, could not support Houston. He brought out Santa Anna's silver wash bowl and, as a symbol of his affection and admiration, bathed and dressed Houston's unhealed wounds. But he wouldn't vote for the hero of San Jacinto. Most of Texas felt the same way.

Houston lost. Fort Worth—typical of the whole state—had no intention of losing its slaves. It felt like the rest of the South and at least in the 1850s, did not mind the thought of seceding from the Union. Secession was a dreaded word for Houston. Few others seemed to fear it—or the Union itself. Houston made one fervent plea for Texas to remain with the Union when a burly Brazos River bottom farmer elbowed his way to the front of the crowd and yelled, "But Gen'l Sam, we can whip them damn yankees with corn stalks." Houston smiled a sad smile. "Son," he said, "you're right. But them damn yankees won't agree to fight with corn stalks."

Chapter 3

The pride and poverty of war

What I Saw in Texas: *This was the name of the 1872 book by John W. Forney in which this Crosscup & West engraving appeared. It was the first recorded picture of Fort Worth.*

In 1860, the storm was no longer brewing. It struck.

More were willing to listen to the beliefs, the philosophies of Sam Houston, but not enough. He had been elected governor again, but the votes had been for his deft plan to cut down the new threat of Indian raids, not his anti-secession platform. Houston had suggested that each county raise 25 volunteers to join the Rangers in putting a stop to the Indian depredations.

That idea was popular. He also pled for Texas to cast its allegiance, for all time, to the Union. That idea was not popular.

Fort Worth had opinions favoring slavery. But it was not particularly ready for open conflict. Those Lincoln-Douglas debates seemed so far away. So did war.

It was not.

Abolitionists—dedicated to freeing slaves for the good of all mankind—worked underground, spreading fear and rebellion and anger where there was none before. Perhaps they did their cause more harm than good. They picked up few converts. Instead, they inflamed many men who would soon seek vengeance rather than reason.

Anthony Banning Norton was one of the converts. He founded Fort Worth's initial newspaper, *The Chief,* then packed it with his own personal pro-Union, abolition dogma. He found a lot of readers. Norton made most of them mad. He was a little odd—a self-anointed radical who campaigned nationally for Henry Clay in the 1844 presidential race (which James K. Polk won). Norton took the loss harder than Clay. He arose and announced, "The country might be going to hell, but I'm going to Texas."

He did, vowing to never cut his hair or trim his beard until Clay sat in the White House where he belonged. Fort Worth thought Norton was a strange sight with even stranger ideas. He left George Smith as editor of *The Chief* and ran off to Austin amidst the ugly rumors of slave rebellions and abolitionist plots.

The fuse for violence had been lit. It did not burn long. In Austin, Norton established *The Intelligencer,* but he continued to faithfully mail his views to *The Chief,* knowing sooner or later the right eyes would find them.

Suddenly, the rumors were no longer merely whispers in the night. On a hot July day, the slave insurrection—small but devastating—erupted.

Fire swept through downtown Dallas, erasing every building on the western and northern sides of the square, leaving behind a $400,000 loss. Flames cut down property at Pilot Point, Ladonia, Wilford, Honey Grove and Waxahachie. Twenty-five kegs of gunpowder stored in a hogshed in Denton exploded—another $80,000 gone. And Archibald Leonard's Mill, only eight miles away from Fort Worth, collapsed in ashes.

After the burnings came the hangings. Dallas wasted no time at all. As District Judge Nat M. Burton reported:

"Mr. Cameron who lived on the Fort Worth road 12 miles from Dallas had a Negro boy about twelve years old, who came to town every Sunday to get the mail. When he returned home that Sunday after being in Dallas his master saw the smoke from the burning town and asked what it was. He replied that Dallas was burning. He was asked how he knew it. He said that as he was going to Dallas that morning Uncle Cato who was then a notorious Negro in these parts told him to look out that Dallas would be burning before he returned home.

"Old Cato was captured and he implicated the other two Negroes who were hanged with him. Their stories were corroborated by other Negroes. They stated that two white preachers from the North put them up to it, and a committee waited on the preachers. . . . Whipped them and told them to leave the country."

Most of the settlers brought their slaves into town to witness the hanging, planting the seed of fear, hoping to prevent the necessity of any more executions. A committee was even appointed to give every Negro in the county a good thrashing. Retaliation would be swift and tempered with neither mercy nor

Rangers yes, Union no: Governor Sam Houston wanted more Rangers to stop the Indians and settlers agreed. His plea for Texas to join the Union, however, was about as popular as Texas abolitionists.

leniency.

In Fort Worth, *The Chief* editorialized: "The divine nature of slavery must be clear to all. To every man must spread the truths of slavery." To many, such a message was meddling. They thought the abolitionists should merely shut up, mind their own business and go back to the country that raised them. Others struck back. An angry mob got together and promptly voted to leave every abolitionist it could find dangling from a tree. The anger did not cool. Neither did the threat. On July 17, according to the *Houston Telegraph*, "Fort Town's men hanged an abolitionist in the early morning . . . on a pecan tree near the banks of the Clear Fork, three-quarters of a mile west of Fort Worth. They left him hanging there. All through the day people thronged to gaze upon an abolitionist."

Fort Worth had been salvaged from the prairie by the hands of men who were not afraid to work or fight for what they believed in. Many believed in slavery. They were all convinced that no "damn yankee" had any authority to trespass on their soil and raise hell against them.

But still the "Mystic Red," whoever they were, moved in secrecy, placing pistols in the pockets of slaves, urging a widespread deadly riot. Fifty of the weapons were uncovered among slaves on farms that surrounded Fort Worth. And on an August day, a half-barrel of strychnine was discovered hidden away on another farm—poison (rumors said) for the mouths of slave holders.

Fort Worth found itself caught in the middle of an invisible war. An enemy was lurking in its midst. But the enemy had no name.

Paul Isbell, a slave trader, gave it one. He came riding into town from his plantation with a letter he said he found hidden on a nearby farm, swearing of its authenticity under oath. He was a respected man, one whose words were never doubted. And Isbell told Captain Daggett and Nathaniel Terry, "The lid of Pandora's Box is about to be lifted."

Deputy County Clerk T.M. Matthews took the letter, leaned back in his chair, and read: "We need more agents—appoint a local agent in every neighborhood in your district. Brother Leake recommends a different match be used about towns. Our friends sent a very inferior article, they emit too much smoke, and do not contain enough camphine—I will reprove you and your co-workers for negligence in sending funds for our agents but few have been compensated. You must call on our colored friends for money."

It was sent to a preacher, a brick mason, and a Northern Methodist who, farmers had long known, laid more foundations for "Northern sentiments" than they did for buildings. He was Anthony Bewley. His associate was called Crawford. If Bewley were guilty, Fort Worth leaders reasoned, so too was Crawford.

Fort Worth waited. The days and nights grew quiet, yet restless.

And in September, the *Texas State Gazette* in Austin reported a story with a Fort Worth dateline: "No more fires or abolitionists hung within the last few weeks. Several are running however just in time probably to save their necks." One named Willet fled into the Texas woodland thickets, living on nuts and herbs, staying a step ahead of the vigilantes, finally making it back home to Kansas. Bewley and Crawford should have gone with him. They were given their warning. They did not listen. When they did decide to run, it was too late.

Ned Purvis—called a loyal slave by the Purvis family—had publically denounced the abolitionists, referring to them as "De tools of de debbil." One night he crawled beneath the flooring of a church on the Clear Fork and listened while Bewley spoke to the slave congregation. He heard a lot, and it persuaded him that "De debbil wa'r unchained. Dees Yankee men tol' de colored folks to rise up agin'st dar marsters."

The masters rose up against Bewley, capturing him near the Indian Territory border, dragging him back to Fort Worth wrapped in a rope that would take his life. The Reverend was charged "with implication in a nefarious plot to poison wells, fire towns and residences and in midst of the conflagrations and death to run off with the slaves."

Bearded abolitionist: Anthony Banning Norton was a radical politician who vowed not to cut his hair or trim his beard until Henry Clay was elected U.S. President. He arrived in Forth Worth in 1849 to found the city's first newspaper, the Forth Worth Chief, *then left for Austin. He started the* Austin Intelligencer *but continued to file his pro-Union opinions with the* Chief *by mail.*

But still the "Mystic Red," whoever they were, moved in secrecy, placing pistols in the pockets of slaves, urging a widespread deadly riot.

At age 25, James Jones Jarvis completed his law degree in Illinois and traveled to Shreveport, Louisiana. Texas needed lawyers, they told him. He decided to find out. It was the winter of 1856. Jarvis thought he might buy a horse for a long journey, but $100 was all he had and that would not buy a nag. He started out on foot and walked the entire distance from Shreveport to the east fork of the Trinity River, then doubled back to Quitman in Wood County. Jarvis arrived with $60. He loaned $55 to a needy friend and began a most successful legal career with only $5 for a new suit and pair of shoes.

Bewley, in no mood to face eternity with an uncleansed conscience (it was said), confessed to the charges while the vigilante hangman adjusted the noose around his neck. The letter had been authentic and had been intended for him. He was guilty but only of the things he believed in. He and Crawford both died that night, tied to the same limb of a pecan tree. Their bodies were left there, swinging slowly in the wind, a macabre warning, Tarrant County said, for any "Black Republicans" amongst them.

Charles Mitchell, whose father had served as one of Fort Worth's earliest teachers, later wrote: "I don't know how long their bodies stayed there. People forgot about them during the war and my family went to Dallas but after we got back—you know how kids will do—Eph Daggett and I crawled up on the top of the Turner & Daggett store roof and saw their bones, right on the top of the roof and bleached white. As far as I know the two were never buried, not even their bones."

Fort Worth had a sudden, paranoic distrust for every new face it saw. One of them belonged to Harry B. Catlett, and he later pointed out, "Excitement was very high in Fort Worth preceeding outbreak of war. Every newcomer was closely scrutinized. His sentiments probed and if his proclivities were towards the North, woe unto him. He was a branded man and his best bet was to get away while the getting was good."

Fort Worth had had enough of the Mystic Red and its bold plan to tear apart Texas, thus linking the Great Lakes with the gulf and surrounding "slavery by land and water." The city backed its resentment with resolutions aimed at wiping out those who sought rebellion, those who had placed themselves— as far as Fort Worth was concerned—"beyond the pale."

Two lists were drawn up. One bore the names of Black Republicans in need of being watched, people like the hated editor Norton who had attributed to the fires. The Black List held the names of criminals to be immediately hanged. And (the resolutions asserted) anyone who did not concur with that brand of justice probably belonged on one of the two lists. There would be no exceptions at all.

Fort Worth leaders were never content to just stand around and be trampled on without fighting back. The hangings had not been legal. But the Grand Jury in Parker County commended Fort Worth on the executions and even suggested that Norton should be hanged as well.

Fort Worth was always ready to defy anyone who tried to take away what belonged to its people. It bristled at the thought of rebellion on its farms, aroused by the zealous deeds of abolitionists. But the men of Fort Worth generally were not that anxious to depart the Union, even if it did not agree with the Union's firm stand against slavery.

The vote on secession seemed imminent.

Fort Worth opinions were divided, even confused. A few wanted to secede just because the South favored it. Others thought it better to get out of both the Union and the Confederacy, be independent again, align itself with neither. In a public meeting, residents even voted to raise the Lone Star flag over Fort Worth as "the banner of our liberties." They wanted slaves all right. But they were a little leery of war, especially one waged against family and neighbors and their old homeland.

Many had heard the words of Sam Houston: "Some of you laugh to scorn the idea of bloodshed as the result of secession. But let me tell you what is coming. . . . Your fathers and husbands, your sons and brothers, will be herded at the point of the bayonet. . . . You may, after the sacrifice of countless millions of treasure and hundreds of thousands of lives, as a bare possibility, win Southern independence . . . but I doubt it." They had no reason to doubt him, either.

The proposition heated up the never bashful tongues of Fort Worth. As C.B. Mitchell recalled, "It got so that up to four and five nights a week we'd hear debates and speeches in the Masonic Hall."

They probably did little good. The die would be cast in Montgomery, Alabama, with Colonel Nathaniel Terry sitting in to listen to the pros and

In 1836, at age 18, William M. Harrison began a career as a merchant in Red River County, Texas. His total worth at the time was less than $1,500. In 1849, Harrison bought a plantation and increased his holdings to $150,000 by the Civil War. Four years later, he was forced to sell his war-ravaged estate for $10,000.

It might have crippled another man's dreams. But Harrison returned to his roots in merchandising. In less than ten years, he had enough capital to invest in a Jefferson, Texas, bank. He then moved to Fort Worth, initiated the charter for the State National Bank in 1884 and quickly became president. At his death, William M. Harrison was among Fort Worth's most admired philanthropists. His estate was valued at a half million dollars.

cons debate of the emotional issue of secession. He was a devout Southerner. (He would later be Fort Worth's delegate to the Texas Secessionist convention in Austin.) Terry returned home, fired with the hopes and defiance voiced by the Confederacy. He gathered with his friends at Andrews Tavern, enthused about the almost unanimous vote for secession. "Remember," he pointed out, "only eight delegates voted no."

Fort Worth, however, was haunted by one of those eight—James Throckmorton of Texas. Throckmorton had stood in Montgomery and proclaimed, "Mr. President, in view of the responsibility in the presence of God and my country—and unawed by the wild spirit of revolution around me—I vote no." Throughout the hall, his words were greeted with the sounds of hissing. Throckmorton, undaunted, rose again, saying loudly, "Mr. President, when the rabble hiss, well may patriots tremble."

Fort Worth did not tremble, but it was still in doubt on that February 23, 1861, when 800 of its men gave their answer at the polls. Secession carried, but by only 27 votes.

A thrilled Nathaniel Terry left quickly to cast Fort Worth's decision in Austin. Disappointed, Sam Houston did not even bother to show up at the secessionist convention. He did not think it was legal anyway. And when he failed to answer the roll call, the office of governor was declared vacant. Houston had done all he could do. Texas seemed determined to march away without him. Seated on the south porch of the governor's mansion when he heard the outcome of the state vote, Houston simply turned to his wife and said softly, "Texas is lost."

Terry did not believe him. He had faith in the Confederacy and its preordained triumphs. War was coming, but Terry faced it without fear and with even less sense. He sold his plantation to David Snow, a man who had opposed secession, for $20,000. Snow offered to pay him in gold. Terry refused. He would accept nothing, he said, but Confederate money, a currency safer and far better than gold. Snow obliged. (Colonel Nathaniel Terry would die a broken man, penniless, shortly after the guns were silenced at Appomattox.)

Fort Worth braced for a war that would kill its soldiers but not touch its streets at all.

Yet the toll would be heavy.

Nat Burford, a young attorney who split his time on both Fort Worth and Dallas problems, headed out to join the Texas Cavalry as a private. In less than a year, he would become a colonel and be handed command of the 19th Texas Cavalry.

Volunteers tried to put together an army of sorts under Tom Johnson, but nobody knew much about military tactics, and training was more chaotic than beneficial. Dr. Peak, astride Grey Eagle, rode proudly out front of his cavalry. But he would fall and hurt his back and not be able to gallop off to battle when his men did. William Quayle, and old sea captain, headed up a band of mounted riflemen, riding on Choctaw mustangs and carrying a homemade Confederate flag. Out of the remnants of Birdville came old Withem's Fife and Drum Corps. And Captain M.J. Brinson, a merchant, was busy trying to round up a second company of volunteers from Tarrant County.

Charles Mitchell would later write: "I saw three companies of men formed here and marched off to join the Confederate Army. They all wore homespun clothes and carried all sorts of guns. They had six-foot squirrel rifles, shotguns, cap and balls and whatnot. Each man had one or two six-shooters and a home-made saber that had been fashioned right here in town."

Marching off to war was a glorious experience. The glory ended quickly. Tarrant County's General R.M. Gano watched his 16-year-old troops fight and die at Yellow Bayou as they valiantly kept Union General Nathanial Bank's soldiers from ever stepping on Texas soil. He was a warrior, but one with compassion. William Speer, a friend and historian, wrote of him, "The prisoners who fell into his hands had abundant evidence of his humanity and magnanimity. When, at the close of the war, it was reported that all officers of a certain rank would be arrested, he was advised to leave Tarrant County, at least for

The saga of Cynthia Ann Parker

In 1836, Parker's Fort in Limestone County, Texas, was raided by a band of Indians. They killed most of the members of the Parker family, taking only two or three captives. One of those was a young girl named Cynthia Ann Parker. Cynthia Ann was traded to the Comanches of the Wichita Mountains, where she was raised as an Indian squaw. She was given up for dead by the survivors of the battle.

Thirty years later, the Comanches themselves attacked a village very near the site of the original Parker's Fort. This time, American soldiers were prepared for the attack, fought off the Indians and countered with a surprise raid on the nearby Comanche grounds. An Indian woman and her two sons were among the soldier's captives. They soon realized that the woman was Indian by culture only. One of the generals remembered stories of the initial raid in 1836. He brought a surviving member of the Parker family to the army camp where he recognized the squaw as his cousin. Cynthia Ann returned to live with the Texas settlers and raised her sons there. One son, however, returned to Comanche territory. His name was Quanah Parker—and he became chief of his tribe on their Indian Territory reservation.

Cynthia Ann Parker and her baby Prairie Flower, shortly after their recapture.

Quanah Parker

The Indians who had once buried the tomahawk were pulling it out of the ground again.

a time. He declined, saying that if arrested he would ask to be tried before a federal jury made up of those prisoners of war who had been in his charge."

No one ever came to trouble him. Gano put the memories of carnage behind him, turned down an offer to run for governor, became a minister instead and chalked up more than 4,000 baptisms during the next 15 years.

For those in Fort Worth, the dying seemed far away. Somewhere battles were raging. But Fort Worth remained ignorant of them, unconcerned that any Northern army would ever go out of its way to invade the city.

The most serious threats were much closer to home. The Indians who had once buried the tomahawk were pulling it out of the ground again. The forts built to defend the prairies around Fort Worth were empty, their troops gone off to fight another war. The plains were unprotected, vulnerable. As one Young County resident wrote in 1861, "There must be a frontier at some point. To the north and northwest of us lies a belt of country from fifty to one hundred miles in width, once settled by an enterprising and industrious people, but who have been compelled to recede before the overpowering savages and have fallen back, at each step letting them in nearer to you, and when and where shall this retro-migration cease?"

No one felt safe. No one really was. Some men—ten companies in all—had left Tarrant County to take up arms against the North. Those who stayed wound up in the Frontier Guard, battling the new outbreak of Indian depredations. They were necessary, but not necessarily successful.

The *Dallas Herald* reported: "By private letters from Weatherford we learn that about thirty of Col. M.T. Johnson's men came from Belknap a few days since, foot-back and a-walking, half-starved. Some of them stated they had subsisted several days on what they could pick up by the way, and most of them were barefooted. Their horses were stolen by the Indians and even the blankets pilfered. Rumor has it that out of sixty-five horses fifty-nine were stolen or stampeded, and the company was left without provisions ninety miles in the wilderness beyond Belknap." (Ironically, though, the Indians did not trouble Fort Worth until 1869, after the soldiers had returned from battle, after the city had some semblance of defense again. They tried to trick the settlers with a barrage of fake turkey gobbles, but no one was deceived. So the braves killed a cow, then an aging woman about six miles north of town

The spirit of the frontier: Two Texas Rangers stand ready in 1888.

and wandered on back toward the Red River.)

Fort Worth was not saved. It was neglected.

Captain Lawrence Sullivan Ross, with 70 members of the Texas Rangers, a few volunteers and a detachment of the U.S. Second Cavalry had perhaps broken the spirit of the renegades back in December of 1860 on the Pease River. He whipped the Comanches badly and found among the captives Cynthia Ann Parker who had been stolen by the Indians during a bloody raid on Fort Parker in 1836. Cynthia Ann was grown, and she considered herself an Indian. The rescue broke her heart.

Cynthia Ann Parker, clutching her child Prairie Flower, was brought to Fort Worth, put on display, a folklore heroine for the crowds to gather and gaze upon. Medora Robinson, just a girl at the time, remembered, "She stood on a large wooden box, bound with a rope." She was dressed in torn calico. Her blonde hair hung straight, cut shoulder-length. Tears clung to her eyes, and her words were more like Indian prayers. Medora Robinson could never understand, asking again and again, "Why does Cynthia Ann weep?"

Cynthia Ann Parker wept because she no longer belonged to any people. Her broken heart would kill her.

The Indian threat worried Fort Worth during the early 1860s. But, like the Union troops, the warriors never came. Battles did not ravage Fort Worth. But the war did. A thriving population of 6,000 withered away to only 250. The city was dying. But enough strong-willed people hung on to keep it from being buried.

In the field, soldiers such as George Mulkey found war had no glamour at all. He wrote, "Our job was to confiscate meat for the army. We would go through a man's herd and cull out the beeves that were over four years old, and drive off the steers for the army. No, we were not popular and oftentimes the cattlemen took a shot at us, and we had a pretty tough time in general. It was hard, too, because we did not want to do it."

In Fort Worth, citizens were having a harder time with the Confederacy than with the Union. The High Vigilance Committee Court in Gainesville arrested Dr. Mansell Mathews, a Christian minister and a patriarch of the early days when Fort Worth was struggling for survival. Mathews loved Texas and the South. It was his home. But the dictates of his conscience led him against slavery. Fort Worth had no quarrel with him. As a whole, its residents respected and tolerated the minister's personal beliefs. After all, Mathews neither sought nor caused trouble.

The court of the Confederacy was less lenient. As far as the judges were concerned, Mathews had the sins of treason upon him, so he was jailed and found himself facing the death penalty. Captain Eph Daggett was furious. (The

Cash was rare. People bartered, secured credit or did without. But they outlasted the hard times.

Indians had described Daggett as "too big for a man, not big enough for a horse.") He stomped into the holy High Vigilance Committee Court and stood firm in behalf of the evangelist. Dr. Mathews, he argued, had committed no overt act of treason. His mind might be with the North, but his heart surely lay with the South. "If that be treason," Daggett shouted, "then I, too, am guilty." Hang Dr. Mathews, he concluded, and you might as well save a place on the gallows for me. Even the High Vigilance Court knew better than to quarrel with Eph Daggett.

Mathews escaped the death penalty, but the committee decided he ought to at least remain in jail for three days thinking he was going to die. Punishment would thus be the agony of suspense, wondering when the rope would burn his neck. After all, Mathews had watched for days as men no more guilty than he were marched out to the noose.

Daggett fumed. The punishment was cruel and inhuman to say the least. He asked to see the minister, but he was forbidden to go alone. A guard would stay with him, and Daggett was ordered to not even hint at the new verdict. Daggett believed that somehow he must get word to Mathews that his fate was no longer dangling at the end of a rope. So he talked with the evangelist about the Bible, discussing theology, quoting scripture. At last Daggett asked, "What is your favorite Bible quotation, the one that gives you the most comfort?" Mathews paused. And Daggett, smiling, answered for him, "Fret not thy gizzard and frizzle not thy whirligig, thou soul art saved." Mathews had reason to smile, too.

Fort Worth did not smile. Depression was upon it. Families—distraught over the plight of the economy—were moving back east. Private schools shut down for lack of tutors. Mail finally arrived by pony express but only after a two-day journey from Waxahachie.

A little coffee was being smuggled in from Mexico. But most drank a substitute—a hot liquid concoction of parched barley and wheat. The well-to-do lit their homes at night with tallow candles. The poor used sycamore balls soaked in oil.

For the most part, county offices were closed. Jails were often empty because there was no arresting officer to patrol the streets. Tom Redding finally agreed to be a temporary marshal, but he did not really want the thankless, unpaid job of cleaning up a drunken little tenderloin nest that was being referred to as Hell's Half Acre. The United Friends of Temperance organized juveniles in Bands of Hope, requiring a pledge of total abstinence. For those who did not take the pledge, the dance halls stayed open 18 hours a day.

News was slow in finding Fort Worth. If it had not been for old Ed Terrell, there would have been little news at all. Once each week he faithfully rode to Dallas to pick up a copy of the *Galveston News*. It was left on the town square for all to read. Prices were out of sight. A hundred pounds of flour cost $15. Corn was $2 a bushel, pork $20 for 100 pounds, cloth $4 to $5 a yard and cotton brought eight cents a pound.

It was a time for sacrifice. Women made the clothes their family wore—cotton shirts, cotton jeans, bedticking suspenders and linsey-woolsey dresses. And they did not forget the soldiers. They made by hand those items that the Confederate government could no longer supply—bandages, knit socks and mittens.

What the women needed most were looms. The men made sure they got them. Members of Masonic Lodge, Chapter 148, even tore the joints from the first floor of their lodge building to make the looms.

Fort Worth persisted. The people hunted wild turkey and prairie chickens on the banks of the creeks, making syrup from watermelons, cooking cornbread, lye hominy cracklings and liver pudding in the hollows of fallen dogwood trees.

Confederate fiscal agents added insult to hardship. They raided Turner & Daggett's department store, seized $3,000 worth of Northern credits and shipped the money back to a government in Richmond that was afflicted with no more poverty than Forth Worth. Cash was rare. People bartered, secured

Prairie Lullaby: The post-Civil-War era brought times of sacrifice to Texans. The well-to-do lit their homes at night with tallow candles. The poor used sycamore balls soaked in oil.

credit or did without. But they outlasted the hard times.

The war ended long before the grief. The chains of reconstruction bound the South up tightly, reaching out to include Fort Worth. The courts were ruled by a lynch law and human life was the cheapest commodity in town. Carpetbaggers or scalawags handed down their own brand of courtroom justice in their own particular vernacular. Judge Hardin Hart once listened as attorney J.C. Terrell tried to amend a pleading, then leaned back, propped his feet up and explained, "Now, Joe, you know you cannot raise at this stage of the game. Gause stands pat on his general denial, and you will have to call or lay down your hand."

The only government around was martial law, a force of one officer and 20 black soldiers who carried orders to round up Tarrant voters for a roll call. Union General Phil Sheridan, the state's military commander, only shuddered and proclaimed, "If I owned Texas and all Hell, I'd rent Texas and live in Hell." Martial law made sure Texas was just about as comfortable.

Yet Fort Worth escaped much of the suffering. Dr. B.F. Barkley, the Birdville proponent who had fought Fort Worth so diligently during the county seat feud, suddenly found himself in the seat of power. He was first named head of the Freedman's Bureau to oversee the freeing of slaves. Then Squire Barkley was appointed county judge in 1867. His time for revenge was at hand—if he wanted it. But Barkley was not carrying old grudges, at least not openly.

Fort Worth resented him because they resented anyone with carpetbag authority. So Barkley made his daily journey between Fort Worth and Birdville heavily protected by an armed guard. He took no chances. It was a wise move.

But tempers, as they have a habit of doing, gave way to order, if not harmony. One night in Andrews Tavern, Stephen Terry, former chief justice for Tarrant County, met with a group of Fort Worth's leading citizens. He had seen how the South was being tormented and vandalized in the name of law and good— though not honest—government. He told his neighbors, "I don't want to intrude my opinion, but have you men considered what Tarrant County has escaped? Spared a carpetbagger or a radical Northerner bent upon spiteful vengeance as the county judge, the key man responsible for enforcing the new order? We should give thanks that Dr. Barkley, our new county judge, is a Tarrant citizen—one of us. We admit that he has an iron will; has in the face of insults and threats, stood steadfastly loyal to the Union party throughout the war. But you cannot deny that he is a man of a good heart and is fair minded." They could not deny it, for he was.

Slowly the town—what was left of it—put its prejudices aside and began to rebuild. Cash was still hard to find. Gold, Fort Worth liked to say, was as rare as a raindrop in a Kansas drought. Surviving on credit was still a way of life.

Press Farmer, the old sutler, rode into town one day in 1869 with a $20 gold piece stuck deep in his pocket. He was a frugal man, one that bought only with wisdom, always telling those new-fangled merchants, "I buy things for their durability, not their flashalarity." The gold piece, however, was the first real money he had touched in years—paid him by a horse trader who had rented Farmer's stalk pasture for awhile. For luck, the old sutler branded the gold coin and paid Dr. Burts who had faithfully looked after his family's

Fort Worth's first merchant: Press Farmer, his wife and daughter were found by Major Ripley A. Arnold living in a tent at the site of the fort when it was established in 1849. Farmer became its sutler—a settler of provisions—and performed the duties of quartermaster.

ills during the war without charging a cent.

With at least one debt off his conscience, Farmer hung around the square all day visiting with friends. Just before he left for home, the sutler heard a man call out, "Wait, Press, I want to pay you some money I owe you." Farmer was handed a gold piece—the same one he had brought to Fort Worth that morning. During the day, that coin had changed hands ten times and had cleared up $200 worth of debts.

The money famine would not end until men who would be cowboys realized they could purchase a rancher's cattle for $3 to $5 a head, move the whole herd up a long trail for about a dollar a mile—$1,500—and sell them in Kansas for twenty dollars apiece.

That trail, in the 1870s and 1880s, would cut through Fort Worth. Its streets would swarm with those " 'roamin' $20 gold pieces." And the cowboys, in time, would bring three million dollars back from Kansas and leave more than their share in the town's hip pockets.

Prosperity was grazing on the plains. It was not far away at all. All Fort Worth had to do to be peaceful again was get rid of carpetbag rule and scalawag demands on its property. Fort Worth grew stubborn, then downright tenacious. It had been pushed around and walked on—not anymore.

Word came that Yankee military officers at Bonham and Marshall were going to order the town to surrender all its Confederate property. That meant everything it had.

Captain Eph Daggett bowed his back. This, he decided, was just one damn tax too many. "We must provide for our own," he said. "That is our first duty." Some of the men met in the Turner & Daggett store. They wanted to fight back, arguing that the Union only had 1,800 soldiers scattered throughout Texas and none close enough to enter Fort Worth if a good militia wanted to keep them out. Daggett, however, was the peacemaker. He reminded them, "There are no disorders in Tarrant County. We have governed ourselves and maintained order." He intended to keep it that way.

Fort Worth indeed had a supply of Confederate property. There was cotton—but for many, life was already a little threadbare. There was corn—but farmers with hungry families needed it for planting. As Turner pointed out, "Too many families—too many Negroes in Tarrant County are without clothes—without shoes—without corn. Men can't let their own suffer."

They were not about to haul the Confederate property all the way to the stations in Bonham and Marshall. It was easier to wait for the Yankee agents to come after it. That would take weeks, maybe months.

When the agents finally arrived in Fort Worth, they found only a small quantity of Confederate goods. The rest—though they would never know it—had been scattered throughout the county, handed out to the settlers and farmers who needed it most to face the harsh winter ahead of them. As Turner said, "Somehow frontiersmen always find a way out of their troubles."

The money famine would not end until men who would be cowboys realized they could purchase a rancher's cattle for $3 to $5 a head, move the whole herd up a long trail for about a dollar a mile—$1,500—and sell them in Kansas for twenty dollars apiece.

Chapter 4

The salvation of horned cattle and hard cash

Houston Street 1876: Everyone gathers for the photographer as he records for history Tivoli Hall, A.J. Anderson's Gun Store and further down the street, Fakes & Company furniture store.

Texas, when Generals Lee and Grant finally shook hands at Appomattox and put their swords away, was an unfenced world, its prairies trampled by great herds of those rangy, rawboned longhorn cattle.

The land was untamed, the cattle even wilder. But men on horseback chased them down, claimed ownership with the fiery end of a branding iron and developed a vast new kingdom of hide and horn.

Fort Worth became its capital.

An estimated 3.5 million cattle were scattered throughout Texas. They were lean and muscled and tough, survivors of the herds that Spanish conquistadores had lost on their long trek across a hostile land. The cattle's mossy horns sometimes reached nine feet in length, causing one old-timer to point out, "Why, a jaybird has to carry rations just to fly from one tip to another."

And, during the 1860s, all a man needed to become a cowboy was a rope, a running iron and the nerve to use them. His reason was a simple one: hunger.

The war had left Texas broke, no money but lots of cattle. Up north, the banks had plenty of money, put there by people who were starving for the taste of beef. And already, the Western Railroad was cutting into Kansas, laying tracks that, by 1879, would span the entire continent. Texas needed money. The northern states needed food. All the cattleman had to do was figure out a way to get those herds to the rail center in Kansas.

He drove them north, through the streets of Fort Worth, and that long, dust-bitten trail would tie a bitter nation back together again.

By the fall of 1865, Captain Eph Daggett had decided that the most viable market for his Cactus Bloomers (as Texans called the longhorns) was in Shreveport. So he turned his herd east from his Fort Worth home and launched, he said later, the most difficult drive of his career.

The route was an uneasy one, lined outside of Marshall with Negro soldiers dressed in blue. Daggett found them much too arrogant to suit him. He pushed his herd into the brush thickets to avoid them, a move that was as risky as it was slow and impractical. In Shreveport, the cattle only brought a six dollar profit per head. For Daggett, the trip hadn't been worth the trouble at all.

The trail would definitely be north, following the wagon ruts of old Jesse Chisholm, who traded with the Indians for buffalo robes and never drove a herd of cattle in his life, who died of cholera in 1868, caused by eating bear grease that had been poisoned by being melted in a brass kettle. No one ever paid much attention to Chisholm, but they struck to his trail religiously. After all, the old trader had found the one route north that took advantage of accessible water and favorable crossings.

In April of 1866, a group of cattlemen rode into Dallas and stopped beside a man standing watch over the community. The cattlemen were after two answers. Where was the best place to ford the Trinity River, and exactly how far away was the Chisholm Trail. The man had neither answer. And the disgusted cattlemen rode on.

One stomped into the Tarrant County courthouse and asked the same questions. He was in a hurry, he said. In less than an hour, a thousand head of cattle would be descending upon the town.

Charles Biggers Daggett, who had opened the first store in Fort Worth, didn't even blink. He grinned and yelled, "Bring 'em on."

A new era was stampeding its way toward Fort Worth.

Daggett, rushing out of the courthouse, quickly rounded up a group of men who immediately mounted their horses and galloped out with the cattlemen to find the most advantageous place for that many longhorns to ford the river.

The spot they chose for Colonel J.J. Myer's herd that spring day would forever be known as Daggett's Crossing. And Fort Worth—whether it was ready or not—had become Cowtown.

It didn't take Fort Worth long to get ready.

The cattle came, millions of them. And the cowboy—a mixed breed of miners,

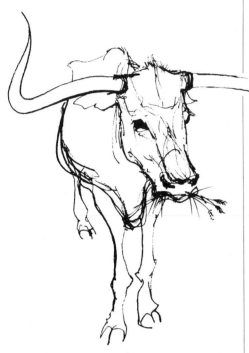

An estimated 3.5 million cattle were scattered throughout Texas. They were lean and muscled and tough, survivors of the herds that Spanish conquistadores had lost on their long trek across a hostile land.

Forerunner of downtown business: P.B. Binyon's modest Transfer Office was the forerunner of Binyon O'Keeffe. Wagon masters kept an eye out for mud holes.

farmers, soldiers, clerks and lawyers —were right behind, chewing dust and the grime of their own sweat, dodging stampedes when, they said, "It was like startin' from the back door of hell on a hot day and comin' out on the run."

Many were looking for opportunity. Some just hoped to make a living. Most were desperately trying to outrun their past and, (it is said) they came whipping a mighty tired pony into Texas. When dealing with men, they believed that "mindin' your own business is your best kind of life insurance." But dealing with a town was more like dueling hell itself.

The cowboy left his brand on Fort Worth.

Fort Worth gave him plenty of chances.

It was the last stopping-off place for supplies before the drovers headed toward the Red River and those long, lonely months on the trail, the final opportunity to gamble away good money on tainted cards, rolling dice and painted women. And the cowboy made the best of it.

Saloons never closed. Many didn't even have locks on the doors. Uncle Bob Winders' Cattle Exchange called itself the "handsomest saloon in Texas." In the back room of Henry Burns' saloon were dog fights, cock fights and even prize fights. And Herman Kussatz's Tivoli Saloon had variety shows and German music to go along with warm, free lunches every day at noon.

John McCoy, a drummer who lived in Fort Worth during its cattle-driving days, knew and observed the cowboys well. He once wrote of them:

"He enjoys a coarse, practical joke, or a smutty story; loves danger but abhors labor of the common kind; never tires of riding, never wants to walk, no matter how short the distance he desires to go.

"He would rather fight with pistols than pray; loves tobacco, liquor and women better than any other trinity. His life borders nearly upon that of an Indian. . . . His wages range from $15 and $20 a month in specie. . . . The cowboy has few wants and fewer necessities, the principal one being a full supply of tobacco."

Another early-day resident of Cowtown, Sam Smith, remembered:

"In the early days cowboys would come into Fort Worth, get drunk, and as they left town they would shoot out every light they could see."

They also made it a habit of shooting at the large coffee-pot sign that hung above James Bradner's tin shop. And, as likely as not, the drovers would ride into a saloon on their cow ponies and fire away at their reflections in the mirror. Of course, the Headlight Bar made it easy for them. It advertised: "Ride right in boys and get bar service in the saddle."

The *Fort Worth Democrat,* under the headline, "The Cowboys' Tear," dutifully reported on a far too common nightly occurrence in a booming town that smelled of rawhide and gunpowder.

The story said: "A dozen or more of the festive cowboys, imbued with the spirit of pure devilishment, mounted their horses and as is their custom visited the several dance houses, caroused and danced with the 'girls', drank when they felt so disposed, and continued their career without much trouble until about 1 o'clock when they all congregated at the Red Light, and after mounting their horses, each drew his six-shooter, and blazing away in the air, fired twenty or thirty shots, at the same time putting spurs to their horses,

they made tracks for the depot, and there reloaded and fired another volley. . . . Three of them were calaboosed after much trouble and six shooters taken from them."

Fort Worth had given its soul to longhorn cattle and the men who pushed them north. Morals may have been low, but the economy was high and, for the time, that was all that really mattered.

The Fort Worth Standard, in editorial, criticized the antics of the cowboy:

"Is there any absolute necessity for riders to rush their mustangs down the streets at breakneck speed? It is done too often and endangers the bones, if not the lives of little children—annoying older people as well."

The merchants didn't mind. They could tolerate most any kind of hazard as long as their cash registers kept filling up. As a saddle maker, C.J.E. Kellner, remembered, he "filled an order once from a drover by the name of Montague for 40 saddles, chaps, spurs, and everything that goes with them. I think the price was $50 a round. He drove the cattle to Montana."

Prosperity wore a pair of mossy horns. Business had spurs.

In 1871, for example, the *Cherokee Kansas Sentinel* reported, "360,000 head of cattle by a careful register have passed Fort Worth! Where is there another route that can count as many cattle?"

And Amanda Blake, the first lady trail driver, also came to realize the importance and popularity of the town, learning the hard way, her patience tested and bruised by floodwaters.

She wrote: "We camped a long time at Fort Worth, waiting for the Trinity River to fall low enough to cross our cattle. I counted fifteen herds waiting to cross."

Tools of the trade: A saddle shop in Fort Worth.

Forth Worth earned money from them all.

Colonel J.F. Ellison returned in '71, ambled along the streets he knew so well, and reported, "That herd of 750 mixed cattle I drove through here last spring on credit paid off. I sold the cattle and outfit at Abilene, came back by boat, paid my creditors, and pocketed $9,000."

"What's the drive this year?" a merchant asked.

"About 1,500 head are through Fort Worth today." Ellison told him. "I'm counting on sending several herds up trail this season and means plenty of bacon to buy."

The merchant smiled. "I can sure supply it," he said.

Fort Worth made quite an impression on cowboys who stayed awhile behind its closed, whiskey-stained doors. Those who drove on through were not particularly awed or overwhelmed at what they saw. W.R. Massengale, who chewed the dust of a herd in 1870, recalled, "We took the [Eastern Chisholm] Trail, went by the way of Fort Worth, which was a small village of one or two small business houses, a blacksmith shop and I think a school house and about twenty families. The Indians were bad in that section and we had a double watch on every night which made it hard for us."

The war years had left Fort Worth in shambles. It was slowly trying to recover, and the longhorn would be its savior. Yet, as Massengale remembered, the Indians were doing their best to keep the town flat on its back. They were hungry. Beeves were rambling through Fort Worth and on across the lands the Indians had once claimed. Beeves were salvation. Tribes took what they could. And they killed anyone who stood in the way and many who did not.

After the railroad had reached Fort Worth, its agent M.B. Loyd published a document that was handed out to any cattleman considering the long overland trail to Kansas. Obviously his purpose was to persuade them to take the train instead. Yet is graphically depicted the hardships that lay ahead within the Indian territory. The document was a letter from the Lee and Reynold's Ranch which read,

"Dear Sir: On the morning of the 2d instant the Cheyennes numbering about 50 strong attacked this Ranche, and were repulsed with

Market day 1877: From the courthouse, Weatherford and Houston Streets and the southwest corner of the courthouse square is crowded with early-day farmers, traders and businessman.

one Indian and one horse killed.

"They killed for Messrs. Lee and Reynolds three horses and wounded two. Half an hour later they attacked two men, two miles from here, on the other side of Red Fork, they killed and scalped one, shot the others horse and run him into this Ranche. At the same place they attacked a man herding cattle for M. Laflin, they running him to the Ranche. On the morning of the 3d a War party of Kiowas and Comanche, numbering about 50 made another attack on the Ranche, but were repulsed; the same day about 4 o'clock in the evening they attacked two men at Red Mound, four miles above Baker's Ranche, and run them five miles. A little later in the evening at the same place they attacked four men with three wagons, they killed and scalped the men and burnt two of the wagons, and two of the men. Kingfisher and Barker's Ranche was deserted, and we are all forted up here. . . . The Osages have been on the trail before the late raids, and have been taking, by force, cattle from the different herds. The wild tribes are well armed with Spencher-Carbines and Winchester Rifles and a drover stands no showing whatever.

"Four herds passed on the 8th all bunched up, the boys all had pistols, but no guns. We do not know whether they have got through safely or not. It is not safe to travel this trail, and I would advise no drover or person to try it."

Still men gambled with their herds, and most of them won. Few got rich, but they generally ate well as long as no one insulted the trail cook. And danger, in those days, was just a part of every day living.

Abilene, Kansas, had beckoned.

And the cowboys came. For most of them, Fort Worth was the last stop on the way north and the first stop on the way home. They paid their money going to buy flour, bacon, beans, dried fruit and coffee. They paid their money coming back just to wash the aches and pains of the trail away.

For there were many. During the first years of the cattle drives, the midwestern states feared tick fever that clouded those Texas herds. The disease infected and killed their own cattle. One farmer remarked, "If I can make any money out of the Texas trade I'm not afraid of Texas fever, but if I can't, I'm damned afraid of it." Armed guards met the drovers at the border with a simple proposition. Either go home or die. One cattleman, Martin Culver, stared down the barrels of the guns and called to his men: "Bend 'em west boys. Nothin' in Kansas anyhow, except three suns: sun flowers, sunshine, and sons of bitches."

Joseph G. McCoy figured out the way to make big money. During the first years of the trail drives, he met with Colonel Myers who had driven that first herd through Fort Worth and told him of a plan to build stockyards in Abilene, a place where Texas cattlemen could find buyers for their stock. Myers told him, "A cattle depot operating upon legitimate business principles is the greatest need of Texas stockmen."

It was a need McCoy fulfilled. Abilene was at the end of the most direct route north from Fort Worth. It had more prairie, less timber, smaller creeks, less flies, no wild Indian disturbances and folks who could care less about Texas fever. They owned no cattle.

In 1867, only 35,000 longhorns went to Kansas. Two years later, because of McCoy, the number hit 350,000. And by 1871, 700,000 cattle were tramping

As Remington saw him: "A Texas Cowboy."

The Texas Cowboy

Come all you Texas cowboys
    And warning take of me:
Don't go out in Montana
    For wealth or liberty.

But stay home here in Texas,
    Where they work the year around,
And where you'll not get consumption
    From sleeping on the ground.

Montana is too cold for me,
    And the winters are too long.
Before the round-ups have begun,
    Your money is all gone.

For in Montana the boys get work
    But six months in the year,
And they charge for things three prices
    In that land so bleak and drear.

This thin old hen-skin bedding,
    'Twas not enough to shield my
    form,
For I almost freeze to death
    Whene'er there comes a storm.

Your chuck is bread and bacon
    And coffee black as ink
And hard old alkali water
    That's scarcely fit to drink.

They'll wake you in the morning
    Before the break of day
And send you out on circle
    Full twenty miles away.

With a "Tenderfoot" to lead you
    Who never knows the way.
You're pegging in the best of luck
    If you get two meals a day.

Yes I've traveled lots of country,
    Arizona's hills of sand
Down through the Indian Nation
    Plum to the Rio Grande.

Montana is the bad land,
    The worst I've ever seen,
Where the cowboys are all tenderfeet
    And the dogies are all lean.

N. Howard Thorp (1908)

the Kansas prairie, most driven by cowboys who feasted on Fort Worth beans and coffee.

The depression was over. Gold again found its way to Fort Worth. And Fort Worth made damn sure the cowboy was treated well. When carpetbag politicians set up brand inspectors to collect exorbitant fees, a Fort Worth newspaper was the first to publically back the cattleman, calling the practice a "genteel system of blackmail." Cowboys defied the inspectors, beat them, chased them, kicked them out of their way, and Fort Worth never got around to prosecuting any of the drovers—at least not seriously.

In 1885, more than 220,000 head of cattle were pushed northward, but that marked the last great year of the trail drives. Herds dwindled. Stockmen no longer needed to make that long trek across unfriendly country. The railroads took some cattle to Kansas, but railroads were expensive, charging as much as $1.50 a head. Like Fort Worth, other cities ultimately built their own stockyards, and buyers found their way to Texas. The drovers became ranch hands and "cussed" any job they could not do on horseback. Yet, it was not until 1896 that "Scandalous" John McCanless drove the last small herd up the broken remnants of the old Texas trail.

Cattlemen had faced their share of problems—slumping beef prices, blizzards, droughts, an overstocked market, stampedes and age that crept up quickly in the saddle.

But the drives came along just in time to pull Fort Worth back on its feet and stayed around long enough to build it into a dynamic, booming city, no longer isolated on the fringe of the frontier.

It was, and forever would be, cowtown.

Its maker was the cowboy, a tough and hardy and special breed. Many of the cowboys had been the sons of British businessmen. Others were outcasts, members of English nobility whose tainted deeds had stained their good British titles. But then, cattlemen believed that "nobody came west save for health, wealth, or a ruined reputation."

Some cowboys were Mexican, the last of the Vaqueros. And quite a few were former slaves in search of a new way of life. Of them all, it was said, "Between the shoulder and the hip belongs to the rider, and the rest belongs to the company."

Cowboys on the trail, generally, were young men, barely 20 and described by an older cattleman as "prematurely bowlegged, responsible, with a streak of hell in their hearts." By the time they were 30, most were either broken or dead from too many long hours in the saddle. They worked from can till can't, from sun to sun, earning about $30 a month and all the beans they could eat. When a cowboy rode alone, he carried between the folds of his yellow slicker a frying pan, some bacon, salt, coffee, flour and a bottle of sourdough. He never knew when he would find the next chuckwagon.

The cowboy firmly believed that God made some men large and some men small but that Colonel Colt, with his .45, made them all equal. Yet he used that gun mostly to cut down rattlesnakes on the trail—a place, one wrote, that was "a hundred miles to water, twenty miles to wood, and six inches from hell."

The trail driver's life was pretty well summed up by one old cowboy who always explained, "We placed our faith in God, a six-shooter, and the chuck wagon, and we trailed cattle to market."

Chapter 5

Making the hard times pay off

Speculation on the prairie: As Fort Worth grew, buyers reached out into the open land, their investment would bring dividends. This land office was at the corner of Main and Lancaster Streets.

Major K.M. Van Zandt turned his face west. The war was behind him, and he thought he would just leave its memories where they lay. He had marched off to that conflict with Bass's Grays—the pride of Marshall, Texas. Van Zandt had fallen into Union hands after the Confederate calamity at Fort Donaldson up in Tennessee, served some time at Johnson's Island on Lake Erie and was exchanged just in time to charge into the bloodbath at Chickamauga and Missionary Ridge. The battle left him weak and ill, though not injured. He had returned to East Texas in a last-ditch attempt to dig up new recruits when Robert E. Lee called an end to the struggle.

Old dreams were buried in Confederate gray. New ones, perhaps, lay to the west. Khleber Miller Van Zandt was ready to find them and latch onto a couple, without being bothered anymore "by the many carpetbaggers and undesirable characters" who had crossed his path.

Many shared his outlook. Few were willing to ride far enough to take advantage of it. He would write, "As we journeyed West, the distance between villages grew greater, and the way grew lonelier. The enthusiasm of the men with me began to wane. One by one they said, 'You are going too far,' and they turned back." By the time Van Zandt reached Fort Worth, he was riding alone.

Below him, on the day in 1869, clustered the bits and pieces that were to be Van Zandt's future. It was not yet badly scarred by the hoofprints of cattle, but the town looked and smelled of ruin.

Van Zandt later wrote of that day:

"Fort Worth, as I first saw it . . . presented a sad and gloomy picture. The town had been laid out according to the general style, with a square in the center with stores surrounding it. A courthouse had been started in 1860. The rock walls had been built up as high as the first story, and there the work had stopped. The very looks of those walls accentuated the picture of desolation. . . . On the south and west sides of the square there were a few business houses, some of them stone or brick and two stories high. All of them had the shelves empty and the doors locked.

"The town had lost much of its former population due to the war. The

Fort Worth in the late 1870s: Looking east from the courthouse, Rusk Street is in the foreground, Belknap Street is on the left; Weatherford Street is on the right. Rusk Street gained a lurid reputation because of Hell's Half Acre. City fathers apparently believed the street dishonored General Thomas J. Rusk, hero of the Texas Revolution, for whom it was named; they changed the name to Commerce Street. Home of Major K.M. Van Zandt (top); on his first day in Fort Worth, he was not impressed.

Richard Moore Wynne at 17 was a staunch Texas secessionist. One of the first to enlist, he was promoted to lieutenant within a year's time and served with the Tenth Texas Regiment throughout the Georgia campaign. Severely wounded at the battle of Murfreesboro, Wynne left action only long enough to recover. He was shot at the last battle of Nashville, almost completely paralyzed on one side and left on the field to die. He was taken to a northern prison where he remained until the Confederacy surrendered. He returned to a desolate Texas, where he chose to lead the Reconstruction process, first as sheriff and later as an honored Texas legislator.

Colonel Wynne relaxes in his Victorian parlor (below).

young men had nearly all gone into the Confederate Army. Many of them had fallen on the field of battle, and those who had returned home had fallen prey to the apathy of the old men who remained at home and became weary with four long years of watching and waiting. . . . There were many more houses than there were people to occupy them."

Fort Worth, in essence, was a dry, dull, floundering frontier village—with neither a post office nor saloon—with no way to go but up and no one to really show it the way. Major K.M. Van Zandt would be the man.

It would have been easy for the major to turn away from the destitution before him and ride on. But Van Zandt had a feeling about Fort Worth, a good one. He talked and he listened. He learned enough, he said, "to make me realize the possibilities of the place and to decide to cast my lot here and grow with the town."

Van Zandt's impact was strong and it was felt immediately. He rented a house and established a mercantile store, even risked the shocking sum of $300 to purchase an entire block of downtown Fort Worth.

The major did not wait to see if the city would grow. He was determined to make it grow. He was the new lifeblood that Fort Worth needed, the kind of man who would ultimately sell off a chunk of his land for $200, then donate the money to the members of the First Christian Church to build themselves a prayer house.

Fort Worth was still staggering beneath the weight of reconstruction. The sound of bawling cattle was heard, but was still not close enough. The jangle of money broke the silence. And men went out of their way to discover the cures and evils of hard whiskey again.

Affluence, as Van Zandt believed, was slowly finding the round-about road back to Fort Worth, a road that had been empty for a long time, one still marked by the potholes of reconstruction. People had a little gold and silver for a change, but few places to keep it, usually depending on merchants and storekeepers to tuck it away in some vault for them. Gold and silver were heavy, bulky, hard to manage. But the coins were better than that paper currency floating around, much more trouble than it was worth. Texas, after the war, had no banking system at all. Those notes, likely to be counterfeit anyway, could not be exchanged for cash until merchants sent them up to the New York Reserve Bank by stagecoach. That took a long time. And stagecoaches were beset by too much misfortune to be a good bet. Besides, no one ever knew when one of those faraway banks was apt to lock its doors and clean its vaults.

Martin B. Loyd, who had served in the war as a Confederate cavalry captain from Mississippi, arrived in Fort Worth with $40,000 in gold. He needed a good, safe place to hold it. When he could not find one, he sat down and founded a one-room bank, calling it an "exchange office." It gave Fort Worth a little dignity. It would be a Godsend to cattlemen. Seven years later, in 1877, the exchange office would be incorporated as the First National Bank, opening with $72,000 worth of deposits and winding up the year with $220,000—even declaring a dividend of 12 percent.

Fort Worth was taking shape. Two brothers, fresh out of college, hit Fort Worth in 1869 with a fervor and fever for the necessity of higher education. They were appalled by the town's lack of it. Addison and Randolph Clark found fast, firm support from Van Zandt, Dr. Peak, John Peter Smith and the Christian Church. With more faith and fortitude than money, they organized Add-Ran College.

In a short time, the institution offered ancient languages, English, mathematics, physical sciences, mental and moral sciences, social and civic history. It also made sure women got a good solid course in "embroidering and cutting" (if they wanted one).

Classes were tough. The rules were even tougher. All students attended church each Sunday and were never allowed to partake of tobacco or any beverage form of alcohol. And none could attend any "exhibition of immoral tendency," which automatically cut out the "race course, theater, circus, billiard-saloon, bar-room or tippling house."

The coming of the tarantula: Overcoming severe obstacles, the railroad arrived in Fort Worth in the summer of 1876. Citizens pose (above) with a Texas & Pacific woodburning locomotive in the 1880s. Captain Buckley B. Paddock (below), editor of the Fort Worth Democrat (1872–1884) was well-known as a civic promoter. Paddock popularized the "tarantula map," a diagram of north Texas showing all railroads leading to Fort Worth.

Fort Worth did not yet have all those immoral exhibitions but it would. And Add-Ran college was ready for them. The Clark brothers would be shocked at the behavior of cowboys and the sin that sprang up from their footsteps. And when Fort Worth began actively seeking a railroad, the Clarks dreaded the "riff-raff" those tracks would bring. (Fate was unkind to Add-Ran. The college—in spite of its constant ministering against moral decay—eventually found itself jammed into the iniquitous corner of Hell's Half Acre.)

On a July morning in 1872, Fort Worth was as feverish as the weather. The people had long heard rumors surrounding the coming of the railroad. They realized that towns fed by trains were destined to endure, while those without the rails were cursed to labor with little hope of growth or good fortune. Fort Worth wanted those tracks. At last, Colonel Thomas A. Scott, honorable president of the Texas & Pacific Railroad, was in town to look over Fort Worth's assets, to study its potential as a rail point. He arrived with Texas Governor J.W. Throckmorton and a party of Eastern capitalists, all looking for a way west, all casting a narrow eye on the attributes of Fort Worth, if there were any at all.

Colonel John Forney, editor of the *Philadelphia Press*, made the trip with Scott, and he later wrote:

"The town of Fort Worth contains some twelve or fifteen hundred habitants, several churches, good schools, and a large court-house, in the centre of the plaza, constructed of yellowish limestone, resembling Joliet marble. It remains in unfinished condition. . . .

"The prospect from this plateau is grand beyond description, decidedly the finest we enjoyed during our visit to Texas—especially in the western direction and the course pursued by the Texas and Pacific Railroad. For fifty miles away there lay stretched before us a succession of cultivated fields, interspersed with belts of timber, wide expanses of prairie lands with the natural grass, and in the dim horizon, so far off as to be barely distinguished from the clouds themselves, a succession of lofty mountains. The hotel accommodations at Fort Worth need to be greatly enlarged, but there are comfortable private dwellings, and the citizens are kind, courteous, and hospitable. The breezes at this elevation far surpass anything we experienced.

"Fort Worth is a city set on a hill, and as the point of junction between two branches of the Texas and Pacific, is particularly enviable. . . . Lands in the vicinity of Fort Worth have been selling at exceedingly low prices, but they will be greatly enhanced on account of the proposed railroad facilities."

Scott also liked what he saw. He was ready to deal. Blunt and to the point, he told the town leaders, "I want 320 acres of land south of town. . . . In consideration of this, I will proceed as rapidly as possible to build the Texas and Pacific Railroad to your town."

Before dark, Van Zandt, Eph Daggett, Colonel T.J. Jennings and Judge H.G. Hendricks had all signed a "promissory obligation" for the land and slapped it firmly into Scott's hand. Fort Worth was not about to drag its heels, not over something as important to its existence as a railroad.

The Texas & Pacific did. Fort Worth waited, and it waited in style. Within a year, the population had doubled. Lumberyards came in and readied themselves for the boom, along with wholesale grocery stores, livery stables and even an ice cream parlor. But, most important of all, B.B. Paddock strode briskly into the life of the town. It would never be quite the same again.

Paddock, at 16, had been too young to enlist for duty in the War between the States, but he joined anyway. A year later, he was one of the South's youngest officers. He had practiced law for awhile, but Paddock had other ideas and none of them included a courtroom.

He was not bashful. Paddock walked into Van Zandt's store, introduced himself to the major and announced he had decided to call Fort Worth home. "What would you like to do?" asked Van Zandt.

"I would like to run a newspaper, sir," he answered.

Paddock was talking to the right man. A year earlier, Van Zandt had traded a wagon load of wheat for a printing press once used in the publication of

Harnessing horses and dogs: Nobby Harness Company (top), 600 Houston Street, sold to the cattlemen as they headed north through town and to local pet owners (note dog harness lower center). H. Dugan's wagon yard (above), located in the 200 block of West Weatherford Street, reportedly was a good place for the latest out-of-town news and local gossip.

the *Quitman Herald.* He had launched the *Fort Worth Democrat* just so the town would have some semblance of a newspaper, then run through a quick succession of editors, none of whom had impressed either Van Zandt or Fort Worth.

B.B. Paddock would. (He ultimately would be the self-appointed critic, conscience, voice, defender and number-one salesman for the town.) In one of his earliest articles for the *Democrat,* Paddock wrote with pride:

"The society of Tarrant County is better than is usually found in a new country. The gentlemen are generally well informed, shrewd, and many of them cultivated and refined. The ladies compare well with those of the older states, in point of health, beauty, style, and cultivation; all are social and agreeable. . . . Lands are worth from three to five dollars per acre for unimproved and from ten to forty dollars for improved lands. The price varying with the locality and quality of improvements. . . .

"The population of Fort Worth is about two thousand, and is increasing daily. Scores of the best men in the country are coming to and locating in Fort Worth, and are going to work with energy and determination to build up the place and make it what it is inevitably destined to be— the city of Northwest Texas."

Paddock was the prophet. Fort Worth had to grow—Paddock would not let it quit. "All classes of people who are willing to pull off their coats and go to work are in demand," he advertised. All classes of people read and they came. The gentlemen were rather well-informed, shrewd and cultivated, even if they did wear mud and cow dung splotched on their boots. And the women—regardless of style and beauty—worked and sweated right alongside

Author of the city charter: J.Y. Hogsett poses in his office in the Powell Building.

of them.

Then the panic of 1873 knocked Fort Worth back to its knees.

Banks failed in New York. Property values, once so high, were suddenly so low. The crowds had flooded into Fort Worth to find a home. The same crowds were now on their way out of town.

Paddock had told them in his editorial columns, "Bring your lumber, buy your lots, build your houses and settle down; for Fort Worth is bound to go ahead and be the railroad center of the West." But with the whole country being financially strangled, the Texas & Pacific was not going anywhere.

Paddock bragged, "The health of Tarrant County is unsurpassed. The climate here is said to be very beneficial to those affected with lung or bronchial complaints—many have been restored to health."

But that, as panic gripped the country, was just about all Fort Worth had to offer anymore.

In Kansas, Texas cattlemen found no market for their herds. Money— especially after the New York Stock Exchange shut down for ten days—ran scared, then dried up altogether. Some trail drivers gambled for a good spring and leased grassland up north. But a severe blizzard raged across the plains and froze their cattle. Other drovers killed the longhorns themselves, salvaging the hides and tallow. They would not make much money, but their pockets, at least, would not be empty.

Fort Worth depended on the profits of those cattlemen. Trail herds were the most reliable high-finance industry it had. But they were suffering even worse than the rest of the nation. And Fort Worth felt the blow.

Only a year earlier, George Van Winkle and A.P. Wroten opened a private bank with a trunk load of gold mined from the rich hills of California. Now the trunk was empty. The bank locked its door. It could have been a bad omen for Fort Worth. But the town did not choose to waste away while standing around and watching for a train to end its misery, a train that did not come. Instead, Fort Worth made 1873 pay dividends. The reason was simple enough to Paddock. Its citizens, he said, "possessed a quality of enterprise not to be found in the ordinary frontier village." They did not weaken just because the dollar did.

And, for the first time since a defeated army came shuffling home, the men of Fort Worth found themselves with the time-honored right to vote. They made the most of it. Scalawags could start packing. As one citizen remarked, "Didn't the Bible say, 'There's a time to plant, a time to pluck up, and a time to cast away?' Well, the time has come to cast away them carpetbaggers."

The men supported Horace Greeley, a Democrat hard at work roasting the contemptible U.S. Grant. They could not budge the Republicans nationally. But the Republicans did not stand a chance at home.

C.B. Mitchell remembered, "When we went to vote we had to pass between a row of Negro soldiers at the old stone courthouse, and they all glared at us. We voted them out that time." Tarrant County elected Democrats to both Congress and the Legislature and passed an amendment making Austin the permanent capital of Texas.

Major K.M. Van Zandt became Fort Worth's voice in the House of Representatives. And one of the most important documents he was to carry to the 13th Legislature that year was the charter draft, written by J.Y. Hogsett, to incorporate Fort Worth as a full-fledged city. The Charter was obtained from the state in 1873.

Those 2,688 acres within the city's boundaries needed a mayor to rule over them. That position would not be hard to fill. But a mayor needed help in the fine art and responsibility of decision-making—and that posed a problem. As the *Democrat* lamented, "Everybody wants to be mayor, but no one wants to be alderman."

Four men filed for the office. The vote went to William P. Burts. It seems most people had forgiven the good doctor his superstitions about jackrabbits. They merely remembered all those ills he had treated during the war without ever bothering to send a bill. (Burts had felt responsible. He had been the

Then the panic of 1873 knocked Fort Worth back to its knees.

Early fire fighters: The first fire station in Fort Worth (above left) was located on Main Street between 11th and 12th. When it opened in 1883, a 3,000-pound bell was placed in the tower to sound the alarm. The Central Fire Hall (right) was erected on Throckmorton Street, in 1899 and subsequently razed in 1938.

only doctor left in town.)

Fort Worth finally rounded up five aldermen off the streets who, like Burts, agreed to serve without pay until the city was able to dig back out of a depression again. During their first week, in a flurry of civic duty, the officials passed ordinances regulating gambling and gambling houses and shooting galleries, restricted the carrying of deadly weapons, ordered the building of sidewalks, protected shade and ornamental trees and prohibited mobs.

In a sudden fit of dignity, Fort Worth created laws, but it desperately needed a police force to keep them all from being broken. One town marshall had no chance at all doing it by himself. On April 10, 1873, that first police department swung into action. It boasted four officers to support the mandates of Marshall Ed Terrell. Thirty days later, they were out of a job. It had taken all the city's money to build a new jail, and now there were no funds left to pay the police who were supposed to keep it full.

Paddock, for one, was even more concerned about the wanton deficiency of fire protection. "Burn and pray for the bucket brigade"—that had been Fort Worth's motto far too long. The town's collection of flimsy wooden buildings—all heated by fireplaces and wood stoves—was flirting with disaster. Paddock demanded a fire department, but few listened to him. When a building on the square went down in flames, people merely stepped around its ashes without (as he wrote) taking any steps "to prevent a recurrence of the fearful event." The editor, undaunted, twisted a few arms, stomped a little more, yelled a little louder and at last persuaded a few of the town's leading businessmen to gather at the courthouse and organize a fire company.

A blue norther kept them all away. Only Paddock showed up. And he wrote in the Democrat, "We took our position on the steps of that edifice and although it was a little cool, we heroically held our position until patience ceased to be a virtue." Alone, he walked inside and, he wrote, "We took our seat amid the most profound silence." The meeting needed a chairman. Without opposition, Paddock elected himself, then promptly voted himself in as secretary, treasurer and a committee of five to draft a resolution which, he pointed out, "we immediately proceeded to adopt . . . as a whole without debate." He continued, "Now the fire company is ready to extinguish fire in any part of the city on short notice. All orders promptly executed, day or night."

Feeling cynical as usual, Paddock even went so far as to offer the

company's services to Dallas. He explained, "If you will let us know a day or two before you intend to have a fire, we will be on hand with our machine."

Of course Fort Worth had no machine. The only hook and ladder equipment Fort Worth had for battling a blaze, Paddock wrote, was "a five foot ladder, a walking stick with a hook on the end, a pint cup, and a wet blanket."

Paddock had Fort Worth's attention. At a second meeting, May 2, 1873, the editor had company. And the group put together a 60-member unit, manned primarily by clerks and mechanics in town. The men even took up a collection among themselves and came up with enough money to purchase an actual hook and ladder wagon.

The wagon came by train to Dallas, then members dragged it home and waited for the outburst of flames. By now, they were almost eager for a fire. They could fight it for a change. Times were improving, in spite of the monetary crisis.

But they were still only one short step above rock bottom. Fort Worth was not standing still, but it was not really going anywhere either. And as the days dragged on without confirmation of a railroad, the town began to wallow in its misery, then sink again.

The railroad had become a busted dream. Only 30 miles away from the outskirts of Fort Worth, the Texas & Pacific laid its last track. Its backers—those eastern capitalists who had been so smitten by Fort Worth—had gone broke.

The consequence was devastating. As Paddock wrote: "Professional men from all over the country who had left comfortable homes and good businesses to come here and begin their fortunes anew, faced inevitable ruin. The population dwindled as fast as it had grown. Stores and dwellings were vacated by the score. Business was at a stand still and gloom and despondency were everywhere visible. . . . The decimation of Fort Worth left here about one thousand people. Many of them stayed because they could not well get away. Others remained because their faith in the ultimate growth and preeminence of the city was not shaken by this disaster."

One of those unshaken was Major K.M. Van Zandt. Paddock printed his beliefs in the *Fort Worth Democrat*. Van Zandt supported his with money. He could have left. He had the chance—a tempting one. He was offered a partnership in a Houston bank, an honest gesture by friends who thought the major might be in the midst of a panic as severe as that suffered by the rest of the country. But he refused. Van Zandt suggested, instead, that those bankers come to Fort Worth and enter into business with him. He was not joking. These were not the days for jest.

Van Zandt had an eye on owning his own bank. Thomas A. Tidball and John Wilson had one, but Wilson was ready to pull out and go back home to Missouri. Van Zandt—along with old reliable John Peter Smith, J.J. Jarvis and Tidball—decided to invest a total of $30,000 and reopen the private institution under the name of Tidball, Van Zandt and Company.

He also met with Fort Worth's merchants and told them that if Fort Worth had any hopes at all of becoming a city, something had to be done and done quickly.

Bank and banker: Fort Worth National Bank (top) and period transportation. Khleber M. Van Zandt (above) was the oldest son of Isaac Van Zandt, congressman and Republic of Texas minister to the United States. He surveyed for the railroad and practiced law in East Texas before coming to Fort Worth following the Civil War. Van Zandt was president of the Bank of Tidball, Van Zandt and Company, which later became Fort Worth National.

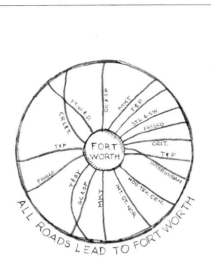

The tarantula map: The importance of transportation to a city can be understood by the extravagant maps and claims made during early growth years. The famed "tarantula map" of Captain Paddock (above) was often printed in his paper. Another promotional map (below) took certain liberties with geography to make its point.

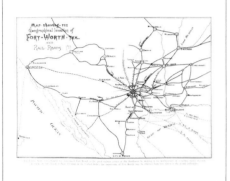

In the meantime, B.B. Paddock astonished his readers by creating his "tarantula map." It pictured Fort Worth with nine crooked legs coiling out of its downtown square. Each leg represented an imaginary railroad that linked the town with every major section of the nation. The railroads would come, Paddock predicted. He was willing to bet on it.

Yet none were in sight. People in Dallas merely shook their heads and ridiculed the drawing. They called Paddock a "slightly tetched dreamer." Dallas could afford to scoff. Dallas had a railroad. And Fort Worth was gripped in lethargy and despair. More than 3,000 citizens had run away, the lights of their campfires at night burning could be seen all the way to Dallas.

A former Fort Worth attorney, Robert E. Cowart, even wrote in the *Dallas Herald* that the little town on the twin forks of the Trinity had become such a drowsy place that a panther had even been found asleep in its street.

Fort Worth did not laugh. The town tried to make the best of it. The fire department adopted a real live panther for its mascot. So did the Keg Saloon, but the panther asleep behind its bar woke up long enough to scalp a man.

Paddock was not pleased about his hometown being referred to as "Panther City." He even wrote that Cowart had "a keen sense of the ridiculous and verbiage that can make an Indian's hair curl." Yet, he concluded, "No attempt was made to deny or explain the charge. It was accepted fact."

A railroad would change all of that. Fort Worth rolled up its sleeves, took a deep breath and went after one. Its plan—devised and presented by Van Zandt and four other civic leaders—was as outlandish as Paddock's "tarantula map." But it made sense. The major met with Frank S. Bond, vice president for the Texas & Pacific in Marshall, and told him bluntly that the lack of money for rails need not hold up the railroad because rails could be bought on credit. Bond merely shrugged and explained, "We have no money to pay for grading the road."

Van Zandt smiled. "We will take the contract for grading the road," he said, "and accept your note due in a reasonable length of time."

Bond was flabbergasted. Fort Worth was serious. He agreed to discuss the proposal further. By the time he arrived in Fort Worth, the Tarrant County Construction Company was already organized and boasted subscribed capital stock of $25,000.

Bond was just as eager to get the railroad on the move again. He had no choice but to accept the plan. When he left, crews were covering his footsteps with work on the road that would lead the Texas & Pacific to cowtown.

All eyes were on Fort Worth. And most of them had either amusement or contempt for the grassroots effort to attract a railroad. Fort Worth, in its ignorance, had undertaken the impossible. The *Sherman Register* editorialized: "The probability is that their scheme will terminate just as many a one before, and exhaust itself ere they commence work."

Paddock answered back, "The *Register* never made a greater mistake. The people of Fort Worth heretofore have held town meetings and made buncombe speeches, and it all has ended with 'resolved.' But this time they have put their hands deep down into their purses and have gone to work with a vim and energy worthy of the importance of the work at hand, and they will not abate their vigor until the road bed is completed from Eagle Ford to Fort Worth."

But 30 miles would take three years. Work was slow, then cut to a crawl during the damp months of winter. January rolled around and with it came forfeiture of the land that had been donated for a depot and sidings. A deadline had been set and missed. The donation would not be extended again until October 23, 1875, carrying with it the stipulation that the railroad would have to be completed within two years.

Paddock tried to remain optimistic. He could always see the good side of Fort Worth. He wrote: "The news having gone abroad of the organization of the Tarrant County Construction Company and their determination to resume work on the T & P, between [Fort Worth] and Eagle Ford, has already produced a good effect on the business of our town. It has infused a new life and vigor

Some call Colonel J.P. Smith "the father of Fort Worth." At the age of 12, he lost both parents. Smith moved to his cousin's Kentucky farm where he studied language and mathematics during the winter months. In 1853 he moved to Fort Worth and established the town's first school. He later took up surveying, studied law on the side and was accepted to the Bar without the benefit of a formal legal education.

Although he was opposed to secession, Smith nevertheless served in the Confederate Army. He was badly wounded twice. At the war's end, he returned to Fort Worth, juggled a law practice, cattle trading and real estate dealings and collected large amounts of the city's prime property.

In 1882, he was elected mayor and initiated an ambitious road paving project—Fort Worth's first—which won him a second and third term of office. But Smith declined nomination as governor of Texas— he preferred Fort Worth to state politics.

into our people which reacts on those coming here with good results. Vacant houses are filling up; hotels are crowded; stages and hacks come in loaded, and everything is beginning to assume the appearance of life, activity and enterprise, which was shown here in the early days of 1873."

But Fort Worth was facing still another dilemma in its race with the rails. The Legislature established a time limit for the Texas & Pacific to finish laying its tracks to Fort Worth. The railroad was emphatically told to get those rails spiked down by the end of the 1876 legislative session or it would lose its rich land grant. Texas & Pacific, after all, had been promised 16 sections of land for every mile of track it completed. That was a lot of dirt—too much to squander by fooling around and wasting time.

Paddock, in the *Democrat,* was preaching prosperity: "We know of no term that expresses more fully the condition of affairs in Fort Worth at the present time than 'red hot.' In every line of business there is great activity which increases day by day as the time when the steam whistle shall wake the echoes in our city approaches."

But the whistle might not blow for Fort Worth. In June, the tracks were still far away. The T & P could not afford to gamble away all of those sections of land on the sweat and skills of unskilled laborers. The railroad immediately voided its contract with the Tarrant County Construction Company and put its own crews on the right-of-way.

Fort Worth's feelings were not hurt, however; they pitched in to help. It would take every available muscle in the county to beat the deadline. The stakes were high. But so were the risks. And from Austin came rumors that the legislature had decided to adjourn and no extension would be given the Texas & Pacific. It appeared as if those three years of fighting the odds had created false hopes and no railway. The shouting dimmed, but persistence did not.

If a man anywhere in the county was able to work, he was immediately dispatched to join those burly, cursing section hands who kept up a steady sledge-hammer beat, driving spikes and rails into place. Businessmen turned their employees loose, then locked their doors and went themselves. All day and far into the night, women brought coffee and food to the sore and weary workers, even watering the mules for them so no strong arm would have to leave the job at hand. Few rested. Even fewer slept.

Fort Worth asked the legislature for one last extension, but the legislature turned away, saying it had probably given the railroad too many extensions already.

Fort Worth had one chance—it had to stall adjournment. A motion was offered in the House chamber to call it quits and go home. It was beaten. The halls rang with the arguments of a desperate filibuster. Day after day, the vote was taken for adjournment only to be defeated by the slimmest of margins. Tarrant County's representative, Nicholas H. Darnell, was ill in bed and in no condition to be moved. But for 15 consecutive days, Darnell's cot was carried into the House so he—with a voice much weaker than his determination—could cast his vote against leaving Austin.

In Fort Worth, both fear and excitement gripped the town. The *Democrat* reported that interest was spreading, as well as curiosity: "There is a continual and incessant stream of buggies, carriages, hacks and persons on horseback going to and from Sycamore Creek, who gather there every day to witness the throngs of men, who are at work like bees on the bridging and piling on the bottom. On Sunday there were hundreds of spectators on the grounds all day. Some of them came long distances, and many had never seen a railroad or anything pertaining to one, and were much interested and highly entertained by the sight of the engines and the busy workers."

The Legislature fretted but lingered. Fort Worth and the Texas & Pacific worked without ceasing, laying a mile of track a day. Nothing could stop them now, but Sycamore Creek was trying. The crew realized it had no time to build a proper trestle, so the men merely stacked up enough lumber and cross ties to span the water then kept right on going.

Early-day disaster: The railroad made it into town just under the wire of the Legislature's delayed adjournment, but the trains did not always make it across the bridge. A bridge collapsed on the Trinity River around 1881.

If a man anywhere in the county was able to work, he was immediately dispatched to join those burly, cursing section hands who kept up a steady sledge-hammer beat, driving spikes and rails into place.

Fort Worth was in sight. But the railroad was running out of time and, in Austin, the sympathetic legislators were running out of "no's." The filibuster was losing its voice.

Workmen said to hell with a roadbed. Building one would take the hours they lacked. Instead, they laid the tracks on a dirt road, weighting down the rails with big rocks, and headed into Fort Worth. Behind them, a train—old Number 20—crept along, bringing the town ever close to the one spark it thought it had to have for greatness. Paddock wrote of the makeshift mile: "It was as crooked as the proverbial ram's horn, but it bore up the rails."

From out in the prairie, the train whistle could be heard on the downtown streets. And on July 18, Paddock appealed for proper respect to be shown the iron horse that Indians referred to as the "big puff wagon." He wrote: "It is suggested that Fort Worth men, women, and children, old and young be present and give them a rousing welcome. Let every one bring a basket with boiled hams, light bread, cold chicken, salads, pickles, wines, anything, everything that is good, and give the hard-handed strong-armed men who have been at work night and day, a rousing welcome. Let there be no standing back."

No one did. At 11:23 a.m. on July 19, Number 20—burning the air with the acrid aroma of wood smoke—came rolling into town as the *Democrat* headlines shouted:

"At Last.
"The day has come.
"Hope Ends in Fruition."

Dr. R.F. Line—only five years old at the time—watched the grand entry. He did not remember the firing pistols, the yelling, the passing around of that barrel whiskey. But he did have a vivid impression of the day. He later recalled, "There were covered wagons all over the place, must've been one hundred at least. It was a little ol' engine. The smokestack was the biggest thing about it. It had black smoke and a coarse whistle and big bell that scared me. I'd been threatened all my five and a half years with boogers. By golly, I thought, there's the booger."

And *The Democrat,* as usual, spoke for all of Fort Worth about the coming of the train; how it "uttered its shrill scream within the corporate limits arousing the 'panther' from his lair, startling the birds from their nests in affright, and carrying joy to the anxious hearts who have waited long and patiently for the sounds that then reverberated through the hills and valleys around the beautiful city of Fort Worth."

Morgan Jones, one of the construction bosses, sat down on the sidewalk and rested. He had not had time to change clothes for the last two weeks. Lawyers, store owners, bankers, doctors, druggists, clerks, ranchers and farmers all rolled down their sleeves and went back to the jobs they knew best. Down in Austin that afternoon, the legislature at long last got its adjournment. And a few days later, Nicholas Darnell, whose "no" votes had kept the House in session, was dead.

The three-year battle for a railroad had, like a jealous mistress, demanded

A sign of prosperity: Trader's National Bank of Fort Worth, February 18, 1886.

and obtained most of Fort Worth's selfish and civic consideration. Yet the town prospered and, as it had done so many times before, wiped the mud of depression off its boots.

By now a group of Germans operated a brewery. For amusement, men who dared to be caught in such places either went to the race track on the north side or wound up betting loose change on a cock fight, dog fight or foot race. A new government law prohibited every man east of Parker County from toting his pistol downtown, and, as Charles Mitchell remembered, "A man would rather be caught without his pants than his six-shooter in those days." West of Parker County, the Indians could not be trusted. But the law was trying hard to make places like Fort Worth feel civilized and, more importantly, act like it.

Fakirs were common—they often wandered the courthouse square looking for someone gullible enough to pay a few coins for an impromptu exhibition. "One fakir," C.J.E. Kellner recalled, "claimed to pull teeth with a buggy whip, and it is said that he pulled about a wagon load of teeth."

Policemen returned to the streets, though the town still could not afford to outfit them with proper helmets, clubs or badges. They walked in pairs, well-dressed in blue uniforms and black slouch hats, and they did what they could to keep the jail full. There were only two cells and a dungeon, but on a good Saturday night, the jailer had little problem squeezing in as many as 30 drunks.

Paddock, at the *Democrat,* kept the faith in Fort Worth, but even he took no unnecessary chances. He announced, "We take all kinds of produce for subscriptions . . . corn, wood, oats, butter, eggs, chickens, etc. taken in payment. We take cash only for 'ads.' "

And on the morning of September 10, 1874, a new-fangled invention jarred the minds of Fort Worth. The telegraph was thrust upon the town, putting it in immediate touch with the rest of the country, cutting away the lonely feeling of frontier isolation.

Two days later, Mayor Burts wired the Honorable W.L. Cabell, mayor of Dallas: "Today another link has been completed which joins us to your growing and prosperous city. May it increase your happiness as it has ours—and may prosperity of both be advanced thereby."

On September 14, Mayor Cabell replied: "Dallas responds to your greetings most heartily and extends to her sister city Fort Worth its congratulations in at last being able to tell of her glories in electric words, and trusts that the near future will bind us with iron bands as well as by the great electric tongue of thought."

Diplomacy out of the way, Fort Worth and Dallas—as the towns would always do—went back to fighting and feuding and fearing that one would outgrow and ultimately outlast the other. The rivalry kept them both reaching up beyond their grasp, hanging onto nothing but hope until prosperity came their way again.

The rails gave Fort Worth stature. But, by 1876, the dusty old cattle trails—virtually forgotten—were again thick with herds and money. Cattlemen were always an optimistic lot, the kind who could stand on their front porch, stare into the face of a drought and proclaim, "Well, we're one day closer to rain than we've ever been before." They had survived the panic and blizzards and heavy losses and were following the longhorns back down the road of good fortune. "The trail is swarming with cattle," *The Democrat* commented. Five herds—12,000 beeves—belonged to one man, Major Seth Mabry. And before the drive ended that year, 204,438 cattle had tramped through Fort Worth.

Within a few years, Fort Worth would be the end of the trail for the cowboy. No longer would the drover suffer that three-month trek to Kansas, branded by lightning, thirst, flood waters and his own loneliness. The trains leaving Fort Worth would cover those unfriendly, back-breaking miles for him.

B.B. Paddock (though first) was not the only voice of optimism to understand the importance of the railroad to the town's once and future economy. Paddock

A most unlikely team: The driver's name was Harrell, a Fort Worth resident who drove the team of buffaloes throughout West Texas during the 1880s.

had a competitor, M.M. Brannan and *The Fort Worth Standard.*

In October of '76, Brannan took a stroll down to the tracks then bragged to his readers: "The depot is still there, and so are the many trains which are loading with cotton, wheat, and all kinds of produce, which seek Fort Worth as an outlet to the great marts of the continent." He was impressed (he wrote in a later article) by the "thousands upon thousands of feet of lumber, innumerable bales of cotton awaiting shipment, box goods, heavy groceries, bagging and ties, and every article of merchandise in crowded profusion."

The year of '76 was a good year, one that shook Fort Worth out of its doldrums and set its feet on the pathway of the rich, if not the righteous. It was also tragic. The courthouse burned. In his headlines, Paddock reflected on the adversity of it all: "Total Destruction of the County Records! Loss Incalculable." He lamented, "Had the records of the courts been saved, the loss would have been slight, as the better workmanship and modern improvements that can be utilized in rebuilding the house would compensate for the loss incurred. . . . If it should transpire that the fire was the work of an incendiary, as it is believed by many, we hope the fiend may be discovered and punished."

No incendiary was ever found. So Fort Worth kicked away the rubble and made plans to build a new courthouse, one (as Paddock explained) that "would be an ornament and do credit to our county."

By November, *The Standard* was ready to report that "The old Courthouse has been torn down and a great pile of 'gray sad rocks' is all that remains of the grim old ruins from this whilom temple of justice. . . . The foundation of the new Courthouse has been commenced."

Fort Worth was in the agony of growing pains. Its downtown had been all right for a frontier village, but now it had to hurry to catch up with progress or be left behind. Paddock chastised. He wrote: "There are so many loose stones in the streets that the progress of vehicles is greatly impeded. . . . No city in northern Texas can boast such a limited supply of good sidewalks."

Cotton stop: The Boaz and Battle Cotton Yard at the corner of Main and 14th Streets was one of the stops of the mule car operated by the Fort Worth Street Railroad.

Paddock had a reason for wanting better streets. On Christmas day, after a two-year wait, a mule—the pride and joy of the Fort Worth Street Railway Company—began pulling the town's first street car over a single track from the courthouse to the depot. It wasn't much, but it beat trudging through the mud and mire of the street. The transportation company had been incorporated by Major Van Zandt, John Peter Smith and Jesse S. Zane-Cetti for $50,000. The tiny street car was met with immediate approval. It was a carnival ride without the music. As John Renfro remembered, "The novelty attracted more passengers than anything else. Within a year or two after the company started, it was carrying 400 riders a day and by 1878 was making $7,000 a year profit."

The businessmen had to be farsighted. In 1877, the net profit was only $22. But the little car rolled along, powered by a mule that Paddock described as being "something larger than a West Texas jack rabbit."

When it rained, the driver frantically searched the sidewalks for strong-armed men, then offered them free rides. His reasoning was sound. As one rider recalled, "A bunch of the railroad fellows were loafing on our day off when we saw the car. The man that runs the car asked if we wanted to ride. Of course we got on, to our sorrow. About every block the car jumped the track, and got stuck in the mud. That's what he asked us to ride for—so we could lift the darn thing out of the mud."

Chapter 6

Refinement from the ashes of vice and violence

High rise: The first two-story home in Fort Worth (circa 1890) was built in 1872 by David Boaz at 611 East Bluff Street.

In that centennial year of 1876, Fort Worth found out that the wages of sin were generally profitable enough to keep living on easy street as long as the right streets were easy to find. With growth had come the multitudes—all out to make their own fortune or take someone else's.

One visitor to the western cattle towns carefully observed the strange mix of people who gathered there: "Here you see in the streets men from every state and from almost every nation: the tall, longhaired Texas herder with his heavy jingling spurs and pair of six-shooters; the dirty, greasy Mexicans, with unintelligible jargon; the gambler from all parts of the country, looking for unsuspecting prey; the honest emigrant in search of a homestead in the great free west; the keen stock buyers; the wealthy Texas drovers; deadbeats; cappers; pickpockets; horse thieves; a cavalry of Texas ponies; and scores of the demimonde."

Fort Worth was no exception. It had its good and its bad. It was not unlike Ellsworth, Kansas, which always bragged that on Saturday night, "hell was in session."

Its earthy view of life was best typified by its unsophisticated, rub-their-faces-in-the-dirt attitude about the '76 presidential race between Republican Rutherford B. Hayes and Democrat Samuel J. Tilden. Little support at all could be found for a Republican. Too many remembered U.S. Grant—the general and the president—and too many did not like what they remembered. (*The Standard* had labeled Grant's administration as "a desperate clique of robbers," even blaming the former Union general for the bankruptcy of several English ironmasters, a panic in Portugal and religious riots in China.) Fort Worth—with malice aforethought—descended on the polls, with *The Standard* editorially warning them that they could not vote more than once and that anyone carrying guns or a Bowie knife would not be allowed within a half-mile of the ballot box.

Early telegraph reports were in error. They indicated Tilden had won. Fort Worth Democrats went wild, putting out the word to round up anvils, powder and "all auxiliary for a magnificent display, and shoot as much as we blame please." But the election was thrown into the House, and Hayes—as *The Standard* bitterly complained—was "pronounced" president. During his term, Hayes was known in *The Standard* newsprint only as "his fraudulency."

But Fort Worth found ways to recuperate from such disappointments. The first theater, the Adelphi, made a stab at being legitimate with the production of "Struck by Lightning." The owners stayed open just long enough to run up a debt of $800, then packed up and sneaked out the back side of town. A month later, the stage was called Theater Comique, and the manager used a tightrope walker out front to attract crowds. One resident later recalled, "We all thought we were tough but the toughest guys used to sit in the balcony at the old Theater Comique and for pastime they used to shoot the keys off the piano." And, on the second floor of B.C. Evans store, Josh Billings made the audience laugh, Romeo embarrassed them, and Madame Rentz's Female Minstrels shocked them by performing "for the first time in this city the Parisian sensation, the Cancan."

Fort Worth was not easily shocked. Dance halls and bars were tucked around almost every corner. As J.B. Roberts remembered, "The screeching of fiddles and the foghorn voice of dance callers could be heard all along Main Street at all hours of the night; and it was not uncommon to see a policeman at the head of the set, while the chief of police might be upstairs betting a stack of reds on a high card. . . . Saloons never closed. . . . The drinking places didn't bother the churches and the churches didn't bother the saloons."

Touched by moral indignation, the city made one effort to cut down on the wickedness that transgressed its streets. It passed a hard-hitting series of ordinances that shut down gambling and prostitution and prohibited the wearing of guns in town. As a result, the city almost died. Morals did not seem as important when the town found itself going broke. The cowboys stuck their money in their own pockets and kept it there, not even bothering to come

He lived by the gun: T.I. (Long Hair Jim) Courtright, who liked to gamble and who once rode with Annie Oakley, was Fort Worth marshal from 1876 to 1879. He was killed in a well-publicized gunfight with saloon owner Luke Short.

Fort Worth, circa 1880: "The drinking places didn't bother the churches and the churches didn't bother the saloons."

into a town that had swept its dirt away. A newspaper ad, bought by merchants, pointed out: "We notice especially this year that, contrary to custom, almost all of them remain in their camps a few miles from the city and give as the cause the too stringent enforcement of the laws closing all places of amusement that attract them."

Fort Worth was not about to make a mistake, then suffer for it because the town was too strict and stubborn to correct it. The town again put a price tag on sin and corruption and politely stepped out of the way.

The laws were loose. So was the man chosen to enforce them—"Long Hair Jim" Courtright. In reality, he was only told to try to "keep the peace" without causing any problems for the big spenders—but, of course, without letting the town fall completely into the hands of the lawless. Courtright was a survivor of the War between the States. He saw his first action as a 17-year-old drummer boy, suffered three wounds and earned high praise for his courage at both Fort Donaldson and Vicksburg. "Long Hair Jim"—the alias of Timothy Isaiah— was a tall man with a slightly crippled hand that never interfered with his quick draw. His nerves were unbroken. His hair dropped to shoulder length. And he always carried his pistols in a sash. He was tough, deadly on murderers, horse thieves and train robbers. But he left the gamblers pretty much alone.

"Long Hair Jim" was himself a gambler. That, he said, was a gentleman's privilege, and he took advantage of it every chance he had while serving as town marshal. He was even arrested one night for playing pool.

For a time, his wife ran a shooting gallery. "Long Hair Jim" rode with Buffalo Bill Cody's Wild West Show, shoulder to shoulder with Annie Oakley. She was good. But Courtright was fast. No one, desperadoes claimed, was faster. Few tested him. None tested him twice.

So "Long Hair Jim" and his men kept an eye on the thirsty men at the Headlight Bar, The Occidental, Tivoli Saloon, Waco Tap, Our Friends, Our Comrades, The Beer Garden, Trinity, The White Elephant, Bon Ton, Horse Head and Cattle Exchange. And they paid special attention to The Red Light, a dance hall that kindly furnished its own girls. Couples were paired off, and they danced until so tired they felt obliged to leave for one of 20 small rooms

Guarding the town honor: Pat Morrison, deputy sheriff of Tarrant County, attempted to keep the peace in a city well known for cowboy fun in the saloons and dance halls of "Hell's Half Acre."

It was all right for "Long Hair Jim" to arrest a drunk, the town said— but not until he had run out of money and was worthless to the Fort Worth economy.

that encircled the dance floor. The music never lasted long.

This was Courtright's lair. This was the heart and soul of Hell's Half Acre.

Merchants detested violence, but they loved to hear the jangle of good money. It was all right for "Long Hair Jim" to arrest a drunk, the town said— but not until he had run out of money and was worthless to the Fort Worth economy. When Courtright became too zealous, he was promptly sent out of town to track down bandits who loved to rob trains so they would have enough pocket change to throw away in Hell's Half Acre.

They all came to the seamy side of town. Fort Worth was a refuge. It sheltered a bad breed. It might not forgive their transgressions on the road, but—for a while at least—Fort Worth was willing to forget them.

The road was a treacherous place to be.

Mrs. W.L. Baird of Big Spring recalled the time her stagecoach was robbed:

"In mid afternoon, as we entered a dense grove, two masked men with revolvers suddenly appeared, shouting 'Halt!' Our driver complied, as a revolver was trained constantly upon him.

"The second bandit jerked open the door and, pointing his gun at us, told the man within 'to get out and reach for the sky!' He obeyed, though trembling violently and protesting he had no money.

"Meanwhile we girls were crying and beseeching mother: 'Oh, please give'em your money!'

"Whereupon the bandit said: 'You needn't be alarmed, madam, we never molest ladies.'

"On hearing this, she began interceding for her fellow traveler, whose pockets were being ransacked. Thirty-five cents was found in a vest pocket. This the robber dropped back, saying: 'We don't want this.'

"Just as the robber reached the man's pants pocket, my mother was saying: 'Where do you expect to go when you die?'

"The robber paused, slapped his intended victim's back and said: 'Get back in the coach.' To the driver, 'Drive on and don't look back.'

"As soon as we felt ourselves safely away, the man turned to my mother and drew a wallet from his hip pocket.

" 'Madam,' he said, 'if they don't molest ladies, please keep this for me until we reach Fort Worth. It contains $65.' "

Most were not so fortunate. Gunmen prowled the Trinity River bottom on the Weatherford Highway. They stalked the travelers who crossed Mary's Creek just beyond the halfway stage stand. On one occasion, they took several gold watches (as well as four or five hundred dollars) from five passengers.

The sound of a train whistle also made the bandits' blood run hot. The *Democrat* reported: "The mail and express train due here last night at 1:20 . . . was stopped at Eagle Ford on its arrival there at 12 o'clock, by four masked men armed with shotguns. . . . They were all apparently young men, seemed to be old hands. They put their plunder in a small bag and threatened, if there was a shot fired on their leaving, to return and raise 'merry h--l.' They quietly disappeared behind the depot on the north side of the tracks. None of the passengers was molested."

Many citizens—as did "Long Hair Jim" Courtright—probably sat with the bandits behind a deck of cards somewhere in Hell's Half Acre. Sam Bass and his outlaws spent a lot of time hiding away in the saloons. Temple Houston—an attorney as eloquent with his words as his guns—came riding in from time to time, usually wearing his rattlesnake hat band. Luke Short— the dandy, the gambler—preferred a stovepipe hat, and he was as fast with his pistols as "Long Hair Jim," men whispered. And Doc Holliday—coughing off attacks of consumption—always found a good poker table as soon as he found Fort Worth.

The painted women loved them all for a price and, more than once, wandered into the line of some high-riding drunk's gunfire. The *Democrat* would dutifully report, "Another soiled dove crossed the river."

The Standard took a dim view of the heathen half acre, fussing, "There is a class of beings infesting the city needing the closest surveillance." It was

Protecting the valuables in transit: The Texas and Pacific hired armed guards to protect valuable shipments from train robbers such as "The Wild Bunch."

all up to "Long Hair Jim." He would have loved to bury a few, but the merchants did not want to see anyone's bankroll put underground, or anyone with money ride away angry. So the piece of pandemonium around Rusk and Twelfth went virtually unchecked, despised but pardoned. *The Democrat* was quick to add wit as well as wisdom: "A young man under the influence of liquor informs us there were 300 fights in town Saturday night. If that isn't lively for a peaceable interior town of 2,200 inhabitants, then what is?"

But Fort Worth was not just mired in the cesspool of Hell's Half Acre in the 1870s. It had another side as well—a progressive one that was determined to grow even if it had to use the tainted money of gamblers and prostitutes to do it (which it did).

The Mansion Hotel opened, and by '82 its owner W.W. Dunn advertised, "This house is in the business center of the city, convenient to all street railways. . . . It now has 60 of the most pleasant rooms in the city, and offers special inducements to the commercial traveler and the quietude and comforts of a home for families." Reverend Randolph Clark said of his school, "We promise its patrons that no pains will be spared to give their children a good, thorough education." The only real pain was the half acre of sin. The Rev. Clark, in time, would simply stare at it, shudder and declare piously, "A lad living here and then retaining anything of moral character could stomach two trips to Chicago."

Sanger Bros. had the Cheap Cash Store. The Go-Ahead Dry Goods merchants vowed to "keep ahead of all other merchants in North-West Texas [sic] for low prices and first class goods." W.D. Thomason—to add a little recognition for his stock of dry goods—stuck a sign out front of his two-story, brick store that read: "Here's Whar the Panter Lay Down." Mitchell & Thurman, carpenters and joiners, advertised, "All kinds of work done on short notice, and in genteel style. We keep coffins on hand all the time." Mitchell numbered houses for a nickel. The Peers House, a hotel, boasted "female waiters." And *The Standard* endorsed the females by saying they were "exceedingly useful" as well as "ornamental."

The court voted in a little welfare, agreeing to $5 a week to support "pauper

Frank McCown." Commissioners only voted themselves $4 a meeting. C.B. Daggett was awarded a franchise to run a ferry service across the Trinity for teams, wagons, horses and riders. And in the courthouse, judges dismissed ten times as many cases as they tried, pointing out that most of the files and evidence had been destroyed in the '76 fire.

But it was John Lockwood, coming down from New Jersey, who had the most intriguing proposition for Fort Worth. He gathered a group of aggressive businessmen around him and said, "I'll put up $10,000 and build a gas plant if you'll subscribe an additional $10,000."

They did. And he did. And in 1877, street lamps fueled by artificial gas, jerked Fort Worth out of the darkness. Each night, a lamplighter rode along on his black pony, stopped at each lamp and stood in his stirrups to ignite it.

Fort Worth just could not seem to outlive its need for the horse. It had tied itself to the sunrise side of the country with steel rails. But horses carried Fort Worth further west. By 1878, the town had become the easternmost point of the world's longest stage line. Yuma, Arizona, lay 1,560 miles and 17 days away, lodged in the bosom of a country ruled by Comanches and Apaches and rattlesnakes. It was a tiresome run in desert heat. As Paddock wrote, "The 17-day journey was too long. The coyotes and horned frogs that inhabited most of the country beyond the Concho could not afford to wait that long for their mail and so the Second Assistant Postmaster General, at the earnest solicitation of the inhabitants and contractors, agreed to increase the compensation 100 per cent if the trip could be made in 13 days—which was easy. . . . The mail left Fort Worth in a Concord coach pulled by six horses and ran to Thorp Springs, where it was transferred to a surrey with two horses. These went as far as Brownwood, where a buckboard and two bronchos took it the remainder of the way, if they were not interrupted."

The commissioners that year got a new courthouse but soon outgrew it and voted another half million dollars to replace it. A few businessmen began tossing around the idea of developing a meat-packing center for Fort Worth. They realized that those states which still guarded against Texas cattle, still ran scared of tick fever, would not be opposed to receiving healthy frozen carcasses. Stockmen could sell more cows, earn larger profits, ride fewer miles. Paddock suggested that Fort Worth should go ahead and build stockyards, "become the great cattle center of Texas, where both buyers and sellers meet for the transaction of an immense business in Texas beef." It would be several years before the idea rooted.

Fort Worth found itself stricken with the ailment of political reform—an issue to be debated, cursed, praised, fought and fought over. Attorney R.E. Beckham led the reform forces into battle, pledging to clean up the dirt in Fort Worth. He was angry and not a bit shy about attacking Mayor G.H. Day every chance he had, which was many. Beckham charged that the city was on the verge of bankruptcy, it was without credit, and, besides, hogs ran loose in the street. The reform candidate promised to declare war on gambling and prostitution, enact tougher laws, and enforce them. Nor did he like those street salesmen who blocked traffic to peddle their wares.

At a March rally in '78, Beckham accused Day of always handing down $3 fines in his own court, then tacking on the inevitable court costs of $9.85. He roared, "The city administration is just one little police court!" A second candidate, J.M. Peers, stood and proclaimed, "Them's my sentiments exactly."

Mayor Day ambled to the platform and mixed verbal molasses and politics. "I come here filled with the milk of human kindness," he said. "I love everybody here. I offer myself as a sacrifice to the dear people for the good of the country." The voters promptly sacrificed him.

Vice lost. And Beckham was good to his word. He got rid of the hogs on the streets and cleaned up the stench of their mudhole wallows. But it took a public referendum to kick them out of town. The hogs barely lost—377 to 324.

As he had promised, Beckham also cracked down on Hell's Half Acre. He should not have. Merchants suffered when sin went broke. They started

Fort Worth just could not seem to outlive its need for the horse. It had tied itself to the sunrise side of the country with steel rails. But horses carried Fort Worth further west.

Posing on the prairie: The Fort Worth & Denver City train helped expand Fort Worth's business prospects.

doing business on the cattle trail. Baylis John Fletcher, following along after 2,525 cattle, recalled, "Solicitors from the big grocery stores of Fort Worth met us on horseback several miles from the city, bringing such gifts as bottles of whiskey and boxes of fine cigars." Fort Worth wanted the cowboys to know they were still welcome in town. The cowboys wanted women and whiskey.

It was not long before the *Democrat* announced, "The dance halls are in full blast again." Courtright was disgusted. He threw in his badge and left town, heading for New Mexico to guard a silver train that kept tempting Mexican bandits. Unfortunately, he got a little careless with his guns and shot down the wrong men. He left a couple of cattlemen lying in the dirt of their own ranch. At least that was what the grand jury said. Courtright, with his companion Jim McIntire, headed back to Fort Worth to hide out in the commotion of the half acre he had wanted to wipe out. Courtright hit town, opened the T.I.C. Commercial Detective Agency, settled down and waited, hoping New Mexico would someday forget. It never did.

The new decade of 1880 began—as the old one had ended—in confusion. The *Dallas Herald* wondered if any county judge or county attorney candidate in Tarrant County would ever propose the enforcement of gambling laws in case they were elected. It asked, "Are they all running on free gambling, free whiskey, and free grass platforms?" Most were.

The Roman Catholics got their own cemetery—on the far side of a river that had no bridge. Getting to the burying ground was tough indeed. Funerals were best attended when the water was shallow. And the finest compliment a man could receive was, "He is a good friend, he will follow you all the way across the river."

And in the distance could be heard the sounds of another approaching train. The Texas & Pacific had company. Coming from the north, over the tracks of the old Baxter Springs cattle trail, was the Missouri-Kansas-Texas Railroad. On a May day, the first Katy train rumbled into Fort Worth, offering to carry carloads of cattle all the way back up to St. Louis. It was tempting. But the cars were too small. And the horns on the rangy old steers were too long. Cowboys were destined to eat dust for a few more years.

Paddock's "tarantula map" had another leg. He went after a third. Paddock heard that owners of the Gulf, Colorado and Santa Fe Railroad—operating between Galveston and Belton—had decided to reach out for a northern market. From Cleburne (the story is told) the Santa Fe was either headed to Fort Worth or Dallas. It really all depended on who came up with the first $75,000. Paddock was not about to be outbid by Dallas. Businessmen huddled together. John Peter Smith laid down the first subscription, totaling $5,250. Major K.M. Van Zandt and Dr. Peak had $2,250 apiece, while B.C. Evans and Boaz and Ellis came up with $5,000 each. Evans and Martin found an extra $3,250. And even store clerks and everyday laborers stopped to donate what little they could.

The Santa Fe promoter had gone on to Dallas, but Paddock was right behind. He was waiting the next morning when the railroad representative came down the hotel stairs. Paddock handed him a contract. "We signed," he said, "now

On a May day, the first Katy train rumbled into Fort Worth, offering to carry carloads of cattle all the way back to St. Louis. It was tempting. But the cars were too small. And the horns on the rangy old steers were too long. Cowboys were destined to eat dust for a few more years.

you sign." The promoter was flabbergasted. He tried to brush the editor aside, saying he had not had time to make the same offer to Dallas.

Paddock was firm. "That's too bad," he said. "You told me the town that signed first got the railroad." In December, the Santa Fe rolled into Fort Worth.

During the 1880s, the town launched the next three railroads themselves, laying tracks for the Fort Worth and Denver City, Fort Worth and New Orleans, the Fort Worth and Rio Grande. Paddock's fabled "tarantula" was reaching out and making tracks in all directions, just as he had predicted. Perhaps Paddock was not as "teched" as the newspapers had said he was.

On an Indian summer day in 1881, Dr. Julian Feild (whose father had built the first gristmill then served as the town's first postmaster) became perplexed enough to demand a change in Fort Worth that would forever affect its outlook and its hearing. Feild had spent most of the day riding out to Everman to call on a farmer who was reported to be seriously ill, perhaps dying. Doctors usually paid no attention to the discomforts of the miles. But this ride was different. The hours were long and hot, and Dr. Feild—much to his chagrin—found the farmer out plowing his garden. He was neither bedridden nor knocking at death's door.

The good doctor—his temper as warm as the summer—returned home and announced to his family and patients: "This is the end. They're fixing to put in telephones here, and from now on all my patients have to have telephones. I'm not riding to Everman to watch my patients plow fields anymore."

His phone was installed on September 15. His number was 1. Before the year had ended, 40 others, never knowing when they might need medical treatment, paid for their phones as well.

The newspaper, *The Democrat-Advance,* would remember: "1881 was very kind to Fort Worth. It found the city hovering on the ragged edge of uncertainty, as to whether it would remain an overgrown village or develop into a city. It leaves it without a doubt in the minds of any, the most prosperous and progressive city in the state, the admiration of all, and with a future before it full of hope, and which excites the envy of all its rivals."

John Peter Smith took the oath of office as mayor in '82 and engineered wide-sweeping improvements throughout Fort Worth. He paved the first streets, beginning with Weatherford, Houston and Main. He saw that a property tax was initiated to pay for free public schools. Eight hundred students took advantage of the education in the spring of '83, and the roll totaled 1,200 that fall. They attended classes in vacant houses and churches until honest-to-goodness schools could be constructed.

The new mayor built the first sanitary sewers giving the 1886 city directory a reason to brag: "Fort Worth is the only completely sewered city among her many sister cities of the state, having upwards of twenty miles of piping laid."

Typhoid fever struck the town in 1881. A year later, smallpox stalked the streets. A new health officer, Dr. H.W. Moore, believed his only hope to shut down the epidemic was to make drastic changes in Fort Worth's water supply. It was unhealthy, badly polluted by the runoff from stables and outhouses. John Peter Smith built a pump station near the courthouse to take care of four million gallons of water a day. It was lifted out of the Trinity and run through six miles of pipe. Within four years, that supply was enhanced with the drilling of 90 water wells.

Fort Worth's enterprise did not escape the *New York Daily Chronicle.* It reported in 1882, "The city is cosmopolitan. It has the rush and energy of a frontier town with strange contrasts of nationality. It smacks of Mexico and New York. Broadway and ranch brush against one another."

So often they did their brushing down in the dim lights and loud music of Hell's Half Acre. "Long Hair Jim" Courtright still hung out there. And the Rangers came riding after him. In New Mexico, he was still a wanted man. The *Dallas Herald* recorded: "It would seem the pursuit of Jim Courtright

Leaders-to-be: Students at the old Fort Worth High School, 1880s, look forward to a growing city and a tamer country.

by the New Mexico authorities would never cease. Several parties of rangers as well as officials from the Territory have been here at different times, but have always gone back without serving their warrants. . . . A day or two ago four Rangers met A.W. Woody and told him they were going to Fort Worth to get a bad man. Woody suggested they go to Courtright and get his assistance. 'That's the very man we're after,' was the reply."

They found him on a fishing picnic at Marine Creek. But Courtright was waiting for them. *The Herald* reported: "Courtright deliberately loaded his Winchester, held it across his knee, faced the horsemen and waited. The horsemen turned their animals and rode back to the city. The four were watching the saloons and hotels last night, but if they are after Courtright they will have . . . to go away without him."

Courtright had always vowed, "If I go back I will be murdered . . . and I prefer to die where my friends are. I will not be arrested alive, that's all." He carried a $2,000 price on his head. No one dared to try and collect it. But the Rangers almost made it. Together with Albuquerque Chief of Police Harry Richmond, they lured Courtright to a room at the Ginnochio Hotel, asking him to check out some photographs to see if he could identify any wanted men in them.

He sat down and was handed the pictures. When "Long Hair Jim" looked up again, he was staring at three pistols, all eager to fire if given the chance. Courtright was not quite ready to die. Word of his capture raced through town. An angry crowd numbering almost 2,000 gathered on the street below. Its mood was ugly.

And Tarrant County Sheriff Walter Maddox told the Rangers, "You can't take that man away from here. That crowd won't let you and I can't control them." The Rangers were not used to backing down. They sent an attorney, William Capps, down to talk to the crowd. While the mob listened, the Rangers slipped Courtright out the back door, dragged him down a back alley and had him locked up in the county jail before any of his friends knew he was gone.

That should have been the end of the road for "Long Hair Jim." But he got hungry. And the lawmen, with more compassion than good sense, took him to the Merchant's Restaurant to eat. Old gambling companions had conveniently hidden pistols beneath the tables. Courtright dropped his napkin. He asked Richmond to get it for him. But the Albuquerque sheriff snapped, "Pick it up yourself." It was the wrong command. "Long Hair Jim" went down for the napkin. He came up with the guns. And minutes later he was on a train bound for Galveston.

By the mid 1880s, cattle were no longer coming to kick dust and dung and dollars over Fort Worth. Fences had closed the long trails. A new breed of cattle was being developed, one that had more beef and shorter horns, one that fit quite well inside those railroad cars. The Indians, too, were riding the rails, coming to town to sign grazing leases on tribal lands. Yellow Bear, who had hit town with Quanah Parker (Comanche chieftain and son of Cynthia Ann), did not leave. At the Pickwick Hotel, he blew out the light but not

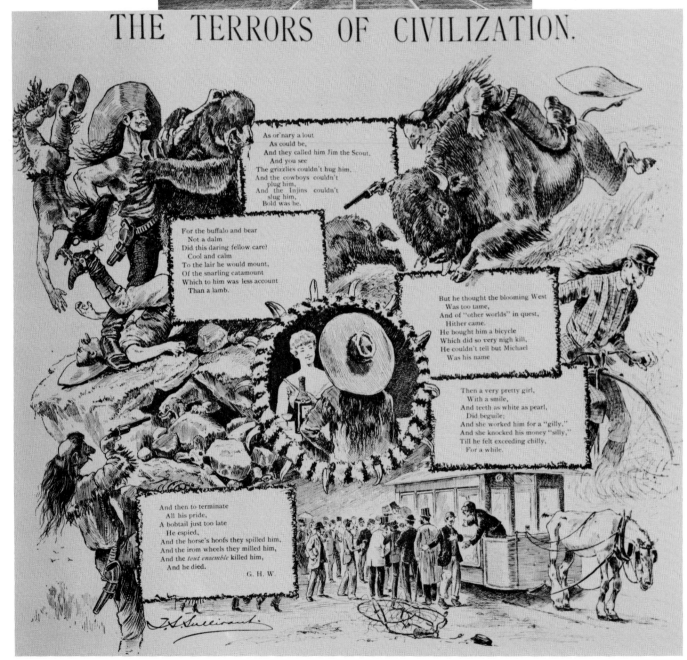

Capt. G.H. Schmitt's Company Texas Rangers, on duty, in Ft. Worth railroad strike, 1886. Left to right: Will Owens; Henry Putts; J.C. Barringer; Sam Pickett; Charles Kuhley; G.H. Clark; J.R. Robinson; Corp. J.W. Durbin; Lieut. A.C. Grimes; and Capt. G.H. Schmitt.

Civilization: Street car rail repair (left) was hard work at low pay, while the cars themselves proved too much for Jim the Scout. Captain G.H. Schmitt (above right) and his company of Texas Rangers was sent to Fort Worth in 1886 to keep the peace during a bitter railroad strike. The strike was called when the Knights of Labor tried to break Jay Gould's hold on the country's railroads; it spread to Fort Worth in March 1886. Quanah Parker settled on the reservation in Indian Territory (below) but maintained friendship with several Fort Worth cattlemen such as Burk Burnett.

the gas. He never woke up again. Quanah Parker was found 13 hours later, gasping for breath, sick but alive. A year later, those gas jets were gone, replaced by the magic of electricity. It would also power streetcars and send those faithful mules out to pasture.

Alarm boxes were scattered throughout Fort Worth, giving the town the state's first electric fire-alarm system to go along with a new central fire station. And Mrs. Belle M. Burchill, a school teacher who became a postmistress, first began home delivery of mail, hiring five letter carriers.

But growth was not without its headaches. Railroad workers were restless. Jay Gould and the Wabash Railway Company had a stranglehold on the trains, and the Knights of Labor were damned and determined to break it, dying if necessary. Workers wanted more money. They struck.

The Wabash did not come to Fort Worth, but the Knights of Labor did, piling railroad ties across the tracks to keep all trains out of town. Not even the state adjutant general on his way to the agitation at Alvarado could get out of the depot. A crowd shoved its way into the railroad yard. Men were dragged off to jail. The strikers stood their ground.

As the *Austin Statesman* reported:

"Fort Worth is in the hands of the mob. The citizens' posse, summoned by the sheriff to assemble this morning at the Missouri Pacific Yards, met some 300 strong, according to orders. Most of the citizens were unarmed. About 400 strikers, armed, desperate, and ready for bloodshed, were on the scene. Fifty well-armed officers were also on hand. A freight train was made up, and the Missouri Pacific engine came along to pull out the train. A grand rush was made by the strikers for the engine. Arms were presented on both sides. The engine was not molested, but all the cars were uncoupled, and even the nuts were taken out of the draw heads. Some of the Knights were arrested, and the engine was sent back to the house, and all attempts to move trains abandoned."

Women and children sat down on the tracks. Engines, running strong, tried to frighten them away, threatening to run them down. One woman yelled, "Come on, run her through, but remember when you do, it will be over our dead bodies!"

The engines were parked. The trains had shut down.

Fort Worth did what it had to do. It turned again to "Long Hair Jim" Courtright. Courtright had ended his year of exile, surrendered to stand trial and had been easily acquitted. When Fort Worth needed a gun, it always called on "Long Hair Jim," even appointing him U.S. deputy marshal. Courtright jammed his pistols down into the sash around his waist. Backed by an armed guard, he climbed aboard the engine, promising to lead it out of the city, to get it on the move again. Throughout Fort Worth, the switches had been spiked down to eliminate any threat of derailment. Beyond the city limits, however, Courtright and his men were on their own. They could only gamble that no one had tampered with the tracks. It was not a safe bet.

But on April 3, 1886, the train cautiously pulled away from the depot. At Buttermilk Junction, the strikers were waiting. Four men quickly threw a switch, halting the train, then hastily walked away.

Courtright ordered them to stop. His guards swung down to the ground beside him. They ran to the men, searched them and found no weapons. Courtright could breathe easier now. The strikers were apparently more interested in causing trouble than harm. He turned back toward the train and saw five men lying in the tall grass that hid the edge of a gully.

The strikers were more than a hundred yards away, Courtright guessed, far out of the range of his pistols. And they were armed with Winchesters. "For God's sake, don't shoot!" the marshal yelled.

Gunfire tore at the ground around him. Dick Townsend, a Tarrant County Deputy Sheriff fell dying. Courtright's guards ran for cover. Behind them, a second band of riflemen concealed by a pile of lumber opened fire, catching the train in a deadly crossfire of bullets. A shot ripped through Officer Charlie Sneeds's face. Another officer went down wounded. Two bullets slashed through Courtright's hat. The fight was brief—less than 15 minutes.

Courtright and his guards slowly retreated, backing the train down the tracks and into the shelter of Union Station. Fort Worth braced itself for war. The strike was out of hand. And the *Fort Worth Gazette* reported: "Rumors of the most sensational character were rife in early portions of last night. Nearly every male citizen of the town was armed and prepared for trouble. It was reported that the strikers intended to raid the gun stores and burn the Union depot. It is also said that they threatened to clear the city of 'scabs' within three days. Sheriff Maddox has arranged to give three taps continuously of the fire bell as a danger signal . . . if another collision occurs it will, in all probability, result in a more serious loss of life than that of yesterday."

Mayor John Peter Smith wired Governor John Ireland. The message was direct and simple. It said, "We are threatened with serious trouble here. The presence of one or two companies of Rangers or state militia would prevent a riot. Can you furnish the troops?"

The Rangers came. One company took a special train from Harrold. Two companies rode out of Austin, and two more were dispatched from Dallas. As the *Gazette* observed: "The city is very quiet at this midnight hour. . . . There is no loud talk or bluster. No strikers are to be seen. . . . Some predict further trouble today, while others are inclined to the opinion that the worst has already happened, and that no further bloodshed will ensue."

The blood dried but not the anger. One Union leader said, "It has been demonstrated that strikes are failures. We must try something else. You may look for us at the ballot box and in the primaries."

Out of the bitterness came the Dark Lantern Party, an assorted collection of Farmers Alliance men, Greenbackers, a few Republicans and members of the Knights of Labor. It was, Fort Worth Democrats conceded, a serious threat to their power, but it was at least legal. An Austin newspaper called the Dark Lantern party the most powerful foe the Democrats had ever had to contend with in Texas.

As election time dawned on Forth Worth, both parties staged torchlight parades. About 1,150 men marched behind the Democrat banner. Only 320 Dark Lanternites showed up. On voting day, the city had a 900 majority for the Democrats. Out in the county, the Dark Lantern party boasted an 800 majority. It was not enough. No Dark Lantern candidate made it to office. Peace moved back to downtown Fort Worth.

And a year later, Paddock, who had purchased the *Gazette,* would report with pride:

"Refinement follows wealth according to the law of cause and effect, and social pleasures increase and multiply as refinement ploughs its way into rugged western life. This has been noticeable in the social status of Fort Worth during the last three years. . . . The previous seven years in history of the city had been spent with everybody in pursuit of money. . . . But the year 1883, with its era of public improvement, caused a revolution in social affairs. Homes were improved. The city began to have a finished appearance. Shrubbery and shade trees were cultivated. Men of wealth built costly residences. Sidewalks sprang into existence in all parts of the city. . . . The churches increased in numbers. Their

Women and children sat down on the tracks. Engines, running strong, tried to frighten them away, threatening to run them down. One woman yelled, "Come on, run her through, but remember when you do, it will be over our dead bodies!"

Fort Worth in the 1880s: The city moves toward civilization.

congregations swelled and the social garden budded and blossomed in proportion to the development of business enterprises. The roughness of frontier life was passing.

The city prospered. Everybody prospered, and life in Fort Worth commenced to adorn itself with "comforts and delicacies."

Unfortunately, "Long Hair Jim" Courtright was not able to hang around long enough to appreciate them. He symbolized the frontier, a way of life that Fort Worth was trying to sweep behind it. Trouble and controversy always followed in his footsteps. After the violence of the railroad strike ended, a *San Antonio Light* editorial said, "Jim Courtright is largely responsible for the Fort Worth massacre; but who is responsible for Jim Courtright?" Mayor John Peter Smith merely stared back at the critics and commented that those who break the law have no right to choose who might arrest them.

But "Long Hair Jim" turned in his badge. He went back to his detective agency, got in a quarrel with Luke Short and died in the streets of Fort Worth. It was a quarrel with a friend.

Short had been a cowboy. But gambling was an easier way to make a living, so he dealt cards rather than cattle, even opening up the famed White Elephant Saloon in Fort Worth. Vigilantes had cut short his poker days in Dodge City.

Some said Courtright had a bad habit. When he ran out of money, he simply reached over and took a handful of chips from the dealer's pile. It was not stealing. He always paid the money back. But he irritated a lot of good folks that way. One was Luke Short. The two men met in front of Ella Blackwell's shooting gallery, about a half block away from Short's saloon. Vic Jossenberger the lamplighter, watched in the darkness. So did Jake Johnson, Short's friend, whose testimony would ultimately lead to the gambler's acquittal.

As the men talked, Luke Short suddenly lowered his hands. "Don't pull any gun on me," Courtright declared.

"I have no gun there," the gambler replied.

Short smoothed his vest, his hand coming ever closer to the pistol on his hip. "Stop that," Courtright ordered.

Both men drew. Short's first bullet slammed into Courtright's right thumb. "Long Hair Jim" could not cock his pistol. He executed the famed border shift, pitching the gun to his left hand. The pistol was still in the air when Short's second bullet struck him.

Jossenberger said he watched as Courtright, lying on the ground, looked up and said, "Shoot, Luke, or give me your gun."

Cowboy-turned-gambler: Luke Short, owner of the White Elephant Saloon, shot and killed the notorious "Long Hair Jim" Courtright. He was acquitted.

"Goodby, Jim," Short said softly.

"Goodby, Luke," Courtright replied. And the gambler shot "Long Hair Jim" right between the eyes.

Some said Courtright had been trying to force protection money out of Luke Short. Others said a band of merchants had hired Courtright to stop Short from fleecing many of Fort Worth's young men at the keno tables. Perhaps it was jealousy. Short did try to marry "Long Hair Jim's" widow. But it did not matter. "Long Hair Jim," who had lived by the gun, died by one. And his funeral procession stretched out six blocks long, a parade of friends, mourners, enemies and the curious.

Courtright's death was merely the most sensational of many in Hell's Half Acre. Those who kept their life generally lost their money—sometimes to keno, sometimes to cards, sometimes to gunmen. The odds were about the same in either game.

Prostitutes—known to the press as fallen angels—had a bad habit of committing suicide when they ran out of both love and money.

But Sally did not commit suicide. No one ever knew why she died. And no one ever knew who drove those nails into Sally's hands and feet. Fort Worth just woke up one morning and found Sally crucified on an outhouse wall.

The town was horrified. New Mayor H.S. Broiles was appalled. He and County Attorney R.L. Carlock vowed—as many had before them—to cleanse Fort Worth of that whiskey and blood-stained half acre. Broiles and Carlock were serious. New restrictions were placed on police officers expressly prohibiting them from walking off their beats to enter saloons, variety theaters or brothels except, of course, in the line of duty. Their pay was raised to eliminate the temptation of bribery. The police cracked down. And Hell's Half Acre began to wither with shock.

The cowboys were gone. Jails were crammed with the "riff-raff" that usually crammed the saloons. And, by 1889, the notorious half acre of sin for sale was virtually shut down.

But it refused to die.

Chapter 7

Battling into the twentieth century

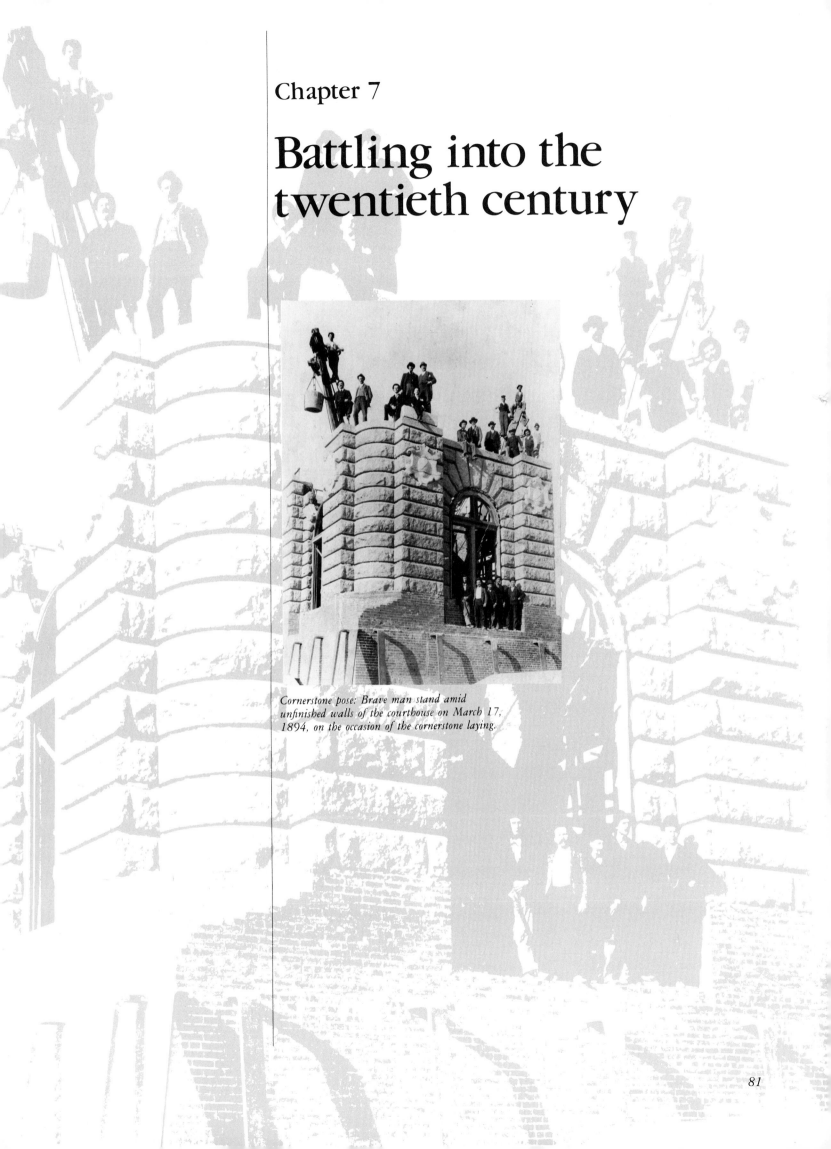

Cornerstone pose: Brave man stand amid unfinished walls of the courthouse on March 17, 1894, on the occasion of the cornerstone laying.

Fort Worth was ready to kick its way into the realm of refinement and high society, even if it had to use the back door. As Albert S. Leach recalled, "Many times I have seen ladies with evening gowns and gentlemen with tops and tails on the streetcar going to or from Greenwall's Opera House when some of the stars of the Gay Nineties were here, or maybe a dance at the old Worth Hotel, which was quite a gathering place for both cattlemen and society."

And women wanted a library. They had teas and dances and cake walks to raise money. They would boldly walk up to a cigar smoker on the street and ask him politely to donate the price of a cigar toward the construction of a library. Mrs. D.B. Keeler even had the nerve to write Andrew Carnegie. And on June 30, he replied, saying he would give Fort Worth $50,000 for the building if the city agreed to provide the site and $4,000 a year to maintain it. So the women in the city took Mr. Carnegie's money and built the library they wanted.

Eastern gift brings western civilization: Like many other cities, Fort Worth constructed its public library with a gift from Andrew Carnegie.

B.B. Paddock, who in 1884 had retired as an editor but not as a promoter, decided that Fort Worth should be known nationally for something other than shootings, prostitution, railroad strikes, hell-raising cowboys and the death of "Long Hair Jim" Courtright. He wanted the town to sponsor "an exhibition of the products of the field, forest, orchard, and garden." The result was the fabulous Spring Palace.

Paddock was named president of a company to raise $50,000 for the monumental structure. The price tag would ultimately be $100,000.

The Spring Palace was two stories high, made entirely of Texas lumber and agricultural products. The roof was granite. Its towers were draped with shelled corn, oats, wheat, millet, cornstalks, cactus, alfalfa and even Johnson grass. Over the grand entrance was a panel of sea shells, and the great seal of Texas was fashioned out of two colors of corn. In the music room was a grand piano, its case made from red pepper. Millet heads formed a harp, and a bass violin was put together with sugar cane, using strings of straw. The windows were curtained by a delicate combination of popcorn and peas.

The exposition was named, "Karporama—the fruits of the earth." Publicity proclaimed that the Spring Palace "will be for Texas, all and much more than the great Paris exposition was to Paris, or even our great centennial celebration was to the United States." One wrote that it "will show the world we have the intelligence, energy, and enterprise to utilize our natural resources and that there is to be found in Texas quite as much culture and refinement as exists in other portions of the country."

The Spring Palace—with a wheat-crested dome that rose up almost as tall as the nation's capital—was (the brochure said) "Nature speaking for itself." Paddock called the Oriental architecture with Moorish towers, "easily the most beautiful structure ever erected on earth." He carefully planned the opening for spring, a time "when there were no other places of entertainment and amusement anywhere in the country."

Special trains from as far away as Chicago and Boston rumbled into Fort Worth, carrying gossip-tongued socialites and black-tie dignitaries whose appearances gave the exposition even greater importance. On opening day, May 10, 1889, the governor of Nebraska spoke, and the music came compliments of the Elgin Watch Factory Band of Elgin, Illinois.

In an editorial, *The Democrat,* called the Spring Palace the "pride and glory of Texas." It may have been. It impressed a lot of people but lost $23,000. Nevertheless, Fort Worth, with hopes as high as always, geared up for the second season, with cities and counties from throughout the state competing

The Texas Spring Palace: Constructed in 1889 near the railroad station, the palace was built to house a trade fair honoring the state's produce. Promoted by Fort Worth merchant R.A. Cameron (above), the structure was 225 by 375 feet and its dome was 150 feet in diameter. Fort Worth women decorated the $100,000 structure with wheat, corn stalks, cactus, rye, moss, Johnson grass and cotton. Individual counties, such as Rusk (above left), had their own display space. The palace ended in near tragedy a year later (above right), when on May 30, 1890—with more than 7,000 dancing inside to the music of the Elgin Watch Factory Band—"a boy stepped on a match near the base of a decorated column." Quick action resulted in only one death, that of Al S. Hayne. A monument to Hayne, who fought to save other lives, is located in a small park at the corner of Main and Lancaster Streets.

for prizes for the most attractive decorations. The loss was erased that next year, and the Spring Palace began showing a gratifying, if only slight, profit.

But at a dress ball, on May 30, 1890, it all went down in flames. More than 7,000 people had crowded into the palace, many of them dancing to the music of the Elgin Watch Factory Band, when the fire struck, racing madly through the dry grass and straw decorations.

Edwin B. Randle recalled that he "saw people rushing out and headlong down the stairway which led from the outside to the ground below. Many of them were just rolling down the stairs, and I saw one man run right across this rolling mass of humanity. I called out at once for them 'to take your time,' but there was so much excitement that didn't do much good."

Men and women jumped, breaking legs and ankles. Children were thrown from the second-story window—anything to escape the flames.

A hook and ladder company knocked down the high board fence that surrounded the palace and charged the fire. As Paddock wrote: "In four minutes the building was a mass of flame, inside and out. So rapid was the spread of the fire that firemen, who were stationed in different parts of the building with their hoses connected to the fire hydrants, did not have time to turn on the water.

"Why hundreds did not perish is a mystery. . . . About 30 people were injured, more or less seriously. . . . Low-necked and short-sleeved dresses of the ladies exposed them to the falling cinders."

Within eleven minutes, the fabled Spring Palace lay in a blackened, splendid pile of ashes. It claimed but one life.

Frank Leslie's Illustrated Newspaper reported an eyewitness description:

Culture in the city: Conrad Rhau (above) was a violinist and teacher in Fort Worth, 1885. The Waldo Quintette (below) was one of the popular groups of the Fort Worth Mandolin Club.

"As the panic . . . increased, and it seemed probable that many would be burned to death, Mr. (Al) Hayne gave himself to the work of rescue. He picked up fainting women and terrified children, and dropped them out of the second story windows into willing arms waiting to receive them below. After all had left the building but Mr. Hayne and one woman, who had fainted, the flames enveloped the entire building. The fainting woman was several feet away from the window and her dress was already ablaze. The hero did not hesitate a moment, but ran to her, picked her up, and, without a thought of self, leaped from the window with his senseless burden in his arms. His clothing was ablaze, and in the fall he broke several bones. He died three hours later, but his name will long be cherished as that of one who gave his life for others."

It was a tragic loss. But, as *Frank Leslie's Illustrated Newspaper* concluded, "Fort Worth is one of the most enterprising cities in Texas, and it is safe to say that even the destruction of its magnificent Spring Palace, which has attracted visitors from every section in the Union, will not dampen the ardor of its citizens nor lessen the magnificent prosperity which it rightfully enjoys."

They were right. Arlington Inn (at the corner of Merrick and Crestline) opened its doors, charged four dollars a night for a room and was described in *Baedeker's: A Handbook for Travellers* as "a winter-resort commanding a splendid view of the Trinity Valley." (But, alas, fire took it also.)

During the next decade, the good life snuggled up to Fort Worth. The grand homes of Burk Burnett, Winfield Scott and Tom Waggoner became social gathering places. Culture bounded onto the stage of Greenwall's Opera House with performances of "The Mikado," "The Burgermaster" and "The Toreador." One night, the curtain rose on "The Virginian." and the critic for the *Fort Worth Record* called it "a splendid dramatization of the novel; the very heart of the book is presented and nothing of any consequence is lost. The cowboys were cowboys; they did not play at being cowboys." And the next night, Joseph De Crasse presented his production of "The Merchant of Venice," followed by "Hamlet." The Greenwall had diversity if nothing else. To its stage came Edwin Booth, Lilly Langtry, Lillian Russell, Douglas Fairbanks, Sarah Bernhardt and all the Barrymores—John, Ethel, and Lionel. When John Phillip Sousa and his band played, the critic wrote, "No other musical celebrity now before the public has put the newspaper reviewer to such continuous strain in their hunt for laudatory adjectives."

Fred Laue recalled, "Every occupant of the third balcony was either a man or a boy, as ladies would occupy the first floor and balcony. On special occasions, a famous play would come to the city and seats would be hard to secure. In order to take care of as many customers as possible, ladies were allowed to sit with the men, but this was only on rare occasions. It made the men so nervous having the ladies sit with them that they could not enjoy the show."

A 'pyrotechnic drama,'—"The Last Days of Pompeii" exploded over Fort Worth, as 7,000 residents actually "participated in games in vogue at the dawn of the Christian era." Laue remembers, "It covered five acres including a man-made lake 'Bay of Naples,' which was filled with three million gallons of water. The background was 10,000 yards of oil paintings. The finale was a 'million dollar' fireworks display," probably every bit as loud as the volcano that turned its fury on Pompeii in the first place.

The growing pains were now less painful. St. Joseph's Hospital opened in 1889, followed by All Saints' Hospital six years later. William and George Monnig launched Monnig's and lived on the second floor of their building for several years. Nat Washer came down from Tennessee to join his brother in Washer Brothers. And a young Bowie merchant, W.C. Stripling, established a branch store in Fort Worth, even though he had nothing to use for counters except packing cases. H.C. Meacham had a small drygoods store. And Leopold August left Jacob Washer to run his own A. and L. August Clothing Store.

In 1881, Polytechnic Institute (later Texas Wesleyan College) appeared in Fort Worth. Eight years later, its president, Reverend Oscar Fisher, changed its name to Fort Worth University. By 1894, it boasted the third medical

Higher education on the prairie: Fort Worth University in 1910 included (from left) Cadet Hall, Science Hall, a gymnasium and an administration building. Founded in 1881 under another name, it included a law school and a medical school. First term medical students pose (right) in January 1895. Texas Christian University moved to Fort Worth in 1910, and FWU eventually became Oklahoma City University. Margaret Bunnel (above left) shows her support. Coach Charles Wilburn Leigh (above right)—also a math instructor—stands tall in 1897.

school in the state. Its first dean was the honorable Dr. Bacon Saunders who, several years earlier, had diagnosed a case of appendicitis. Saunders had read about the ailment in his medical journal and admitted he had never removed an appendix before but thought he probably could. The patient told him to go ahead. He had little to lose. Dr. Saunders anesthetized the man with chloroform. He boiled his catgut ligatures in olive oil, then boiled sheets in order to drape a semi-sterile environment around the patient who was lying on his kitchen table. Saunders operated, the man recovered. And the doctor would forever be remembered as the physician who performed the first appendectomy in Texas.

In his advertisement of Fort Worth University, Reverend Fisher said bluntly, "Increase your knowledge, your brain power, and thereby your capital, by study in one of our schools. Fifty-one teachers, eight hundred students. Military school for boys. Homelike accommodations for girls. Expense moderate."

As the century drew to an end, Fort Worth had lost an old friend, albeit a wild and bawdy one. The cattle trails—once its economic lifeblood—had shriveled up and blown away with the dust. The drought of 1885 had left the vast prairies littered with the sun-bleached bones of cattle that had found no water. Pasturelands were ashen. Cattle went mad and cattlemen went broke. As one rancher said, "I sold my spread and moved to town so I'd never have to listen to the awful sounds of a thirsty cow again."

Prices crashed. The value of cattle plunged from $35 a head to $10 a head, and most did not sell at all. By 1887, stockmen were earning only a $9 profit on each steer in Chicago—not enough to make those three-month-long trail drives worthwhile. The cattle stayed in Texas.

Yet, Fort Worth still followed the dollar-mark brands of cattle into the

Taking early stock: The Fort Worth Stock Show (top), one of the city's most popular current attractions, began in 1896 under the shade trees along Marine Creek on the north side of town. Stock pens (right) covered dozens of acres by 1903 when both Swift and Armour were in full operation. A genuine Texas Longhorn (above) was among the first animals sold in the newly-opened Fort Worth Stockyards in 1904. The Stock Yards Club (above right) included a saloon and pool hall on the northeast corner of Main and Exchange Streets, circa 1907.

Presidential appearance: President Theodore Roosevelt spoke in Fort Worth on April 8, 1905, planted a tree, then left for Oklahoma to see a man capture a coyote with his bare hands.

A high price for justice: In 1894, county commissioners decided a "palace of justice" should replace the old courthouse, which had burned. The commissioners, shown at the cornerstone laying, were voted out of office when voters objected to the proposed building's $500,000 price tag.

twentieth century. Back in 1883, the Continental Meat Packing Company had built a processing plant. It had quickly failed, but others did not. The Texas Dressed Beef and Packing Company, established with a capital of a half-million dollars and boasting some of the state's most influential cattlemen as its stockholders, purchased the old Continental site in 1890. On the north side of Fort Worth, a stockyard was constructed and, in 1893 the new owner, G.W. Simpson, offered Texas ranchers fifty cents more a head than they could get in Kansas City. Herds were again turned toward cowtown.

In 1896, rancher Charles McFarland stopped stockyard official Charles French on a Fort Worth sidewalk and made a simple suggestion. "A show of fine stock sure would do a lot to develop our livestock industry," he said. French agreed. A year later, cattlemen staged their first livestock exposition in Fort Worth, down under the oak trees that shaded Marine Creek. Four exhibiters showed up. In 1898, the exposition featured six shorthorns and two herefords, two lots of hogs, but no sheep.

L.B. Brown of Smithfield became the first Texan to ever pay $1,000 for a registered bull. And as banker K.M. Van Zandt looked over the check, he merely shook his head and muttered, "Poor Louis is losing his mind."

Sterling P. Clark, who one day would be sheriff of Tarrant County, tried hard to enter chickens in the exposition. But Frank Hovencamp told him plainly enough, "We don't want any two-bit rooster wakin' up a thousand dollar bull." During those early days, Hovencamp's daughter was busy driving around town in her father's buggy, collecting prizes that the merchants donated—blankets, a harness, buggy whips, even a parasol.

In 1906, the exposition left the oak trees and moved up to the stock pens. Management decided folks should pay admission to see those blue ribbon winners, and they did. Cattle was again king in the Fort Worth economy.

Swift & Co. and Armour & Co. made the difference. Fort Worth almost did not get them. It was 1901 and both companies were looking favorably upon the town beside the Trinity. But Fort Worth needed to come up with a $100,000 bonus to insure that the two companies would choose cowtown for their location. Money was hard to find. Businessmen held meetings, rallies and confrontations with their own bankers.

And *The Fort Worth Register* wrote, at the end of that last dramatic meeting:

"Fort Worth made history for herself and Texas last night. Fort Worth today will be on the lips of every man, woman and child who reads. Fort Worth, the packing house center of all the South and Southwest. . . .

"Fort Worth started on her road to greatness last night. At 11:35 o'clock Monday night, October 7, 1901, the die was cast, and J.W. Springer of Denver, Col., standing on the rostrum of the city hall auditorium, in front of the packing house soliciting committee and before a vast multitude of Fort Worth citizens, ladies and gentlemen, from all the better walks of life, announced that:

FORT WORTH IS IT

"She having succeeded in raising $100,000 packing house bonus, with over $600 to spare. Of this amount, $15,669 was raised in the city hall last night. At this announcement, pandemonium took possession of the audience—hats went up, handkerchiefs were waived, handshaking was unanimous."

Swift & Co. and Armour came. And their impact was felt foremost at the bank. By 1909, the two companies were processing 1,200,000 cattle and 870,000 hogs each year. And the town's population had jumped from 26,688 to 73,312.

Fort Worth was definitely on the move, and it had the railroads it needed to make it go. A dozen trunk lines cut into the city, with switchyards handling as many as 1.5 million cars a year. The number of railroad lines linking Fort Worth to the rest of the nation had even surpassed the dream of Paddock's "tarantula map."

President Theodore Roosevelt took one of the trains into the city, met a crowd of 20,000, offered his sympathy when a roof collapsed under the weight of 50 spectators, stayed long enough to plant a tree in the lawn of the library,

Sweet memories: Neighborhood children (right) pose in front of the George B. Hendricks home, 704 West 7th Street, April 26, 1896. Men of the Fort Worth Club (below) found joviality in the snow in 1896. Ladies hem linen napkins (bottom), circa 1894.

then rode on north to Oklahoma, joining Burk Burnett and Tom Waggoner on a wolf hunt.

Tarrant County completed a new courthouse in 1894 but it was not particularly appreciated by voters. The courthouse was grand, even massive. But it cost almost $500,000. Taxpayers were outraged by the extravagant cost. It was too large, they said. Such a structure had no place in county government. So the first chance they had, voters went to the polls and defeated every commissioner who had had a hand in building the courthouse (which was all of them). In a copper box beneath the cornerstore of the structure, however, Fort Worth placed its legacy for future generations—$100 in Confederate money, a bottle of Tarrant County wine, a prescription for the Grippe written by Dr. Julian Feild, a lock of hair from Judge Robert G. Johnson's child, the original oration of Henry M. Furman at the cornerstone ceremonies, a few copper cents and all sorts of rosters with names from lodges, churches, government officials and the Chamber of Commerce.

On an August day in 1903, Colonel R. Peterson—driving a $2,600 automobile—set the first automobile speed record between Fort Worth and Dallas, making the 30 miles in one hour, 35 minutes. The *Fort Worth Telegram* called the automobile "a large machine, belonging to the 'Red Devil' class." A man named Cromer (who sold bicycles on easy terms) registered the first car in the city in 1904. When he pointed his Rambler toward the country, Cromer carried along a wire cutter to cut fences when he needed to make a detour through somebody's pasture, a pick to chop down the high center of the old dirt roads and a shovel for digging out of sand beds. He was not too popular, especially with farmers. That same year, Fort Worth recorded its first hit-and-run accident. An attorney from Gainesville, George H. Giddings, was standing on a street corner at Seventh and Houston when the vehicle struck him. He explained that it was "a benzine wagon which turned the corner noiselessly and at a rapid speed."

Throughout Fort Worth came the sounds of culture—from the Mandolin Club, the Arion Club, the Literary Society, military bands and theatrical groups. Paddock would look back on the era and write, "There were picnics in the daytime and by moonlight, when the moon was in commission. Everybody was happy and tried to make his neighbor happy. Good old days."

They were not doing too badly either down around the awakening saloons and brothels of an aroused Hell's Half Acre. For a time, the area had been pretty much under wraps and quiet, though still tainted and tempting.

George Leroy Parker—handsome, handy with a gun—regularly hung around Fannie Porter's house. He had picked up quite a reputation stealing horses, then robbing trains and banks, but no one in Fort Worth knew about it. He

Turning the century: Although street cars were in evidence, transportation in 1896 (above), the new court house is in the distance at the end of Main Street. And in December 1900, photographer C.L. Swartz was visited by the infamous "Hole-in-the-Wall Gang" for a formal portrait. This touted group of criminals made Fort Worth their home between jobs. From left, standing, Bill Carver and Harvey Logan. Seated, Harry Longbaugh (The Sundance Kid), Ben Kilpatrick, and George Parker (Butch Cassidy).

While Pinkerton's detectives combed the Hole-In-The-Wall country for him, Butch Cassidy played cards and drank whiskey in Hell's Half Acre.

called himself Jim Lowe, but that was as false as the impression he gave of being a genteel gentleman.

His friends dropped into Fannie Porter's to stay a spell—Harry Longbaugh, Harry Tracy, Kid Curry, Sam and Blackjack Ketchum, Elza Lay, Deaf Charley Hanks, Ben Kilpatrick and Bill Carver. They knew that Parker (alias Jim Lowe) had been taught the fine art of armed robbery by a man named Cassidy, that Parker himself had once worked as a butcher and—at least on wanted posters—was known as Butch.

Harry Longbaugh—who referred to himself as the Sundance Kid—knew Butch Cassidy best. The rest of the gang was simply called the Wild Bunch. It was an apt description. While Pinkerton's detectives combed the Hole-In-The-Wall country for him, Butch Cassidy played cards and drank whiskey in Hell's Half Acre.

Sundance fell in love with a new girl at Fannie Porter's—Etta Place. She would accompany Sundance to South America while Cassidy, wanting one last "raise," hit the Great Northern Train in Wagner, Montana, on a July day in 1901 and rode away with $40,000 in nonnegotiable currency.

He brought it all to Fort Worth. Fannie had a few girls who knew how to write, and they worked with Cassidy for days, scribbling phony signatures on the unsigned notes. A Dallas banker discovered the forgery and contacted Pinkerton. The detectives rushed down into Hell's Half Acre.

Butch Cassidy was gone. He was bound for South America. Cassidy and Sundance, when funds ran low, made it a habit of robbing village banks while Etta held the horses for them. But the girl was stricken with a severe attack of appendicitis and Sundance, not overly impressed with Argentina's medical facilities, brought her to New York by boat, then on to Denver.

Etta Place underwent surgery. But Sundance vanished, heading back to South America. He never returned. He and Cassidy promptly took the payroll from an Alpoca Silver Mine mule train, and a Bolivian cavalry rode down upon them.

The outlaws wedged themselves in a small hut, their last fortress. Sundance fell wounded during the night as the Cavalry encircled them in the darkness. Before morning, he had bled to death. And just before the sun rose, so the Bolivian report goes, Cassidy—realizing the futility of it all—put his final bullet into his own head.

College Avenue Baptist Church, January 18, 1914.

Etta Place walked out of the hospital and disappeared, though some believe she returned to Fort Worth and, under the name of Eunice Gray, operated the Waco Hotel for 40 years. She spent a lot of time talking about South America. Eunice Gray died in a fire at the hotel in 1962, leaving behind an estate valued at $90,000. She was 77.

County Attorney Jefferson Davis McLean tried to use the law to exterminate the evil from Hell's Half Acre. J. Frank Norris used the pulpit. McLean was a crusader, Norris an exorcist of sin. One used the grand jury, the other damnation. McLean died.

McLean was a devout opponent of open gambling. On the afternoon of March 21, 1907, McLean saw Sheriff Wood—along with several deputies—preparing to raid the faro and poker games of William Tomlinson's gambling room. McLean halted his buggy, told his wife to wait for him and hurriedly walked down the street to assist Wood.

The equipment was confiscated and the County Attorney headed back toward his buggy. He passed One-Armed Bill Thompson, the gambler whose games were being hauled away. Thompson sneered, muttering, "There goes the ————who always gets in when he ain't got a chance to get a piece of the pie for himself." McLean stopped and turned. One-Armed Thompson drew his pistol and fired. McLean clutched at his throat and crumpled into the street. Duff Purvis, a county commissioner, was standing beside the attorney when he fell. Purvis recalled:

"After shooting McLean, Thompson, with his smoking weapon in his hand, bolted through the Stag saloon, which was filled with people.

"I saw Jeff fall. I realized instantly what had taken place. I cried out to the crowd, 'Bill Thompson has shot Jeff; catch Bill.' I then turned to McLean. I wish I could describe the look on his face. He appeared to be entirely satisfied. He looked like a man who had done his whole duty unflinchingly and he was not ashamed of what he had done. . . .

"Jeff never spoke during this time. He was breathing naturally. The crowd got to pressing around him. . . . At this point Jeff, in his natural tone of voice, said: 'Don't let them crowd me' . . . Then I saw the pallor of death creep over his face."

One-Armed Bill Thompson reached the Roe Lumber Yard before police caught up with him. He could not escape. He tried to shoot it out with officers and lost. A crowd of 3,000 gathered around, and Thompson pretended he was dead in a desperate effort to prevent the angry mob from lynching him. He missed the rope but died a few days later in jail.

Most of the members of the Texas Legislature (in town attending the Fat Stock Show) were shocked at the shooting. They quickly returned to Austin and, feeling righteous, passed a state law against gambling. Hell's Half Acre shuddered.

Reverend J. Frank Norris called down brimstone onto that Sodom and Gomorrah corner of Fort Worth. Hell's Half Acre ducked. Norris was not a man to be ignored nor reasoned with. He had first gained notoriety at his First Baptist Church by preaching one Sunday morning, "Why Dallas Beat Fort Worth in Baseball." Norris said softly, "Dallas beat Fort Worth because Dallas was better prepared. Boys, you had better get prepared for this game of life." Then he wept. And he shouted. And he gnashed his teeth, saying, "Old Devil, you think you've got these boys tonight. But, oh, Devil, you haven't! You haven't! These boys are going to knock a home run for Jesus Christ tonight." Norris jumped into the aisle and exhorted, "Come on, boys, knock a home run for Jesus." Sixty weeping souls did.

J. Frank Norris knew how to make hellfire so hot his congregation felt the heat. Some even swore, as much as a Baptist would dare, that they could smell the sulphur.

Hell's Half Acre would smell it. But then, J. Frank Norris was, he believed, the chosen. He had watched liquor destroy his father. He himself had been shot at the age of 15, lying paralyzed for three years. And when he recovered, Norris told his mother, "God has laid his hand on me to preach the Gospel."

Reverend J. Frank Norris called down brimstone onto that Sodom and Gomorrah corner of Fort Worth. Hell's Half Acre ducked.

The cowboy's staple: Beer was served at the Stag Saloon at 6th and Main Streets by proprietor W.A. Hornbeak and Tony Porter. The supply of suds was maintained daily by the Anheuser-Busch Brewing Association (right).

In Fort Worth, the long, lanky preacher found trouble within his own soul. He said, "I was the most knocked down, run over, chewed up, fired preacher in the world. I was drawing a big salary, wearing tailor made suits, preaching in the midst of a city of over a hundred thousand people, none paying any attention to me. . . . I was not causing a riffle. My moisture was turned into the drought of summer, my soul was poured out like water. . . . Something had to happen."

It did. J. Frank Norris learned—then polished to perfection—the power of sensationalism. He became a showman, a controversy himself. But people paid attention to him. He caused not only riffles but wars.

Norris condemned bootleggers in his sermons, busting fruit jars of illegal moonshine against the side of a galvanized tub. He displayed monkeys as part of his fundamentalist wrath against the falsehoods of Darwin's evolution. He even filled a number-two washtub with rattlesnakes, just so the crowds would come—and they came.

For J. Frank Norris, the wages of sin were always death, and Hell's Half Acre was the best place in town to draw back pay. It sizzled. Norris persuaded

Upward mobility: The Fort Worth Hotel and A & L August Clothiers occupied the corner of 7th and Main Streets at the turn of the century (above). Fort Worth's first skyscraper was the Flat Iron building—patterned after its New York City namesake—built by Dr. Bacon Saunders.

the minister's association to hire a detective and investigate the innards of the acre. The man's report frightened, then intimidated, the ministers. He had found filth all right, the detective said, in 80 houses of prostitution. He even had a list of the miserable owners who ran these hellholes of degradation. The ministers swallowed hard. Eight of the owners were among Fort Worth's most influential and socially prominent leaders. They were big money men with a penchant for donating heavily to the church. One was even a deacon. The ministers backed off.

Norris smiled. "If a preacher is not stirring up the devil, he is dead, already sold out," he said. He did not sell out. Norris remembered, "The arrangement was that each minister would get up the following Sunday night and read out publically the names of the owners of those houses of ill repute. You understand this agreement was entered into before we found out who the men were. But I, being young and unsophisticated, thought the other brethren would carry out their part of the agreement. Therefore, I proceeded to read the names."

He preached on "The Ten Biggest Devils in Town and Their records given." The battle had begun.

Hostility took Fort Worth by the shoulders and shook it. In 1911, Norris fought for state-wide prohibition. Gunmen tried to assassinate him, firing two shots into his study as Norris prepared his next sermon against them. His congregations grew. They became so large that they spilled out of the church house.

Norris bought an old circus tent once used by Sarah Bernhardt, put it up and launched a 90-day revival. He preached hard and long against the transgressions of alcohol. Six days before the liquor election, firemen chopped the tent down, saying it was unsafe, a fire hazard. The wets won by more than 6,000 votes.

Norris—believing that God's word was indeed a terrible swift sword—attacked Mayor W.D. Davis and the city administration. The good Lord, he believed, had definitely paved the way for his new verbal assault. After all, the state comptroller had discovered that $400,000 in tax revenue was missing. And that made for just about the best sermon topic around, if any preacher had guts enough to preach it. Norris did.

Davis was furious. He called Norris a "fanatical outcast, [not] worth killing with a dollar ninety-eight-cent pistol." Then the mayor had other ideas. He requested a town meeting, urging every adult male to attend but excluding "boys under 21" and "women."

After a two-hour bombardment of accusations, Davis concluded by saying, "This is a time for heads of homes to act and not a time for sissy boys. If there are fifty red-blooded men in town, a preacher will be hanging from a lamp post before daylight."

Two days later, at 2:30 o'clock in the morning, the First Baptist Church exploded and burned to the ground. Norris' home also burst into flames. The preacher promptly moved his congregation to a theater and blasted the persecution that had been heaped upon his bowed and weary shoulders. He told them, "If anybody thinks a bunch of these machine . . . politicians can make a fight on my wife's husband, and I will do a flop-eared, pot-licker, suck-egg hound, when he tucks his tail between his legs and runs down tin can alley—well, they have another think comin'."

So did J. Frank Norris. Ten days later he was indicted for arson. Outside the courtroom, boys passed out religious tracts while women held afternoon prayer sessions. Norris would later preach that his trial was like "Luther in front of the Diet of Worms." But he was acquitted. As the verdict was read, an old lady stood and shouted to the judge, "Woe be unto you." And immediately the crowd broke out in song, "Nearer My God To Thee."

Norris never acquitted Hell's Half Acre. He, alone, could not rid Fort Worth of its most cancerous eyesore. But the Acre never fully recovered from his Sunday morning thrashings. By 1917, it wilted at last, then began drying up as the bawdy houses and booze dispensers scattered elsewhere.

Trains, cops and fiddlers: The office of the Fort
Worth & Rio Grande Railway Company (above).
The city's police department (below left) shortly
after the turn of the century. The Old Fiddlers'
Contest (below right) on April 13, 1901, drew
a bearded assortment.

The days of hats and a slower pace: Clowning around in front of the boat house at Hust Lake (above). An outing at the lake in 1907 (below left). Picnicking, fishing and an assortment of head apparel at Hust Lake in 1907 (below right).

Gathering in the park: While the womenfolk tend to their duties, the men ponder life at the park; in the left center with the derby hat is Captain B.B. Paddock. Forest Park, looking south, November 7, 1909 (left).

Building for tomorrow: Students at Arlington
Heights School pose, circa 1905 (above).
Construction workers (below) pose at the site of
the old Fort Worth High School on Jennings
Avenue, January 1911.

Pretty and courteous: James A. Walkup advertised the "prettiest and most up-to-date Soda Fountain in the city" in 1912 (above). It was located in the Walkup Pharmacy at the corner of Main and 15th Streets. That same year, "courteous treatment" was offered at the barber shop in the Western National Bank Building (below).

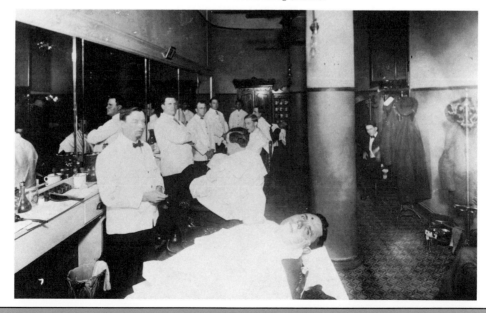

Yesterday's store, today's flea market: The place
for tools and household supplies was at J.B.
Burnside's "old hardware corner" (below) at 5th
and Houston Streets, February 1912. J.L.
Pummill's meat market and delicatessen (above
left). The Norvell Corset Shop in the Westbrook
Hotel Building (above right) in 1912.

Industry on parade: The Fort Worth Shirt Company (top), 209½ West 11th Street. The Westland Cigar Manufacturing Company's (center) best sold for 15 cents in 1911. The Texas Cleaning & Dyeing Company (bottom) in 1912.

The wonders of electricity: Electric wires skirt the ceiling of the Progressive Print Company (right), which featured a linotype machine. The drafting room at Waller & Field, Architects (below left) located at 209½ West 8th, had an electric blue printing machine. The offices of W.M. Coleman, J.W. Bondurant and C.H. Duffield (below right).

Flowers and fires: The Fort Worth Flower parade and festival in May 1900 brought flower-bedecked carriages and jovial spirits to the city; among celebrants, the Mulkey boys (above left) with their "float" called "During Paddock's Time." In 1904 townspeople watched the Texas & Pacific station burn (right).

Chapter 8

Reaching for the sky and finding oil

The oil boom days at Burkburnett.

Amon Carter touched the streets of Fort Worth in 1905, stopping long enough to kick the unpleasant memories of San Francisco off the bottom of his shoes before launching into a campaign to sell advertising cards for those electric street cars. San Francisco, he believed, had not paid his talents enough money or attention, creating severe problems for the grand lifestyle he pursued. But Fort Worth would pay.

On a cold winter day, he walked with a salesman out into the stockyards to watch the demonstration of a new product—oil-soaked cow manure—sold to those thousands who could not afford other kinds of better-smelling fuels. Carter nodded at two reporters, A.G. Dawson of the *Dallas Morning News* and D.C. McCaleb of the *Fort Worth Record*.

They had come merely because duty demanded that they write about the strange new heating fuel, one that cowboys had used for years out on the open prairies. The day would change their lives.

Carter and the two reporters clustered around the cow-chip fire and discussed the possibility of creating a new daily afternoon newspaper to contend with the *Fort Worth Telegram*. The reporters knew how to write and edit. Carter was a genius when it came to selling advertising space. The trio would, they believed, be a natural team, even though their faith was much more substantial than their bank accounts. There, amidst the choking smoke of dried cow-chip coals, was birthed the *Fort Worth Star*. Colonel Paul Waples rounded up a few friends and they laid out $50,000 to finance McCaleb's and Dawson's new paper. Amon Carter, alas, had no money to invest at all. But Louis Wortham was named Publisher/Editor and Carter strolled aboard as a $35-a-week advertising manager. Dawson had wanted to pay him twenty bucks a week, but Carter held out until he got what he wanted. Carter was like that.

And, in time, Amon Carter would replace another newspaperman, B.B. Paddock, as the most devoted, determined and downright fanatical promoter Fort Worth could have. He believed in his city. He made sure the whole world shared that belief, even if he had to go tell them himself (which he did).

It was Carter who coined the phrase that became the most legendary description of Fort Worth—"Where The West begins." Franklin Roosevelt used it in his speeches. Bob Hope joked about it. And Will Rogers laughed to reporters that Fort Worth is where the west begins and "Dallas peters out."

Carter began all his speeches by shouting: "Texas forever! Fort Worth now and hereafter!" And, likely as not, he would tell the audiences, "The chief occupation of Texans is trying to keep from making all the money in the world," or "You do not belong to society as constituted in Texas unless your front gate is 18 miles from your front door," or "If all Texas steers were one big steer he would stand with his front feet in the Gulf of Mexico, one hind foot in Hudson Bay, the other in the Arctic Ocean and with his tail brush off the mist of the Aurora Borealis."

He was quite a peddler.

The early news in Carter's *Fort Worth Star* pretty much summed up the highlights of 1906. C.W. Post, who had once lived in the city, was back in town promoting his Grape Nuts as a medical cure for every disease. Out in Brownwood, Charles Hale struck a match to see just what was inside his new gas-powered automobile and wound up "terribly burned." A 40-year-old wife petitioned for a divorce, charging "intolerable cruelty." In 24 years of wedlock, she had mothered 27 children. The original New York cast of "Mrs. Wiggs of the Cabbage Patch" was bringing its production to the stage of Greenwall's Opera House. And F.O. "Painless" Cates was willing to extract a tooth for 50 cents.

Fort Worth's population had hit 40,000, and Amon Carter wanted most of them to read the *Star*. The newspaper had good times and more than its share of bad ones.

The Star had always walked a financial tightrope. By 1908, it was in serious trouble. The original investment of $50,000 was gone, and the Star had fallen

In search of a lifestyle: Amon Carter, publisher of the Fort Worth Star Telegram *(left) and Louis Wortham, the newspaper's editor who also wrote a five-volume history of Texas.*

It was Carter who coined the phrase that became the most legendary description of Fort Worth—"Where The West Begins." Franklin Roosevelt used it in his speeches. Bob Hope joked about it. And Will Rogers laughed to reporters that Fort Worth is where the west begins and "Dallas peters out."

Fort Worth fourth estate: The Star-Telegram *building (above). The composing room of the old* Fort Worth Telegram *(right), purchased by the* Fort Worth Star *to become the present* Star-Telegram.

another $27,000 in debt. McCaleb and Dawson had left before the newspaper's first anniversary. And the successful *Fort Worth Telegram* was eagerly trying to hire Carter away, dangling a $75-a-week paycheck in front of his eyes.

Carter refused.

"Then," said C.D. Reimers, the publisher of *The Telegram,* "We'll put you out of business."

"Hop to it," Carter retorted. (Carter would later confess, "We were failing, so we decided to expand.")

He and Wortham decided to buy the *Telegram.* All they needed was $92,500, plus a down payment of $2,500. Carter walked down to the Fort Worth National Bank and used four diamond rings and a diamond and pearl scarf pin as collateral for the down payment. And Colonel Waples, though hesitant at first, again came to the financial aid of the struggling *Star.* He, W.C. Stripling, W.G. Burton and H.C. Meacham came up with the cash.

Colonel Waples, in a fit of generosity, offered Carter and Wortham corporation shares. Carter wound up with ten percent, even though he had to borrow a "piece of swamp land" down in Florida from a friend in order to secure his shares. Carter was still having trouble keeping money on hand.

But he was, at last, part owner of a newspaper. And the *Star* and the *Telegram* was, and forever would be, one. And Carter did not stop until he owned it all.

Fort Worth, for a change, was on the threshhold of acquiring a certain degree of respectability. Add-Ran College had fled the city back in 1896 when the Clark brothers turned their backs with anguish, anger and despair, on their neighbors, the raucous little night-life joints of Hell's Half Acre. They had taken their stern lectures and discipline to the safe, comfortable bosom of Waco. But a fire in 1910 burned them off the Brazos. Fort Worth held out a generous hand, one worth $200,000 and a campus site of 56 acres. The Clark brothers decided that Fort Worth had repented enough and brought their school, along with 326 students, back to the Trinity with a new name— Texas Christian University. That same year, the Southwestern Baptist Theological Seminary, too, left Waco and found a new home in Fort Worth, looking for enough space to keep from being cramped and crowded. Within five years, a third major school—Texas Women's College—located in the city with 101 students. The opportunity for book learning was plentiful. Fort Worth had become concerned about growing minds.

Speeding things up: The Interurban's inaugural run between Fort Worth and Dallas brought out officials of the Fort Worth Traction Company to pose, praise and eat barbecue (above).

It also made arrangements to take care of injured bodies, regardless of how ill a person's pocketbook might be. Patients who could not pay for their treatment were either sent to the charity ward of St. Joseph's Hospital or to a makeshift hospital in the basement of the medical college. And in 1912, Mrs. Ida L. Turner, a former postmistress, got tired of just worrying about the lack of medical facilities for children. She and Mrs. J.H. Strayer and Mrs. Charles Sheuber (chairmen in the city Federation of Women's Clubs) held a charity ball to raise money. They talked lumber company owners, furniture dealers and hardware merchants into donating their merchandise. Then they persuaded carpenters, brick masons, plumbers, painters and electricians to give their time and talent to fashion that merchandise into a building. And from such city-wide effort came the creation of the Fort Worth Free Babies Hospital.

But it was from the skies where Fort Worth heard its future calling. Those strange, new-fangled flying machines, with pilots strapped inside their innards, were coming to town amidst the echo of hard-core ministers who preached, "If God had meant for you to fly, he would have given you wings."

It was 1911 and a trio of international barnstormers—two Frenchmen and a Swiss—were hopscotching their way across the country. They had planned an air show in Dallas, but Amon Carter was not about to let them get that close without tight-roping the skies over Fort Worth as well. Carter dispatched R.E.L. Costan to Dallas with an offer of $5,000 for the pilots to turn their flimsy aircraft toward the twin forks of the Trinity. They agreed, promising to appear January 12 and 13, high above the old Driver's Club.

More than 15,000 crowded into the park to witness the daredevil feats of the "International Aviators." But the winds were strong, and the pilots refused to leave the ground. After all, they had already lost one of their group, John B. Moisant, who had been killed during a performance in New Orleans. The pilots kept fiddling with their planes. Four hours passed. The crowd grew restless but did not walk away. The aviators tested the winds with kites. And, at last, one climbed into his plane. *The Star-Telegram* reported:

"The first actual thrill of the afternoon came when Edmond Audemars in his little yellow Demoiselle leaped into the air, even though the Swiss aviator could not control the little trick machine in the cross currents of air that swept to and fro near the earth. The sputtering of the Demoiselle's engine made the crowd forget its long wait, and there was a buzzing expectancy of seeing for the first time a heavier than air machine leave the ground. The Demoiselle skipped swiftly across the field, and as it neared the judge's stand it made a jerky leap into the air. Audemars' flights, however, were unsuccessful Thursday, and the best exhibition that the Demoiselle could furnish was a series of 'hops.'

"The aviators were aware that the crowd was becoming disappointed and lapsing back into its former restlessness.

" 'I'm not going to see them disappointed,' said Roland Garros, the French aviator, who only two hours before had shaken his head significantly and commented to his fellow birdmen on the peril of attempting a flight in the puffy wind that he knew was in the air.

"Rene Simon, the 'fool flyer' himself, grasped Garros by the arm almost in fright, and told him he must not try to fly at the risk of his life. Simon and the other aviators were still pleading with Garros when the mechanicians started the engine of the 'Statue of Liberty' monoplane and Garros climbed into the machine. . . .

"When it mounted gracefully into the air and moved steadily upward for several hundred feet, the crowd burst into applause. Every head bent upward and not an eye left the machine. . . . So high was the monoplane when it passed over the heads of the spectators that the terrific throbbing of its powerful engine could be heard only as a murmur . . . persons on every side were heard explaining that Garros was lost, that he already had lost his directions. . . .

"It was when the monoplane turned backward and sped toward the aviation field that thousands of people realized the peril of Garros. As

"Daredevil Cal" Rodgers piloted the first plane to Fort Worth in August 1911, under the sponsorship of the Vin-Fiz grape drink. Rodgers landed his "Vin-Fiz Flyer" in Ryan's pasture as he stopped in Fort Worth enroute to the first transcontinental flight in history.

the machine neared the field it could be seen rocking in the gusts of wind, and when it swerved almost to turn topsy-turvy the crowd held its breath. Before Garros reached the grounds of the Driver's Club, he pointed the nose of the machine downward and it looked as if he would plunge into the crowd at the north end of the track. The machine held its poise, however, became steadier, and the daring Frenchman alighted gracefully. . . .

"The crowd was wild and the big police squad patrolling the track could not stay the rush that started for the infield."

The next day, only 10,000 showed up. The "Fool Flyer" himself, Rene Simon, flew. The Demoiselle was seriously damaged. And the "International Aviators" rolled away from Fort Worth with $6,300 for their troubles.

Fort Worth would be captivated by the sky forever and by the men and machines who conquered it. C.P. Rodgers, old "Daredevil Cal," kept the fever running hot. On September 17, he flew out of New York, sponsored by the makers of a grape drink called Vin-Fiz, and was off on the first transcontinental flight in history. A month later, he touched down in Fort Worth. He barely made it. On his last stop before Fort Worth, "Daredevil Cal" hopped out of Denison at 9:25 a.m. and, above Whitesboro, followed the wrong railroad tracks out of town. He was lost. Fort Worth scanned the skies. It saw nothing. Ten thousand had gathered in Ryan's pasture to await the Vin-Fiz Flyer. School was out. Bells were ringing. Telegraph and telephone operators frantically tried to alert Rodgers that he was nowhere near Fort Worth. Above Bonita— 70 miles out of his way—"Daredevil Cal" finally got the word. He turned back toward Fort Worth. At 3 p.m., the speck in the sky grew larger. It was Rodgers looking for a place to land. But he could not find one—the excited crowd, tired of standing and waiting, had rushed onto the field, swarming over his landing site.

"Daredevil Cal" made a quick calculation and headed to the far side of the field, pretending to set down there. As the multitudes raced toward him, he quickly banked the bi-plane, sailed over the throng at 75 feet and landed a half block away, pretty much where he wanted to be in the first place.

Welcome the car: Life changed dramatically with the coming of the motor car, as did appearances of Fort Worth drivers.

Rodgers climbed out of the plane and handed Amon Carter the first airmail letter ever delivered in Fort Worth. A newspaper reporter tried in vain to interview the pilot of the Vin-Fiz Flyer. But Rodgers had only one comment for him—"It was pretty cold up there today."

Fort Worth had slipped into a mechanized age. By 1909, Henry Lewis, a 19-year-old policeman, had been outfitted with a five-horsepower Indian motorcycle to chase down speeders who rode too hard in those fancy-dan automobiles. The fire chief even had a Maxwell passenger car, with a fire extinguisher attached to the left runningboard and a spotlight mounted proudly where the windshield once had been. By 1910, fire trucks ruled the roads. And in 1913, fifteen policemen patrolled the streets on bicycles. Officers strongly believed that the two-wheel bikes were much more adept at running down burglars because they were so quiet.

Pleased at its progress, Fort Worth was at peace with itself. The rest of the world was not—and would not be for a long time—and would drag Fort Worth into the conflict before anyone got around to settling it. The *Star-Telegram* kept publishing stories from the turmoil in Europe, stories that pointed to the outbreak of war. In 1914, it broke. Yet war seemed so remote, so far on the other side of a big ocean.

Benjamin D. Foulois brought it closer to home. He was a young army captain who had registered fifteen minutes of flying time with the Wright brothers. So the U.S. Army—obviously impressed with his experience—put him charge of the military's first airplane in 1910.

It was Foulois who led seven planes—the nation's entire air force—into Ryan's pasture on a November day in 1915. He was headed for San Antonio to set up a permanent headquarters at Fort Sam Houston, but Foulois stopped long enough in Fort Worth to dine at the Metropolitan Hotel with a host of city leaders. He boldly predicted that, in case of war, the government would spend $100 million for the development of air power, shocking most who heard him. A few months later, Foulois himself drafted the first aerial appropriations bill, asking for $640 million. Fort Worth was destined to get a big chunk of it.

Foulois told them, "If Germany comes out victorious in this war, she will have the strongest army in the world. . . . If Germany cared to take issue with the United States after this European war, she could land troops anywhere she pleased along the Atlantic coast and take every munition factory we have. . . . Our little army today would be wiped out in the first good fight we had."

At Fort Worth, perhaps, the tide was turned.

The Canadians came first—the gallant, reckless members of the Royal Flying Corps. General Hoare had been sent to Texas to check out Dallas, Fort Worth, Waco, Austin, Wichita Falls and Midland, searching for places to build three air training fields.

He located all three of them in Fort Worth—Carruthers Field at Benbrook on the west side, Taliaferro Field on the north side and Barron Field at Everman to the south. After all, Fort Worth had broad open spaces, a clear atmosphere and no forests to reach up and knock down their fragile flying machines.

The training was as deadly as the war. Planes—flown by unskilled hands—kept dropping and crashing. More than 50 lost their lives. The 51st was Vernon Castle, an internationally famous dancer and instructor at Carruthers Field. He was a favorite of Fort Worth society, living at the elegant Westbrook Hotel, performing at camp shows, where admission was as cheap as a dime. His last flight ascended on a February morning in 1918. As Castle prepared to land, he was forced to pull his plane up sharply in order to avoid collision with another craft. Castle's airplane stalled, seemed to hang in the sky, then

A wing and a prayer: The entire United States Army Air Corps visited Fort Worth in 1915. The pilots landed seven planes in Ryan's pasture and were treated to dinner at the Metropolitan Hotel.

*The good and bad of training: Canadian pilots
training in Fort Worth (above right) found the
local company charming. Captain Vernon Castle
(top) was the most famous of the Canadian pilots,
shown here with friend Jeff. Castle was killed at
Carruthers Field, near Benbrook, when he forced
his plane into a rapid climb near the ground to
avoid a student pilot; the plane stalled and crashed.
The casket (above) was part of a solemn
processional leaving Robertson's Funeral Parlour.*

plummeted into the ground 75 feet below. He died instantly. He was 31.
But his skillful maneuvering of the plane, witnesses said, no doubt saved the
lives of his cadet passenger and the pilot of the other aircraft.

When his wife and dance partner, Irene, heard the grim news, she said
softly, "It was a brave man's death and it is not a woman's part to complain."

Maury Jenkins, who trained at Barron Field, recalled, "The Canadians were
already living like there was no tomorrow." He soon found out why. Jenkins
explained, "When the cadets weren't waltzing, there were planes to fly and
crash. . . . We trained on Thomas Morse Scouts and Curtiss JN's, called
'Jennys.' And a lot of us didn't make it. . . . It was just you and a few pieces
of wire, canvas and boards, and a primitive engine."

The headlines on that April 17th morning, 1917, gripped a nation in fear
and unrest. The *New York Times* put it dramatically:

> "America in Armageddon;
> Country Is Called to War;
> All Its Forces Mobilizing."

For many, their first step toward the trenches in France, the bloody road
to Berlin, began on Fort Worth soil.

In June, an army commission sat down with Fort Worth leaders to find a
potential site for a large training camp. Businessmen had mapped out two
locations. One was just south of Southwestern Baptist Theological Seminary,
and a second proposed area sprawled near Lake Worth. But an old veteran
of the Mexican Expedition, in town to recruit Army doctors, thought he had
a better idea. Colonel Holman Taylor told the commission, "I know the best
site in Texas for an Army camp. It's there in Arlington Heights, between
the streetcar line and Stove Foundry Road."

Taylor had once considered it himself for a National Guard Camp. He
chauffeured the brigadier general to the area and told him, "Just look at that
gravel surface, General. It just quit raining an hour ago and in a couple of
hours more it will be dust here again."

It was a possibility, the general said. He drove to two more sites, then
returned to Arlington Heights for one last look. Just as the colonel had promised
him, dust rolled up from his automobile tires. It was his kind of place, the
general said.

Immediately civic leaders began talking about the large number of civilian

Camp Bowie

*A new way of life: The cavalry band (right).
Troops stand for regimental colors at reveille
(below). The 144th Infantry Regiment relaxing
(center right). Communications drill (far right).
Sundays were shared with civilians (lower right).*

Stutz and strutting: J. Clarkson (top) takes his Stutz Black Hawk out for a spin. Children prepare for a parade (above) for the Red Cross in June 1917.

Camp Bowie was hammered into existence without the luxury of wasted time and wasted dollars. As many as 3,500 carpenters were at work, most living in a tent city, earning a nickel an hour more than their usual wages.

---

employees near Arlington Heights, the existing streetcar line, nearby lumber facilities and a close connection for spur railroads. A month later, the general gave his official blessing for the construction of Camp Bowie.

Arlington Heights had been the dream that failed. Land speculators had grabbed all the farmland they could, even built houses. But home owners did not beat down their door at all. Few came, and Arlington Heights tumbled. One broker traded his lot for a typewriter. Another investor swapped his piece of land for a set of tires.

As Robert McCart Jr., remembered, "Father always had great faith in the Arlington Heights area and when it started going downhill be bought up a considerable amount of territory at cut prices. Then when the Army started to build, he donated about 1,000 lots."

Camp Bowie was hammered into existence without the luxury of wasted time and wasted dollars. As many as 3,500 carpenters were at work, most living in a tent city, earning a nickel an hour more than their usual wages. A 13-year-old boy, Claude Sims, toted a two-gallon bucket of water up steep ladders so the workers would not have to stop long to quench their thirst.

The camp ultimately became the training ground for men who would learn to march, shoot, survive and kill when the alternative was being killed. It had barracks, rifle ranges, gas warfare instruction houses, 15 mess halls, a base hospital, an ammunition magazine and endless acres of tents.

Captain Proctor, the commissary officer, received a telegram, notifying him that the first detachment would crowd into Camp Bowie by sun up. He hastily ordered 1,000 hams and 1,000 cases of eggs for breakfast.

Only 100 men straggled in. But they were the first of the 100,000 who would go into combat with Camp Bowie training fresh on their mind.

They did not fight all the time. Hell's Half Acre raised the sleepy eye that J. Frank Norris had blackened but not shut. Sin was back in business. Nothing had changed except the prices. And again the saloons badly outnumbered the churches in downtown Fort Worth—178 to 16. The theater even had the gall to name itself Pershing in honor of the general who had been chosen to lead the U.S. forces against the Kaiser. On the marquee was written: "High Class Musical Comedy." What was inside was a basic, show-and-tell, now-you-see-it-now-you-don't, girlie burlesque show. But anyone who was really patriotic felt obligated to attend the Pershing, and all the soldiers did.

The puritan crusaders were up in arms. *Pass In Review,* the Camp Bowie newspaper, reported: "Uncle Sam has rolled up his sleeves and started in to make a genuine cleaning out of 'houses of ill fame, brothels, or bawdy houses.' These places of the devil and aides to the kaiser will not be asked to move. They will be made to clear out. . . .

"The district extends five miles everyway from all camps. It that district the lewd women must stay out.

"And auto livery drivers must refrain from carrying passengers to such places. Suggesting the whereabouts of such a place is punishable.

"Patrons of these hell holes will suffer likewise."

The publication would also point out, "The best thing in Fort Worth is the Chamber of Commerce. They insist that there is nothing too good for a soldier."

From Camp Bowie came the famed 36th Division—the T-Patchers from Texas and Oklahoma. After seven months of training, Major General Edwin St. John Greble, their commanding officer, led the 36th on a parade through the streets of Fort Worth.

Watching them from his reviewing stand, Governor William B. Hobby remarked, "This is the greatest crowd I have ever seen in Texas."

A reporter asked him, "Would you go with these boys to France?"

"Good Lord, yes," the governor replied.

And one newspaper reported: "Yes, the Texas-Oklahoma Sammie is ready for action. He may be here another week, two weeks or two months but he is ready to fight and die for his country. After seven months of gruelling training—all gone through that you and yours looking on will be safe—he is

Preparing to give lives: A review by the 36th Division through the streets of Fort Worth.

part of a war machine perfected by the iron-handed yet kind-hearted General Greble."

Within six months, the T-Patchers from Fort Worth would be charging across France and into battle. One regiment, the 142nd, had the Millionaire Company whose roll call bore such names as Big Bear, Rainbow Blanket, Bacon Rind and Hohemanatubbe, all Indians whose reservations sprawled across Oklahoma oil lands. They were buck privates who carried thousand-dollar bills in their pocket.

Capt. E.M. Matson remembered, "The Oklahoma Indians ploughed their way through the German machine gun nests like their forebears of old. Nothing could stop them, although a large number were killed." Another regiment lost 691 men during its first day of fighting. And during 23 days, the 36th Division won two Congressional Metals of Honor, 30 Distinguished Crosses and 128 Croix de Guerres. It cost them 1,300 lives.

The war did not go well at Camp Bowie either. A Spanish influenza epidemic went on the rampage. And Ralph Lamb remembered the day he marched out with the troops to watch a gun crew demonstrate the firing of a trench mortar.

He said, "After a few minutes, a shell jammed in the gun and before it was realized, another shell was dropped on top of it, and it exploded both shells at the same time. I was stretched out on the ground about 30 feet from the gun . . . and a piece of shrapnel came past my nose, close enough, I felt the heat from it. And it buried in the ground about two feet past me. The explosion killed 15 and injured about 20."

Training was so dangerous that the *Star-Telegram* was duty bound but

Gate crasher: Not all planes came down like they were supposed to in 1918.

surprised to report: "Not a death occurred at Camp Bowie Base Hospital during the 24-hour period from noon Tuesday until noon Wednesday. It has been over a month since a similar report came from the hospital."

Peace! It finally came on November 11, 1918. The next day, the newspapers carried Woodrow Wilson's proclamation: "The Armistice was signed this morning. Everything for which Americans fought has been accomplished."

Fort Worth celebrated the news, as one report said, "in true Western style . . . as noisy as could be made. Automobiles with old iron tubs and pieces of tin attached dashed through the streets; cowbells were used to increase the din, and shots were fired into the air from revolvers and shotguns."

For a moment, even a day, Fort Worth forgot all about its refinement.

Oil kept the smudge on its face. Oil brought riches, but it also brought back the same loud, lusty, libertine spirit of the trail-driving days. The wealthy wore overalls and had plowshare blisters on their hands. They had more money than they knew what to do with. The slick-haired dandies knew what to do with it—take it off the farmer's hands, ease their problems somewhat.

Oil had long taunted the insatiable greed of Texas. Traces of the black gold had been found in water wells as far back as 1887. The first semblance of an honest-to-God oil field did not shadow north Texas until 1911 when a driller hit a pool on the Stringer Ranch near Electra. By 1917, the war machines were crying for oil, and more wildcatters than ever began testing the deep earth around Fort Worth.

The town of Ranger belched forth black gold.

All of Texas had been agonized by an agricultural and economic drought. Money was scarce. The land and its people both were suffering. In Ranger, John M. Gholson and Cull Moorman took a long-shot bet. They met with W.K. Gordon, superintendent of the Thurber Mine (owned by the Texas Pacific Coal Company), and they offered him 30,000 acres of lease land if his company would dare drill a well.

Gordon had no reason not to gamble. He moved a wooden rig in on Nannie Walker's farm and promptly hit a gas pool. Failure! There was no market for gas. Gordon thought about quitting but finally hauled his rig on over to

John McClesky's place.

He drilled again. Gordon reached the depth where geologists had hoped the oil would be gathered. The hole was dry. And Texas Pacific Coal Company officials wired their superintendent: "Think we have made a mistake; better quit."

Gordon wadded up the telegram, stuck it in his pocket and kept right on drilling. He had gone too far to turn back now. He said he had faith. Others said he was just plain stubborn.

In October, it all paid off. The gusher exploded upward, climbing two-thirds of the way to the crest of the derrick, then raining out across the land. Frank Champion, a roustabout, walked a mile into Ranger, brushed the oil from his face and said softly, "The McClesky is a well."

Boom time.

Ranger was choking on money, not dust any longer. The town was irrigating its crops, whether it wanted to or not, with oil instead of water, which was fine since there wasn't any water anyway.

Within months, the population of Ranger topped 30,000. The sanctity of its cemetery was violated with oil derricks, and nobody cared. The derricks towered over churches, even a school playground. Farmers, in debt for breakfast, were millionaires by dinner time. A single week's worth of building permits in the town totaled $420,000. Houston, that week, could only manage $53,000 worth of permits. And the Texas Pacific Coal Company turned down an offer of $120,000,000 for its holdings.

B.B. Paddock wrote, "The discovery of oil in north central Texas came at the end of a year's drought, and the enormous amount of money spent for leases and development relieved a very serious financial depression. . . ."

Over in Burkburnett (named for an early day Texas Ranger), S.L. Fowler was getting ready to sell his farm and pack up his wagons and move on. But his wife wouldn't leave. There might be oil under us, she told him. And Fowler laughed. After awhile, he stopped laughing. His wife wouldn't budge, demanding that at least one test well be drilled on their farm before she told it goodbye. Fowler sighed, decided to humor her a little, and talked friends into putting up $12,000 for the well. He wasn't excited about it at all.

The wagon, bringing in a load of timber, bogged down in the sand a good 50 yards shy of the spot Fowler had chosen for his test site. He wasn't perturbed. He told his men, "Oh, well, unload her here." One chunk of farm land, he

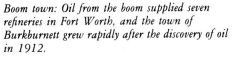

Boom town: Oil from the boom supplied seven refineries in Fort Worth, and the town of Burkburnett grew rapidly after the discovery of oil in 1912.

Winners and losers: E.T. Ambler and his chauffeur (top) in a Rambler, circa 1909. Carl Schilder (below) won a bet from Albert Shockley, who chauffeured a wheelbarrow.

Ranger was choking on money, not dust any longer. The town was irrigating its crops, whether it wanted to or not, with oil instead of water, which was fine since there wasn't any water anyway.

thought, was as good as another. All he wanted to do was get that ridiculous drilling out of his way so he could move.

On the night of July 26, 1918, he was awakened and told that the well had come in. A driller explained, "We've got 1,200 barrels of storage filled and now she's running down the cotton rows." Fowler stayed.

Within three months, more than 200 wells had been drilled inside the city limits of Burkburnett. Why not? Oil was selling for $2.25 a barrel, and Fowler's well was gushing 3,000 barrels a day.

Four railroads rushed to build spurs to Burkburnett.

Hogtown was not about to be left out. It only had 50 residents and most of them called the town Desdemona. A gusher roared up on a September night in 1918, sending flames across the Joe Duke farm. The drill bit had struck paydirt at only 1,000 feet. And the soaring column of fire was so bright, it was said, that people could read a newspaper in the three buildings of downtown Desdemona a mile and a half away. Those 50 Hogtown citizens were soon joined by 16,000 neighbors, living in tents and shacks. And as many as five producing wells would be ganged on a single acre.

Oil poured out of Cisco, Eastland, Breckenridge and other west Texas towns. And it all poured toward Fort Worth—the railroad gateway to the rich fields. The city already boasted the Gulf refinery, the Pierce Fordyce Oil Association and Magnolia Petroleum Company. And by 1922, Fort Worth would be the home of 22 refineries.

Oil men fought for space within the city. It became a boiling pot for legal and illegal petroleum transactions. Everyone wanted a piece of rich dirt. Approximately 2,100 corporations or syndicates were jammed into every corner of the city. Within a year after those gushers begat greed, there was no office space available anywhere in Fort Worth. So business was generally conducted on the run inside the Westbrook Hotel, called the "piece de resistance of Fort Worth hotel and heritage" by its owner Benjamin J. Tiller. He had reason to be proud. After all, the Westbrook was seven stories high, had more than 200 rooms (and each had a bath), a $20,000 air conditioning system and a price tag of one million dollars, all coming from the estate of J.T.W. Tiller.

During the boom, though, all furniture had to be dragged from the lobby so more oil speculators could crowd their way inside. A curvaceous Roman statue on a pedestal would ultimately be dubbed the "Golden Goddess" because, it was said, she watched over so many oil deals. She could just as well have been called the harlot of heartbreak.

Oil company representatives shuffled their way through the lobby, selling shares from such whimsical companies as "Alamo," "Hog Creek," "King Midas," "Heart of Duke" and "Hercules." And—believe it or not—they sold. It was said that a man could begin with shares on one side of the lobby and make his fortune by the time he crossed to the other.

Sid Richardson dug his wealth out of those oil field mud bogs with hard work, more than his share of self-confidence and a hefty dose of good luck. But as Richardson always said, "I'd rather by lucky than smart 'cause a lot of smart folks ain't eatin' regular."

Richardson came out of Athens, Texas, with the belief that he was destined to earn his keep by trading horses. And he dealt enough horseflesh to keep his pockets filled with ready cash. But the black of oil caught his eye.

He was seated in a Wichita Falls hotel room one night in 1919, staring at a losing poker hand, when his boyhood friend, Clint Murchison, ambled up beside him. Murchison whispered his message. An oil scout, he said, had told him that a top secret well was to be tested that night. Was Richardson interested?

"Let's go see if it's a real well," Richardson whispered back. He quietly folded his hand and walked away from the poker table. Outside the hotel, the two young men jumped into an automobile and raced away into the darkness. It was 3 a.m. when they pulled to a stop beside the well perched on the bank of the Red River, between Texas and Oklahoma. The crew believed Richardson and Muchison owned the well and were eager to find out if there really was oil buried beneath the earth. They all brought the well in. And

Tanking up: The Montrose Oil Refinery, near Hodge Station north of Fort Worth, was one of many in the area that processed oil from the West Texas boom. Businessmen kept in close contact with the fields with five round-trip Texas & Pacific passenger trains to Ranger each day.

the two speculators roared away before the dirt had time to soak up the oil.

By nine o'clock the next morning, Richardson and Murchison had bought up $75,000 worth of acreage surrounding the well. And they promptly sold off five percent of that land for $200,000.

Within two years, both men had earned $2 million each in the oil game. And Sid Richardson, on his way back to Athens, was haunted by the fact he still owed Murchison's bank $6,000. He hit town driving a brand new Cadillac. Richardson recalled, "I swung around that dusty square twice so's all the bench warmers would see me good, and then I marched into the bank and paid back Mr. Murchison his money in cash . . . 'fore the dust had settled, all those old boys got off their benches and started for the oil fields. They said, 'If that dunce can make so much money, we'll go, too.' "

Richardson went busted as quickly as he had gotten rich. In 1921, the price of oil plummeted to a dollar a barrel, and Richardson found himself wiped out. Eight years later, he hit a producing well on the Edwards lease up in Ward and Winkler counties. Richardson picked up a couple of cheap drilling rigs and began acquiring leases at bargain prices. Oil was making him wealthy again.

But in 1930, the big east Texas oil fields rocked the petroleum industry, and again, the price of oil took a profit-crushing nose dive, earning a mere dime a barrel. In January of '30, Richardson had been making a comfortable $25,000 a month. By June, his monthly check was $1,600, and the banks were grabbing all of that in hopes of paying off Richardson's $250,000 debt.

Richardson later told Eleanor Harris of *Look* magazine, "I've been broke so often I thought it was habit formin', but there was only one night when I didn't turn the light off and my mind off at the same time . . . I'd just lost a

Furnishing furniture: The Kemble Furniture Company sold new furniture, bought and sold used furniture and furnished rent houses, according to its 1912 ad. The firm was located at 300 Houston Street.

Sid Richardson drilled 385 wells, and only 17 of them came up dry. In 1957, Fortune *magazine called him the wealthiest man in America, if you counted his $500 million in proven oil reserves.*

million dollars, and that day I'd had a dry well. I knew I was flat broke. But it wasn't those thoughts that was keepin' me awake—it was a kidney infection hurtin' me."

Sid Richardson never worried about money. He was never in awe of his own bank account. In 1930, he no longer had one. So he did what he always did best. He started over, in March of 1932, with nothing more than four $10 bills between him and the poor house. A former boss, Bill Little, let Richardson have $15,000 worth of pipe on credit. He secured his drilling equipment with just a promise to pay. And he even hired his workers on credit. Richardson gave them all $100 a month to live on, then wrote down $10 a day for each of them, "payable when possible."

He drilled and hit a dry well. He drilled again. Another dry well. Richardson braced himself, found that his crew was willing to stick with him, and he tore into the earth for a third time. And the ensuing gusher pushed him out of poverty forever.

Sid Richardson drilled 385 wells, and only 17 of them came up dry. In 1957, *Fortune* magazine called him the wealthiest man in America, if you counted his $500 million in proven oil reserves.

Richardson even had more oil land holdings than many of the country's top oil companies. And, in '53, when Secretary of the Treasury George Humphrey introduced Richardson as "one of our best clients," the Fort Worth oilman told him, "No, I'm one of your best partners."

But Richardson, who died in 1959, never took the time to be impressed with himself. And he never took the time to stop working. He once said, "If I didn't keep working I'd get lonesome. I'm working for fun and charity. I'm just trustee for a lot of money, that's all." Once asked, "What's the size of your bankroll?" Richardson merely smiled and answered, "Well, after the first hundred million, what the hell?"

Richardson and Murchison (who would later own the Dallas Cowboys) played the oil game by their own set of rules and they won big. They were not alone. During the oil boom of the 1920s, speculators either hit the jackpot or the road out of town. One oilman in the Westbrook Hotel grabbed off a fortune, took a thousand dollar bill, set it afire and calmly lit a cigar. But unfortunately, so many of those shares running loose on the street were worth no more than the burnt-end of that cigar.

As B.B. Paddock wrote, "Men with vivid imaginations, extensive vocabularies and an elastic conscience provided themselves with blueprints, fountain pens and blank stock certificates, and with these as their total assets sold stock to unsuspecting, confiding, and gullible people without limit. Many persons parted with their hard-earned money for beautiful green stock certificates, setting forth that they were the owners of so many shares in some oil company, the location of which they, subsequently, were unable to discover. . . . Many who had never seen Texas before set forth their extravagant claims, reaped the harvest, and moved on to new fields where the inhabitants had not heard of their nefarious practice elsewhere."

One who did not move on fast enough was Dr. Fred A. Cook. In 1909, Cook had stirred imaginations and controversy by claiming to have beaten Robert Peary to the North Pole. He was down and out, profane and penniless up in Wyoming, when he heard of the Ranger strike. Cook rolled into Fort Worth, promptly capitalized the Texas Eagle Oil Company based on a non-existent field near Hogtown and sold $1.5 million worth of stock without ever having to show anything of value. It took him a mere 12 months to merge with 413 other companies, placing them all under one name, Petroleum Producers Association. He put together a list of two million people, spread his offices throughout one entire floor of a downtown building and mailed out those cards, letters and promotional literature peddling dirt that, he intimated, was filthy rich. Many who had already been fleeced once, got in

Another year: The second annual sales convention of the Panther City Oil & Grease Manufacturing Company on December 26, 1924.

line to invest again. The mails brought in box loads of cash.

The mails did him in. Dr. Cook could not outrun the federal boys. U.S. Attorney Henry Zweifel charged him with fraud, presented 200 witnesses and 900 exhibits and got a conviction. Cook was sentenced to 14 years and nine months in a federal prison and also fined $12,000.

And still there were frantic, impatient oil speculators on street corners, yelling at shady operators who were waving worthless paper, pleading with them "to save some for me."

One who lost his money to oil swindlers was J. Frank Norfleet, a 50-year-old west Texas rancher. The bunco artists picked on the wrong man. They took the rancher for $45,000. At one point, however, inside his Westbrook Hotel room, Norfleet became suspicious of the smooth-talking swindlers and drew his pistol. He recalled:

"One of them grabbed the Bible off the dresser. He held it over his heart, raised his right hand, dropped to his knees and sobbed, 'I swear by my mother's grave that I am not trying to trick you, that I am no crook. Don't kill me.' The other man claimed to be a member of a lodge of which I am a member. He put his arm around me and said, 'Frank, haven't I always been square with you? Haven't I kept every promise.' Their appeals renewed my confidence in them. I let them go, thinking my money was an investment."

By morning, the swindlers and the $45,000 were gone. And J. Frank Norfleet swore, "I am going to get them if I have to spend the rest of my life at it." He relentlessly trailed the men for 14 months. His son Pete quit college to help the rancher. And one by one, the swindlers were stuck behind bars. Norfleet found the last one, Joe Furey, in a Jacksonville, Florida, cafe. He remembered:

"He recognized me as quick as he saw me . . . I drew my pistol. 'I am an officer—I have a warrant for your arrest.'

"Furey began screaming, 'Bandit, robber.' People jumped up. As the crowd gathered around me Furey started to push his way out. I grabbed him by

Gas gathering: Company officers, city officials and the press turned out for the turn-on ceremony of a Lone Star Natural Gas gate in the 1920s.

the collar—it must have been a death grip. They grabbed me and pulled me across the restaurant. . . . But I didn't turn loose of Furey. He bit my hand, took a part of my finger off, but I held on."

Furey's yells brought the one man J. Frank was hoping to find, a police officer. Norfleet said, "Furey was a mad man. He kicked and cursed me. He fought as hard as a man could fight. I didn't want to harm him. We were nearing the end of a long, long trail. . . . My chase was almost over. Therefore, I didn't shoot him. But God knows I had reason to."

Furey, like his accomplices, was convicted. And Norfleet returned to his IXL Ranch in Hale County, saying, with pride, "I tricked the trickster and I showed the master mind that the man they picked as the sucker was the man who brought him to justice." Fort Worth District Attorney Jesse Brown, who directed the pursuit and who prosecuted the swindlers, could always look back on J. Frank Norfleet and say, "In horses, dogs, and men, it is character that counts."

Chapter 9

The sign says "Fort Worth for entertainment"

Fashionable sport on the plains: A Fort Worth hunting party of questionable skill.

PART OF
SKYLINE of FORT WORTH
Biggest City of its Size
in the United States

Oil had reached out and shook Fort Worth with the hallelujah fervor of a brush arbor revival. Believers were everywhere. And newspaper advertisements gave them every opportunity to ante up. One said boldly: "WANTED! 200 people who will take a chance for big stakes. I am drilling a wildcat oil well—and am ready to spud a second well—on two large blocks of acreage in south Texas. First well already down 807 feet. Excellent geology. A wonderful gamble to open up a new oil field. Write immediately for full particulars."

The betting men wrote. The winners shoved Fort Worth upward. Oilmen snapped up every bit of office space they could find. Rent increased so rapidly that professional men, doctors and lawyers, were forced out of their offices and exiled to the suburbs.

Then came the skyscrapers. The first ones to rise up, then look down on Fort Worth, were the Life of America, Sinclair and W.T. Waggoner buildings.

Marvin and O.P. Leonard opened up a small grocery store, promising themselves that it would never be completed. They made their first sale in 1918, getting a nickel for a can of condensed milk. A year later, they added automobile tires to the bread and eggs and butter. Within four years, the Leonard brothers had bought all the property that fronted two blocks of Houston Street.

Those trying days in the early 1920s—Dr. R.J. White recalled, "The heat— I don't know how we stood it then. People used to have a lot of what was called ether convulsions, but I always believed it was the heat. I can remember operating in August, and the sweat would run down my arms into my rubber gloves. When I finished an operation and took off the gloves, it would make a puddle."

Dr. Robert Baker remembered a physician in Burleson. "For stomach ache," Dr. Baker said, "he would prescribe castor oil and camomile for three days. Then, if they weren't better, he would conclude it was acute appendicitis and send them up to Fort Worth for surgery. . . . Sometimes they lived, and sometimes they died. Mostly, they lived, because people are tough."

Out at the stockyards, the International Butcher's Union was hot and ready to prove just how tough it was. It struck for more money. And Fred Rouse was hired to break it up. He started a riot instead. Rouse—feeling courageous behind a gun—fired into a frustrated crowd that became an angry mob. The strikers broke from their picket line and charged Rouse, beating him severely, cracking his skull and leaving him for dead. The ambulance was on its way to the mortuary when Rouse suddenly raised himself up from the stretcher, blinked once or twice and looked around.

The flourishing city: The skyline (left) with the old City Hall in the foreground and the W.T. Waggoner Building rising high in the background; the inscriptor was a master at doubletalk. Phillips Egypt Theatre (upper left), an architectural oddity, and the pavilion at Lake Como (above).

His days still were numbered. Five nights later, a group of men brushed their way past a pleading nurse, grabbed Rouse and dragged him kicking from his hospital bed. Fort Worth found Fred Rouse the next morning, hanging by the neck and, this time, quite dead.

That was 1921, the year that Amon Carter began his self-centered scheme to own one of those fussy little pieces of new electronic machinery called radio. He did not just want the box. He was not content to listen. He wanted to talk, too. And radio concerned him somewhat because it was, after all, competition for the almighty dollar. A friend in New York even told him that radio was destined to kill off newspapers and bury them in an early classified grave.

Carter told his *Star-Telegram* circulation manager, Harold Hough, "If this radio thing is going to be a menace to newspapers, maybe we'd better own the menace."

Hough took $300 out of petty cash, went down and invested in a homemade rig, stuffing the fragile transmitter in an old tomato crate and dragging it back to the *Star-Telegram.*

And the *Star-Telegram* was on the air.

Reception was poor and transmission illegal. Hough later purchased a more powerful transmitter—the 16th unit manufactured by Western Electric—and applied for a license. Herbert Hoover, the secretary of commerce, gave him the call letters of WBAP, explaining that they mean "We Bring A Program." On may 2, 1922, with a 70-foot broadcast tower, Carter heard his first legal transmission on WBAP.

W.T. Waggoner heard it too. He promptly telephoned the station and reported the signal was coming in loud and clear. He was impressed. He lived two miles away.

Carter's station, like his newspaper, took a deep interest in the problems of west Texas agriculture. WBAP became the first radio station in the country to broadcast regular reports of the cotton and grain exchanges. And many times, it gave ranchers the warning they needed when a blizzard was on the way, gave them time (for a change) to protect their stock without suffering the customary heavy financial loss.

Fort Worth's sudden riches had been yanked from far beneath the ground. Yet Fort Worth kept looking toward the sky as well. Perhaps it still remembered the words of a Como, Texas, boy, Lieutenant O.L. Locklear, who had shocked the city in 1919 with a daring exhibition of flying above Barron Field. He would ultimately be called "The Demon of the Sky." And he said, "I don't do these things because I want to run the risk of being killed. I do it to demonstrate what can be done. Somebody has got to show the way. I want to do things people feel can't be done. . . . I am convinced that some day we will all be flying, and the more things that are attempted and accomplished, the quicker we will get there."

Fort Worth got there in 1924. It almost did not.

After the war, Barron Field had become an integral part of the Army Air Corps' Model Airways System, an experiment that would link military bases by plane. In '24, the system was abruptly scrapped. Barron Field, it appeared, would become nothing more than a deserted ghost town. Sergeant William G. Fuller arrived from San Antonio to make the shut-down official. Fort Worth Mayor H.C. Meacham was not pleased with the military decision. Fuller remembered, "He came out and tried to talk me into not closing the field. But I told him I was just a sergeant and was only carrying out orders."

The next time Fuller saw H.C. Meacham, the mayor was seated in Major Harvey Burwell's office at Kelly Field in San Antonio. Fort Worth needed aviation, Meacham said, and, as Fuller recalled, "He finally talked Major Burwell into putting a field at Fort Worth. In return, Mayor Meacham promised to find land for the field on the north side of the city, to build a residence for the field operator, and to dig a well and build a 'shop' for spare parts."

Fort Worth purchased 100 acres of land for $100. Fuller—ordered to help the mayor set up the airport—promptly got a handful of prisoners out of the

That was 1921, the year that Amon Carter began his self-centered scheme to own one of those fussy little pieces of new electronic machinery called radio. He did not just want the box. He was not content to listen. He wanted to talk, too.

Yesterday and today: Meacham Field with single engine plane and tower in 1942 (right), and a sleek prop jet at Meacham in 1980 (above).

county jail to clear cactus off the field. And, once each week without fail, the Army dispatched a plane from San Antonio to Chicago, with a major stop in Fort Worth, testing the feasibility of regular airline service. National Air Transport took over the route, flying in a mail plane. A hangar was constructed in 1926. And in '27, Fort Worth Airport was officially dedicated as Meacham Field. By 1962 it would be designated as the tenth busiest executive airport in the nation. A one million dollar improvement was implemented, and Meacham Field wound up ranked second only to Love Field in Dallas as the most active airport in the FAA's Southwest traffic region.

More and more, Fort Worth became a stopping place for celebrities, some wanting to be seen, some wanting to hide. Tex Rickard, the persistent fight promoter, caught up with Jack Dempsey in Fort Worth in 1926, eager to sign up the Manassa Mauler's fists for a championship bout. Dempsey had dynamite in those fists, but his philosophy surprised reporters. Polite and polished, with a brand new nose job, he told one, "If you get a boy or girl started right, they will keep it up. The youngster has got to be given every chance. He must be taught. A businessman should not fire a boy when he makes a mistake but should teach him how to do better." Then Dempsey, escorted by Amon Carter, sat down with Tex Rickard in the Texas Hotel and gave a youngster a chance. He signed for "the fight of the century" with a soft-spoken Gene Tunney. He would live to regret it.

In 1927, the celebrated Charles A. Lindbergh, the "Lone Eagle," flew into Fort Worth. He held his audience spellbound, recounting those long, agonizing hours to Paris, saying, "All in all I couldn't complain of the weather. It wasn't what was predicted. It was worse in some places and better in others. In fact, it was so bad once that for a moment there came over me the temptation to turn back. But then I figured it was probably just as bad behind me as before me, so we kept on toward Paris."

In the late 1920s, Kathryn Kelly walked into a Fort Worth pawn shop and bought her husband George a present. She drove home and handed him his first machine gun. Thus began the violent, greedy escapades of Machine Gun Kelly, the scourge of banks in the Southwest, a kidnapper who found Fort Worth to be the best place possible to hide out when the heat was more than he could stand.

He and Kathryn spent much of their time in a fashionable home at 857 East Mulkey. They aroused their neighbor's curiosity because George Kelly insisted on driving his 16-cylinder automobile along New York Avenue which was unpaved and potted with chug holes. Kelly knew Fort Worth. Police only checked the paved streets. The bad ones were omitted from their patrol. Machine Gun Kelly and an accomplice, Harvey Bailey, kidnapped an Oklahoma City oilman and talked his family out of $200,000. Fort Worth police, on special assignment with the FBI, tracked down Bailey at Boss Shannon's home in Paradise. Shannon told them, "I've got nothing to hide, boys. Harvey Bailey is in the backyard asleep in his bed." The FBI took Bailey, but first dared him to escape, saying, "There's your guns. Grab for them if you want to." He did not. Kelly was arrested in Memphis and sent on to Fort Leavenworth before he could get back to the unpaved streets of Fort Worth again. The '30s were not good at all for Kelly. Nor did they treat Fort Worth too kindly.

Fort Worth had been in hopes that the opulence of it all would last forever. When the W.I. Cook Memorial Hospital was completed in 1929, its reception room dazzled with travertine marble walls from Italy inlaid with 18-carat gold.

But the good times crashed right along with the stock market. Fort Worth hated to admit it. In a front page editorial, Amon Carter said the depression was, in reality, nothing more than "ridiculous spectacle brought on by idle gossip, unfounded rumors, and a state of hysterior [sic]."

Men elbowing their way into soup lines did not believe Carter. But then, men elbowing their way into soup lines could not afford to buy the *Star-Telegram* so they were not aware that their hunger was a mere "ridiculous spectacle."

The First National Bank found out otherwise. Its doors had not even opened yet on the morning of February 18, 1930, when a thousand people crushed into the street out front and began screaming for their money. Other depositors got word of the stampede, and they hurried downtown, hoping to grab their money, too, before the cash was all gone.

The First National was a large bank with a stated deposit of $24,139,069.37, at least a million dollars of it on hand. The million did not last long. The stampede was on. The mob could not help but remember that only two weeks earlier, the Texas National Bank (stricken by a bad case of bad loans) had collapsed. They did not want to take the chance of it happening again.

The bank was in a panic. Sheriff Red Wright was called. Texas Ranger Tom Hickman came on the run. At least a dozen policemen suggested to officials that they should be given their cash deposits before the crowd became too hard to handle.

Fort Worth's business leaders backed the bank. Amon Carter crawled out of a sick bed, shuffled off to the bank and climbed atop a table, speaking loudly: "This is the safest bank in the world and you'll soon find it out. It is paying off every dollar as fast as you are passing in your checks and for every dollar it is paying you it is taking in six more. Why, right now $2.5 million is coming from the Federal Reserve Bank in Dallas."

He nodded. And from the wings came heavily-armed men, all toting large U.S. paper currency pouches and smaller coin bags. Carter was always a genius with his timing. He continued, "See there. What did I tell you. You can't take your money out as fast as they can bring it in. Let's boost for our city. Let's not go mad like this. Let's go home and in the morning your money will be right here for you. The organization I represent has a hundred thousand

The eye of the beholder

The history of an environment is documented first in the mind of the artist. Two examples in Fort Worth: The Farm Securities Administration paid photographers including Arthur Rothstein to take pictures documenting the work of the organization throughout the country. During January 1942, Rothstein photographed the Fort Worth area and some of his work is seen in this book. He captured interesting elements of the city's lifestyle and signage and took pictures that many photographers miss. In contrast, Samuel P. Zeiglar preferred a softer, traditional approach to picturing the city. Zeiglar, born in 1882 in Pennsylvania, and a student of fine arts, moved to Fort Worth in 1917 to become music professor at Texas Christian University. Two years later, he founded the TCU art department and was its only instructor until 1947. He retired five years later and died in 1967.

Samuel Zeiglar's artistic renderings of Fort Worth included construction of the W.T. Waggoner Building (left), the First Presbyterian Church (lower left), and the University Christian Church (lower right).

Three Rothstein scenes: Photographer Arthur Rothstein captured these scenes in January 1942: a roadside cafe on U.S. 80 between Dallas and Fort Worth (top); the Chalk Hill Drive-In Theatre on U.S. 80 (above); and a tire company sign on West Lancaster Street (right).

Off to the races: Arlington Downs race track entrance as pictured by photographer Arthur Rothstein in 1942. A 1936 race at the Downs (right), located on U.S. 80 between Fort Worth and Dallas.

dollars here and I expect to leave it here."

W.T. Waggoner, an old rancher who always grumbled because his men kept hitting oil when they drilled for water wells, stood behind Carter. He said, "I have been a cowman . . . and have swung onto many a cow's tail in a stampede, but this is the first stampede like this I ever saw in my life. I am here to tell you this stampede is worse than cattle stampeding and I want you to stop it and go on home. This bank has been in business for 50 years and will be in business here long after we are gone." Pappy Waggoner paused. He held his right arm high and said, "I hereby pledge to you every cent that I own or possess in this world that you shall not lose a single dollar in this bank. I will sell every cow and every oil well if necessary to pay for any money you lose here."

W.P. McLean told the crowd, not quite as nervous as before: "All of you know Bill McLean hasn't got much, but I'll bet every last dollar in the world I have on this bank. If any of you don't believe that, go on home now, I will give you my personal note for your deposit and pay you on demand Wednesday."

The withdrawals slowed, but the crowd was still restless. It lingered. Sheriff Wright passed amongst the depositors, handing out hot dogs. Carter sent out for cheese sandwiches. Flasks of whiskey were smuggled in. The Texas Hotel orchestra played "Home Sweet Home" on the east end of the lobby, while Newt McCrary conducted another orchestra in "Singing In the Rain." Carter, still ailing from the flu, stood again and announced that bank passbooks were good for free admission to the Majestic Theater, and 200 immediately left to watch William Boyd star in "Officer O'Brien," a talkie.

The next morning, the *Fort Worth Press* (an evening newspaper) delivered a morning edition, draped in a black bordered box. On the front page, it pointed out, "The Press desires to bring you all the latest information regarding the present unrest following the run on the First National Bank . . . Press carrier boys were called out of bed to get it to you. If you think it's worth it you may pay the carrier boy an extra two cents when he comes around to collect his bill this week."

The banner headline said it all: "FIRST NATIONAL NIPS RUN WITH MORE THAN ENOUGH CASH."

Fort Worth had again survived crisis.

The trial hit again in 1932 when the city council appropriated $100 a month for the operation of a soup kitchen. And a year later, the stockyards were on the brink of collapse. The depression had hurt. The drought was lethal. The grasslands were burnt, water soaked up in a selfish soil, and feed withered. Cattle, sheep and goats died of thirst and starvation by the thousands. About 400,000 head of cattle were shot to avoid the cost of transporting them to slaughtering plants. Another 1.5 million cows were sent out of state so they could find something to eat.

The rains stormed down on August 25, 1934. The rains brought salvation, as well as irony. Two flash floods swept over the Fort Worth stockyards, and ranchers—who had been praying and pleading for rain—lost another 61 mules, 500 sheep, 80 hogs, 10 registered bulls and 80 horses.

Fort Worth, however, was digging its way back to respectability if not prosperity. And Amon Carter was dreaming another dream. He wanted to bring the Gulf of Mexico to Fort Worth, and the Trinity River seemed the best way to do it. That cranky old river, he thought, could be a great canal— an industrial and economic coup for the city. Why, Carter even envisioned ocean liners pulling up to the docks at Fort Worth! He drove Will Rogers out to the banks of the Trinity, and told him his dream. The humorist, who called Fort Worth his second home, frowned.

"Well, what do you think?" Carter asked.

Rogers stared at the publisher, glanced back at the river and rolled his eyes reverently to the sky. "I can see the sea gulls now," he said.

In his syndicated newspaper column, Rogers wrote:

"Fort Worth is several hundred miles from the nearest seagull but Amon

Tale of two competitors: When Dallas hosted the Texas Centennial in 1936, Fort Worth established Casa Manana, a show organized by New York producer Billy Rose. A large sign in Dallas (above) advertised Fort Worth and fun. The 1936 Stock Show parade in Fort Worth (right).

Big cowboy: Famed big band leader Paul Whiteman teamed up with Billy Rose to give Fort Worth a formidable attraction to compete with the Texas Centennial celebration in Dallas.

wants to give Fort Worth the benefit of a tidal wave. They have had droughts, floods, bollweevils, cattle fever, ticks and were struck by two visits of [Governor] Jim Ferguson, but they have never tasted seawater. It's the only thing they haven't tasted in a bottle.''

For Amon Carter, life itself was on a grand scale. And Fort Worth was his life. An epigram in his office said: ''Most everybody can get results when kindly encouraged but give me the man who can get there in spite of hell.'' He could.

In the midst of hard times, Texas—because of the date on the calendar not the joy in its heart—felt obliged to celebrate its centennial in 1936.

And the Centennial Commission—a bank of holier-than-thou historians—made Fort Worth mad. None of the three million dollars appropriated for the celebration would be given west Texas because west Texas, they deemed, contained no history to commemorate. Dallas, only an unblemished spot on Texas soil in 1836, not even a town, got the money because Dallas came up with more seed money than anyone else.

Carter was furious. He would, he said, show Dallas ''how the cow ate the cabbage.''

Fort Worth would have its own centennial with or without the blessings of the commission. It made Carter no difference. He had Billy Rose—all 5'3" of him; the highest paid impressario in the business; the producer of Broadway's ''Jumbo;'' the husband of Fannie Brice, the nation's funny girl. Carter had no trouble selling Billy Rose on the idea of creating a centennial extravaganza for Fort Worth. After all, he had offered to pay Rose a thousand dollars a day for 100 days.

A *Star-Telegram* editorial, said, ''Faces which a few months ago were sobered by the depression are tanned and smiling, for there are jobs again.''

Rose flew in and told a crowd, ''You people stick with me and I'll make a big state out of Texas.''

A reporter asked, ''Will you miss Broadway?''

''Hell,'' Rose snapped, ''I am Broadway.''

And he made his promise. Rose said, ''I'm going to put on a show the likes of which has never been seen by the human eye . . . it'll be a five million dollar show.''

Dallas had planned to spend $15 million to portray Texas, with proper pomp and circumstance, with refinement and culture and the best of taste. It was to be an exposition that would inform and enlighten. How could Rose compete? He said, ''We'll give them a bold ball of fire. . . . We'll have a 'Lonely Hearts Ball' weekly where all the lonesome women can come and find a partner in a drawing. . . . I'll get Shirley Temple, Mae West, Guy Lombardo, Jack Benny. I'll get 1,000 beautiful girls for the Frontier Follies. I'll have a Texas pageant to be called 'The Fall of the Frontier' . . . 'The Battle of San Jacinto' . . . or some other Texas name. I'll have 2,000 Indians and 1,000 cowboys, and guess who wins? I'll have a chorus line of 500 pretty girls. . .

''Dallas has all that historical stuff so we don't have to worry about that. We can just show the people a good time. I plan to drive Dallas nuts. Everytime Dallas says something about its exposition, I'll give'em Shirley Temple. . . . This'll make 'Jumbo' look like a peep show.''

Billy Rose had spoken.

It would have been a mistake to sell him short.

Dallas kept 10,000 men working for a year on its exposition. Rose put his together in a couple of months. He hired Comanches, Apaches, Navajos, Hopis and Sioux to participate in the pageant. He auditioned Gonzo the mind-reading dog, a 75-year-old bareback rider who had worked for P.T. Barnum, Joe Peanuts and his 16-piece all monkey band, a strong woman who bent nails between her fingers, a frog circus and a man with a human spine spiked with Indian arrows. His billboard ads proclaimed: ''BIGGEST ENTERPRISE DEVOTED EXCLUSIVELY TO AMUSEMENT IN THE HISTORY OF THE WORLD. . . . Monkey Mountain. . . . 92 other attractions of Magnitude

Fun in Cowtown: With the slogan, "Dallas for education, Fort Worth for fun," the city hoped to lure some of the millions of 1936 visitors to Cowtown. Casa Manana was the place to be (above) when a Casa Manana dancer (right) flapped her feathers.

*On stage and side show: Two celebrants ponder
the Bug House (above), one of many Casa Manana
side shows. Singers and dancers in Billy Rose's
production (left).*

Main Street, Fort Worth: Rothstein captured a downtown scene in the early 1940s (above). Amon G. Carter presents a deed to Big Bend National Park to President Franklin D. Roosevelt (right).

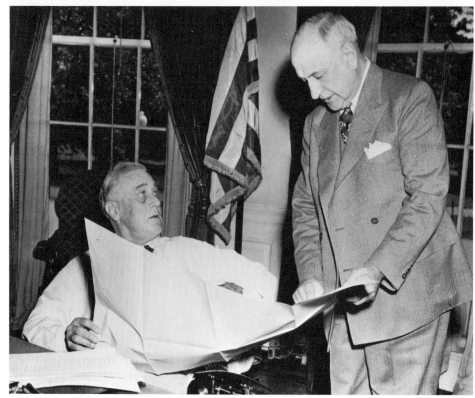

and Merit. . . . Not Cheap Catch Penny Peep Shows. . . . Take your Entertainment Sitting Down.''

Rose decided on a rodeo because, he said, "it was grand opera on horseback.'' And he presented square dancing, with the caller saying, "Hurry, girls, and don't get lazy, big fat hogs and lots of gravy, *Star-Telegram,* full of news, grab that gal with the high-top shoes.'' The focal point would be Casa Manana. His press agent called it "something at least a decade beyond the dreams of any showman in the world. The largest cafe-theater in the universe. The most fabulous outdoor entertainment arena in existence. A structure of such sweeping magnitude that its stage alone might house a millionaire without discomfort to his family and retinue of servants. House of Tomorrow.''

What's more, the ads were filled with bare-breasted girls.

A Baptist minister, S.H. Frazier, said angrily, "If I had the money, I would rent a concession stand and preach morning, noon, and night, and distribute religious material out there.'' Fort Worth's General Minister's Association even adopted a resolution condemning Rose's advertising and the centennial's lack of religious orientation. But Carter was only really concerned about one Fort Worth preacher.

He called J. Frank Norris. "Are you going out of town this summer?'' he asked.

"I might. Why?''

"We've got this centennial show and some nude girls, and we're going to sell liquor.''

"I see,'' said Norris. "I've been intending to hold some revivals. I guess I could start them early.''

He did. The fire and brimstone preacher traveled 2,700 miles that summer, delivering the word of God, while Sally Ann Rand hid her naked body behind fans and balloons as she danced away the troubles of Fort Worth. November 6 was even designated as Sally Rand Day, and Fort Worth publically thanked her for bringing "culture and progress to Tarrant County.''

Pioneer Palace served 10-cent beer in a honky-tonk atmosphere while slot machines rattled and pigs raced on a 40-foot-long bar. And the "Last Frontier'' was Rose's long-promised western showpiece, presented in an outdoor theater. The advertising told it all. "Vivid, Visual Saga of the March of Civilization. . . . THE OLD WEST LIVES AGAIN. . . . See Attack of the Hostiles. . . . Womanhood in Jeopardy. . . . Thank God the Rangers! Battle of Arroyo Grande. . . . and The Mail Goes Through.''

Two million saved up their hard-earned depression dollars and immersed themselves in the centennial celebration. They obviously believed Fort Worth's slogan—"Dallas for Education, but Fort Worth for Entertainment.''

Fannie Brice looked it over and told her husband, "Good Heavens, Billy! It's better than your publicity. It's a goose's dream.'' And the irrascible Damon Runyan called it "thrilling . . . gorgeous . . . colossal . . . a dream come true.'' When Runyan attended the New York World's Fair in 1939, he was disappointed, writing, "No hits, no runs, no Carters.''

As Billy Rose walked away from Fort Worth, a critic asked him what he intended to do to top his centennial production. Billy Rose thought for a moment, then answered, "I'll get one of those little Balkan wars and go on tour with it.''

Carter was delighted. He announced that Dallas did have something Fort Worth did not have—a real city only 30 miles away. And in the back of its mind, Fort Worth kept trying to remember what the depression had really been like. For many, it was merely a fantasy, produced by Mr. Broadway. It had, after all, witnessed the biggest girlie show ever put on a stage.

Fort Worth danced its way out of the depression. W. Lee O'Daniel, a radio announcer with a hillbilly band, the number one pitchman for Fort Worth's Burrus Mills, sang, preached and politicked his way to the good times. Pappy O'Daniel one morning stepped to the WBAP microphone and asked, "What do you think I ought to do about the politicians who have this state hogtied? How would you like me to run for governor?'' The answer came in 60,000

Two million saved up their hard-earned depression dollars and immersed themselves in the centennial celebration. They obviously believed Fort Worth's slogan—"Dallas for Education, but Fort Worth for Entertainment.''

Pigskin prodigies: Football has always been an entertaining and economic factor for Fort Worth fans. Even the horses got to witness the contest between Fort Worth and Dallas on January 1, 1896 (right). Quarterback Davey O'Brien led TCU to the national championship in 1938 and along the way beat Arkansas 21 to 14 (top). Sammy Baugh (above) was an All-American quarterback at TCU and sparkplug for the Washington Redskins.

letters, and most of them had campaign contributions. Pappy felt obligated to run.

He took his Lightcrust Doughboys and headed down a guitar-picking, fiddle-sawing trail to the governor's mansion. He wept. He pleaded. His platform, he said, was "the Golden Rule and the Ten Commandments." And what Texas needed, O'Daniel preached, was "less Johnson Grass and politicians." He sang hymns. He read poems. A fiddler from Turkey, Texas, Bob Wills, would yell, "Pass the biscuits, Pappy!" And Pappy would pass around empty flour sacks for donations. They came back filled. O'Daniel beat back 12 other candidates in the Democratic primary, then won in November of 1937 by whipping the Republican nominee 473,526 to 10,940. Fort Worth had spawned its first governor, and O'Daniel took his lightcrust biscuits from WBAP to Austin.

Ben Hogan attacked the depression with a putter. He learned the fine art

A golfing legend: Fort Worth's Ben Hogan, one of the all-time greats on the professional golfing circuit.

of golfing as a caddy at Fort Worth's Glen Garden Country Club and hit the ball much better than those who owned the bags he toted. In '37, Hogan religiously saved money and told his wife, Valerie, "It's now or never." He turned pro and watched the savings run lower than his tournament scores. January of 1938 found the Hogans living in Oakland, California's cheapest motel, with eight dollars in their pockets and no food on the table. They had been eating nothing but oranges for a month, but Hogan summoned up enough strength to tackle the L.A. Open. He would say later about the final round, "I played harder that day than I ever played before or since." Hogan took second and won $380. He and Valerie would never have to eat oranges again.

Gene Sarazen said of Hogan, he is the "most merciless of all the modern golfers. His temperament may derive from the rough, anguishing years of his childhood or the hostility he sensed he encountered as a young and overdetermined circuit chaser. Whatever the reason, he is the type of golfer you would describe as perpetually hungry."

In 1940, the Texas Iceman was golf's leading money winner. Eight years later, he became the first golfer to win the PGA, U.S. Open and Western Open the same year. He was riding high, taking the title in eleven of his last sixteen tournaments. But on a foggy west Texas highway in 1949, a bus slammed into his car, critically injuring the legendary Fort Worth golfer. A B-29 bomber on a training flight, stopped in New Orleans, picked up noted specialist Dr. Oschner and hurried him to El Paso to rework Hogan's crushed pelvis, fractured left leg, crushed shoulder and broken ankle. Many thought Hogan would die. They were not sure he would ever walk again even if he pulled through. They knew he would never play pro golf.

A year later, Hogan announced his intentions of going back to the L.A. Open. Officials tried to be polite and sympathetic. They invited Hogan to be the honorary starter for the tournament. "Honorary starter, hell," Hogan screamed, "I'm gonna play." He finessed his way to a 72-hole tie with Sam Snead before losing in the playoffs. Hogan, in 1950, was voted Golfer of the Year. And three years later, he won the Masters with a total of 274 that shattered the old record. Byron Nelson would only shake his head and say, "The man who could play for glory better than anyone I've ever seen is Ben Hogan."

But not even the exploits of Hogan could overshadow the finesse and skill of "Lord" Byron Nelson on a golf course. And they saw a lot of each other.

At the age of 13, Nelson began packing around rich men's clubs at Glen Garden Country Club. And on the practice driving range, he and that other caddy, Hogan, began trading shots. Each won a caddy championship. Then in 1932, Nelson tied his gear on a suitcase and drove to Texarkana for his first professional tournament. He finished third and earned $75. Nelson thought he could make a living at the game. At least, he was ready to give it a try. Slowly, he began to change his swing, and the experts shuddered. Nelson was swinging all wrong, they said. He was breaking tradition. He was going to ruin a pretty fair country game of golf.

In his book, *Shape Your Swing The Modern Way,* Nelson recalls, "They said I stayed down too low through the ball, that I had a dip in my swing, that my foot and leg action was too loose. . . . All I was trying to do was find a better way to swing so I could make a living at the game."

He did.

And, in time, those same experts would credit Byron Nelson with being the first player to ever make a complete change from the old way of swinging to the modern method of playing golf.

Nelson convinced them by winning. Between 1937 and 1942, he won the U.S. Open, the Masters and two PGA Championships. He was good, he said, because he had learned to play the game in Texas. He would later say, "Learning golf [in Texas], in the heat, the wind, the cold, you're schooled under different conditions. If you learned to hit it well against the wind, you can sure play when there isn't much wind."

Three of the famed: Jim Swink (top), All-American halfback at TCU who led the Frogs to the SWC championships and to the Cotton Bowl; Mike Renfro (center), All-Southwest Conference wide-receiver for TCU and a member of the Houston Oilers; Bob Lilly (bottom), All-American at TCU and All-Pro for the Dallas Cowboys.

Perhaps no one has ever conquered the pro circuit so convincingly. In 1944, Nelson won seven tournaments. He was hailed as the best. During 1945, Nelson entered 30 of 32 professional tournaments. And he won 18 of them, including 11 in a row. Seven times he was second. And he wound up third in another. That year he pocketed $52,511.32 and promptly bought a 600-acre ranch at Roanoke, just north of Fort Worth and Dallas.

Hogan and Nelson, in the late '30s, kept Fort Worth watching the world's highest-priced fairways. Billy Rose kept it watching naked skin. Sammy Baugh made Fort Worth forget them all.

Baugh—long and lanky, even described as fragile—made his way to TCU from the high school gridiron at Temple, carrying only a baseball scholarship. The Horned Frogs head football coach Francis Schmidt was told, "The kid plays football, too. Maybe he'll make your team." Schmidt laughed. "Not a chance," he said. "He'd be broken in half in our first contact scrimmage. Too skinny."

But Slingin' Sammy Baugh flat knew how to throw a football. Dutch Meyer became TCU's football coach, and the skinny kid fit perfectly into his offensive philosophy. As Meyer would explain, "In our system, only two things are necessary to begin passing. One is to have a team on the field. The other is to have possession of the ball anywhere on the field."

As tailback in the Horned Frogs single wing attack, Baugh made All American. And up in Washington, Redskin Coach Ray Flaherty was paying him a lot of attention. His ballclub had lost to Green Bay in the 1936 NFC Championship game, and Flaherty told his players, "All we need to win is a forward passer." He found one at TCU.

Grantland Rice, the great sportswriter, was concerned. He took Redskin owner George Marshall aside and told him, "If you sign Baugh, you'd better insure his right arm for a million dollars because the tough guys in this league are gonna tear it off him."

Rice was wrong. Baugh was skinny, but his passes were lethal. During one game, the coach diagrammed a play and said, "On this one Sam, the tight end takes 10 steps straight ahead, turns and comes back on a button hook pattern. I want you to hit him with the football right in the eye."

Baugh paused. "One question, Coach," he said. "Which eye?"

He led the Redskins to the NFC title that first year, just as Flaherty had predicted. And he lasted 16 seasons in the pro's, completing 1,709 passes for 22,085 yards. As Dick McCann, long-time director of the Pro Football Hall of Fame, pointed out, "Never mind what other fellows have written about other quarterbacks, Sammy Baugh was the best . . . and is the best . . . and will still be the best, long after the long pass has been thrown by some as yet unborn boy in some distant decade."

Fort Worth wondered. Baugh was gone in 1937. But the magic of the forward pass was not. TCU unveiled a little quarterback, only 5'7" and 150 pounds. He stepped out onto the practice field with huge I.B. Hale. And someone wrote, "That big guy may become the All American tackle that folks predict, but the little fellow will never get off the bench."

As another wrote, "He forgot to weigh Davy O'Brien's heart." All Davy O'Brien did in 1938 was earn All American honors, lead TCU to a 10-0 record and the mythical National Championship, beat Georgia Tech in the Sugar Bowl 15-7 by completing 17 of 28 passes for 225 yards and win both the Heismann and Maxwell Trophies.

Pro football just could not believe what Fort Worth had wrought. Scouts looked at O'Brien, said he didn't have a chance and walked sadly away. Yet in his rookie year, the bantam-weight quarterback was ranked number two passer in the league, and he set three new passing records. In 1940, Davy O'Brien played his last game, and he went out in style, throwing a record 60 passes and completing 33 of them for 316 yards. He had done enough, O'Brien thought. He put the childish games behind him and joined the FBI.

For Fort Worth, the bad years, the hungry years, had also been the glory years.

Chapter 10

Cowtown's unexpected legacy

Creative cowboys: Both Will Rogers (left) and Charles M. Russell, the "cowboy artist," had a strong influence on Fort Worth. When Amon Carter Sr. met Rogers, the world-renowned humorist introduced Carter to the art of Charlie Russell. This led Carter to build one of the largest collections of Russell's art, now housed in the Amon Carter Museum of Western Art. After Rogers died in an Alaskan plane crash in 1936, the Will Rogers Memorial Coliseum was named after him.

On August 16, 1935, *The Fort Worth Press* carried an article datelined Point Barrow, Alaska, that left Fort Worth in shock and sorrow. The lead was a simple one: "Wiley Post and Will Rogers, famous flying companions, were killed at 8:15 p.m. Thursday (12:18 a.m. Friday Fort Worth time) when their plane crashed 15 miles south of here."

A second front-page story pointed out: "Will Rogers probably had hung his slouch hat in Fort Worth more times than any other city—except in fashionable Beverly Hills, his California home . . .

"The city's prominence as a cattle center seemed to place it close to the heart of the former Oklahoma cowboy."

Fort Worth would never forget the humorist and trick-roping philosopher. Amon Carter made sure of it.

When the first idea of a '36 centennial celebration struck him, Carter asked the Public Works Administration to build a coliseum and auditorium for the observance. He had not yet discovered the bigger-than-life imagination of Billy Rose. Then, when Post's plane went down into the snows of Alaska, Carter suggested naming the coliseum after Fort Worth's number one box office attraction—Will Rogers.

Harold Ickes, the interior secretary and PWA director, wasn't particularly impressed. "I can't understand why a memorial to Will Rogers should be built in Fort Worth just because he was Carter's friend," Ickes grumbled. Carter had hoped that the coliseum would ultimately house the Southwestern Exposition, Fat Stock Show and Rodeo. The project, received no respect at all and was dubbed "Amon's Cowshed."

The publisher flew to Washington to meet with Ickes. The PWA director explained that a school building and tuberculosis sanitarium had already been approved for Fort Worth and that both "clearly outranked a livestock pavilion as socially-desirable projects."

Carter washed his hands of Harold Ickes. He sent his plan straight to the White House, with Postmaster General James Farley delivering the message to an old friend, President Franklin Roosevelt. Carter, sitting in an outer office, overheard Farley tell FDR, "Amon wants to build a cowshed."

Fort Worth submitted a formal application. And Farley telegraphed back, "Your proposal received. Was always in favor of large cowsheds." In November of '35, Jesse Jones, director of the Reconstruction Finance Corporation, wrote Carter, "Your cowshed has been approved by the administration."

By centennial time, only one exhibit barn had been completed. But Fort Worth, as usual, had its eye on day after tomorrow.

War interrupted the vision and gave Fort Worth another.

Adolph Hitler was stomping through Europe. Fort Worth never liked to waste time when it was staring into the teeth of a good fight. The city council purchased 526 of Genevieve Tillar's (widow of Benjamin J. Tiller) good acres for $99,750, then donated them to the U.S. Army for a bomber plant site.

When Major General Harry C. Bryant broke ground, he declared, "We're starting to dig Hitler's grave this afternoon." The plant was nailed together by April of 1942, a full two months ahead of schedule. And, during that same month, the first B-24 rolled off the Fort Worth assembly line.

British Ambassador Lord Halifax, with gratitude, said it was "nothing short of a miracle." Within two years, the Convair plant would put 3,000 bombers and transport planes into the air. Next door, the Army had constructed Tarrant Field and was busy training crews to fly the powerful B-24s.

By 1936, a coliseum, auditorium and tower were added to the Will Rogers exhibit barn. Beneath its grand dome would be held war bond rallies, golden glove fights, a boy scout circus, ice shows and the oratory of fire-breathing revivalists.

And the rodeo, looking for a home, found one right where Amon Carter always believed it should be. Those northside buildings—the traditional arena for the Fat Stock Show—were drafted into the war effort, providing facilities for the manufacturing of war planes. In '43, the show did not go on. Ranchers

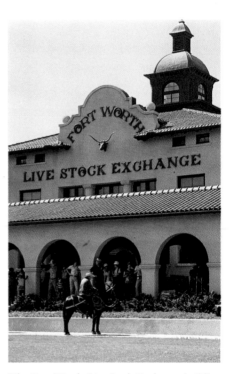

The Fort Worth Live Stock Exchange building.

From revivals to rodeos: The Will Rogers Memorial Coliseum has been the setting for a variety of activities since its construction in 1935 and 1936; 1936 construction (right). The carnival at the March 1944 Fort Worth Fat Stock Show (below).

Coliseum enthusiasm: In the early 1900s, the stock show became so successful that local merchants donated $50,000 to induce the Stockyards Company to build in 1908 the North Side Coliseum. The new show arena became host to the first indoor rodeo in 1917–18, when the Fort Worth Stock Show went from professional entertainment to competition rodeo. Quanah Parker and Comanche braves (left), frequent visitors to the show at the invitation of cattlemen.

Texas Cookin'

I know a man that cooks armadillo
Tastes so sweet he calls it pie
I know a woman who makes pan dulce
Tastes so good it gets you high

Get them enchiladas greasy
Get them steaks chicken fried
Sho' do make a man feel happy
To see white gravy on the side

I know a place that got fried okra
Beat anything I ever saw
I know a man that cook cabrito
It must be against the law

We gonna get a big ol' sausage
A big ol' plate of ranch style beans
I could eat the heart of Texas
We gonna need some brand new jeans

In time, the Southwestern Exposition became the social event of Fort Worth. After watching cowboys scratch leather and eat dirt, cattlemen and sophisticates alike would adjourn to Rainbeau Garden, just around the corner, to dance to Herman Waldman's orchestra, watch the "Dance of Lovers" direct from Follies Parisienne and listen to the songs of the Honey Sisters.

were too busy producing beef, they said, to help win the war and peace.

In '44, it did—inside the Will Rogers Coliseum. Back during the rough and tumble days of 1918, Fort Worth dared to be a little different and staged the "World's Original Indoor Rodeo," with cowboys competing for $3,000 in prize money. Leonard Stroud took most of it home.

As Frank Evans, the exposition's publicity director, tried to point out, "Until recent years, many persons have failed to appreciate the fact that a rodeo is a real sports contest. It is not a circus or so-called 'Wild West Show.' When the rodeo chutes swing open, cowboys and cowgirls match their skill and courage against outlaw horses and wild cattle."

He would later look at bull riding and write, "If you think eight seconds is a short period of time, just imagine your trying to stay for that length of time on the dun-colored hide that writhes with the fury of a tornado and explodes with vicious jumps."

In time, the Southwestern Exposition became the social event of Fort Worth. After watching cowboys scratch leather and eat dirt, cattlemen and sophisticates alike would adjourn to Rainbeau Garden, just around the corner, to dance to Herman Waldman's orchestra, watch the "Dance of Lovers" direct from Follies Parisienne and listen to the songs of the Honey Sisters.

Back in 1937, they swooned over barebreasted Reggie Roth in "Indian Whoopee." And the '38 presentation featured the "World's Fairest Glamour Girls, eye-fetching beauties, daring novelties, a spicy show of talent, beauty, and humor." Fort Worth, at the rodeo, did not think about cows all the time.

Yet the city would always be bound tightly to its ranch-style heritage. In 1944, the Fat Stock Show moved into the comfortable 1.5 million dollar surroundings of the Will Rogers Coliseum. And in a stock show program, J. Frank Dobie, Texas folklorist and historian, gave to the whole world the description of a cowboy: "You'll see him in Fort Worth during the Southwestern Exposition and Fat Stock Show. You won't have to be told who he is, you'll know him. He's that tall, handsome man in a big hat, polished boots, and snug fitting moleskin suit, or is the wiry cowboy in levis, scuffed boots, and well rolled hat. His honest eyes twinkle from a sunburned face and when you shake hands with him you'll learn what a real handshake is. His carriage is unfettered and one knows most of his life has been lived in God's great outdoors. His heart is as big as the country over which he rides. Look at him with pride. He and his father and his father's father built the great cattle

Cowtown hangs on to cowboy image

North Fort Worth is the last pure remnant of cowtown.

It is alive with fine restaurants and chili parlors, saloons and beer gardens, country music and walk-up hotels where drifters find a home for awhile. It is crammed with souvenirs of the Old West—cowhorns, bricks from the Stockyard, armadillo ash trays, feather hat bands, bull whips and barbed wire.

And it is where real, honest-to-God cowboys still come to buy their buckles, boots, beer and belts. And within those old, weather-whipped brick buildings are fashioned some of the finest hand-made saddles in the world.

During June, the Old Chisholm Trail Roundup Days celebrates that cowtown image. Arts and Crafts are set up inside the Fort Worth Live Stock Exchange, once the headquarters of the greatest cattle market in the world.

A cowboy parade, with fiddles, drums and steel guitars all wailing the "Cotton-Eyed Joe," ambles down Exchange Avenue, once thick with cattlemen who came to buy and sell and curse the price of beef.

Inside the Northside Coliseum, armadillos race as handlers crawl alongside them, fanning their rear ends with cowboy hats, urging them on to greater speeds. Those that are hardest to catch make the best racers, James Smith says. He's a member of the New Braunfels Armadillo Association, a group trying diligently to have the little "Texas tank" officially named as the state mammal of Texas.

Outside, men and women alike compete in the quick-draw event. Bob Graham of Conroe is three times World Champion, a man who can draw and fire a .22 in a second. He says, "We're nothing more than professional gunslingers firing at balloons." Graham smiles. "But you know there's a little gunfighter in all of us," he says.

Even the chili cookoff is an integral part of the cowboy era. On the range, cooks cut up a little of everything they carried in the chuckwagon and called it stew. Today, it's referred to as chili. And most ingredients are still a secret.

Maggie's Pop-Eye Chili, it's said, will knock your eyes out. Burning Memories Chili is guaranteed to ward off attacks of "hectic-flush, scours, blind staggers, anthrax and mild cases of chili fever." Marryin' Smert's Wildflower Chili booth offers such free services as "widows wuved [sic] and hugged, divorcees molested, and toms peeped." Marryin' Smert would also perform a "super Dooper Temporary Weddin'" for just under four dollars, then rent out a shotgun, if necessary, for 49 cents."

T. Tom T. Chili, according to the sign, is nothing more than Polish Ambrosia. Perriman's Powerful Panic Stricken Panther Potion will "pucker your palate, pickle your pancreas and pulverize your pelvis. It ain't passive."

Neither was the West.

Happy trails to you: The annual Chisholm Trail Days brings out the fun in Cowtown, from love in a tub to armadillo races, from fiddlers and chili cook-offs to fast-draw shoot-outs, parades and lonesome longhorns.

CHILI . . .
Texas dynamite served on the half-shell

One of Texas most legendary concocters of good chili was the late Hondo Crouch, the self-styled imagineer who went out and bought the little town of Luckenbach so he could guarantee that the beer hall would be open any time he got thirsty.

It was Hondo Crouch who engineered the state's first ladies-only chilibust in Luckenbach, calling it, with pride and passion, the "Amelia Earhart Memorial Hell Hath No Fury Like A Woman Scorned Chili Cookoff."

One of his winners, Aligani Jani of Stonewall went on to capture the World's Chili Cooking Championship in Terlingua. And Aligani Jani remembers well Hondo's own recipe for chili.

He told her, "Dice armadillo into chunks; do not grind. Next, dye them pea green to produce the color for green chili. Use only 'Ysleta Red' chili pods, grown only in Ysleta, Mexico, because the soil is peculiar. Grind three cumino seeds vigorously. Add a jigger of tequila, pinch of salt, slice of lime. (May be either taken internally or added to chili.) For chili thickening, put in a raw egg—two, if they're cheap. And if you can borrow some, add olive oil. It's too expensive to buy. Add green onion tops and finely ground cedar bark. Sprinkle with green spinach or fresh watercress and serve on the half shell."

For the more conventional chili cooks, however, El Lumbre del Sur (Fire of the South) chili was a top ten finisher a few years ago at the Republic of Texas Chilympiad.

Use nine pounds chuck roast; one-fourth cup cooking oil; 15 cloves of minced garlic; five large onions, finely chopped; 10 cups of hot water, three-fourths cup chili powder; one tablespoon oregano; two tablespoons ground cumin; six tablespoons salt; six jalapeno peppers, fine chopped; two squares unsweetened chocolate; two tablespoons masa harina; one-half cup cold water.

Cut meat into small pieces and cook in hot cooking oil until meat turns white. Add garlic, onion and hot water; cover and simmer for one hour or until meat is tender.

Add chili powder, oregano, cumin and salt; cook slowly another hour, stirring occasionally. Add additional water if needed. Taste and add more seasoning if needed. Add peppers and chocolate, and stir until chocolate is dissolved. Stir masa harina (a corn flour; cornmeal can be substituted) into cold water; add to chili and cook and stir until mixture thickens. Serve hot. The recipe makes 12 to 16 servings.

Fort Worth welcome: Stock show staff in front of Will Rogers Memorial Coliseum in 1946 (top). One of the growing number of new motels along Highway 80 in the early 1940s (left).

The Medical Arts Building, once one of the landmarks of the city, was imploded on July 1, 1973.

Since 1927, Fort Worth and Dallas both had dreamed of possessing a great, international airport. But they could not get together, and neither city would step back and offer its support to the other.

industry of the Lone Star State." And the cowboys would never have made it without Fort Worth.

The war came to a halt amidst a mushroom-shaped cloud over Japan. Fort Worth was ready. The city had long relied on the strength of a military-bankrolled economy, and it feared that peace would shut so many doors that its population would all drift away. So the city obtained referendum approval on a $20 million bond issue aimed at increasing public works. It kept its hometown men supplied with jobs—never gave them a chance to get away.

In February 28, 1948, Tarrant Field received a new name—Carswell Air Force Base, in memory of Major Horace S. Carswell, a Fort Worth aviator who was shot down early in the war. He won the Congressional Medal of Honor but lost his life in China. Four months later, the Convair plant rolled out its best-kept secret. Employment had been drastically cut at the plant when war ceased, but several thousand stayed on, working behind closed doors and facing the world with hushed lips. In June, the secret flew—a B-36, powered by six motors, capable of flying 10,000 miles without having to stop for fuel, a threat to deliver an atomic bomb almost anywhere in the world. The B-36 became America's hole card in the cold war, jockeyed by the Eighth Air Force stationed at Carswell. Less than a year later, the B-50 bomber Lucky Lady II took off over Fort Worth skies and returned 94 hours later, ending the first nonstop flight around the world.

Since the day Roland Garros battled the impossible winds over the Driver's Club, the city felt a close kinship with the skies. It had reason. It paved the way for the creation of air power in two world wars. General Dynamics, the successor to Consolidated-Vultee and Convair, produced the sleek, controversial F-111, able to fly three times the speed of sound. For most pilots, the war in Vietnam really began on the assembly line of Bell Helicopter. And Bell's Iroquois established eleven world records for flight.

Amon Carter, for years, had clung to the hope that Fort Worth would become an international air center. In the 1920s, he literally pirated the southern division of American Airlines away from Dallas, flying through "the worst storms I ever saw" to New York to sign the critical agreement papers. The weather was even too bad for commercial planes to be in the air. But Frank Hawks, an old devil-may-care aviator, hauled Carter to New York even though the winds tore the fabric from the plane's right wing. Dallas, in all probability, never forgave him.

Since 1927, Fort Worth and Dallas both had dreamed of possessing a great, international airport. But they could not get together, and neither city would step back and offer its support to the other. Amon Carter once suggested that Fort Worth and Dallas jointly build "the biggest and best airport in the world." A study was made. An engineering form designed the layout of the terminal, but Dallas Mayor Woodall Rodgers refused to go further with the project since the terminal rear end pointed toward his city. He found that extremely insulting.

Carter, just as mad, wrote the mayor, "Some of us in Fort Worth are just plain country folks and while we may still eat with our knife we have felt somewhat encouraged because we have learned to do it with skill . . . while you were willing always for a 50-50 deal we had found that to mean one horse and one rabbit and unfortunately we in Fort Worth had always gotten the rabbit."

Dallas turned back to Love Field. The proposed 1,000-acre "Midway Airport" was dismissed. Fort Worth, with Carter behind the whip, built its own. Greater Southwest Airport, (later named Amon Carter Field) was Carter's biggest failure and most dismal disappointment. It opened in 1953. The opening was the biggest splash it ever made. Fortunately Amon Carter died before he ever learned how big a mistake the airport had been. It later became a training field for American Airlines.

Dallas stuck with Love Field. And it grew. But so did Dallas, and eventually the urban sprawl suffocated any major airport expansion. In 1964, the Civil Aeronautics Board ordered Fort Worth and Dallas to bury their rusty hatchet

Big-time flight: Dallas/Fort Worth International Airport (above). Carswell Air Force Base (top right).

and select a site for an international airport to serve both cities. The Texas Legislature even approved a constitutional amendment that would allow the creation of an authority to govern the airport. In 1967, voters spoke their peace. Tarrant County passed the issue. Dallas County did not.

A regional airport board finally got off the ground with Thomas M. Sullivan chosen to oversee the planning and building of "the last of the great airports in this country." Sullivan had experience. He had designed La Guardia and Kennedy in New York and had served as a consultant for the development of airports in Puerto Rico, Zurich, Paris and London.

Sullivan faced a monumental task, but he was not worried. "I've done three of them," he told the board, "and I don't anticipate any problems with this one." He had learned from his mistakes. As he said, "First I made a list of all the things that went wrong in the New York airports, then I set out to change them."

He did. His concept was revolutionary. But then, Sullivan had 17,500 acres to play with. He would have an airport larger than the entire island of Manhattan. And when completed, Dallas/Fort Worth Airport would be able to accommodate 272 takeoffs and landings an hour. By contrast, the three major New York airports combined, Kennedy, La Guardia and Newark, could only handle 162.

Fort Worth and Dallas both advanced $3 million to launch the initial operations, and negotiations got underway for eight airlines to underwrite $500 million in revenue bonds.

The money ran out before the negotiations.

Sullivan recalled, "At one point, we were two weeks away from being forced to shut down the site work, release the board staff, and leave me in sole custody of a mammoth, $700 million dream."

But banks in Fort Worth and Dallas, along with the Bank of America, purchased $35 million in bonds to finance the preliminary site preparation until negotiations with the airlines could be finally hammered out. It took a

The legend of baseball: The Fort Worth Cats (top) fielded a team well into the 1900s; this photograph was taken in the 1890s. Arlington Stadium (right), the home of the Texas Rangers.

year. But those joint revenue bonds were sold out before the printer's ink was dry.

The dirt flew. And a gray-haired farmer in Grapevine glanced at the heavy equipment and said, "What we've done gone and lost is a lot of good farmland. Used to be a lot of cottonfields out there. Won't be seeing no cotton no more. What they're doin' is plantin' concrete now. And if you'll notice, it's growin' pretty good. Course, they used a helluva lot of cash money to fertilize it with."

In the autumn of 1973, the international airport became a reality. Sullivan called it "the single most significant thing that is happening in the world of

Fort Worth's climb to higher learning

Fort Worth may have been a bold and bawdy cowtown, but religion dragged education to its tobacco-stained doorsteps.

The first institution of higher learning, Add-Ran Male and Female College, graced Thorp Spring in 1873. It would one day be known as Texas Christian University.

That name, however, was bestowed upon the college in 1902, while the campus was anchored to Waco, seven years after Addison and Randolph Clark had gathered up their flock of students and fled the degradation of Hell's Half Acre in Fort Worth.

One teacher would declare, "The town boys, the boys from the farms and ranches, rough but clean were dazzled by the glitter of vice and caught up like insects around the street lamp."

In Waco, the lamp was dark.

A fire chased TCU back to Fort Worth. In 1910, the main building burned and a disheartened Texas Christian University, wounded by lean years, moved its 302 students back home again. Waco had only raised $40,000 to keep the college on the Brazos. Fort Worth did much better. Dallas tried, but it was much too busy negotiating with Southern Methodist University to outbid a reconstructed cowtown.

Fort Worth offered $200,000 and 50 acres, along with city utilities and a street car line. The Board of Trade and the Christian Churches of Fort Worth put up most of the money and the University agreed to remain in Fort Worth for at least 10 years.

It has never seen any reason to leave. And it wasn't long before Van Zandt Jarvis, a rancher who was president of TCU's board, could say with pride, "Next to the packing houses, TCU is the most valuable asset in Fort Worth."

Texas Christian University is presently ranked among the top university-level institutions in the nation, with 60 buildings on a 243-acre campus and an average semester enrollment of 5,800.

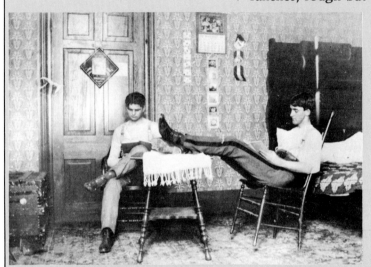

Higher study: TCU students in a dorm (above) when the university was located in Waco. The TCU education building (right) housed the Brite College of the Bible when it was first built.

In 1891, the Methodist Episcopal Church brought Polytechnic College, a coeducational institution, to the cattle-scarred streets of Fort Worth. When Add-Ran fled, Polytechnic became the only thread of higher learning that cowtown could hang onto.

By 1914, the Methodists had established SMU in Dallas and loosened their grip somewhat on Polytechnic. So the institution became Texas Woman's College. Two decades later, men were again allowed on campus and the name of the campus was changed, at last, to Texas Wesleyan College.

Texas Wesleyan presently sprawls

across 50 acres atop Polytechnic Hill, one of the highest points in Fort Worth. It mirrors both the old and the new. Some buildings reflect the contemporary thinking of architects. And some hold onto the dignity of their heritage, rising proudly from behind those Georgian-styled columns.

Like TCU, the Southwestern Baptist Theological Seminary chose to move from Waco to Fort Worth in 1910, with the Southern Baptist Convention gaining control of the college in 1925.

In 1910, the seminary had only one building, constructed for $100,000 and standing alone on a bald hill about six miles from town. Seven decades later it had ten major buildings, housing units for 750 married students, and total assets in excess of $42 million.

Southwestern Baptist Theological Seminary has one basic purpose: "to provide graduate education for men and women preparing for Christian ministry."

It has been successful.

By 1980, Southwestern Seminary had become the largest theological seminary in the world with a record enrollment of 4,336. In addition, Southwestern has provided at least one-third of the seminary-trained leadership for local churches in the Southern Baptist Convention. And one-half of the missionaries appointed by the board are Southwestern alumni.

In the 1960s, Fort Worth became concerned about the educational needs

Halls of learning: The main building of the Fort Worth Wesleyan University (above). The administration building of Texas Wesleyan College (right), the result of combining Polytechnic College and Texas Woman's College in 1935. Texas Christian University in 1913 (below). The tennis courts at TCU (lower right), in front of Reed Hall; once the administration building, it now houses the history and English departments.

Institutional diversity: Fort Worth's range of higher education institutions (clockwise from top): Texas Christian University, Tarrant County Junior College, Texas College of Osteopathic Medicine, Southwestern Baptist Theological Seminary and Texas Wesleyan College.

of those trying to keep pace with technical advances in the work-a-day world. Industries were begging for skilled personnel. And Fort Worth decided to help fill that need. The idea for a junior college, offering a wide-range of studies, was created by Fort Worth Town Hall. And voters, by a two to one margin, approved the sale of $18,144,000 in bonds to establish Tarrant County Junior College.

It all became a reality in 1967, when 4,272 students enrolled, giving TCJC the largest opening enrollment for a new junior college campus in the history of higher education.

Thirteen years later, the junior college could boast four campuses in the county, with about 20,000 students taking credit courses each semester and another 20,000 participating in non-credit courses.

The junior college curriculum has given many older people the opportunity to return to school. Some students are in their 80s. And the average age is 29. About 80 percent of them work, with more than half holding down fulltime jobs. They can take the basics.

Or they can take the kinds of courses that will help them most in their job, such as Air Conditioning and Refrigeration Technology, Auto Body Repair, Ecology, Welding, Small Gasoline Engine Repair, Horticulture, Fashion Merchandising, Food Marketing, Fire Protection Technology, and Law Enforcement.

Tarrant County Junior College has become Fort Worth's affirmative answer to the job market challenges of the future.

City imagery: Downtown Fort Worth as painted by Murray Bewley, 1920s, one of the city's well-known artists. A couple feeds the ducks and enjoys the beauty of Trinity Park (above). The First Christian Church lends a contrast to the Fort Worth National Bank building (right) and to the striking Calder sculpture in the background.

aviation today. We have the airspace and ground space that other cities have run out of. D/FW Airport will be serving people and planes—and doing it more efficiently—long after other major airports have fallen victims to overcrowding.''

As Bayard Friedman, a Fort Worth member of the Regional Airport Board, kept saying, ''Any city is just as good as its transportation system and will rise or fall with it.'' Fort Worth, hand-in-hand with Dallas, came up with the best.

The two cities also joined forces to gang up on major league baseball and tear the Washington Senators away from the nation's capital. They cornered owner Bob Short, realizing he was suffering from a severe lack of wins and attendance dollars and pointed out that two million people lived within 30 miles of newly-expanded Arlington Stadium.

The 20th World Gymnastics Championships were hosted by Fort Worth in December 1979, the first time the event was ever held in the United States. Kurt Thomas (above), one of the United States medal winners, competes in the floor exercise.

Besides, north Texas was traditional baseball country anyway. Fort Worth had fielded its first professional team in 1895. During the late 1940s and early 1950s, the Fort Worth Cats of the Texas League kept supplying the Brooklyn Dodgers with enough talent to send them back to the World Series year after year. And the Dallas-Fort Worth Spurs—the last team to play in Arlington Stadium—had even established a minor league attendance record.

Bob Short saw the light. He packed up his ballclub lock, stock and barrel and trucked them to Texas, even renaming them the Texas Rangers along the way.

The long wait for Fort Worth and Dallas was at an end. As early as 1958, the two cities had struggled to acquire a major league baseball team. But they needed some semblance of a major league stadium. And the sports committee, headed by Arlington Mayor Tom Vandergriff, found it had no authority to sell revenue bonds to build a stadium until it had a team. And it could not get a team without a stadium.

In 1960, Fort Worth and Dallas went after an expansion team. Texas and California found itself in the running for the last team. Amon Carter Jr. and Dallas contractor J.W. Bateson kept knocking on doors, filibustering for a ballclub. When they went to sleep that night, they were assured of a team. When they awoke, the Angels were in California.

Eight years later, the majors again felt the monetary urge to expand. Kansas City got one team because baseball officials had felt badly about letting Chuck Finley move his A's to Oakland. Seattle got another. And Texas, Montreal, Buffalo and Milwaukee were left bidding for the final National League franchise. Fort Worth and Dallas might have pulled it off. But down in Houston, Judge Roy Hofheinz, owner of the Astro's, voted no. He did not want two National League teams in the same state. North Texas had been blackballed again.

Short had perhaps been the area's last hope. He said, "I'm not kidding myself about the move. We need a million fans to stay alive. If we can draw 1,200,000 I'll visit Washington with a brass band."

On a Friday night, sixteen days after the baseball strike of 1972, major league baseball exploded in the Arlington Stadium that hitched Fort Worth and Dallas together. Dick Bosman pitched and won. Big Frank Howard took his first swing on Texas soil and threaded the 400-foot sign in deep center for a home run. Dave Nelson, better known for stealing bases, homered. And Toby Harrah scored three times, the last one providing the winning 7–6 margin. And the newspaper headlines screamed: "Rangers Have the Last Harrah."

Short sold out to Fort Worth and Dallas businessmen, with Fort Worth's Brad Corbett taking the reins as chairman of the board. He would be praised for the trades that worked out, cursed for the ones that did not. But Corbett built a team that could contend. In Washington, the fans had been unhappy because the team did not win at all. In Texas, fans were disgruntled merely because the Rangers did not win it all. They hungered for a pennant. Ted Williams, "the splendid splinter," managed, saying "Practice, dammit, you gotta practice." Fiery Billy Martin managed and came within five games of

Fort Worth champs: 1980 Colonial golf champion Bruce Lietzke receives his trophy (above); three-time Indianapolis 500 champion Johnny Rutherford (below).

the title. When Corbett, tired of coming close, tired of suffering, returned to his Robintech Company, Fort Worth's Eddie Chiles stepped in to make the Rangers run.

Professional sports are deeply ingrained in Fort Worth's day-to-day living. During winter, the Texans—on flying skates—pound the puck around the arena in Will Rogers Coliseum. On every Saturday night, rodeo thunders inside the Northside Coliseum out beside the stockyards that made the cowboy famous.

And in spring, the big bucks chase the little ball around the glory and glamour of the Colonial National Invitational Tournament. It all began in 1946 when 28 players polished up their putters, sanded down their drivers and teed off in pursuit of $15,000 in prize money. Harry Todd of Dallas shot rounds of 71, 70 and 70 for a three-stroke lead going into the final day. Then Todd went out and carded a 69. But Ben Hogan, meanwhile, was tearing the course apart. On number 18, he sank a five-foot putt for a remarkable 65 and walked off his home course with first place and $3,000. Hogan would say of Colonial, "It's the only course I ever played where a straight ball won't work. On one hole you gotta fade. On another you hook. And on some, you gotta do both."

Colonial, long and unpredictable, is full of surprises, the kind of tournament that goes out of its way to knock the legends to their knees. In 1948, the galleries hung onto the hems of Hogan, Byron Nelson, Lloyd Mangrum, Jimmy Demaret, Carey Middlecoff. But it was an unknown named Clayton Heafner who carved out a first round 67. No one paid any attention. Heafner's second-day total was a 68. But nobody cared. They were too busy having convulsions over Hogan's 65. On the last round, a gallery gathered to watch Heafner choke, see one of the greats run him down. But no one caught him. The unknown shot a 69, set a course record of 272 and won by six strokes. He said, "This is the way all golf tournaments should be run. I'd rather finish last at Colonial and get to take part than to be in the money at some tournaments." It was good that he felt that way. In 1949, Clayton Heafner finished last.

In 1951, Dr. Middlecoff won it all by making a 60-foot putt from the concession stand, taking a birdie. Tommy Bolt lost it all by missing a four-inch putt. And Jackie Burke bought an antique putter in the pro shop grab bag, then went out and rolled in putts of 8, 15, 30 and 40 feet to finish second.

And even Arnold Palmer suffered the initiation rites of Colonial. In 1955, he shot a 312 and wound up last. It would take him seven years before he finally won, finally figured out, as Hogan had said, how to hook and fade both on the same hole.

Fort Worth grew out of the sweat and hoofprints of longhorn cattle. It fought the weather (sometimes the worst tyrant of all) and usually lost. *The Democrat,* in an obituary, even blamed the weather for the death of one man, saying, "Like many young men, he came to Texas to seek his fortune, and in his desire to rise rapidly, exposed himself to bad weather."

And it believed, as B.B. Paddock wrote, "God makes the country, but man makes the town."

It had good men, like Dr. A.C. Walker, a surgeon who, it was said, "handled a knife as a violinist handled a bow." It had controversial men, like "Long Hair Jim" Courtright. On his tombstone was written: "Representative of a class of men now passing from Texas, who, whatever their faults, were the type of that brave, courageous manhood which commanded respect and admiration." And it had its plain old mean men, like A.J. Bell who once robbed an old man of $120. And the 1882 newspaper said, "He is one who steals as naturally as the moon draws away light from the sun . . . as soon as he could crawl, no doubt, he stole grass from red ants."

Ed Terrell, the first Anglo to set foot on the ground that would hold Fort Worth, saw the change coming as far back as 1870. He said, "Then the howl of the lone wolf, the shriek of the prowling panther, the neigh of the wild horse, and the yell of the wandering savage caused these hills to send back the startling echoes. Now they reverberate with the roar of the rushing trains,

Nothing too outlandish for Tandy: (left, above and right) part of the realities the dreams of businessman Charles Tandy.

the chime of church-going bells, and the songs of gladness from the congregational worshippers of the Most High God."

The changes came swiftly. No longer did Fort Worth have to depend on cranberries to cure malaria, clam broth to strengthen a weak stomach, breathing the fumes of turpentine to relieve the whooping cough, gargling beer for a sore throat. They may have done it, but they were no longer forced to do so.

Fort Worth, at last, has cleared the dust out of its throat and stuck its Stetson rather regally on the rooftops of skyscrapers. It has become a national manufacturing center, though cattlemen still brag about the stockyards, out in North Fort Worth where the sidewalks are still western wooden, saloons stain the soul with beer and cheatin' hearts, saddlemakers are craftsmen of a rare breed, and snuff-dippin' cowboys hang onto broncs and bulls every snuff-dippin' Saturday night in the indoor arena of the Cowtown Coliseum.

Fort Worth is blessed with the unexpected. It, along with Dallas, ranks as the largest land-locked market in the United States, thanks to a mammoth airport. It is the fifth largest city in Texas, parked within the third largest county. However, Fort Worth (with its population of 420,000) would be the biggest city if located in 28 of the nation's states.

The Tandy subway is the only privately-owned underground subway system in the country. Trinity Park, favored and sometimes revered by hikers, cyclists and picnickers, is a people-place where Mayfest annually brings together such diverse concoctions as fine art, potato sack races and frog jumping contests, along with magicians, jugglers and clowns. Fort Worth's pride, the Texas Boys Choir, usually sings, as it does at command performances around the world.

Constant change: The skyline of Fort Worth, as suggested by New York watercolorist Nicholas Solovioff, upon completion of the Tandy Center.

And the food at Mayfest is the gift of many lands—Italy, Bavaria, Mexico, Germany and even America.

Fort Worth did not slip into the 1980s. It exploded. In fact, the Fort Worth skyline underwent its most drastic changes since the early 1920s, the days when wildcatters' oil greased the city's path to greatness.

But as one developer pointed out, "Fort Worth is the last major city to build in."

And it would be Charles Tandy who would most dramatically reshape that new skyline, building upward and outward on eight square blocks of downtown real estate. By 1978, he had completed two office towers, a galleria with an ice skating rink, a shopping mall with glass elevator and roof garden and the first new department store for downtown Fort Worth in four decades.

Most were shocked when Tandy announced his intention of transforming an aging, decrepit part of the city into a vibrant array of modern architecture. He was laughed at and jeered. City boosters hoped such a dream would not crumble, but it seemed too outlandish to be a reality.

Nothing was too outlandish for Charles Tandy. Besides, he loved downtown Fort Worth and was willing to spend a lot of money to stop that wild exodus of retail merchants to the suburbs. That was Charles Tandy's style.

After World War II, Tandy turned his attentions to his father's business—Hinckley-Tandy Leather Company. He realized that the Veteran's Administration was desperately looking for leather that could be used in crafts to aid recuperating veterans. And Tandy knew there were few leather wholesalers around. He and his father split from Hinckley, formed the Tandy Corporation and, he once said, set out "to make a killing in leather."

They did. Tandy recalled, "As a young man, I saw a lot of people become successful, and I just made up my mind to be one of them."

In 1963, Charles Tandy made a bold move that ultimately shoved him to the forefront of American business. He went to Boston and purchased a small, struggling chain of nine stores called Radio Shack. By 1978, his empire had sales of $1 billion and a profit of $66 million. Tandy was the highest paid chief executive of a publicly held company in Texas, earning a yearly salary

Jim Wright becomes House majority leader

Jim Wright, on that day in 1976, knew all about the role of the underdog. He had been there before. And he knew how to scramble for votes. That was what got him elected to the House of Representatives in the first place.

Now the House was in its ritual of electing a majority leader. And Jim Wright was one of the four who had announced his intentions of seeking that lofty seat. In 1976, during the race for majority leader, his Fort Worth opponents kept saying Wright was too liberal. *The New York Times* and *Washington Post* said he was too conservative. And an aide replied, "If Wright wasn't a politician, he could go to work for the highway department on the center-striping machine. Nobody knows more about the middle of the road than Jim Wright."

John McFall of California had been the early favorite. But he became tainted by the Korean payoff scandal. He was eliminated on the first ballot. Phil Burton of California had 106 votes. Dick Bollinger of Missouri had 81. And Wright was third with 77.

On the second ballot, Bollinger was knocked out of consideration by a mere two votes. He had 93. Wright inched ahead with 95. And Burton kept the lead with 107. It did not surprise Wright that Bollinger stumbled. He had said of his colleague, Bollinger, "He has great intellectual capability, but some members think of him as condescending in that he doesn't listen to them and that he preaches too much."

Wright and Burton squared off for the final vote. And Wright played the subtle game of politics. He pointed out that Thomas P. O'Neill, who had moved up to House Speaker, and John Brademas, the new House whip, were both liberals. If Burton were elected, the liberals would sweep the top three positions in the House. He—Wright—was the only chance the conservatives and moderates had to maintain some influence in important decisions.

Enough listened. Jim Wright won the post, 148–147. Later, he smiled and said, "You know, about 227 members of the House have since come up to me and said how happy they were that their vote made the difference."

of $790,000.

Fortune magazine called the Tandy Corporation in Fort Worth "a giant machine for the creation of millionaires. Tandy has . . . a vibrant faith in the power of money to motivate men." At least 50 of the men who worked with him to put his leather and electronic kingdom together emerged as millionaires themselves, reaping the benefits as Radio Shack became the world's largest chain of consumer electronics stores."

When Charles Tandy died of a heart attack in 1978, the *Star-Telegram* said, "He dreamed the dream of a business and made it international in scope. He dreamed the dream of a builder and gave a downtown a new reason for being . . . He dreamed the dream of an optimist and, even when things looked a bit gloomy, would say, 'yes, we can,' and made it happen."

Tandy's revitalization plan was the impetus for other construction projects that would total a $300 million investment in downtown, providing 2.8 million more square feet of office space and at least 1,500 new hotel rooms.

Sid Bass, too, was willing to gamble big money on the revival of downtown Fort Worth. For several years he had painstakingly acquired old shops and buildings, hoping to convert and renovate them to a kind of turn-of-the century charm along Main Street. He and Tandy were slowly chasing away the porno movie houses and sleazy strip shows that plagued Main, using the power of developmental dollars instead of council legislation.

They would crown it all with a 14-story luxury hotel called Americana/Tandy Center. The 510-room hotel—trapezoidal in design—would cover three blocks; a glass-enclosed bridge would connect to Tandy Center. The hotel and underground parking carried a price tag of $40 million, to be paid for entirely by Bass Brothers Enterprises. In the 2½ blocks he owned on the north end of the downtown area, Bass envisioned a tight-knit creation of unique shops, restaurants and boutiques in small buildings that age, neglect and cheap wine had left behind, all hanging their awnings in shame. "That kind of development fits into the everyday life of downtown Fort Worth," Bass said. "We want to make it a place where people will be happy to go. If the downtown is filled with skyscrapers, the area becomes sterile. We need some mix. It'll give a good image to small firms."

Ray Hunt's Woodbine Development Corporation out of Dallas began altering the time- and secret-scarred face of the Sheraton-Fort Worth, better remembered through the ages and rumors as the Texas Hotel.

As historian William E. Jary Jr., recalled, "The Hotel Texas, for many people, was Fort Worth." Opened in 1921, after 800 Fort Worth residents put up the first $2 million for construction, the hotel has always been an elegant cornerstone of the city's latter-day history. Rudolph Valentino and his wife, Natacha Rambova, danced in the Crystal Ballroom on the 14th floor. During the hard times of the Depression, Lawrence Welk, his accordian, and a nine-piece band tried to sing and play the dark bitter days away. But they were not nearly as successful as Sally Ann Rand who had less than an accordian to hide behind. Ken Maynard, the celluloid cowboy, smartly rode his horse through the lobby of the hotel, eased into an elevator and came galloping out on the 14th floor. Even celluloid cowboys had a soft spot for publicity stunts.

And on November 21, 1963, President John F. Kennedy, in the midst of a political swing through Texas, went to sleep in Suite 850 of the Texas Hotel. It would be his last night. Come morning, there would be a speech, a breakfast, a short flight to Dallas and that long, winding motorcade that would carry him beneath the Texas School Book Depository building.

Woodbine is investing $32 million on the renovation and refurbishing of the splendid old hotel which has a seat on the National Register of Historic Places. By the time it is completed, it will boast a lobby/atrium that rises upward for six floors, as well as a cascading 26-foot waterfall.

Next door will be the Continental Plaza, a 40-story glass skyscraper, providing Fort Worth with another million square feet of office space for only $70 million.

Fort Worth also began watching the downtown Hilton expand; the rise of

A unique people place: The bold and exciting Fort Worth Water Gardens.

Landmarks: The 14-square-block Tarrant County Convention Center (top), Heritage Park (top right) and Thistle Hill (above), the last of the cattle baron mansions.

Sid Bass' two-tower City Center, including the 32-story First City Bank Tower, hiding a four-level atrium; and the development of the Tarrant County Office Administration Building.

The Texas and Southwest Cattle Raisers Association, that first met beneath the shade of the oak trees on the Trinity, will have a new $1.5 million home, along with a Cattleman's Museum and Cattle Raisers Memorial Hall. The Educational Employees Credit Building, as well as the 18-story Trinity Terrace, a high-rise center for senior citizens, is growing up out of Major K.M. Van Zandt's old backyard.

And the Texas and Pacific Building, opened in 1931 when the Fort Worth & Denver City's "Texas Fast Mail" train came rushing in at 6:15 a.m. sharp, has found restoration the quickest way to attract people again. But, by the 1980s, those people were looking for offices not trains. The last passenger train pulled out in the late '60s and the art-deco terminal felt deserted for a long time. With renovation, the proud aging building (on the National Register of Historic Places) where once 50,000 people arrived and departed daily during World War II, is free of neglect again. Halden Conner, who developed the project with John O'Hara, explained, "It was designed in a very romantic period when railroad stations were the heartthrob of a city." Perhaps it still will be.

Fort Worth seldom stands still, at least not for very long. It has too many people who are restless, who do not mind looking for work when they look ahead. As Mayor Woodie Woods pointed out in the spring of 1980, "Our great and strong asset is our citizenry. We have warm and friendly people with a strong work ethic. They have made Fort Worth what it is today through their hard work. And our city staff and city council is making a conscientious effort to work together to promote growth in a manner that is conducive to good living conditions.

"Fort Worth is a viable, growing city with a pleasant climate and friendly people. These assets, combined with our rich western heritage and incoming flights from all over the world into Dallas/Fort Worth Airport, indicate that

Finest pianists: On stage at the close of the 1977 Van Cliburn International Piano Competition, from left, Mrs. Irl Allison, Van Cliburn, Dr. Allison, winner Steven De Groote, second runnerup Jeffrey Swann and first runner-up Alexander Toradze. Steven De Groote (right) performing with the Fort Worth Symphony.

In 1962, the ears of cowtown heard the musical genius of performers from the United States, Russia, Japan, France, Argentina, Portugal and a half dozen other countries on both sides of the iron curtain. By 1977, the competition was drawing 76 contestants from 25 countries.

we also will be developing into a world tourist mecca."

Fort Worth may have been carved from hide and horn. But it surely understood the value of entertainment, the significance of amusing and amazing a surprised, doubting world. No one ever suspected that Fort Worth would wind up as a cultural and fine arts center of international magnitude. Before Franklin D. Roosevelt, out on a fishing boat, flipped the switch that opened Billy Rose's centennial shocker, a critic sneered, "It is like holding the world series in Walla Walla or maneuvers of the battle fleet in the lake in Central Park." After the show, the words were different: "Only two things live up to the claims of their press agents—the Grand Canyon and the Fort Worth Casa Manana."

Fort Worth is still a kingdom of cultural blockbusters. Some are subtle. Thistle Hill is the last of the mansions fashioned by cattle barons who made themselves and their city rich. The Botanic and Japanese Gardens reflect on beauty. The Water Gardens are oblique, perhaps even spectacular. And the Zoological Park, with America's largest herpetarium, puts animals on their natural landscape, rare and exotic birds in a rain forest.

Some are magnificent. The Tarrant County Convention Center, with a domed arena and seating 14,000, spreads its contemporary walls over 14 square blocks that once were tainted by the high-priced love and low-priced whiskey of Hell's Half Acre. When it opened in 1968, manager Louis C. Owens pointed out, "I sincerely believe that, because it was built by the taxpayer, it should be operated for the taxpayer, bringing in opera, symphony, musical comedy, drama, folk and rock music, hockey, boxing, basketball, even pet shows." The diversity of the opening itself pretty much summed up the entertainment philosophy of the center. Sharing the stage that week were the quips of Bob Hope, the arias of "La Traviata," the love-sick ballads of Eddy Arnold and the beauty of the Miss Teenage America Contest.

The Fort Worth Community Theater feels all the comforts of home at the William Edrington Scott Memorial Theater, the gift of the man whose collected paintings and sculpture adorn it. Scott had found most of them in New York, Mexico, Paris, Florence and San Francisco. And he spent much of his time traveling to New York in an effort to keep abreast with the latest trends in opera, ballet and the theater. He brought his ideas home to Fort Worth, and when he died in '61, left his money to keep those ideas alive. The theater was designed by Donald Oenslager who made not a solitary mark on his sketch pad until he met with the ballet, community theater, symphony, opera, Texas Boys Choir and Van Cliburn Piano Competition. He wanted to make sure he could accommodate them all.

In 1958, not long after Van Cliburn had won first prize in the Tchaikowsky

Symphonic variations: John Giordano conducts the Fort Worth Symphony in a concert in the Water Gardens (above). The symphony plays in the less formal setting of a park (right).

Architectural lines, designs: Two views inside City Hall, including its architectural dynamics and the city council in action. The eye-catching sculpture by Alexander Calder (right), outside the Fort Worth National Bank. Huguley Hospital (below).

International Piano Competition in Russia, the young Texas pianist was honored in Fort Worth with a dinner. During the meal, Dr. Irl Allison of Austin, founder and president of the National Guild of Piano Teachers, passed a note to the hostess, Grace Ward Lankford. He had scribbled, "I have an important announcement to make." She nodded. And Dr. Allison stood and explained that the guild had decided to make a gift of $10,000 to be used as prize money in a competition that would carry Van Cliburn's name.

Rumors and whispers fanned through the country's social circles. The competition, they said, would undoubtedly be held in a place of great international stature, probably New York or San Francisco, possibly Boston or Philadelphia. After all, Kilgore's Van Cliburn was not just your ordinary-common-every-day piano player. He had made his debut in Carnegie Hall at the age of 14, took Russia by storm and became the first classical musician ever honored with a ticker tape parade through downtown New York.

Song and dance: The Fort Worth Ballet Association (top) has risen to national prominence with performances such as this world premiere of Rasputin *with legendary Erik Bruhn. Grand Duchess Anastasia, the only living survivor of Russia's old-line royal family, was present for the "Mad Russian Night" reception following that performance. Fort Worth had its early day opera house (above); the current Fort Worth Opera Association, founded in 1946, is the oldest continuous opera company in Texas. Beverly Sills (right) in the 1979 production of* The Barber of Seville.

But Grace Ward Lankford had no intention of letting the Van Cliburn competition get away. She phoned Dr. Allison in Austin with a simple question: "Why not Fort Worth?"

Allison was not surprised. He agreed, providing, of course, that the international quadrennial piano competition "could be carried out on a scale and in the manner the importance of the event warranted."

In 1962, the ears of cowtown heard the musical genius of performers from the United States, Russia, Japan, France, Argentina, Portugal and a half dozen other countries on both sides of the iron curtain. By 1977, the competition was drawing 76 contestants from 25 countries.

Even in the arts—perhaps especially the arts—Fort Worth has always had the uncanny ability to create what it needed most. In 1925, the burgeoning city was devoid of any music, as far as the classics were concerned. It had had a symphony, but many of the musicians marched off to World War I,

Perennial theater: In the early 1900s, the cast was well-costumed for this unidentified local production (right). The Community Theater of Fort Worth, presenting Noel Coward's Hay Fever *in 1979 (above), and the players' home, Scott Theater (below).*

Opera came to Fort Worth in the form of "La Traviata," with Eugene Conley of the Metropolitan Opera singing the leading male role. He was the only out-of-towner.

and few of them returned.

One spring afternoon in 1925, Brooks Morris was talking to Lela Rogers, the society and amusement editor of *The Fort Worth Record.* "Lela," Morris said, "I think it is about time Fort Worth has a symphony orchestra again. Further, I'm not willing to raise my children in a city which doesn't have a symphony orchestra."

Lela Rogers began the campaign in print. Morris hit the streets, trying desperately to round up musicians. He ran down 68 of them. They came from the Majestic and Palace Theaters, the Texas Hotel Orchestra, the Montgomery Ward Orchestra, Texas Christian University, Burns School of Music, the Baptist Seminary, Meadows School of Music and Rosenthal School of Music.

They all filed into the auditorium of the First Baptist Church on the night of December 11, 1925. And 4,000 showed up to hear that opening concert with Brooks Morris conducting. Another 300 were turned away because no seats were available.

The symphony was in business.

It was a precarious business. Only one harp and two kettle drums could be found in the entire city, and all three instruments were usually being used at the Worth Theater. During rehearsals and concerts, however, they were smuggled out to the symphony. They were odd-looking instruments. (And, during those days of bathtub gin, speakeasys, and prohibition, police were always a little leery about odd-looking instruments.) One night, while driving to a concert, a musician was stopped and arrested. Those kettle drums, the officer had suspicioned, were surely being used to distill some of that illegal whiskey. The concert could not go on until Morris finally convinced a police sergeant that the drums made music, not whiskey, and persuaded him to release the musician from his cell. The tuxedo looked a little out of place behind bars anyway.

In 1974, the symphony introduced its "Pops" concert series. It has featured such a wide array of entertainers as Ella Fitzgerald, Chet Atkins, Peter Nero, Nancy Wilson and even Phyllis Diller. And when conductor John Giordano took his Texas Little Symphony to Carnegie Hall in New York in 1980, the performance was praised by *New York Times* critic John Rockwell. He wrote, "It was what one might expect to hear from a good, provincial German orchestra—lyrical, relaxed, idiomatic, expressive."

Opera, like the symphony, wound up in Fort Worth because one day in

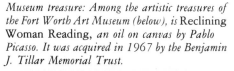
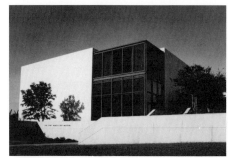
1946 a citizen decided she could not do without it. Eloise Snyder herself had been an opera singer. But her promising career had ended much too quickly when she left the stage to return home and be with her ill husband. She had sung with both the City Center Opera of New York and the New Orleans Opera, and she missed the enchantment of it all.

So did Betty Spain who had also returned to Fort Worth after a year of singing in various musicals on Broadway. Over coffee one morning, Betty turned to Eloise and asked, "Why don't we put on an opera in Fort Worth?"

Eloise Snyder shrugged and suggested, "Why not organize an opera company?"

They did.

Within five months, the two women—assisted by a wide-spread volunteer effort—raised money, recruited the necessary artistic and working organization, found a cast, chorus and ballet, made the sets and costumes, ran down a conductor, launched a publicity campaign and sold tickets.

They did it all with a budget of only $6,000.

Opera came to Fort Worth in the form of "La Traviata," with Eugene Conley of the Metropolitan Opera singing the leading male role. He was the only out-of-towner.

Eloise Snyder herself sang the lead role of Violetta Valery and Mel Dacus was featured as George Germont. Eloise and Mel performed without pay. So did the ballet from the Texas State College for Women, as well as part of the orchestra. Walter Herbert came down from the New Orleans Opera House to serve as the guest conductor. Another remnant of culture had welded itself firmly into the heart of Fort Worth.

The city just seemed to have a knack at coming up with good singing. The Texas Boys Choir, for example, was founded in 1946 by George Bragg in Denton. But, within five years, as many as 35 to 40 Fort Worth youngsters

Modern art: The Fort Worth Art Center (above), a show place for the contemporary. A dance class at the center (below).

were being driven to Denton twice a week for rehearsals.

Bragg ultimately had no choice. He needed the financial support of a metropolitan area. And so much of his choir had homes back in Fort Worth. He, too, came to Fort Worth.

The Texas Boys Choir has sung, and been applauded, around the world. It won one grammy for Monteverdi's "Vespers of 1610," then won another for "Glory of Gabrieli." The famous composer Igor Stravinsky conducted the Fort Worth youths, many as young as eight years old, in Hollywood, then proclaimed the choir "the best boys choir in the world." Critic Algemeen Bagblad of Rotterdam said it, "can sustain comparison with the best in Europe." And *the New York Times* found the choir's performance "irrestible . . . corraling the hearts of the audience."

Fort Worth sowed its own homegrown culture, then made sure it was properly showcased.

The Scott Theater is a significant cornerstone in a broad patch of Fort Worth that has become known as the cultural Acropolis of the Southwest, with Rembrandt, Picasso and Remington all hanging out around the cow barns. It is sophistication in blue denim, Pierre Cardin with snuff streaks on his boots. It is worth millions. It has no price tag. It is the work of the masters, put together by masters in the art world who knew their work and where to find what was lost and who to pay in the dead of night when no one heard, no one saw and no one dared to remember.

Theater is part of it all. In Casa Manana—an aluminum-domed playhouse and namesake of Billy Rose's House of Tomorrow—Broadway has a theater-in-the-round fling with Fort Worth. Neither the likes of "Li'l Abner," "The

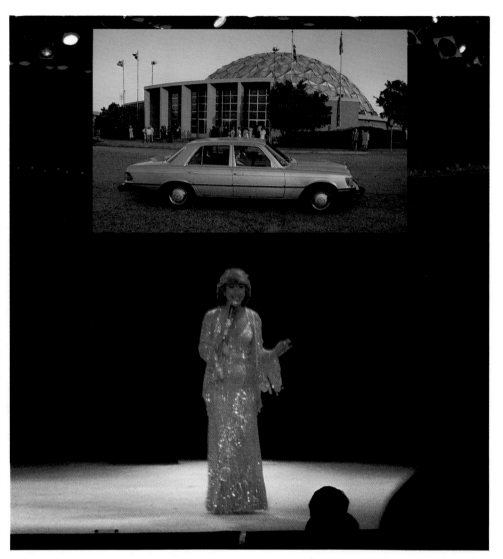

Featured attractions: The Fort Worth Zoo (top). The Pate Museum of Transportation (above). A Shakespeare in the Park *production at Trinity Park (below). Casa Manana outside (insert) and inside with singer Vicki Carr (right).*

King and I,'' or ''The Sound of Music'' need ever feel like a stranger on the Trinity. In addition, Casa Manana is one of the few theatrical organizations in the nation to offer a full season of professionally-produced children's classics.

For the Fort Worth Art Center, the world is contemporary, not always understood, but never boring. It is the twentieth century, celebrated in splashes of color and swirling designs, brushed on canvas, seen through the abstract eyes of men like Picasso. It is a place to experience art, not merely view it, to hike through surrealistic glass and chrome sculpture. The works by Picasso, Kline and Mondrian alone are valued at more than $2 million.

Many fail to understand the unusual forms twentieth century art at the center. Martha Alf, for example, brought her enormous paintings, all brushed on single rolls of toilet paper. ''I'm interested in mystery,'' she said, ''I don't feel you can really comprehend anything.''

Wallace Berman (classified generally as a best generation artist) brought large collages, a threading and weaving of Egyptian hieroglyphs, a woman in a wet T-shirt, a football player, a pope, a gun, an ear and a pair of legs. (Marge Goldwater, the center's curator, explained, ''They're marvelous social documents with lots of space-age symbols.'')

For his part in the ''Los Angeles in the '70s'' exhibition, Lloyd Hamrol created ''Soft Wall,'' a sculpture that seemed to be a pile of hundreds of sandbags. (''It has a very strong presence,'' said Goldwater, ''There's a contemplative space that's created. It's an environmental work.'')

''Much of contemporary art is difficult to understand. It's threatening,'' said David Ryan when he became museum director in 1979. ''I hope to add a little more breadth, a wider variety of disciplines such as architecture, design, folk arts and crafts.''

City Mayor: Woodie Woods

To most people, twentieth-century art remains, for the most part, confusing. "It's very hard to think that much of today's art will prove to be enduring art," said New York art critic Leo Steinberg at a museum lecture. "The art market is so unpredictable that buying art is an act of faith, like electing a president of the United States. It's always like buying a pig in a poke. You don't know what you'll get."

All Kay Kimbell ever knew was that he was getting something he liked. The museum his money built is filled with 4,500 years of art that makes the rest of the world downright envious.

In the mid-'30s when the anxiety of depression was gnawing at most souls, Velma Kimbell talked her husband into attending an exhibition sponsored by the Fort Worth Art Association. Kimbell ambled through the old public library and ran across an English eighteenth-century painting that he decided he just had to have. It was not for sale, Velma explained, it was just an exhibition. That made Kimbell no difference. He had what the New York dealer wanted as well. Kay Kimbell had money. The painting never left Fort Worth.

That was the beginning. In time, Kay Kimbell harvested a fortune in oil, grain, insurance and real estate. And for three decades, he matched his earnings with his art acquisitions, gathering an extensive collection of eighteenth-century British portraits and examples of late European Renaissance works. Kimbell found himself with more paintings than space to hang them, so he loaned bits and pieces of his collection to colleges, universities, churches and libraries throughout Fort Worth.

Kay Kimbell died in 1964. And he left his entire fortune to the art foundation he had personally created for one purpose—"to build a museum of the first class in the city of Fort Worth." No one was ever told just how much money Kimbell had earmarked for the museum, but rumors—those that could be trusted—put the figure at $100 million, give or take an oil well or two.

Louis I. Kahn, one of the world's foremost architects, was chosen to design the $7.5 million building. He dabbled at his sketch pad for a couple of years, he said, waiting for the "idea to become what it wanted to become."

It became Kahn's masterpiece, his last creation, a building with a series of cycloid vaults, resembling (some say) a row of grain elevators blown over by a tornado. Inside are neither columns nor pillars nor windows to interrupt or spoil anyone's concentration on art. Kahn called it "a friendly home in which to enjoy great art."

Richard Fargo Brown made sure there was plenty of great art to enjoy. For seven years he circled the globe, showing up in the most unusual places, traveling with a portable ultraviolet light to detect flaws in the sequestered paintings he found.

And he uncovered those that, some believed, no longer existed. Brown, the founding director until his death, later wrote, "For its size, the Kimbell probably has a higher percentage of discovered and rediscovered pieces of art than any museum in the country."

When the Kimbell Art Museum opened in 1972, the art world was stunned. The Gainesboroughs, Rembrandts, El Grecos, Picassos, Matisses and Goyas were expected. But there was also the medieval "Barnabas Altarpiece," the oldest surviving English painting on wood panel, created about 1250. And there was "Madonna and Child," a Bellini painting, owned by Napoleon III which had disappeared a century before. Suddenly, it reappeared in the Kimbell.

There was an exquisite church apse from a small chapel in southern France. Jerry Flemmons, noted travel editor of the *Star-Telegram,* wrote: "Its walls are painted with pictures of Christ, the apostles and the Annunciation. These were painted about 1150. For centuries the chapel served as a barn, its priceless walls whitewashed. Brown found it. Just how is not known. There is a tale of midnight meetings in rural France and hurried exchanges of money."

Through the years, Brown acquired other impressive pieces—"The Three Crosses" (considered by many to be Rembrandt's crowning achievement); Peter Paul Ruben's portrait of the Duke of Buckingham (lost for two centuries); Rembrandt's "Portrait of A Young Jew," (hidden away in a vault for two

Notable collections: The Kimbell Art Museum opened in 1972 and quickly gained prominence because of the immensity and rarity of much of its collection. In May 1980 the museum obtained Paul Cezanne's Peasant in A Blue Blouse, *for $3.9 million.*

decades and deemed priceless; was one of the best, Brown said, painted at the very height of Rembrandt's powers to see into the human soul and translate what he saw into paint and canvas); El Greco's "Giacomo Bosio," (regarded as one of El Greco's top three portraits and cajoled out of the collection of the Rumanian pretender King).

The Kimbell has seldom gone to the auction block to purchase any of its collection. But when its buyers go, they come back with a blockbuster. In 1966, Brown paid $205,800 for Frans Hals' "Portrait of a Man." It did not worry Brown that the painting was first purchased by a Russian cabaret pianist at a county fair for $7. He had been prepared to spend over $400,000 if necessary to acquire the painting.

And in May of 1980, the Kimbell sent Eugene Thaw to Christie's in New York to bid on Cezanne's late nineteenth century "Peasant in A Blue Blouse." The Cezanne was part of the collection that Henry Ford was selling in order to raise $10 million to help pay off his divorce settlement. Heinz Berggruen, one of Paris' biggest art dealers, thought he had the Cezanne for $3.6 million. But Thaw carted it to Fort Worth for $3.9 million.

Christopher Burge at Christie's said, "The Cezanne was easily the outstanding painting at the sale. It was unquestionably the finest Cezanne to come up at public auction since, well, since it was up before in "58. There will never be another Cezanne as great available again."

Brown was always proud of the three-foot-wide slit running the length of each cycloid, a device that allowed natural light to strike the art. "A work of art was made by an artist working over a period of time, working in different moods, different light and shadow and circumstance," he said. "His art should be seen the same way." In the Kimbell, it is.

Hilton Kramer, art critic for *The New York Times,* wrote, "There has clearly been no shortage of money in assembling the museum collection. There has been no lack of connoisseurship, either. Only a discriminating eye and an informed mind could have brought off this feat of putting together so catholic a collection of such real quality solely in the collecting game."

Kimbell took his inspiration from the old masters of Europe. Amon Carter—first introduced to a Charlie Russell painting by Will Rogers in the 1930s—never had to look further than the American West. It was his country. It was the land Carter believed in, the land he knew best. He borrowed some money and bought a few Russell watercolors in 1935, convinced that Charlie Russell

Art on the prairie: The Amon Carter Museum and a recent acquisition, Ball Play of the Sioux on the St. Peters River *by Seth Eastman (above left and inset), and the Kimbell Art Museum (below left and inset). Hunting for bugs at the Museum of Science and History (above).*

Touching reminder of the past: Log Cabin Village is a collection of old dwellings where a visitor may come to know what it was like to be a pioneer in the days of General Tarrant.

and Frederick Remington—cowboys who could paint as well as they could ride—documented it better than anyone else. (Remington himself wrote, "I knew that the wild riders and vacant land were about to vanish forever, and the more I considered the subject, the bigger the 'forever' loomed.") Remington painted hard to capture it all before it was gone. Amon Carter gave it a place to be seen.

And he did not stop collecting until he died, battling Sid Richardson in a friendly rivalry to see who could ultimately run down and purchase the most Remingtons and Russells. Carter's daughter, Ruth Carter Johnson, said of her father, "His taste in art sprang more from an historic sense than from one of mere aesthetics."

But his will graphically explained what he wanted done with his cowboy art. He had written that he himself was a "part of the heritage of Texas." And he said, "Its pioneer spirit that peopled the wide spaces and laid the foundation of a happy future come down to me in the strain of the blood, and I wish to share it with others who would make Texas their home and inspiration."

From those words came the Amon Carter Museum of Western Art with a permanent collection of 200 Russell and Remington paintings, 60 Russell bronzes and 14 Remington bronzes. Sid Richardson's personal collection—enough to fill the entire first floor gallery and its five exhibit rooms—was on display for the opening of the museum. And those 70 pieces are now on indefinite loan to the museum.

Many of Carter's Russell works came from The Mint, a grand old saloon in Great Falls, Montana, a favorite stopping-off place for the artist, one where he could quench his thirst. And more than once he traded a painting for a drink merely because he had no money.

The Carter Museum, with its Henry Moore sculpture out front, the one he said that depicted "the tenacity of man and his inherent powers of regeneration," was designed by award-winning Philip Johnson. The architect fashioned a great hall with ten adjacent picture galleries. And he explained, "The five segmental arches on tapered columns form an open porch overlooking terraced areas, much as a Greek *stoa* or Renaissance *loggia* overlooking Mediterranean plazas, a shaded place looking on a sunny openness. Behind the colonnade, a glass wall separates the art from the city, the cool from the warm, the peaceful from the active, the still from the windy."

Neither Remington nor Russell nor Carter would have thought that had much to do with cowboy art, but they would have liked its looks anyway.

Helmuth Naumer, former director of the Museum of Science and History, has this theory about Texas and the arts. He said, "Cultured future America will be Texan. Texas—and Fort Worth—provides cultural opportunities to young people that simply can't be found anywhere else. Texans are more natural, more genuine. If they don't like the way I run my museum they come and tell me in plain language. Texas brashness is refreshing. It'll last."

Confrontation reconstruction: The bones of an allosaurus dinosaur confront another prehistoric skeleton in the Museum of Science and History.

The Museum of Science and History is a distinctive corner of the Acropolis. The Noble planetarium is dazzling. The *Los Angeles Times* said of it: "The theater wraps you in image more eye-boggling than any other I know of . . . gives you an unmatched look at the world and at space. The Space Theater is the biggest show in town and you must see it because you have never seen the likes of it."

The museum is even more of a mind-boggler: In it are—tools for brain surgery performed by prehistoric man—the oldest known prescription, collected in Iraq in 2,100 B.C. ("Pulverize the seed of the 'carpenter' plant, the gum resin of the markezi plant, and thyme; dissolve it in beer; let the man drink.")—how Egypt masters kept legions of slaves healthy by feeding vast quantities of onions, garlic and radishes which possessed chemicals that fought off dysentery, typhoid fever and cholera—meteorites, chunks of an ancient planet—mammoth tusks reaching out 12 feet and weighing 200 pounds—The assembled bones of an *allosaurus* dinosaur attacking the bones of another—mannequin in full Samurai armor, used to frighten as well as protect in the sixteenth century—hat from the Philippines made from half a dried pumpkin—the Eskimo raincoat fashioned from a walrus bladder—an Ethiopian witch doctor's paraphernalia—Chinese backscratcher—a lute covered with the skin of a Congo viper.

But, perhaps of most interest, are the traces from old Fort Worth itself. The museum collected an ad from the Spring Palace, "The most unique and attractive exhibit ever presented to the public;" a boot jack, cigar clipper, spurs, snuff box and pistols from the trail drive era; a sash from General Worth's uniform; a photo of Cynthia Ann Parker; the Confederate veteran's blouse belonging to Major K.M. Van Zandt; a check from Loyd's Exchange Office; letters signed by General Worth and Sam Houston.

Fort Worth can never—and does not want to—escape its past.

Not far away from the Acropolis is a small cluster of huts in Log Cabin Village. One was owned by Captain Howard, a farmer, a minute man who held a plow in one hand and a rifle in the other. His only enemies were drought and Indians. Another belonged to John Baptist Tompkins who built the cabin on a hill above Village Creek, peaceful after General Tarrant massacred the Indians there. And a third was the home of Isaac Parker, the legislator from Birdville, whose bill cost Birdville its county seat.

The dwellings are a poignant reminder of a day when life was hard but simple, when families prayed for rain during droughts, then prayed for the floods to dry up and go away. From cabins such as these, a town was born. It brawled. It blushed. It begat children. It boomed.

And it rose up in greatness from the muddy banks of an indomitable old river that ran, for so long, with no name.

Fort Worth. It wore its own brand. Different, perhaps. Defiant, probably. And damn proud of it.

Partners in progress

New technology and free enterprise: Louis Bicocchi's grocery store was the first store in Fort Worth to have a cash register and electric lights.

Making a city grow:

Fort Worth Chamber of Commerce

The corporate community has made dynamic contributions to the growth, development and quality of life in Fort Worth. The city's leading businesses have lent their support and financial commitment to the publishing of *Fort Worth: The Civilized West.* Their corporate histories follow.

It began in 1881.
Captain Buckley Boardman ("B.B.") Paddock and J.W. Spencer took upon themselves to organize the Fort Worth Board of Trade. It was the beginning of what would become the Fort Worth Chamber of Commerce. In those days, such organizations were still rather new in the area. Only two Texas cities—Houston and Galveston—had such a group.

They found 100 people willing to pay $5 a month to help the town. They all wanted to see it expand, to provide services for its people. But their dreams—and the work to be done—were larger than their pocketbooks. And in 1891, ten years later, the fees were raised to $100 per month.

It was a good investment.
The Chamber's duties grew to include such complex services as management of public service, a freight bureau, grain inspection and the Fat Stock Show. The city suddenly found itself a major producer of the nation's beef, grain and natural resources.

That growth was the result of a continual pulling together. Fort Worth's people always seemed willing to help each other. When the Chamber sponsored a street improvement picnic in 1913, over 10,000 businessmen signed up for the wage-free work. The *Star-Telegram* reported, "Rating [the laborers] skill as road builders at $2 a day, the Fort Worth Chamber of Commerce estimates the road improvement to be worth $14,000." It was a way of saving money and still getting the highways so necessary to the community.

But the Chamber's vision was not limited to local growth. In 1918, it played a major organizational and monetary role with three other west Texas chambers in organizing the West Texas Chamber of Commerce. The new group made west Texas "one big family."

This year, the Chamber is 100 years old. It has seen—and had a major hand in—the growth of a small cowtown to a metropolis. Its 2,300 members actively work to support the broad economic base which they have established while still maintaining the city's hometown flavor. That dedication, leadership and knowledge that characterized those early leaders of the business community still exists. For the Fort Worth business community has always believed in teamwork. It has sought growth, but growth to help its people rather than hinder them. The mutual trust and willingness to work for the good of all has made Fort Worth one of America's most livable cities.

The AMF Ben Hogan Company

Quest for perfection revolutionized the golf world

In 1953, just four years after a near-fatal automobile accident, Ben Hogan became the only player in the history of modern professional golf to achieve the Triple Crown of victories — the Masters, the U.S. Open and the British Open. That year he also established his own golf equipment company in his home town, Fort Worth, Texas.

It was a landmark year for golf, but the doors at 2912 West Pafford Street in south Fort Worth opened on December 19, somewhat unnoticed in the bustle of Christmas shopping.

For the previous two months, Ben Hogan had overseen the installation of club manufacturing equipment. The demands for perfection that Ben Hogan required of his own golf game were evident in his manufacturing plant. Slowly the machinery for creating golf clubs filled up the floor space. It was a tedious pace. Six months passed before the first lot of Hogan woods was assembled.

It was a great day for Ben Hogan as he stood before the racks of shiny new clubs that he had designed. But as he took a long hard look, he pronounced them unacceptable.

Hogan affirmed his determination to oversee every aspect of club design and manufacture. The standard of quality he dedicated himself to then, would later make his products some of the most respected in the golf industry.

Ben Hogan's demanding standards were relentless and the first irons and woods to meet his approval were finally completed in the spring of 1955. Only then did a flyer go out to pro shops across the nation announcing the new Ben Hogan line — single models of irons and woods.

It was a modest beginning but the Ben Hogan Company would soon rise to the forefront of the golf industry.

In 1960, AMF Incorporated, which had been looking for the right opportunity to enter new areas in the recreational field, purchased the company. With AMF's financial backing, the Ben Hogan Company was able to accelerate its growth. By 1963 the company had its own sales force and was promoting an expanded line to pro shops throughout the nation. That same year manufacturing space was doubled.

First Ben Hogan Company facility, in 1959.

Four years later, after Ben Hogan was certain his company had the capability of creating an exceptional ball, a ball manufacturing section became part of a $1 million expansion program that again doubled manufacturing space. That same year Ben Hogan, who had served as president since the acquisition by AMF, became chairman of the board and the sales team expanded to seventeen causing the sales volume to soar.

This was followed by one of the most rewarding years in company history, 1968. A new shaft called the Apex had been conceived. With its thinner walls and unique step pattern, the Apex Shaft was lighter than its contemporaries and just as strong. It took the golf industry by surprise. Suddenly design leadership in golf clubs had come to Fort Worth.

In 1972 the Apex name made still another dramatic appearance. This time on a golf ball. By 1973 the Hogan-developed Apex ball had achieved the position of being the leading money and tournament winner on the men's professional tour, a distinction it has held ever since.

In the meantime, plans were being made to expand the Hogan line. In 1972 golf apparel first bore the Hogan label. So successful was this venture that an apparel warehouse and an embroidery facility were added in 1978. By then the Hogan line included shirts, sweaters and slacks for both men and women.

AMF Ben Hogan Company expansion, in 1967 saw opening of new executive offices and construction.

The introduction of the Legend Shaft in 1976 revolutionized the golf equipment world. Since that time Hogan has developed the Apex II Iron, a leading seller in pro shops, and the Director Iron with weight distributed to yield better results on off-center hits. In 1980 Hogan introduced the Vector Shaft, with the flex point near the hands for improved control and accuracy.

The Ben Hogan Company — still at its original location though many times the initial size — employs more than 600 people including a sales force that is international in scope. Under the current leadership of Ben Hogan — still a vital and active chairman of the board — and President Roger L. Corbett, the company produces a full line of equipment and sportswear that sets the standards of quality for the world of golf.

American Airlines, Inc.

An innovative company with deep roots in Texas

A young aviator named Charles A. Lindbergh stowed a bag of mail aboard his little DH-4 biplane at St. Louis on April 15, 1926, and took off for Chicago on the first regularly-scheduled flight of what was eventually to become American Airlines.

Lindbergh at the time was chief pilot of Robertson Aircraft Corporation of Missouri, one of the first private companies to win a government mail contract. In May 1927, the same Charles Lindbergh made history with his solo flight across the Atlantic.

Robertson Aircraft was one of a number of small airlines absorbed in 1928 by Universal Aviation Corporation, which developed a fairly extensive operation in the Midwest.

In the East, Colonial Air Transport flew the first scheduled service — also under a government contract — between Boston and New York, and then expanded its routes through affiliated companies into Canada and between Albany and Cleveland.

The Embry-Riddle Company started service in late 1927 between Cincinnati and Chicago, and Interstate Airlines flew the Chicago-Atlanta route.

Texas Air Transport, of Fort Worth, was awarded mail contracts for two intrastate routes that included such cities as Houston, Galveston, Waco, Austin, San Antonio and Dallas. Mail flights commenced in February 1928, passenger service in 1929.

Texas Air Transport was combined with Gulf Air Lines (a New Orleans company with a route to Houston) in 1929 to become Southern Air Transport. Headquarters remained in Fort Worth.

Colonial, Universal and Southern were bought in 1930 by a holding company, the Aviation Corporation, and formed into American Airways — an airline whose routes lacked any real system and whose fleet of airplanes included just about every type then available. Embry-Riddle, Interstate and many other airlines later entered the American Airways fold.

The various units operated pretty much as separate entities until 1932, when a centralized operations department was organized. Selected to head the department was C. R. Smith — a native Texan who had joined Texas Air Transport as treasurer, risen to become vice president and general manager of Southern Air Transport and established a name

American Airlines drew up the specifications for the famous DC-3, was the first airline to order the airplane, first to put it into scheduled passenger service in 1936 and first to retire DC-3s in 1949. This American Airlines Flagship is shown at Fort Worth Airport during the heyday of the DC-3 (above).

The American Airlines Flight Academy near Fort Worth was dedicated in 1970. It is recognized as one of the world's finest pilot training facilities (left).

for himself by running the most efficient of all the American Airways divisions.

Cancellation of all airmail contracts by the government, in February 1934, resulted in a reorganization of the airline companies and revisions in their route structures. American Airlines emerged from that period as the successor to American Airways, and C. R. Smith was named president.

Except for World War II service as a major general and deputy commander of the Air Transport Command, Smith served as American's chief executive until 1968, when he accepted an appointment as secretary of commerce under President Lyndon B. Johnson.

Smith returned to American as interim chairman from September 1973 until February 1974. Albert V. Casey was elected chairman and president to succeed him. Under Messrs. Smith and Casey, American achieved an enviable reputation for innovation and for excellent service.

The company's many air transportation

"firsts" include the introduction of the famous DC-3 airplane, which it put into service in 1936; scheduled domestic airfreight service, inaugurated in 1944; the family fare plan in 1948; jet service in Texas and across the United States in 1959; a computerized reservations system in the 1960s; super saver fares in the late 1970s and many others.

American moved its corporate headquarters to the Fort Worth-Dallas area in the summer of 1979. Also located in the Fort Worth area are the airline's Learning Center — where flight service and ground personnel are trained; the Flight Academy — one of the most advanced pilot training centers in the world; and the Southern Reservations Office — one of four such facilities on the U.S. mainland.

The airline traces its history to many different cities and to various parts of the country, but its roots probably grow deepest in Texas soil. No part of the nation has left a stronger imprint on the company.

American Manufacturing Company

Mercantile Center epitomizes America's free enterprise system

The wooden walkbridge across Fort Worth's historic Fossil Creek in Mercantile Center is symbolic of the forceful way in which the fledgling business of American Manufacturing Company of Texas bridged its years of growth to enter today's era of personal fulfillment and its pledge to the future of a city it helped build.

Surrounded by lush greenness is a marble stone enscribed with the words "Private enterprise has combined man's craft with the beauty of nature to create the surrounding environment."

Those words are a fitting tribute, indeed, to the founder of AMCOT and a pioneer of the Old West — W. J. Gourley. As a teenager, Gourley moved with his mother, brothers and sisters in a covered wagon from Missouri to Oklahoma. In the early 1920s he acquired the Weatherford Machine and Foundry at Weatherford, Texas. After trips on the road to solicit orders, he would return to work in the shop, doing everything from charging the

Car 100, now located in the heart of Mercantile Center, played an important role in the mercantilism of the South and the United States after the Civil War. This picture dates back to the mid-1930s when the car was used by the railroad to demonstrate to Georgia farmers better beef cattle production methods.

foundry cupola with coke and iron to painting the finished product for delivery.

On May 21, 1925, the corporate name was changed to American Manufacturing Company of Texas. Gourley's determination and drive pushed the plant to keep expanding, increasing its need for multitransportation services. In the early 1930s, it relocated to its present location in northeast Fort Worth.

AMCOT has been recognized repeatedly for its contributions to America's defense efforts. Today, the company continues to serve the world's oil industry by manufacturing oil field equipment.

Even in the days before his death in 1970, Gourley encouraged his family and the business leadership of his company to

A wooden bridge across historic Fossil Creek shows the careful planning and beautiful landscape architecture of Mercantile Center, an American Manufacturing Company investment.

contribute further to the growth and progress of Fort Worth. Together they laid the groundwork for a business development of exceptional quality located in a beautiful environment and dedicated to the principles of the free enterprise system.

The fulfillment of that dream became a reality in the fall of 1980, as Mercantile Center came into its own as a multi-use commercial, retail office and light industrial development. The 1,400 acre project is owned by American Manufacturing Company of Texas and General Industrial Corporation.

Within Mercantile Center, great emphasis is placed on environmental beauty and quality construction. The Woodbridge area of the center is true to its name, as landscaped pathways follow Fossil Creek's meanderings. The area will soon combine, with carefully landscaped open spaces, low profile garden office buildings, a high quality hotel, health services and two office towers.

To the east is a 20-acre site reserved for a fitness center exemplifying the spirit of the overall development. Here will be a conference center, jogging pathways, exercise facilities, and multi-use gymnasium with tennis and handball courts and a swimming pool.

At the heart of Mercantile Center is Mercantile Station and Car 100, emblematic of the timeless commitment to quality and overall uniqueness of this total business environment.

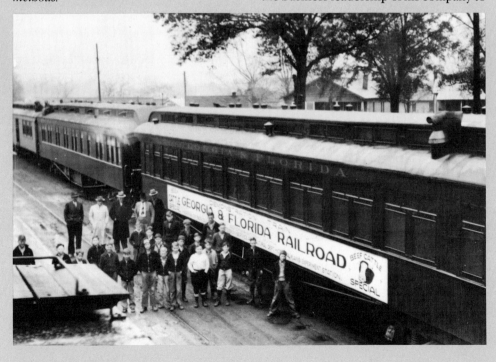

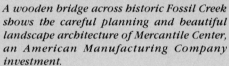

Car 100, a private rail car nearly a century old, is a silent testimonial to the importance of the railroad to Fort Worth's economic history. Ornate brass railings, original cherry paneling and numerous authentic fittings are also symbolic of the permanence to be found at Mercantile Center.

Alongside Car 100 is Mercantile Station. Its wooden frame is one of an old Texas railroad station, rescued from dilapidation and moved to Fort Worth. Completely renovated, the spacious conference area and private offices provide an information center and a meeting place for business leaders.

Together, Car 100 and Mercantile Station are bridging the gap between a prosperous history and promising future. They are the foundation for a total business environment, planned for people and constructed to stand as a permanent monument to America's free enterprise system.

American Quasar Petroleum Co.

Experienced people, important discoveries aided petroleum exploration company's growth

In 1969, five Texas businessmen — whose oil industry roots extended back almost to the turn of the century — found themselves on the verge of an important confluence of ideas.

Their collective opinion was that, as independent oil explorationists, they were destined to fight for the mere scraps among petroleum plays; it was just too expensive for the small operator to go for the really big discoveries that were, by then, to be found almost exclusively in frontier areas or in extremely deep formations.

So they pooled resources and formed American Quasar Petroleum Co. in Fort Worth. A public venture, its stock sold for

View of a pump (foreground) and drilling rig at Quito — scene of American Quasar's initial discovery.

about $2 a share at the outset. They quickly concluded, however, that while going public was a move in the right direction, it would not provide all the funds necessary to pursue the company's primary objectives — namely, big discoveries.

The principals decided then to establish a wholly-owned subsidiary dedicated solely to raising and administering funds for public drilling programs, or "limited partnerships." As a result, Canadian-American Resources Fund, Inc., and later Can-Am Drilling Programs, Inc., came into being. In less than 10 years, Can-Am would grow to represent the largest public exploratory drilling fund in the nation.

Total funds raised for 1970, though, came to a relatively small $3.3 million — almost half of which were spent in explo-

ration and drilling at the Quito prospect, near Pecos, Texas. When the discovery well there was completed as a producer, Can-Am and American Quasar were on their way.

While the discovery at Quito did much to establish American Quasar's credibility, the momentum picked up with the discovery by Quasar Petroleum Ltd. — an 81 percent-owned Canadian subsidiary of AQP — the next year at North Grizzly Valley in British Columbia. Not only did the North Grizzly success underline Quasar's growing reputation for expertise within the industry, it represented an important new find in a promising geologic area: the "Overthrust Belt."

The Overthrust is a petroleum-rich geologic region which, on the map, basically follows the Canadian Rockies south into the United States, passes through the Montana-Idaho-Colorado-Utah border area and touches on Nevada and New Mexico, as well as splitting Arizona diagonally from northwest to southeast, before passing into Mexico.

Quasar's North Grizzly Valley discovery just happened to be the first significant find in the British Columbia foothills portion of the Overthrust. And that wasn't the end of it.

In 1974, drilling at the Pineview prospect in northeastern Utah, American Quasar hit on the first significant discovery in the U.S. portion of the Overthrust, with its Newton Sheep well No. 1. That find literally opened the floodgates to exploration in the Overthrust Belt, in which American Quasar continues to concentrate a great deal of effort — along with a great many other petroleum exploration companies.

But Quasar's full range of exploration encompasses much more of the United States and Canada — including the Southwest, Southeast and the far West.

American Quasar's Newton Sheep No. 1 — at the Pineview prospect in northeastern Utah — was the discovery well that focused wide industry attention on the U.S. Overthrust Belt.

And the company's full range of exploration expertise includes a number of geologists, geophysicists and landmen who cut their industry teeth with giants such as Amoco, Cities Service, Texaco, Shell, British Petroleum, Exxon, Conoco, Chevron, Champlin and Atlantic Richfield.

The secret to American Quasar's success, in other words, has been linked closely to its people, who have helped make it one of Fort Worth's most dynamic and fastest-growing companies.

Bank of Fort Worth

Foresight and planning the measure of the future

Fort Worth entered the postwar era with a population of 323,000 and national acclaim as an aviation, railroad and cattle center. As the postwar development of the suburbs began to shape a new American lifestyle, Fort Worth set an unprecedented pace for the nation in residential construction. In 1947 — the year of the 51st Rodeo and Fat Stock Show — the West Side State Bank was established to keep up with the rapid residential growth on the west side. West Side State Bank became the fourth neighborhood bank in the city and the second bank to be sponsored by downtown Fort Worth National Bank.

The first board of directors — J. E. McKinney, president, C. F. Fry, vice president, Neill Boldrick, Ben Eastman, Raymond C. Gee, Charlie Hillard, R. E. Harding Sr., R. E. Harding Jr., T. W. Loffland, I. C. Parker, John W. Russell and L. N. Wilemon — were confident that their new bank would make a definite contribution to the residential, business and banking communities. So, on July 19, 1947, with a total capital structure of $300,000, five officers and a staff of seven, the West Side State Bank opened for business.

For the first quarter of a century, the West Side State Bank was located at University, West Seventh, Bailey, and Camp Bowie streets — better known to Fort Worthians as "the corners." The new building not only epitomized the latest in

banking furniture and fixtures, but anticipated future growth. However, this farsighted planning was short lived — three major expansions occurred within the first thirteen years, the last one resulting in a two-story addition to the original building.

The original Bank of Fort Worth in 1947.

The Bank of Fort Worth today, situated on a six-acre site between West Seventh and West Fifth Streets.

These expansions were indicative of what was happening in the area. Where the affluent oil and cattle barons were once the mainstay, the ongoing development of residential neighborhoods — Monticello, Crestwood, River Oaks and White Settlement — were bringing in additional resources. Through the dedicated leadership of its management, West Side State Bank capitalized on these resources.

Such dedication was exemplified by five chief executive officers in the 33 year history of the bank — J. E. McKinney, 1947 to 1954, was the organizing president; C. Ferd Fry, 1954 to 1969, in fifteen years of winning friends and building resources, left a legacy which is a constant inspiration; Kleber Jennings, 1969 to 1972, descendant of the notable Fort Worth Van Zandt banking family, brought valuable banking knowledge; Jack Logan, 1972 to 1976, saw the bank enter the '70s as a small neighborhood bank and become a major suburban bank; Barclay R. Ryall, 1976 to present, brings the bank into the '80s with $123 million in assets.

First generation growth, coupled with the cultural influence of the Kimbell and Amon Carter art museums and the Museum of Science and History, made the west side, in the decade of the '70s, a significant financial segment of the city. These factors directly affected West Side State Bank, and it became apparent that the building no longer functioned for the bank, but in spite of it. So, in 1972, on its 25th anniversary, the West Side State Bank moved into new surroundings and took on a new name — THE BANK OF FORT WORTH!

The name change reflected the scope of the bank's services and the geographic makeup of the area it served. The new building, a distinctive contemporary structure, made an architectural statement. With its expanded facilities, the Bank of Fort Worth, situated on a six-acre site bounded by Arch Adams, Bailey, West Seventh and West Fifth streets, accommodated its customers with the ease and efficiency they had come to expect.

In 1978, with assets of more than $100 million, the Bank of Fort Worth (sixth largest bank in Tarrant County) became a wholly owned subsidiary of the Fort Worth based multibank holding company — Texas American Bancshares, Inc.

Throughout its history, the Bank of Fort Worth has taken pride in playing a major role in the economic, social and cultural development of its city. From winning awards in beautification and advertising to providing financial strength and assistance to its friends and neighbors on the west side of Fort Worth, the Bank of Fort Worth has continuously made efforts to bring the latest developments in banking to the suburbs.

Bell Helicopter Textron

Small garage 'plant' sprouted growth of world's foremost helicopter maker

The year was 1941. Inventor Arthur Young had spent thirteen years developing his own set of helicopter design principles and sought a backer to transform his almost perfectly stable flying model into a full scale helicopter. His attempts to interest several aircraft companies had been unsuccessful.

Then Young met Lawrence D. Bell, a man who had founded Bell Aircraft Corporation only six years before in the midst of the Great Depression. Bell recognized Young's genius. Despite his firm's preoccupation with the manufacture of fighter planes as World War II became reality, Bell gave the inventor the chance to build and test one of those newfangled machines.

Test pilot Floyd Carlson learning to hover a development model of the helicopter in 1943. Cables kept the helicopter from taking off.

He isolated Young and his small staff in a small, leased garage in Gardenville, New York — away from the Buffalo airplane plant, so they could concentrate on their unique mission. Long hours and dedication paid off. On March 8, 1946, the Bell Model 47 was awarded the first commercial helicopter license and a new industry was born.

Bell's unique XV-15 tilt rotor converts from helicopter to airplane.

It was one of many helicopter firsts for Bell. Among others were the first convertiplane with a tilt rotor system (XV-3) and the first gas turbine-powered helicopter (XH-13F).

Actual production began in 1946 and the first sale was made that year, with military forces purchasing their initial Bell in 1947. But it was the Korean Conflict in the early 1950s that became the proving ground for helicopter concepts. Eighty percent of front-line evacuations were credited to the Model 47.

Following the transfer of Bell Aircraft's rotary-wing division to Fort Worth, Texas in 1951, the company established a growth and development pace that has been unequalled in helicopter history.

Advent of turbine powerplants led to Bell's famous UH-1 "Huey" helicopter, which gained fame for its mission versatility in Vietnam. During this conflict, the company also developed the AH-1G HueyCobra, the first helicopter given attack designation by the U.S. military. Concurrently, commercial helicopter sales and applications began to accelerate.

In 1960, Textron Inc., of Providence, Rhode Island purchased various Bell Aircraft properties, including Bell Helicopter Corporation — renamed Bell Helicopter Company — and, in 1976, became Bell Helicopter Textron.

Wind-down of Vietnam production enabled Bell to capitalize on the tremendous potential of helicopters in worldwide civil applications. The company has been a leader in development of aircraft for use in petroleum, agriculture, construction, public safety, emergency medical, corporate and other areas.

Bell is now Textron's largest operating

unit, with 9,000 employees in greater Fort Worth, and contributes more than $200 million annually to the area's economy. The company has eight facilities with 2,600,000 square feet of enclosed space on 1,200 acres.

As the world's largest manufacturer of helicopters, Bell has produced 2,500 aircraft for its military and commercial customers — a figure that surpasses the combined total of all other rotorcraft manufacturers.

In addition to work on a dozen different production models, the company is involved in more than 150 research projects. Among its most notable advanced technology programs is the XV-15 tilt-rotor research aircraft, which combines the best features of helicopter and conventional turboprop airplane.

Bell has entered the 1980s with a diversified product line ranging from five-place to nineteen-place helicopters, and is fully dedicated to the design and development of new aircraft to meet the requirements of the next decade and beyond.

Gordon Boswell Flowers

Canaries and carnations were only the beginning

Man does not live by bread alone. The firm of Gordon Boswell Flowers has built a business in Fort Worth based on this philosophy, developing through the years into one of the largest florists in the Southwest.

When Gordon Boswell and his young bride, Fredrieka, opened their first small downtown flower shop in 1919, they shared a building with the C. C. Miller Piano Company. Just in case there was not enough demand for carnations, they also carried a goodly collection of canaries. Fortunately, both sold well — well enough, in fact, that in a few years they moved to 702 Main Street, next door to Herman Jones' Coffee Shop, one of the few places to eat in downtown Fort Worth at that time. Wormser's Hat Shop was located on the other side of the flower shop.

The Boswells' daughter, also named Fredrieka — now wife of Felix Ankele, president of Gordon Boswell Flowers — was a young girl at the time and remembers that the store was very narrow — only nine feet wide. The refrigerator occupied so much space that one could barely squeeze by to get from the sales area to the work room.

This location for their shop proved to be ideal. Gordon Boswell, now chairman of the board, recalls that Fort Worth National Bank was on the corner of their block and Western Union was just across the street. "In those early days of wire orders for flowers, Western Union would often receive telegrams addressed simply, 'Leading Florist, Fort Worth, Texas.' They would bring them across the street to us. It was quite helpful."

By 1928 the shop had grown to need much larger quarters. Gordon Boswell Flowers moved out of the "high rent district" of downtown to 1220 Pennsylvania Avenue, the location of the store today.

Gordon Boswell Flowers opened this shop in 1928 at 1220 Pennsylvania Street in Fort Worth.

The Boswells lived in a large two-story brick home adjoining the store.

The new shop featured a conservatory and ample work space. Mrs. Ankele recalls that the design area had one large table, 9-by-12-feet in size, and all the designers worked around this one area. "In the summer when the business was often slack," said Mrs. Ankele, "the employees played ping-pong on that table."

When Fredrieka Boswell married Felix Ankele, he was working for an oil company in west Texas. In 1946 Gordon Boswell persuaded his son-in-law to trade his derricks for dahlias and join the flower industry. Ankele recalls that the first year he joined the shop there was a glut of gladiolus. Growers were begging them to buy at almost any price. Gordon Boswell Flowers bought a thousand dozen and sent them to customers and other friends.

In 1946 the size of the store was more than doubled. "We were very lucky in our location," Ankele says. "When the store was moved to this location, there was no hospital around. Now we are in the heart of Fort Worth's hospital district."

In 1954 a second store was opened at 6200 Camp Bowie Boulevard to serve the booming west side.

In January 1978 a disastrous fire struck the store at 1220 Pennsylvania. The Ankeles were on the first day of a Caribbean cruise — the first real vacation they had taken in years. They flew back at once. Friends, with many competitors among them, rushed to the rescue. Employees literally worked around the clock. The shop, with the help of the west side store, did not miss a day of business. The store was completely rebuilt and greatly improved in time for the 1978 Christmas season.

A strong policy of advertising and promotion together with active participation in business and community affairs has al- ways been a major part of the working philosophy of both Gordon Boswell and Felix Ankele. Both have served as president of the Texas State Florists Association and have held high positions in Florists' Transworld Delivery and the Society of American Florists. They have both been deeply involved in the civic affairs of Fort Worth ranging from the Jewel Charity Ball to the Air Force Association.

For 61 years, the firm of Gordon Boswell Flowers has grown with Fort Worth. It has made a business of providing Fort Worth residents with that something special that flowers bring to life.

Cantey, Hanger, Gooch, Munn & Collins

Law firm instrumental in Fort Worth's growth for 99 years

The present law firm (a partnership) had its origin in 1881 when William Capps and S. B. Cantey, Sr. formed a partnership under the name of Capps & Cantey. Its original office was on the second floor of a two-story building located at Seventh and Main Streets in Fort Worth — the site of the present Continental Life Insurance Building.

The firm was instrumental in having Armour and Swift locate its meat packing plants in Fort Worth, and also in the formation of the Stockyards Company, which acted as a gathering and sales place for supplying livestock to the meat packers for slaughter and processing.

Around the turn of the century, the firm represented the two largest electric holding companies in the nation — American Power & Light Company and Electric Bond & Share Company.

It was able to interest those two firms in what was then an infant electric generation and transmission business in Texas and particularly in Fort Worth. Cantey, Sr. was the principal negotiator. A merger resulted in the Fort Worth Power & Light Co., which ultimately became Texas Electric Service Company — the utility presently serving Fort Worth and large areas of west and north Texas.

The firm was able to interest Stone & Webster of New York in attempting to put together an integrated mass transportation system for Fort Worth. After considerable time, all systems were combined by either purchase or merger, and the Fort Worth Street Car Company was created. It was later reorganized into the Fort Worth Transit Company.

W. A. Hanger, who had served as state senator for Tarrant County, entered the firm shortly after the turn of the century and was primarily responsible for the "street car" emergence and existence.

Also coming with the firm in the early years of the 20th century was William

Samuel Benton Cantey, Sr., one of the firm's founders, about 1914.

Short; and the firm name became Capps, Cantey, Hanger & Short.

Short served for a number of years as president of the Fort Worth Independent School District in its early days.

Soon after the turn of the century, the firm moved to the eleventh floor of the Burk Burnett Building. It remained there until September 1, 1930, when it moved to the newly constructed Sinclair Building at Fifth and Main. It occupied the fifteenth and sixteenth floors until its move, in 1961, to the present location at First National Bank Building, where it occupies the top three floors.

Capps died in the late teens and Cantey died in the early 1920s. Mark McMahon and W. D. Smith came with the firm shortly after the turn of the century. In the early '20s Alfred McKnight and Gillis Johnson came with the firm, and were followed by S. B. Cantey, Jr. and R. K. Hanger, and, a little later by Warren Scarborough and J. A. (Tiny) Gooch. Gooch recently completed 50 years of active practice with the firm and is a past president of the Fort Worth Chamber of Commerce.

In 1930 the firm consisted of a total of eleven partners and associates and its name was changed to Cantey, Hanger & McMahon. A succession of "end" names were added and subtracted throughout the years that followed. Cantey, Hanger now has 42 partners and associates and employs an average of 50 non-lawyer personnel.

The firm has been active in all civic affairs of the city of Fort Worth and three streets in Fort Worth bear the names of deceased partners of the firm — Capps Street, Cantey Street and Hanger Street. Emory Cantey, the grandson of the founder, is an active partner in the firm.

Cantey, Hanger handles corporate, utility, taxation, labor, civil rights, antitrust, oil, energy, probate, insurance and civil trial matters.

Central Bank & Trust

Commitment to South Fort Worth led to bank's growth

South Fort Worth State Bank, 716 West Magnolia, in the 1950s.

When the South Fort Worth State Bank opened for business in July 1947, its location, 716 West Magnolia, was on the south side of the city in the heart of the medical district and only minutes from downtown.

But with the rapid growth and expansion of Fort Worth it was inevitable that the name South Fort Worth State Bank would become outdated and inaccurate. Downtown was getting closer and closer and south Fort Worth was getting further and further south of the bank's location. For this reason, in February 1972 during its 25th anniversary year, the name was appropriately changed to Central Bank & Trust.

To supplement the name change a new logo was developed. Graphically, it was a red C surrounding a blue state of Texas symbol with a white circle in the center. The purpose of the logo was threefold. The C which is nearly a circle is the symbol of strength and denotes an unbroken line of service. The state of Texas indicates the home of the bank and the white circle shows the ever-growing central area that it serves. The colors, red, white and blue are for the colors of both the state and United States flags.

During the '60s, after two major building additions of 4,000 square feet to the original 6,000 square feet, bank personnel saw that they were still outgrowing the facilities and began to think about a new building. The M.J. Neely School of Business at Texas Christian University conducted a survey in early 1970 and determined that in order to properly serve the area a banking facility of approximately 40,000 square feet was necessary.

Instead of moving out of the neighborhood when the original building had been outgrown, Central Bank and Trust expanded in its old location because, as bank officials put it, "we are committed to this neighborhood" — a basic policy which has lasted over the years. Additional land was purchased in the same vicinity and plans started for the new bank to face Rosedale at Hemphill on four city blocks.

Groundbreaking ceremonies took place on June 15, 1972 and the new complex was opened on October 1, 1973. Located at 777 West Rosedale, it occupies an entire block, and is bounded by West Rosedale on the north; Hemphill on the east; Magnolia on the south and Lipscomb on the west. The twelve drive-thru banking facility with commercial window is situated just west of the main building, surrounded by surface parking area. The adopted identification line, "Centralized Convenience" well describes the location, service and accessibility offered by this facility.

Central Bank again proved its commitment to the community when it began a long term mortgage financing program in 1978 in an effort to revitalize what it calls the "Mid South" section of Fort Worth. This neighborhood, which is the nearest residential area to downtown Fort Worth, adjoins the city's Health Services District, and contains a large number of medical facilities, hospitals, clinics and doctor and professional offices. Much of the residential property in the area had been run down and used as rental houses, but it was hoped that the long term mortgage financing, including the money it would take to restore the homes, would attract buyers to that section of the city. Another attractive and important feature of the neighborhood, especially when people became more energy conscious, was its central location and nearness to downtown Fort Worth where so many people work.

Central Bank invested heavily in the promotion of the "Mid South — An Era Reborn" program. It consisted of the fulltime attention of an assistant vice president, a color slide presentation, printed brochures, elaborate metal yard signs at houses the bank had financed, and a stained-glass logo depicting the style of the period, at the turn of the century, when most of the houses were built.

Few banks are willing to handle long term mortgages and even fewer go out and solicit them. Central Bank & Trust's goal in its "Mid South — An Era Reborn" program was to turn some of these old homes, mostly built in the early 1900s, back into prestigious places to live. Further proof of its policy that it is "committed to this neighborhood."

Central Bank & Trust today.

Champlin Petroleum Company

Spirit of adventure sparked creation of energy enterprise

On a chilly Christmas Day in 1916 in Enid, Oklahoma, Champlin Refining Company was born. H. H. Champlin, a 48-year-old Enid banker, had invested $12,000 in a well that was to be a one-time thing if no oil was found. As it turned out, oil did come in on the Garber-Covington oil field in Garfield County, Oklahoma.

The infant company began to grow and prosper. As output increased, the insightful Champlin saw the need for a refinery to process the oil being brought to the

Champlin Petroleum Company headquarters at 5301 Camp Bowie.

surface. Under his supervision, a refinery was built in Enid, just a few miles from the initial find.

With its ever-increasing size, Champlin Refining Company was becoming an attractive candidate for growth-oriented investors. The company to recognize Champlin's potential was The Chicago Corporation, a group of Chicago investors who were involved in natural gas exploration, in addition to their investments. The corporation seized the opportunity to merge with Champlin in 1954. The Chicago Corporation had its gas exploration and production operations based in the Continental Life Building in

Fort Worth. Soon after the merger, Champlin came to Fort Worth as Champlin Oil & Refining Company — a fully-integrated oil and gas company.

Fort Worth was to become home for Champlin. In 1955 Champlin built its offices at 5301 Camp Bowie Boulevard, which today remain the corporate headquarters for Champlin.

During the early 1950s, phenomenal growth occurred in the automotive industry, bringing about increasing demand for petroleum products. In light of this new market, Champlin initiated a major refinery expansion and modernization program in 1955 for the Enid Refinery.

Growth continued through the mid-1950s, with new exploration undertaken in Calgary, Canada, in 1957. Several retail stations were opened in the midwestern United States in the early 1960s.

Another merger materialized in October of 1964, with Champlin Oil & Refining Company becoming a wholly-owned subsidiary of Celanese Corporation — a diversified international producer of chemicals, fibers, plastics, paints and forest products. With this merger came Champlin Petroleum Company, the company's present name.

The year 1967 brought with it a major expansion of refining capacity — the addition of the Pontiac Refinery Corporation in Corpus Christi, Texas. In January 1970 Champlin and the Pontiac Refinery were sold by Celanese Corporation to Union Pacific. Champlin's size was doubled, as the Union Pacific oil and gas interests were consolidated into Champlin Petroleum Company.

Today, Champlin Petroleum Company is the largest of four operating companies of the Union Pacific Corporation. The fully-integrated oil company is engaged in exploration, development and production of crude oil and natural gas, the refining, transporting and marketing of petroleum products, and the manufacture of petrochemicals.

Champlin has experienced enormous growth with refining operations now in Wilmington, California; Corpus Christi,

Texas, (the old Pontiac Refining Plant); and in Enid, Oklahoma — the birthplace of Champlin Petroleum. All of these refining facilities have been expanded or are being expanded and modernized, increasing their capabilities by at least 50 percent. Champlin is exploring in countless locations all over the United States and Canada and operates or has interest in 23 natural gas plants found predominantly in Texas, Oklahoma and Wyoming. It is also involved in a world-scale ethylene plant in Corpus Christi, Texas in an effort to branch out into the area of petrochemicals.

The growth of Champlin Petroleum Company has paralleled that of the Fort

Worth area. The international airport just 25 minutes from downtown and the establishment of headquarters in Fort Worth for many large corporations are indicative of progress made in recent years.

In this encouraging economic climate, Champlin's revenues in 1979 exceeded $2 billion and its total assets climbed to nearly $1.5 billion. The company is now one of the largest in the Dallas/Fort Worth area.

Champlin has come a long way since that Christmas morning in 1916. Growth with Fort Worth is just as much a part of the company's future as it has been its past.

Color Tile, Inc.

From one do-it-yourself store to major chain

More than a quarter of a century ago, in 1953, the first Color Tile store opened its doors. The innovative concept, introduced in Joliet, Illinois, specialized in selling a broad assortment of floor and wall tiles and related products for the do-it-yourself home improvement market. Its unique merchandising techniques are still in use today.

The idea of the home-improvement "supermart" caught on and, by adding one new store per year, Color Tile grew to a chain of fourteen stores in 1968. In that year, Color Tile was acquired by the Tandy Corporation — headquartered in Fort Worth — and continued to expand during the following seven years with an average of 25 stores opened annually. In 1975, following the spin-off by Tandy Corporation of its businesses unrelated to consumer electronics, the Color Tile operations were transferred to Tandycrafts, Inc. In April of 1979, following yet another spin-off, Color Tile became Color Tile, Inc. — a major independent, publicly held corporation.

When the company was founded, the farsighted decision was made to focus its marketing strategy on the do-it-yourself homeowner. The first store was an 800 square foot, one story building — a humble beginning that would eventually lead to a nationwide chain. The unique concept called for large quantities of products to be neatly displayed in plain sight — supermarket fashion — to give full cash refunds on all unused tiles, to lend special installation tools, to provide friendly, personalized service, and to give free professional advice. The products

One of Color Tile's first retail stores.

and services give customers the more attractive alternative of improving their present homes rather than purchasing new ones.

By March, 1980, Color Tile operated 420 stores in 39 states, with plans for the next several years calling for new store openings at a fifteen to twenty percent growth rate over the prior year's number of stores. Three distribution centers — located in Texas, Maryland, and California — provide more than 220,000 square feet of warehouse space. Color Tile's first manufacturing facility, a wood parquet tile plant located in Melbourne, Arkansas, became operational in early 1980.

The company's executive offices are located in the Tandy Center complex in Fort Worth. Community involvement — an important part of Color Tile's philosophy — has prompted, in recent years, sponsorship by company executives of Junior Achievement projects and Career Day training sessions at local high schools, among other civic endeavors. All 2,400 employees are encouraged to participate in community affairs.

Chairman of the Board, President and Chief Executive Officer is John A. Wilson, of Fort Worth.

A contemporary Color Tile retail outlet.

Continental National Bank

Helping Fort Worth grow for more than 75 years

When J. G. Wilkinson became the first president of Continental Bank and Trust Company in 1903, Fort Worth was still living up to its cowtown image.

The advent of the railroad had just about put an end to the massive trail drives of longhorn cattle. But the dusty city where the West begins was still a stop on the old Chisholm Trail.

Joe Wilkinson knew the times were changing Fort Worth. And he liked what he saw. He'd been persuaded by his uncle, George Thompson Sr., to visit Fort Worth in 1902 and check out the possibility of establishing a bank.

Thompson had assembled a group of prominent local businessmen to form a new financial institution, and all agreed that if Wilkinson joined their venture, he would become the first president.

Wilkinson knew an opportunity when he saw it. He'd already been very successful in his home state of Tennessee, in the mercantile and banking business. By 1903 he and a partner had organized and were operating eleven banks throughout the South.

Texas was next on his list. On April 20, 1903, a new era in Fort Worth banking history had begun. With Thompson and Wilkinson as co-founders, Continental Bank and Trust opened in a small frame building on the corner of Houston and

Continental Plaza, the 40-story office tower bounded by Sixth and Seventh, Main and Commerce Streets, will become Continental National Bank's new home when completed in 1982.

Third. Under the careful management of Wilkinson, the new enterprise flourished, and in 1905 it moved to the corner of Seventh and Houston, into the former post office building.

It remained there until 1921, when the bank merged with the National Bank of Commerce. After the merger, the bank moved into the W. T. Waggoner Building at the corner of Eighth and Houston and changed its name to Continental National Bank.

Nine years after the merger and move, Wilkinson handed the financial reins over to his son. Harry H. Wilkinson was skillful in guiding the bank through the troubled times of the Great Depression. In the ten-year period ending in 1940, Continental National Bank increased its deposits from $9,859,354 to $19,570,089.

After pulling the bank through the Depression era, Wilkinson sold the greater portion of his stock to Ed H. Winton who succeeded him as president. Winton held the post until 1950, when the son of co-founder George Thompson Sr. took over. One of George Thompson Jr.'s first projects was to move the bank into a new building at its old location, Seventh and Houston.

With an exterior of Swedish marble and pink Roman brick, the five-story structure was heralded as one of the most beautiful in Fort Worth. A part of the old building remains in use today, comprising the base of the 30-story structure that currently houses the bank.

Under the leadership of Robert W. Gerrard — who became president in 1971 — the bank became affiliated in 1972 with Southwest Bancshares, a billion-dollar holding company headquartered in Houston.

Gerrard became CNB's fourth chairman of the board in November 1975 and John M. Stevenson succeeded him as the ninth and current president.

Under the guidance of Gerrard and Stevenson, Continental has continued its role as an innovator in Fort Worth banking services. With assets currently well in excess of a half-billion dollars, CNB has grown through aggressive, professional commercial lending skills and a retail program which offers its customers longer business hours and multiple downtown locations. Staffed by a young, imaginative team of officers, the institution has gained in market share through its commitment to the community and its successful campaign to serve, effectively, the middle commercial market.

A new off-shore branch in the Cayman Islands signifies CNB's commitment to growing international markets while Fort Worth area customers will be better served following the completion of CNB's new 40-story downtown home, Continental Plaza.

As a dynamic force behind the growth and prosperity of Fort Worth business, CNB helped a cowtown become a vital part of the ninth largest metropolitan area in the United States. With that same dedication, Continental National Bank will play an even greater role in Fort Worth's bright future.

This redstone building, originally the Fort Worth Post Office, corner of Seventh and Houston, was Continental's home from 1905 until 1921.

Dillard's Department Stores, Inc.

High principles contribute to phenomenal growth

The Dillard's Department Store success story began in 1938 when founder, William T. Dillard, invested $8,000 in a small store in Nashville, Arkansas, his wife's hometown.

By the start of the 1980 decade the Dillard's Department Store group had grown to 50 stores operating in seven states with sales nearing a half-billion dollars. Twenty-nine of the stores were in Texas, with others located in Arkansas,

Kansas, Louisiana, Missouri, New Mexico and Oklahoma.

It had long been William Dillard's belief that success in business results from opportunity, ability and the courage to follow convictions.

This philosophy, coupled with the company's three basic operating principles, are directly related to the phenomenal growth the company experienced.

The first principle of Dillard's is that

the customer is presented with the best merchandise available in famous name, nationally advertised products. Second, cost-control techniques and volume buying allow Dillard's to offer outstanding values at pleasing prices. The last principle, truth in advertising, is summed up by a plaque in Dillard's office: "Business without integrity is not good business, and in the long run will not be successful."

The growth program of the company had been two-pronged: acquisition and expansion through construction of new stores. Dillard's first move into Texas involved the 1956 acquisition of Mayer-Schmidt, the leading old-line department store serving East Texas. Dillard's Department Stores, Inc. was now a reality. Seeing the great potential of the Texas market, especially the Dallas-Fort Worth area, William Dillard set his sights on eventual expansion throughout the state.

Before he made this move, however, Dillard acquired Brown-Dunkin, a leading Tulsa retail institution, in 1960. In 1963 he acquired Pfeifers of Arkansas, with stores in Little Rock and Hot Springs. The Blass Department stores in Arkansas

A current Dillard store.

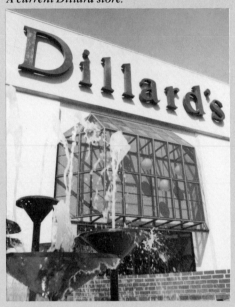

came under the Dillard's banner in 1964. In 1971 he acquired five Fedway stores from Federated Department Stores, entering four new markets in Corpus Christi, Wichita Falls and Longview, Texas, and Albuquerque, New Mexico.

Dillard's entered the Fort Worth market in 1974 with the purchase of the Leonard stores from the Tandy Corporation. These stores were steeped in the tradition and history of Fort Worth, having been established in 1918. The original acquisition included stores in downtown Fort Worth, Arlington, Irving and Northeast Mall.

The second part of Dillard's two-pronged growth program involved construction of new stores. The first Dillard suburban store was built in Austin in 1964. By the start of the 1980 decade 42 new stores had opened, with 23 located in Texas.

His early goal of entering the Dallas-Fort Worth market having been realized, Dillard in 1976 opened a 200,000-square-foot store in Ridgmar Mall — the first regional air-conditioned mall in Fort Worth. The next year, the 100,000-square-foot, totally remodeled downtown store opened and was one of the leading attractions of the unique Tandy Center. In October 1978, Dillard's added a 129,000-square-foot store in Seminary South, the first shopping center in Fort Worth. This new store meant customers could now find a Dillard's store in close proximity throughout Tarrant County.

Dillard's expanded into the Dallas market by opening stores in Valley View and Richardson Square Mall in 1979.

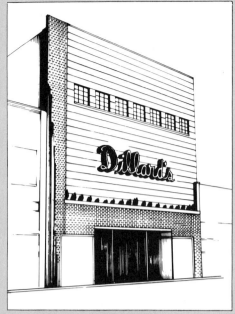

Drawing of original store in Nashville, Arkansas.

Further evidence of Dillard's belief in the Fort Worth area was the building of a 582,000-square-foot central distribution center at Northstar Industrial Park that same year. Engineering provisions were made for future expansion to double the initial size of the center.

Dillard's Department Store plans for the future are simple — to strengthen market position through the acquisition and construction of more stores in the rapidly growing Southwest, as well as continually up-dating and modernizing existing stores. It's the formula William Dillard has used for more than 40 years, and it has worked phenomenally.

The Dunlap Company

From the 1890s to the 1980s... a family tradition continues

The roots of The Dunlap Company reach back to 1893 when H. G. Dunlap opened his first store in Wagoner, Indian Territory (now Oklahoma). The Star Store sold dry goods and groceries, livestock and coffins — usually on credit to surrounding farmers who leased their land from the Creek nation. When the federal government cancelled all Indian land leases, Dunlap was unable to collect his accounts and was forced to close his store. He joined his three sons, Ira, Carl and Clyde in nearby Coweta, to help run their cash store. The store proved so successful that in a few years they had expanded to twelve stores in small eastern Oklahoma towns.

At the age of fifteen, in 1916, Retha R. Martin went to work full time for the Dunlap Brothers. Their offer of $25 per month was too good to refuse! The company continued to open new stores in Oklahoma and by 1919 had 20 stores. In 1920 business was profitable and the Dunlap family retired. They began closing their stores and in 1921 moved to California.

After closing the eleven remaining stores, Martin was to follow and start a new group of stores in the Los Angeles area. Instead, he stayed in Eufaula, Oklahoma. Borrowing $2,000, he purchased, in 1923, 40 percent interest in the last store under the Dunlap name. Although sales that year were only $40,000, Martin paid a $10,000 dividend. It was the new beginning for a business that was already more than 30 years old.

During the Depression, profits were small but the company prospered. Four new stores were opened in 1933. By 1943 there were fourteen stores located primarily in west Texas and New Mexico, so the company moved its headquarters from Oklahoma to Lubbock. That same

year majority ownership was acquired by the Martin family.

Shortly after acquiring Stripling's of Fort Worth in 1977, headquarters was moved to Fort Worth.

Interestingly enough, in the same year that H. G. Dunlap was opening his store in Wagoner, Wesley Capers Stripling — the founder of the W.C. Stripling Company — was opening his first store in Fort Worth. He had previously opened stores in Alvord and Bowie. The store was 25 feet wide and located on Houston Street between First and Second Streets, near the construction site of the new Tarrant County Court House. His fixtures for the store were made from wooden packing cases in which his merchandise was shipped. In his entire first year of operation in Fort Worth, he spent only $8 for advertising. In 1900, Stripling moved his family to Fort Worth and closed his other facilities.

As business prospered the store became larger and by 1912, Stripling's occupied all of the Houston Street side of the block. Will Stripling, eldest son of W. C. Stripling, joined his father as a prominent figure in the store and became president after his father died in 1934.

Due to rapid growth of the store and the city, Will Stripling set about acquiring additional buildings on Main Street and by 1936 had purchased the balance of the

By 1912, Stripling's had expanded to include this building on Main Street and mounted the second largest over-the-street sign in the United States (left).

Sidewalk sales were popular even in the early 1900s at Stripling's one price cash store. The original Houston Street store is the building to the left (below).

block. Stripling's had become a landmark in downtown Fort Worth.

With the growth of the city, suburban stores became popular. In 1962 Stripling's opened its first branch store at Seminary South Shopping Center, followed by another store in North East Mall in 1971, and one in Ridgmar Mall in 1976.

Today, The Dunlap Company remains family owned and operated by Retha R. Martin and sons, Reginald and Edward, and is comprised of 20 specialty department stores in Texas, Oklahoma, New Mexico and Missouri. These include: Dunlap's of Lubbock, Midland, Odessa, Big Spring, Pampa, Victoria, Farmington, Hobbs and Santa Fe; Grissom's of Abilene; Goldstein-Migel of Waco; Vandever's of Tulsa and Bartlesville; The White House of El Paso and Las Cruces; Hirsch's of St. Joseph; Vandever-Ramsay of Joplin; and the most recent acquisition, Stripling's of Fort Worth.

The Martins are committed to the concept of local autonomy for each of their stores — a tradition that has served well in the past and bodes well for the future.

Equitable General Insurance Group

Fort Worth's largest insurance company built on satisfying, automated services

The search was over. The stage was set. After two years of intensive research and study, The Equitable Life Assurance Society of the United States had found the perfect vehicle for marketing property and casualty insurance through the company's nationwide sales force of more than 6,000 life insurance agents.

The pursuit was consummated in December, 1974 when The Equitable purchased Houston General Insurance Company — a medium-sized Fort Worth insurance concern selling multiple lines of insurance in 38 states. From the sale emerged two distinct and separate enterprises now comprising the Equitable General Insurance Group. The first was Equitable General Insurance Company, which would launch The Equitable's efforts into the general insurance field, and the second was a new Houston General.

When The Equitable acquired the company, it presented Equitable General with an unparalleled challenge — to put together in the short period of eleven months a complete operating and service facility to begin marketing activity in eight states in the Southwest.

The odds were great. Never before had such an undertaking been accomplished in so brief a time. Equitable General was given the opportunity to build an insurance operation to its own specification. In January 1975, a determined project team under the leadership of President Glenn B. Morris, began preliminary plans to create a new and distinctive property and casualty concern.

Equitable General's twin nine-story tower complex (above).

Coy Eklund, president and chief executive officer of The Equitable, and Glenn B. Morris, president and chief executive officer of The Equitable General Insurance, break ground on December 9, 1976 for Equitable General's new home office building.

At first there was nothing but empty space at the company's modest headquarters located on two floors of the Ridglea Bank Building. Soon offices began to spring up and countless projects were established. Time and cost frames were created. Critical paths were set — all forming a network of action pointing to "Go" on January 2, 1976.

Meanwhile, adjacent to the home office, the crux of Equitable General's operation — the SERV-U CENTER — was being developed. Advance technology was implemented and individually designed systems were set in motion. All efforts were geared toward the creation of a productive telephone contract facility which would serve policyholder needs quickly and efficiently.

During the first eight months of 1975, systems and procedures of the SERV-U CENTER were carefully planned and utilized. The remaining months were devoted to simulating operations and testing the effectiveness of numerous integrated systems. On January 2, 1976 the center had surpassed all expectations. As Equitable General's first policy rolled off the computer, The Equitable's property and casualty facility unfolded a new era of automated business processing.

At the same time, in detached offices located in downtown Fort Worth, Houston General was engaged in a separate operation — writing all forms of property and casualty insurance through independent agents in Texas and several adjoining states. Although supporting and complementing the activities of Equitable General, Houston General was dominated by specialists in commercial lines of insurance. It was destined, therefore, that in December 1977, the company became an exclusive commercial lines insurance carrier. Since that time, Houston General has constantly strengthened its financial base and service, becoming recognized throughout the area as "The Commercial Lines People."

Anticipating the dramatic growth of Equitable General Insurance Group, approval was granted by The Equitable in fall 1976 for construction of a new nine-story home office building. The structure was completed in May 1978, and in 1980 a second tower was added to help house the group's more than 1,100 employees.

Presently serving 25 states and committed to nationwide expansion in the years to come, Equitable General now operates in a totally automated environment. Recognized worldwide for the resolute marriage of many unique and individual systems, hundreds of insurance executives from countries around the globe have visited the facilities of Equitable General — referred to by IBM as "The Paperless Insurance Company."

Governed by the doctrine of "Coming Right with People," Equitable General Insurance Group will continue, as in the past, to substantiate and uphold the American way of life by meeting the company's social responsibility in all facets of its operations. That is why in its short and exciting history, Equitable General has grown into the largest insurance concern in Fort Worth and reigns supreme among the larger southwestern insurance companies of the nation.

Ernst & Whinney

Since 1919 an effective contributor to Fort Worth

Ernst & Whinney was organized in June 1903 in Cleveland, Ohio by brothers A. C. and T. C. Ernst with the firm name of Ernst & Ernst (changed in 1979 to Ernst & Whinney). This two-man accounting practice has since grown to more than 14,000 people with over 300 offices in some 70 countries.

Building an accounting practice was a difficult task in those early days, and in October 1906, T. C. Ernst elected to withdraw from the firm and go into the commercial laundry business. Annual billings for services by that time had reached $34,300; today the annual figure is more than $550 million.

A. C. Ernst, who continued as managing partner until his death in 1948, early recognized the potential growth of Texas. By 1922 the firm had opened offices in Fort Worth, Dallas, Houston and San Antonio. The Fort Worth office was opened in 1919 with offices in the Burton Building. Ernst & Ernst was the first national accounting firm in the city.

The firm's success is largely due to A. C. Ernst's emphasis on three principles. First, offer clients a wide variety of high-quality business services; second, build staff and grow from within (there have been few mergers); and third, each office should do everything possible to be an effective contributor to its community.

In the early 1920s, the firm pioneered in offering diversified services to its clients, such as industrial engineering, financial planning, organization and personnel studies, various other management consulting services, and in more recent years, a high degree of specialization in computer technology. The firm also stressed industry specialization and established leading positions in a number of industries — notably banking, insurance, and health care.

Included among Ernst & Whinney's U.S. audit clients are about 50 of the 200 largest banks (including Bank of America), about 50 of the 200 largest life insurance companies, and about 30 of the 100 largest nongovernmental hospitals. The firm presently has 27 active industry committees, each geared to follow developments within those 27 industries and available to counsel with its professionals and clients.

The "growth from within" concept is best illustrated by the firm's National Education Center in Cleveland. This 30,000 square-foot facility — the only one of its kind — incorporates the best features of contemporary teaching techniques in a setting conducive to study and is attended by more than 7,000 staff members each year.

Two notable exceptions to the "growth from within" principle were the mergers with the accounting practices of Whinney, Murray & Co. of the United Kingdom in 1979, and S. D. Leidesdorf & Co., a prestigious New York-based firm, in 1978. For more than 50 years, services to clients in Europe, Africa, Australia and Asia were principally through affiliation with the London-based Whinney, Murray & Co.

A. C. Ernst, managing partner until his death in 1948.

After years of study, it was decided that much would be gained, particularly for clients, by merging the two firms, which was accomplished on July 1, 1979, with the name appropriately changed to Ernst & Whinney. With the name change, the firm became truly international in every respect.

The emphasis on "community service" is well illustrated by the support, both in time and money, of the Fort Worth community by the firm's Fort Worth office. Executives and staff have been active through the years in the Chamber of Commerce, United Way, the Arts Council and its related organizations, Junior Achievement, Rotary Club, Youth Orchestra, Casa Manana, and many similar organizations, serving in capacities ranging from president to campaign worker to fund drive chairman to committee worker.

Of course, the principal activity has been service to the business community, contributing to the economic growth of Fort Worth. A representative list of clients back in the 1920s would include Carter Publications, Monnig's Dry Goods, Acme Brick, Mrs. Baird's Bakery, Texas Hotel, Tandy Leather, Texas Christian University, All Saints Hospital, Burnett Estate, Chamber of Commerce, Fort Worth Independent School District, Fort Worth National Bank, Fort Worth Children's Hospital, Pangburn Company, the old Fort Worth Baseball Club (Fort Worth Cats), and many other pioneer companies not only in Fort Worth, but throughout west Texas.

Ernst & Whinney has always believed strongly in aid to education, conducting educators' symposiums, supporting doctoral fellowship programs, career education programs, and generally recognizing the importance of education to the future of the accounting profession, the business community and the nation.

In the 77-year history of the firm, there have been only four managing partners — A. C. Ernst, Hassel Tippitt, Richard T. Baker, and currently Ray Groves. In the 61-year history of the Fort Worth office, there have been only six executives in charge — George Carlson, Ben Irby, George Kirby, John Walker, Norwood Dixon, and currently R. E. Wilkin.

In its literature, Ernst & Whinney describes its purpose — "to provide professional services that we're proud of, to clients that we're proud of, for fees that are fair and reasonable to both our clients and ourselves."

The First National Bank of Fort Worth

Helping Fort Worth grow for more than 100 years

When Captain Martin B. Loyd, a Civil War veteran and native Kentuckian, drove his wagon into Fort Worth in 1870, he was settling into a young town just coming of age with saloons, gambling houses and hotels, yet thirsting for the banking services he would soon establish.

Faced with a demand for beef by the industrialized eastern states, Texas became the state the Easterners turned to for satisfaction. Texas cattle drovers began driving herds of longhorns along the Baxter Springs and Chisholm Trails, and Fort Worth soon became a popular trail town — the last friendly stop before drovers crossed the Red River into hostile Indian territory. The town also became a stopping place for adventurers heading for the California hills, but before long Easterners began migrating to Fort Worth to settle, not just to pass through.

But the bank notes which the Easterners brought with them were foreign to area merchants. The collapse of the banking system in the West and the South during the Civil War left only gold and silver in Texas tills. The bank notes were used widely in the East, however, where conversion to standardized national currency was widespread after the enactment of the National Banking Act in 1864.

Recognizing the importance of the notes to the local economy and the potential profit to be made, Loyd made it his business to exchange the notes for coins. In 1873 he joined Clyde P. Markley of California to form the California and Texas Bank of Loyd, Markley and Company. But it soon became apparent the

Captain Martin B. Loyd, founder of the First National Bank of Fort Worth.

national bank notes had acquired a reputation for soundness, so Loyd withdrew from the California and Texas Bank and in January 1877 he and several associates, none of whom was a professional banker, organized the First National Bank of Fort Worth. The original board included a doctor, several cattlemen, storekeepers and veterans of the Confederate Army.

First National acquired the distinction of being the first bank in the city to receive a national banking charter, granted on March 21, 1877. It was the ninth national banking charter granted in Texas

and number 2,349 in the nation. On April 23, 1877, First National Bank of Fort Worth opened its doors for business with capital of $50,000, and at the close of the first day's business, deposits were $72,000.

At the end of 1877 the bank's deposits had increased to $220,000, and in January 1878 the board voted to pay a dividend of twelve percent, the first ever declared in the city. And just one year later, First National became the first bank in the city to invest in United States savings bonds, to the tune of $50,000.

The growth of the First National Bank paralleled that of the cattle industry, and a young cattleman, Samuel Burk Burnett, joined the original board of directors in 1883. He married the daughter of Captain Loyd, and today their descendents still take an active role in the life of the bank, serving on the board of directors.

In 1912, the same year as the death of Captain Loyd, First National moved into the city's first "skyscraper," a ten-story building at Seventh and Houston. The last remembered words of Loyd were, "Damn my soul, you'll never fill that building," but it had to be doubled in size in 1926.

On February 19, 1930, the threat of a run on First National was successfully avoided when some of the town's most prominent businessmen stood atop desks in the middle of the lobby pleading with depositors to leave their funds in the bank. Sheriff Red Wright circulated through the crowd passing out hot dogs, and depositors were told they could use their passbooks for free admission to the

Majestic Theatre, which promptly diverted the attention of 100 of them.

A newspaper account of the attempted run told of the Hotel Texas orchestra playing "Home Sweet Home" at one end of the lobby while another played "Singing in the Rain" at the opposite end.

After avoiding the run and keeping its doors open for business, First National continued its pioneering growth. By establishing an installment loan department in 1935, it became one of the first banks in Fort Worth to offer consumer loans.

When downtown banks were just beginning to offer free parking and motor facilities in the late 1950s, First National began searching for land for a new home, and in 1961 the present eighteen-story

Fort Worth's first "skyscraper," at Seventh and Houston, in 1912. Captain Loyd said, "You'll never fill that building."

structure across from Burnett Park was completed. At the time, Anne Burnett Tandy was as concerned about the new building being too small as her great-grandfather, Captain Loyd, had been about the old building being too large.

In 1972 a move was made to form a new corporate image — that of "First of Fort Worth" — and the now familiar "1FW" symbol, which identifies the bank to all Fort Worthians, was designed. In the same year First National became the lead bank in the newly formed First United Bancorporation, a multi-bank holding company which today numbers thirteen subsidiary banks and two bank-related businesses.

Still enjoying a prominent position in the life of Fort Worth, the First National now ranks 138th in the nation in size with total assets of $1,310,636,000.

Fort Worth & Denver Railway

Development of Texas a part of company's rich tradition

Known historically as "Fort Worth's own railway," the Fort Worth & Denver Railway was chartered by the Texas legislature on May 26, 1873, to build a railroad from Fort Worth in a northwesterly direction to the Texas-New Mexico border.

The charter was drafted by Colonel Warren H. H. Lawrence, a Fort Worth business and civic leader and was the pet project of another early Fort Worth pioneer, Major K. M. Van Zandt, a member of the legislature. Thus, Fort Worth had its first railway, at least on paper.

Fort Worth & Denver directors dispatched an engineering crew on September 8, 1873, to survey a suitable route for the line. Only 10 days later, however, the crew was dismissed because the failure of the New York brokerage house of Jay Cooke & Company set off a nationwide financial panic.

The resultant depression was a crippling blow to Fort Worth & Denver backers, and it was to be eight years before the first spike on the new railway was driven. In the meantime, the Texas & Pacific Railroad became the first railroad to serve Fort Worth.

In 1881, Fort Worth & Denver directors made an agreement with General Grenville M. Dodge, famed as the builder of the Union Pacific Railroad, giving him complete control of construction. Grad-

The Fort Worth yard and roundhouse about 1888.

ing began at Hodge, about five miles north of Fort Worth, on November 27, 1881.

By the summer of 1882, the line had reached Wichita Falls. Three years later, FW&D rails were joined with those of the Denver, Texas & Fort Worth Railroad (now part of the Colorado & Southern Railway Company) at Union Park, New Mexico. Through train service between Denver and Fort Worth began on April 1, 1888.

The railway operated over Texas & Pacific trackage between Hodge and Fort Worth until 1890, when Fort Worth & Denver Terminal Railway Company was

chartered to build from Hodge to Fort Worth and to construct terminal facilities in Fort Worth.

In 1908, the Colorado & Southern Railway Company, as well as the trackage of the Fort Worth & Denver Railway Company, were acquired by the Chicago, Burlington & Quincy Railroad, which had pushed its lines from modest beginnings in 1849 through the Midwest to Denver and beyond.

Today, the words "Burlington Northern" appear on the big green locomotives and rolling stock seen with increasing frequency throughout the Fort Worth area.

Burlington Northern was formed by the merger of Chicago, Burlington & Quincy with the Great Northern, Northern Pacific, and the Spokane, Portland & Seattle railways on March 2, 1970. Burlington Northern's predecessor companies brought a rich heritage to the new enterprise. These pioneer lines, which played a major role in the opening of the West, were traditionally carriers of farm, forest, and mine products — still the backbone of Burlington Northern's commerce. Non-rail natural resource activities assumed increased importance as the years passed.

Burlington Northern is a diversified transportation company *and* a growing natural resources company, offering a unique combination of assets to a world facing increasing shortages of food, fiber, energy and minerals.

As a member of the Burlington Northern family, the Fort Worth & Denver Railway maintains the rich tradition it has shared during the development of Texas and Fort Worth. Today, Fort Worth & Denver operations span the nearly 800 miles between Texline and Galveston. But the Fort Worth & Denver Railway is linked to its headquarters city in many ways. Officers of Fort Worth's three largest banks had a part in the railway's history. Major Van Zandt, who secured passage of the charter legislation, was for many years head of the Fort Worth National Bank and served on the Fort Worth & Denver board of directors until his death in 1930 at the age of 93. Captain M. B. Loyd, one of the founders of Fort Worth's First National Bank, was a signer of the railway's articles of incorporation. Colonel Morgan Jones, longtime Fort Worth and Denver president, was chief executive of the Continental Bank & Trust Company, predecessor of the present Continental National Bank. Jones was also responsible for construction of Fort Worth's first street railway (mule drawn) as well as the city's first electric power plant.

A unit coal train near Estelline, Texas enroute to Fort Worth.

In 1925, the corporate headquarters of the Fort Worth & Denver Railway were moved into the newly-completed Fort Worth Club Building, making it possible to finance the construction of what is now a Fort Worth landmark. Fifty-five years later, the Fort Worth & Denver Railway remains as the building's only original tenant.

The Fort Worth National Bank

A bank...and the city whose name it proudly bears

Since 1873 Fort Worth and The Fort Worth National Bank have been growing together. Their histories are inextricably intertwined — for the same people who built the bank to its present position as a billion dollar financial institution were also builders of Fort Worth. Their efforts and handiwork are ingrained deeply in the fabric of the city's history, past and present.

The Fort Worth National Bank came into existence in January 1873 as a private banking house founded by two Confederate veterans — Thomas A. Tidball and John B. Wilson — who migrated to the frontier town of 2,000 residents in the aftermath of the Civil War, hoping to begin a new life. Tidball and Wilson, Bankers, began operations in a two-story building on Weatherford Street. In August 1874, their firm was reorganized under the name of Tidball, Van Zandt and Company, with Major K. M. Van Zandt as president — a position he was to hold for the next 56 years. The private bank became The Fort Worth National Bank in 1884 with the issuance of a federal charter, and embarked on an odyssey of sustained growth paralleling that of the city whose name it proudly bears.

Major Van Zandt died on March 19, 1930, and the presidency passed to Robert Ellison Harding. To Harding and his associates fell the task of guiding the bank through the perilous years of the Depression, the challenges of World War II, and the post-war boom. With Harding's election as chairman of the board on January 9, 1952, Estil A. Vance became the bank's third president. Harding's 49-

In an 1876 edition of the Fort Worth Democrat, *Captain B. B. Paddock, editor, wrote "Tidball, Van Zandt and Company are having some elegant touches made to the office furniture of their banking establishment. The counters and desks have been varnished and polished and the iron railing painted and gilded, indicative of the character of the firm — as solid as iron, as pure as gold." This is a view of the bank's interior. In 1884, the private bank was renamed The Fort Worth National Bank.*

year career with The Fort Worth National ended with his death in February 1952. He was succeeded as board chairman by H. B. Fuqua, chairman of the board of Texas Pacific Coal and Oil Company.

In August 1952, the bank moved into its fifth home, a new fifteen-story building at Seventh and Houston streets. Lewis H. Bond, who had joined the bank in 1952 as a petroleum engineer, was named successor to Vance, who died in March 1959. In January 1969, in the largest downtown real estate transaction in the history of the city, The Fort Worth National announced the acquisition of more than four blocks as a site for a new bank building and connecting motor bank and parking garage. Construction on the new building began on April 29, 1971, and the formal opening of the 37-story glass-sheathed tower took place on April 22, 1974.

Fuqua retired on January 19, 1971, after 22 years as a member of the board and eighteen years as chairman, and on January 27, 1972, Lewis Bond was elevated to chairman of the board of the bank and Bayard H. Friedman became The Fort Worth National's fifth president. Friedman was elected board chairman on January 22, 1976, and Joseph M. Grant succeeded him as president.

The Fort Worth National Corporation, a bank holding company, was organized on April 30, 1970, with The Fort Worth National as its lead bank. Lewis Bond was named chairman of the board and O. Roy Stevenson became president of the holding company. On April 25, 1974 the name of the corporation was changed to Texas American Bancshares Inc. — to more accurately reflect the statewide scope of its operations. At the end of 1979, Texas American Bancshares had twelve member banks located in key areas of the state, with total assets in excess of $2.9 billion.

The Fort Worth National Bank has played a major role in the growth of the economy of Fort Worth and of West Texas — first as a major factor in the fight to bring the railroad to the city and later by providing financial support and credit expertise in the development of the meat packing, grain, cotton, and oil industries.

With total assets in excess of $1.5 billion at the end of 1979, The Fort Worth National Bank today is one of the Southwest's largest banking institutions. Its staff of more than 900 officers and employees has a heritage of dedicated service to community and customers dating back more than a century.

Now, in its second century of service, the bank and its people are dedicated to a continuation of this heritage.

This 37-story glass-sheathed tower, with Alexander Calder's "The Eagle" in the foreground, is the current home of The Fort Worth National Bank, the sixth in the bank's history dating back to January 1873. The building, designed by architect John Portman, was formally opened on April 22, 1974.

Fort Worth Star-Telegram

Success of Fort Worth parallels that of newspaper

Amon Carter, the future and prosperity all arrived in Fort Worth about the same time. The year was 1905 and Fort Worth finally was rising above its past boom-or-bust cowtown origin. West Texas, on the eastern rim of which the city had been built, was still a great prairie void. Carter, a master salesman, was preparing to join a new publication, the *Star,* as advertising manager.

His title was misleading. Not only was he ad manager, he was the entire sales staff, and when the newspaper began publishing early in 1906, Amon Carter sold every ad in the first edition.

From that moment, ascension of Amon

The Fort Worth Star-Telegram has never missed a day of publication or delivery in three-quarters of a century. Subscribers received their newspapers even when they were delivered by one-mule-powered vehicles.

Carter, Fort Worth and West Texas were bound together, and the success of all parallels that of the *Star-Telegram*.

Chronology of the *Star-Telegram* is simple enough. First published February 1, 1906 as the *Star*, the newspaper merged with the *Telegram* three years later, New Year's Day 1909. November 1, 1925, the *Star-Telegram* absorbed the Fort Worth *Record* and became a full-time morning and evening publication. November 8, 1974, the *Fort Worth Star-Telegram* was purchased by Capital Cities Communications, Inc.

The substance of the *Star-Telegram* and its history, however, is capsulized in the words of Dr. DeWitt Reddick, a nationally recognized journalism expert and scholar. He said of the *Star-Telegram,*

"I don't believe any newspaper, anywhere, at any time, ever gave so much to its area."

Amon Carter, who rose from ad manager of the tiny *Star* to become majority owner-publisher of the *Star-Telegram* and an international celebrity, early devised the formula for success of his newspaper. "When the lake rises, the boat will rise, too," he said, and set his newspaper on a course of public service for Fort Worth and West Texas.

Within three decades the *Star-Telegram* became Texas' largest newspaper, the first with a circulation of 200,000, then the largest newspaper in the southern half of the United States.

Its constituency lived in a 250,000 square mile region west of Fort Worth, one of the largest circulation areas in newspaper history. The *Star-Telegram,* by the 1940s, was delivered more than 700 miles west, from the Texas panhandle to the Rio Grande, into 1,100 towns with thirteen separate editions.

However large the newspaper became, its focus always was on public service to Fort Worth and West Texas. The *Star-Telegram* is credited with causing the creation of Texas Tech University and Big Bend National Park, innumerable state parks and highways, even town libraries in small villages of early West Texas.

Meanwhile, in Fort Worth, the newspaper helped build the city in all ways, from formation of the first zoo society to fund-raising for the Texas Christian University football stadium, from sponsorship of public Christmas celebrations to

The Fort Worth Star-Telegram at 400 West Seventh Street has grown from a one-room business to these modern structures which spread over most of two blocks.

musical concerts, to the raising of millions of dollars for charities — and always maintaining its First Amendment responsibility of providing local, state, national and international news to readers.

Under Carter's direction, and later that of his son, Amon Carter Jr., the *Star-Telegram* covered the news events, then provided more. Disasters, for example, would be reported fully in the *Star-Telegram,* then the newspaper's second face would establish a fund and raise money for victims of tornadoes and floods and other natural catastrophes.

When Amon Carter died in 1955, his communications empire had grown from a small fledgling newspaper to become the state's largest morning and evening publication. There was a television station (the South's first) and one of America's most powerful radio stations.

But Amon Carter also left behind a legacy of public service that continues under the direction of President and Editorial Chairman Phillip J. Meek, and Capital Cities Communications, Inc.

In the first five years after being sold to Capital Cities, the newspaper's annual charitable contributions to Fort Worth and Tarrant County increased fourfold. In addition, at the request of the *Star-Telegram,* Capital Cities Foundation made grants to Fort Worth institutions of nearly $100,000.

In three-quarters of a century, the *Star-Telegram's* involvement in Fort Worth and West Texas has ranged from a time when its reporters traveled by horseback and slept on the prairies to coverage of America's latest space explorations.

Its technology has gone from early pen-and-ink-written stories to computer print-outs. West Texas has grown from a vast, almost empty plains to one of Texas' most valuable agriculture and oil regions. Fort Worth, the little cowtown "Where the West Begins," has moved from a stockyards economy to the diversity of aerospace.

And the *Star-Telegram* has been there to assist the growth, to report on the development of a town and a region. The *Star-Telegram* still is rising with Fort Worth. In the late 1970s the *Star-Telegram* was the fastest-growing major metropolitan daily newspaper in America.

Freese and Nichols, Inc.

Designing solutions to environmental problems for eight decades

Freese and Nichols, Inc., has evolved from a one-man engineering practice founded in 1894 into one of the leading consulting engineering firms in the Southwest.

John Blackstock Hawley came to Fort Worth in 1890 to install the city's new water works system. Hawley believed the United States was destined to become a nation of great cities, and he knew this growth would bring many environmental

This side channel spillway on Eagle Mountain Lake was constructed to supplement the original spillway designed by the firm in the late 1920s.

The Rolling Hills 80 million-gallon-per-day water treatment plant is part of the Fort Worth water supply system designed by Freese and Nichols, Inc.

problems, with the most crucial relating to water supply and sewerage. In 1894, after the completion of the new water system, he established his practice as a water and sanitary engineer in Fort Worth.

He served as city engineer for the City of Fort Worth from 1897 to 1907, a position which permitted him to take outside engineering assignments. Typical of his work then was the design of a well water system for the city of Itasca, Texas, in 1897. The standpipe for the system is still in service.

As cities grew, so did John Hawley's engineering practice. During the next decade his assignments included work in Mexico, Cuba and Panama, where he estimated the cost of completing the Panama Canal for a group of private investors. He continued his involvement with the water needs of Fort Worth as a member of the engineering planning committee for Lake Worth.

In World War I Hawley was commanding officer of the 503rd Engineers, AEF, and engineer-in-charge-of-construction for the docks at Saint-Nazaire, France. After the war Major Hawley returned to Fort Worth, and in 1921 he designed and supervised construction of a water purification and sewage disposal system

for Fort Worth.

In 1922 Simon W. Freese joined the firm, and in 1927 was named a partner. That same year Marvin C. Nichols started to work for Hawley and Freese and became a partner in 1928. The firm's name was changed to Hawley, Freese and Nichols in 1930 and remained so until Major Hawley retired from active practice in 1938.

Throughout its growth the firm continued its involvement with the water needs of Fort Worth and in 1927 designed the Eagle Mountain and Bridgeport Reservoirs on the West Fork of the Trinity River. These reservoirs were among the first in the nation designed for water supply, flood control and recreation.

During World War II the firm designed and furnished engineering supervision for fourteen military facilities in Texas, Louisiana, Mississippi and Florida. These facilities included the Pantex Ordnance Plant at Amarillo, Texas — one of the largest in the country — and a Naval Air Base at Houma, Louisiana.

In 1946 the company became involved with the newly formed Colorado River Municipal Water District, which pioneered the idea in west Texas of cities forming an association to provide water for member cities. Today it provides water for several west Texas cities, the Permian Basin Oil Field for the secondary recovery of oil, and recreational facilities for 1.25 million people.

In 1968 a branch office was opened in Austin. The firm was incorporated in 1977, and Simon W. Freese was named chairman of the board — a position he still holds.

Today Freese and Nichols' projects can be found throughout Texas. Many of the dams, treatment plants and other facilities designed by Major Hawley are still being used, including parts of the masonry structure of the Fort Worth Water Works installed in 1890. One of the most complete civil engineering libraries in the nation is housed in the firm's offices on Lamar Street in downtown Fort Worth. Freese and Nichols has played vital roles in the design of the Dallas/Fort Worth Turnpike, the DFW Airport and the expansion of Arlington Stadium for major league baseball. Currently it is working on plans for meeting Fort Worth's water needs through the year 2020.

While Major Hawley's original specialties of waterworks and sewerage remain a major aspect of the firm's work, Freese and Nichols has expanded to meet new challenges. It offers comprehensive service in environmental control for cities and industry, municipal engineering and planning, feasibility studies and in other areas of civil and hydraulic engineering and regional planning. Freese and Nichols will continue to meet the new needs of people and their cities in the tradition established by Major Hawley.

Gearhart Industries, Inc.

Success is in its numbers

Gearhart Industries, Inc., 1980.

In a tin shed — with $10,000 and their own family cars — two dynamic, innovative young engineers started what is now a multimillion dollar oil well service and supply company.

Gearhart Industries, Inc., "born and raised" in Fort Worth, celebrated its silver anniversary in 1980. And for Marvin Gearhart, president, chairman and co-founder, there was much to celebrate. Gearhart saw his small, ambitious company develop into a high technology industry leader. But like any American business-hero story, the young company has had many obstacles to overcome.

Go Oil Well Services Inc. — as the company was first named — had its first job in Corsicana, where oil was being found at shallow depths. An independent oil operator had a well that needed logging and perforating. Even with their "handmade" truck unfinished in the shed, the two engineers, Marvin Gearhart and Harold Owen, couldn't pass up such an opportunity. They rented a trailer to carry supplies and made a jet-perforating-gun to shoot the well. Their profit was small but the project resulted in the formation of a new company — Go Wireline Perforating.

The first big break came in Oil City, Louisiana. With a half-ton panel truck purchased on credit, the partners set off to find some perforating work. But no one would hire them, paying little attention to their claim of having the "world's best" perforating charges. Finally an independent oil operator gave them a chance to work, with one small catch — they'd have to do the work "for free." They took the job and with it established their reputation. The well operator hit a gusher — big enough that people began to go out of their way to find Go Wireline.

Go was trying to enter the growing "jet" perforating field which was quickly replacing the older "bullet" form of well perforating. Seven companies had carefully pooled all of their patents, however, making it difficult — if not impossible — for outsiders to get a license and break into that segment of the market. When Go couldn't obtain a license to operate within that pool, it perfected its own charges. The new charges, using a unique copper liner manufacturing process, were estimated to penetrate 20 percent deeper into formation for half the cost. One entity of the pooling seven sued

Go, alleging trade secret knowledge. Hoping for a breakup in the pool, Go fought back with two lawsuits of its own.

In the event of a breakup of the seven (which would leave the wireline service field wide open), Go had a major decision to make — to stay in the wireline service business company, or become an equipment supplier. It decided on the latter. Go Wireline won its suits, and the pool breakup finally occurred in 1962.

Go's decision to become a supplier was at that time correct. It remained in wireline business, but as a manufacturer and supplier this time, for several years. With the availability of perforating supplies and equipment, dozens of independent wireline service companies were formed, and Go supplied them. In fact, six independent wireline service companies that Go now supplied were its own spinoffs. Not only did Go supply the companies, but also helped them get started financially and offered technical advice.

In the spring of 1969 the company made its first major strategic maneuver. The six wireline companies that had spun-off into independent wireline service companies were back, forming a subsidiary called Go International, Inc. This series of acquisitions quickly made Go International the nation's fifth largest electrical wireline service company.

In October 1973, Arab oil-producing states embargoed all petroleum exports to the U.S. It was a slap in the pocketbook to the consumer, but for domestic oil business it was a shot of adrenaline, creating fantastic opportunities in drilling and well servicing.

During the mid '70s, there was a grow-

Gas oil well services in 1958.

ing difference of opinion between Gearhart and Owen on corporate direction, and in 1977 the longtime partnership split. Gearhart stayed with GOI, dealing solely in wireline business, while Owen spun-off the non-wireline related business under the corporate name of Pengo.

Today Gearhart Industries, Inc. is still perceived by the industry as a high technology company. In 1977 it introduced Direct Digital Logging to the wireline service, which reduced engineer error in tool calibration and the manual operation of surface equipment. Measurement While Drilling is another innovation of Gearhart Industries, Inc. This process puts logging tools in the drill collars and permits monitoring downhole parameters during the drilling operation.

The proof of the company's success is in its numbers: In an industry where the growth rate is an expected 15 percent, analysts have stated an expected growth rate of 25-30 percent. The company has doubled its size every three years since its inception.

The growth, the innovation and the success of Gearhart Industries, Inc. keeps the American small business hero story alive and growing.

General Dynamics' Fort Worth Division

Dedication to quality the standard for company's success

Shovels dug into the sandy loam on the shores of Lake Worth April 17, 1941, and construction was underway on the sprawling aircraft plant that is now General Dynamics' Fort Worth Division.

A sense of urgency filled the air in those early World War II days. Nine months later the mile-long plant was completed and Consolidated Aircraft Corporation was producing the first of more than 3,000 B-24 bombers, C-87 transports and B-32 heavy bombers.

In 1943, 20 years after its founding, Consolidated merged with Vultee Aircraft, Inc., and became Convair. By then, monthly production was soaring like the temperatures of typical Texas summer days, 95…100…105. At the time, 30,600 people were working at "the bomber plant," and Fort Worth had a major new industry — one destined to remain the economic backbone of the community.

With the end of the war, recession hit the aircraft industry. Employment dropped to about 6,000 in 1946, just a year before the era of the global bombers began and the giant B-36 bombers became a production-line reality. By 1951, employment had jumped to 31,000 and production continued until August 1954 when the last of the 385 "Peacemakers" was delivered to the Strategic Air Command. It was also in 1954 that Convair merged with General Dynamics Corporation. In May 1961, the plant was designated the Fort Worth Division.

As work on the B-36 was phased out, production turned to Convair's B-58 supersonic bomber, a plane that while in Air Force service set nineteen world speed, payload and altitude records and won five of aviation's major awards — the Thompson, Bleriot, Mackay (twice) and the Bendix trophies.

The first flight of the delta-winged bomber, nicknamed "The Hustler," was made Nov. 11, 1956; and the last of 116 B-58s rolled off the assembly line Aug. 13, 1962. The Air Force retired the B-58 in 1970.

In November 1962, the Department of Defense announced that the Fort Worth Division had been selected to develop and build a supersonic tactical fighter-bomber, the F-111. It was the first U.S.

A pair of sophisticated weapons, the F-16 fighters produced by General Dynamics' Fort Worth Division (right).

General Dynamics B-24 assembly line during World War II (below).

aircraft to be designed for use by two military services, the Air Force and the Navy.

The F-111, a technical marvel with variable sweep wings that can be extended and retracted during different phases of flight and with terrain-following radar that keeps the plane at a set altitude without pilot control, made its maiden flight in December 1964.

In nearly one million hours of flight, the F-111 has compiled a safety record comparable to, or better than, any other U.S. high performance fighter produced during the last two decades. Although the last of the 562 F-111s left the assembly line in September 1976, modifications and upgrading of the craft are expected to continue for years to come.

In 1975 the Air Force called on the Fort Worth Division to build an advanced air combat fighter, the F-16 and initially ordered 650. A few months later, four NATO nations — Belgium, Denmark, Norway and The Netherlands — signed contracts to buy 348 F-16s to be built under a European coproduction program. The U.S. Air Force later announced plans to procure a total of 1,396 F-16s.

That coproduction program, the first of its kind in the history of military aviation, is being conducted here as well as in Amsterdam and Gosselies, Belgium.

Early in 1980, Israel became the sixth nation to fly F-16s, and the U.S. government announced Egypt would be the seventh. The trend was for F-16 sales to top 2,000 during the year as international interest continued in the advanced fighter. Division sales approached $1.5 billion.

Since it opened and under the leadership of such men as George Newman, August C. Esenwein and the current Vice President and General Manager Richard E. Adams, the Fort Worth plant has been known as one of the most innovative, "can-do" operations in the aerospace industry. Aircraft produced at the plant have been the fastest, the first-of-a-kind, the most sophisticated, the biggest and most fuel efficient. With this success story as a pattern, the division's future looks bright. Fort Worth can look forward to a substantial and positive financial impact from this important General Dynamics operation for many years to come.

General Steel Company

An integral part of Fort Worth's growth

General Steel Company was incorporated under the laws of the State of Texas on March 17, 1947 to engage in the general fabrication and erection of structural, reinforcing, and plate steel products. Its incorporators were T. U. McAllister, president, Jack C. Pace, secretary, H. C. Pfannkuche, treasurer, and Paul Brandt and Oliver G. Girsham, directors. Upon the death of T. U. McAllister in March 1958, Jack Pace became president of the corporation and continues to serve in that capacity.

In the early part of 1948, it became apparent that the Fort Worth Structural Steel Company would be liquidated and some of the personnel from the latter company were interested in becoming associated with General Steel Company. General Steel Company purchased the physical assets, including inventory, of Fort Worth Structural Steel Company and sold stock to several former employees of that organization.

The company plant was originally located outside the city limits, in the southwestern part of Fort Worth, Texas, on five acres of land leased from the Gulf, Colorado and Santa Fe Railway. Later, two five acre tracts were purchased and the firm became heavily involved in the furnishing of heavy structural steel and plate products for high rise buildings and, also, the power plant industry. Additional purchases of properties included three acres to the west and another ten acres to the east, making a total of 23 acres with six acres under roof and an employment of 220 people. Steel has been furnished in the "lower 48 states" and to some fifteen or 20 foreign countries.

In December 1972, General Steel Company, through a stock swap, became a wholly owned subsidiary of Howell Instruments, Inc. Howell Instruments purchased most of the publicly held stock and subsequently became a privately held corporation with a parent company set up as Howell Management, Inc. There are four wholly owned subsidiaries of Howell Management, Inc.: Howell Instruments, Inc., General Steel Company, Lewis and Lambert Metal Contractors, Inc., and Childs Construction Company.

It has been the goal of the company since its inception to furnish steady employment for its employees by bringing work from other areas into its plant for fabrication and shipment to the jobsite.

Throughout the years, General Steel Company has reinforced its growing reputation as a quality fabricator and manufacturer.

General Steel Company employees H. E. Burden and Glenn Long punching steel beam in 1951.

General Steel Company office and plant at 3001 West Pafford Street, in 1948.

Geren Associates

Providing quality architecture for more than 40 years

In 1934, the very depth of the Great Depression, the late Preston M. Geren Sr. could see no greater opportunity in Fort Worth than to utilize his 22 years of experience in architecture, engineering, education and construction by going into business for himself: hence the beginning of Preston M. Geren, Architect and Engineer.

His foresight was keen. The combination of existing railroads, stockyards, and the production of oil in nearby west Texas provided base industries for continued growth, even during the lean years.

There were better times to come, and Geren, by virtue of his education and experience, offered clients a variety of skills and expertise seldom found in one man. Recognizing opportunities and meeting needs with expanded services, Geren would guide his fledgling firm to grow through a diversity of practice.

Among Geren's first commissions were several educational facilities, including key buildings at Texas State College for Women in Denton, Arlington Heights High School in Fort Worth, and a new school in New London to replace the one destroyed by a tragic explosion in 1937. During the decades to come, the firm would design and complete many more buildings of classrooms, laboratories, gymnasia and administrative facilities for educators. Clients would include Texas Christian University, Texas Wesleyan College, Baylor University, Texas A&M University, and the University of Texas at Austin and its regional campuses.

Miller Brewing Company, Fort Worth plant, for which Geren Associates were architects.

World War II and the years that followed spurred tremendous growth in Fort Worth. The city became a center for sophisticated defense industry manufacturing and the population expanded by more than 55 percent during the decade.

New facilities were needed to house the community's expanding public, commercial, and industrial activities. The firm, now Geren Associates, helped to provide them, working on such diverse projects as hospitals, Fort Worth City Hall, banks and office buildings.

As the years passed, Geren Associates enhanced its reputation for meeting the needs of a broad spectrum of clients, in-

Western Company of North America headquarters office building, another Geren project.

cluding industrial facilities for: Miller Brewing Company, Universal Mills, U.S. Cold Storage Company, Mrs. Baird's Bakeries, Coca Cola Bottling Company, Fort Worth *Star-Telegram*; utilities: Southwestern Bell Telephone Company, Lone Star Gas Company, Texas Electric Service Company; research facilities: Alcon Laboratories, Sid Richardson Carbon Black Company; financial institutions: First National Bank of Fort Worth, Fort Worth National Bank, Central Bank and Trust, Ridglea Bank, Riverside Bank, Overton Park National Bank; corporate headquarters buildings: Justin Industries, Enserch Corporation, Champlin Petroleum Company, Western Company of North America, Equitable General Insurance Corporation; and, as associate ar-

chitect to Louis I. Kahn for a project of international acclaim, the Kimbell Art Museum.

The 1970s saw the world's largest airport constructed between Fort Worth and Dallas. Geren Associates participated in the mammoth project as associate architect and, in addition, provided complete architectural services for the American Airlines terminal, including interior design. More recently, the firm has been selected by the Dallas/Fort Worth Airport Board to provide a master plan for passenger terminal expansion through 1990.

Today, Geren Associates is the oldest and largest architectural firm in Fort Worth and among the top ten in Texas, having completed more than 1,600 projects, representing an aggregate cost of more than $1 billion. Looking to the future, the firm's staff of 75 persons combines skills which extend beyond traditional architectural practice to include the fields of master planning, interior design, structural engineering, and total project administration.

Haws & Garrett General Contractors

Partners set Fort Worth construction trends

Charles Haws, a country boy from Oklahoma, climbed out of his bomber at the end of World War II and, with his bride, settled in Fort Worth. He started to build houses.

Kenneth Garrett Jr., who grew up on Fort Worth's west side, wanted to follow his uncle as a contractor. His degree in civil engineering led to an estimating and purchasing position with a major contracting firm in north Texas. But Garrett was restless.

A casual introduction sparked a unique synergism between the two ambitious entrepreneurs. Garrett's formal training and budget wizardry and Haws' construction capabilities and experience were officially combined on January 1, 1955. They pooled their total capital of less than $5,000 and began business together.

The prosperous partnership lasted 22 years — until Haws' death in 1976. Today the name of Haws & Garrett General Contractors, Inc. is synonymous with the straight-forwardness and top-notch quality the two builders rendered their clients for nearly three decades.

The partners officed for eighteen months in little more than a storage closet (six by fifteen feet) in what was then the Mutual Savings and Loan Building at Eighth and Throckmorton. Garrett recalled the "absolute magic" of the estimate he submitted for their first job at Carswell Air Force Base. The team came in $53 under the next bidder to win the $26,000 contract.

At the end of the first calendar year, the partners' income tripled. From that point on, there never was a "backward step." When most builders were looking toward public jobs for their bread and butter, Haws and Garrett analyzed the biggest profits could be made by running counter to a trend, or at least ahead of the pack. As their successes mounted, the company began setting the trends for other builders to follow.

During the growth years, building buildings became secondary as Haws and Garrett strived to build regular customers through budgetary responsibility and personal service. The company pioneered the turn-key concept in the Fort Worth/Dallas area. Haws & Garrett General Contractors were one of the first to offer a guaranteed price for a project — from design to building completion.

An integral part of the design/build concept is the principle of total construction management which goes from the contracting phase through the actual supervision of the entire building pro-

Haws and Garrett General Contractors built the world's first private subway in downtown Fort Worth in 1963. The 1,400-foot long tube connected a parking lot with Leonards Department Store.

cess. Thus, the scope of the company's expertise became virtually unlimited — plumbing, heating, air conditioning, electrical contracting, floor coverings, roofing, painting, interior finishing, and even land acquisition and interim financing.

Construction of the world's first privately-owned subway brought Haws and Garrett worldwide attention. Publications from around the world described how crews excavated two city blocks, erected a three-and-one-half story, one block-square building, and connected it to a parking lot with a concrete tube — in a hole 40 feet deep and 1,400 feet long — in little more than a year. The building was Leonards Department Store, now torn down to make way for the Tandy Center. But the M&O Subway is still operational today.

Haws and Garrett began using tilt-up designs at least fifteen years before the concept came into general use in the Fort Worth/Dallas area. Now, according to Garrett, virtually all warehouse construction in north Texas hinges on the tilt-up system.

Although the company moved to Dallas in the mid-1970s, Garrett and Haws have contributed immensely to the prospering community of Fort Worth. Haws was active in community affairs until the time of his death — as board chairman of the Fort Worth Parks and Recreation Department, president of the Community Theatre, board member of YMCA, Fort Worth Arts Council, and Trinity Valley School.

Civic involvement has also been a way of life for Garrett — president of Goodwill Industries, secretary of Fort Worth's Building Code Committee, board member of the Rotary Club, the Streams and Valleys Committee, and the University Christian Church are only a sample of his contributions to civic affairs.

The partnership of Garrett and Haws was built on an enterprising business philosophy. Its success resulted from the belief that the best service they could render the city of Fort Worth was to do a good job building their own business.

The company's future now rests with its heirs and their continuation of the same solid, honest practice of an art perfected by Garrett and Haws.

Huguley Memorial Hospital

A crucial link in a benevolent chain

"People caring for people...This concept, engendered by consciousness of God's pervasive love, is an American tradition of helping our neighbors. It undergirds the establishment of this health center. And in each generation the consciousness of this purpose will elicit and nurture willingness to share the influence, resources, time and knowledge essential to human well-being."

—Statement from Huguley Hospital Memorial Wall

Like some futuristic mirage, Huguley Memorial Hospital looms on the horizon in Fort Worth on Interstate 35W — a landmark in contrast with the expanse of Texas plains, and tangible evidence of a city's faith in its growth and a church's commitment to the health needs of people.

It is no accident that the 220-bed ultra-modern facility towers over these Texas plains. It is there because Dr. H. Taylor Huguley, Dallas dentist and real estate investor, bequeathed the majority of his estate, worth more than $7 million, to build a hospital in honor of his parents.

And it is there because Fort Worth citizens and her leaders worked tirelessly to bring the hospital to Fort Worth. Foundations, individuals and corporations contributed more than $3.25 million to the hospital. Individual citizens and small satellite communities near Fort Worth have donated thousands of dimes and dollars to build the hospital in their own backyard.

The Fort Worth Leadership Committee, chaired by Louis J. Levy, M.D. and in concert with Adventists, conducted the successful capital campaign. Members of the Leadership Committee included William C. Conner, H. B. Fuqua, Robert W. Gerrard, B. G. Jenkins, E. H. Keltner Jr.,

Huguley Memorial Hospital at 11801 South Freeway in Fort Worth.

Thomas H. Law, William G. Marquardt, J. C. Pace Jr., J. Howard Shelton, and Harry K. Werst. The $3.25 million campaign was the largest voluntary support effort for a hospital Fort Worth had seen until that time.

Nearly $2.5 million was contributed to the project by seven major funding sources. Leading the list was the Sid W. Richardson Foundation with $800,000. Other major contributions came from The Amon G. Carter Foundation, Paul H. Pewitt, the J. E. and L. E. Mabee Foundation, The Kresge Foundation, The Fort Worth Clearing House Association, and the Texas Electric Service Company. The partnership with those who initially gave continues.

Adventists are not new to the health care field. They operate 350 medical facilities throughout the world including Loma Linda Medical Center in California; Kettering Medical Center in Dayton, Ohio; Florida Hospital, Orlando, Florida; and six hospitals in Texas. Besides providing a full range of medical services and a 24-hour physician-staffed emergency room, the $20 million Huguley facility places considerable emphasis on preventive medicine.

A full-time Health Education department schedules classes in areas such as stress management, stop smoking, weight management, prepared childbirth, cardiopulmonary resuscitation (CPR), cancer detection, and nutrition and cooking. Hundreds of area residents attend the classes each year. This department enhances the hospital's role as a provider of total health care.

Huguley Hospital's heritage in health care dates back to 1866 when advocates of healthful living established what was to be called the Battle Creek Sanitarium in Michigan. Before this time medicine had seen some changes, but little improvement. "Bleeding" a patient was still proclaimed by some to be the sovereign remedy. Drugs and opiates were freely sold and prescribed. And anyone who wished to try his hand at healing could do so.

In this atmosphere, those at the Battle Creek Sanitarium began practicing "rational" medicine, using natural remedies, fresh air and water, nutritious foods and medication when needed. Dr. John Harvey Kellogg, director of the sanitarium, wanted to find a way to make nutritious food more appealing to his patients. It was his experimenting in the sanitarium kitchen that produced the first ready-to-eat breakfast cereals. It was John Harvey's brother, W. K. Kellogg, who made corn flakes, and many other cereals, household staples in the early twentieth century.

More sanitariums were established. Later they became hospitals. In 1905 land and buildings were acquired which were described as including — "a fully furnished, beautiful hotel building, with an amusement center, five cottages, a farmhouse with implements, horses, carriages and cows on a seventy-six acre tract, with eighteen acres of bearing orchard and fifteen in alfalfa — for about $500 an acre." Now known as Loma Linda University, the expansive center is a fully-accredited university which prepares hundreds in medicine, dentistry, nursing and other allied health fields.

The heritage which led to the establishment of Huguley Memorial Hospital is summed up in this way by Chairman of the Board Ben E. Leach:

"This health center is a link in the chain of Adventist installations encircling the earth to benefit all people. In their goal of helping people maintain good health, enhance the dignity of mankind and serve the Creator, church leaders and institutional trustees are pledged to provide health education and quality professional care for residents of north/central Texas."

Justin Industries, Inc.

Doing the common uncommonly well — from frontier times to the future

In 1879 20-year-old H. J. Justin left his Indiana home and ventured to Spanish Fort, Texas, where he repaired worn footwear from a small room off the town's barbershop. Justin quickly recognized the serious need of the working cowboy for reliable footwear that could withstand the dry climate, harsh sunlight, and alkali waters of the region.

Using $35 loaned him by the town barber, Justin began his boot-making business. He soon earned the reputation of being a good craftsman and a good businessman, and demand for his cowboy boots grew rapidly. Eventually, the boot-making operation developed into a family business, which is now part of a diversified company that is the largest manufacturer of brick in the United States; a major producer of concrete products; builder of cooling towers throughout the world; publisher of fine books; and a national leader in the production of top-quality western boots.

Pioneer determination was at the root of another company that would become an important part of Justin Industries. In 1891 the Acme Press Brick Company began operations at the site of a high-quality shale deposit about fifty miles west of Fort Worth, Texas. It satisfied an expanding need for brick in rapidly growing Dallas and Fort Worth and surrounding cities. Now known as the Bennett Plant, named after Acme's founder, the original facility is the oldest brick plant in Texas. Its product is still in heavy demand, recognized for its outstanding quality.

Innovation and foresight also led to the formation of the Ceramic Cooling Tower Company as Acme Brick sought new

Acme brick delivery trucks, circa 1920.

ways to utilize the line of ceramic industrial products it then manufactured. The first cooling tower with a ceramic fill was built by CCT in 1948. The concept that a ceramic fill would result in a cooling tower far superior to competing products has now been firmly established. Today, that first cooling tower is still operating at maximum efficiency, a feat previously thought impossible.

A few scattered concrete products plants were added in the late 1960s and, with diversification under way, the First Worth Corporation was formed in 1968, with Acme Brick as the major holding. The Justin Companies (boots, belts and leathergoods) merged with First Worth in December 1968. A year later, John Justin Jr., grandson of the boot company's founder, became chief executive officer of the then struggling conglomerate. First Worth was renamed Justin Industries, Inc., in 1972.

Northland Press of Flagstaff, Arizona, joined the fold in 1973, and Justin gained a small but prestigious regional publishing house noted for its award-winning books about the art and history of the West.

Expansion continued the following year with the purchase of Sanford Brick Corporation, the largest brick producer in North Carolina. The acquisition gave Justin a position in the important brick market along the Atlantic seaboard and made the company the largest producer of face brick in the nation.

Justin became a major force in concrete products used in buildings and highway construction with the acquisi-

An early photograph of the Justin boot-making operation.

tion of Kingstip, Inc., and its subsidiary, the Featherlite Corporation, in 1976 and 1977. The step established Justin as the largest producer of concrete products serving the Southwest and Mid-South markets.

The company's operations were significantly expanded when, in late 1976, an intensive review was started of every building materials plant in order to establish market potential, locate production bottlenecks and identify expansion opportunities. Between 1977 and 1979, dramatic expansion, improvement and modernization of Justin's brick and concrete plants were achieved at an investment that substantially exceeded the company's total 1976 net worth.

Justin Industries, with its corporate headquarters located in Fort Worth and nearly fifty plant locations in the Southwest and Southeast, is a unique combination of businesses. Emphasizing quality in its people, its products and its service, and with the determination to expand the markets for its superior products, Justin Industries entered its second century in 1980 — doing the common uncommonly well.

KXAS-TV

First southwest television station still leading the way

The late President Harry S. Truman left his legacy in history books, and became part of the history of KXAS-TV as well. President Truman, standing on the steps of the old Texas and Pacific Railroad station, was the first image to fill the television screens in the great Southwest. WBAP-TV went on the air September 27, 1948 and the live transmission of the 49-minute presidential visit was sent to a handful of receivers.

This marked WBAP-TV's first broadcast. Through the efforts of media entrepreneur and WBAP founder, the late Amon G. Carter, it became the first television station south of St. Louis, east of Los Angeles and west of Richmond, Virginia. Two days later the official station dedication ceremony was broadcast. Jack Gor-

Locally produced programs such as "Saturday Night Barn Dance," filmed in the WBAP-TV studio. The station's "Video Lane" could accommodate everything from livestock to setting the stage for a bootin' barn dance!

On September 27, 1948, the crowd gathered at the old Texas and Pacific Railroad station to hear President Truman speak, while WBAP-TV covered the event and broadcast the presidential visit to a handful of receivers.

As news coverage became more and more sophisticated and the station converted to electronic journalism, WBAP-TV changed ownership. The sale transpired in November of 1974 and LIN Broadcasting Corporation, in accordance with F.C.C. regulations, changed the call letters to KXAS-TV, appointing Blake Byrne President and General Manager.

Since then, the station's commitment to be the best has grown even stronger, keeping pace with television's expanding capabilities and sophistication. Another first, under new ownership — one of the first international live feeds to a local station was to KXAS-TV in 1978. A group of Metroplex business leaders flew to London, England to discuss the direct commercial flights from that city to the Dallas/Fort Worth Regional Airport. An event full of local interest, KXAS-TV covered it live!

In September 1979, KXAS-TV news adopted a new name — Action News. Action News reflects the KXAS-TV news effort to provide fast-paced coverage of local news throughout the Metroplex, and a news format which includes more stories and expanded live coverage.

In October 1979, Channel Five obtained a fully equipped Jet Ranger III helicopter, Chopper 5, which provides Action News with the flexibility to cover stories anywhere in the area faster than ever before.

In 1980 Action News received three national awards including — the 1979 Sigma Delta Chi bronze medallion for Public Service in Television Journalism, the Investigative Reporters & Editors Association 1980 Best Investigative Story Award, and the American Bar Association 1980 silver Gavel Award.

Today television's responsibility to the public has grown. KXAS-TV is proud to represent and support Fort Worth, Dallas and the surrounding area.

don, amusements editor for the *Fort Worth Press,* wrote after that broadcast, "A part of Fort Worth's inaugural television show last night looked like our first roll of home movie film. But a good deal more of it was excellent — enough so to convince the stubbornest critic that television is here to stay."

WBAP signed on two days early in order to cover the Truman visit — the first indication of the station's commitment to its viewers to bring them the best possible news coverage. This pioneering spirit of The Texas News made it the best newscast in the country as selected by the Radio and Television News Directors Association later that year.

The station's enthusiasm for firsts led it to new areas of programming. It was first to telecast live college and high school sports; first to produce a daily newsreel and one of the first to acquire a fully-equipped remote unit, which made possible the Wide Wide World presentations broadcast from places like Carlsbad Caverns and the White Sands Missile Range in New Mexico. October 1949 marked the first professional weather reporting program and the station was the first NBC affiliate in Texas to transmit the network's color programming in 1954.

Over the years, the station has received countless awards and citations. During the chaos and trauma of President Kennedy's assassination in Dallas, WBAP's extraordinary efforts won national recognition when Sigma Delta Chi (Society of Professional Journalists) honored the station for its excellent and comprehensive national coverage of the tragedy.

Ben E. Keith Company

Growth marked by quality in merchandise, excellent service and fair prices

To survive, a business must change with the times. To flourish, it must be one step ahead of them.

Upon these principles, the Ben E. Keith Company grew from its modest beginnings in 1906 as the Harkrider-Morrison Company in Fort Worth to become one of the largest distributors of food products

in the Southwest and one of the largest Anheuser-Busch beer distributors in the nation.

In its early years, the Harkrider-Keith Cooke Company delivered produce in Fort Worth by horse-drawn wagons and made shipments by railway express to nearby cities. One of the young salesmen

soliciting orders in a horse and buggy was Ben E. Keith. Business was good during the winter, but sales were slow in summer when people grew their own vegetables. The summer slump caused Keith much concern.

So, in 1928, three years before he took full control and changed the company name to its present form, Keith journeyed to St. Louis where he met with Adolphus Busch. He obtained the distributorship for Anheuser-Busch products, complementing the seasonal produce delivery.

These were prohibition years and Anheuser-Busch's major products were ice cream syrups, baker's yeast, bevo (a beer substitute), Budweiser Draught Near Beer (sold in wooden kegs) and malt syrup, which could be added to yeast and water to make home-brewed beer.

But with the repeal of prohibition in 1933, the top blew off the beer industry and the Keith Company was ready. Although refrigeration as it is known today was still in its infancy, it had long been a necessity to produce dealers. The Keith Company had refrigerated facilities to keep the unpasteurized keg beer cold and became Anheuser-Busch's beer distributor for north, east and most of west Texas.

The brisk beer sales which started in 1933 have never slowed, with beer distribution now comprising a substantial portion of the company's current sales. Meanwhile, the produce division grew to include frozen foods, groceries, sundries, paper products and cleaning supplies. Gourmet food items and gift packages of fruit are featured in Keith's Fanci Food's annual holiday catalog.

The steady growth of the company was coupled with its concern for the community, inspired by the guidance and example of its president, Ben E. Keith. A Fort Worth native, Keith was born in 1882, and became a founding junior partner of the company at age 23.

Active in organizing the West Texas Chamber of Commerce, he was the Fort Worth Chamber of Commerce's youngest president. Keith helped persuade officials to locate what is now Carswell Air Force Base in the city and was also instrumental in site selection and construction of Will Rogers Coliseum. His civic involvement has set an example for the corporate good citizenship of company operations in each community it serves.

Keith's concern for people was also apparent in policies concerning employees. The Keith Company established a pension plan and profit sharing program in 1943 — one of the first companies in the country to provide these employee benefits.

Over the years the firm expanded, buying existing produce companies or establishing branches in Wichita Falls, 1910; Abilene, 1914; Dallas, 1920; Lubbock, 1925; Shreveport, 1966; Amarillo, 1968; and Little Rock, 1972. Beer distribution centers were located in Breckenridge, Mineral Wells, Dallas and Fort Worth, 1933; Palestine, 1969; Commerce, 1974; and Denton, 1979.

Upon Ben E. Keith's death in 1959, control of the company passed into new hands — but old employees — and R. D. Erwin became president and later chairman. Gaston Hallam, an employee since 1924, was named president in 1963. When Hallam became chairman in 1973, John Beauchamp succeeded him as president with W. P. Warner serving as executive vice president. In 1979 Hallam's two sons, Robert and Howard, became chairman and president of the company, respectively, with Gaston Hallam and Beauchamp moving to the executive committee and Warner serving as senior executive vice president.

With the finest quality merchandise, unmatched delivery service and fair prices, the Ben E. Keith Company remains one of the leading food and beverage distributors in the Southwest. Face-to-face communications with employees, close personal relationships with customers and concern for the community continue to keep the Ben E. Keith Company a positive and progressive force in the areas which it serves.

Early salesmen for the Harkrider-Morrison Company (Ben E. Keith Company) made their calls by wagon. The Budweiser billboard in the background forecasts the company's eventual association with Anheuser-Busch.

Delivery service for Harkrider-Keith-Cooke (Ben E. Keith) Company customers was provided by mule-drawn wagons.

Law, Snakard, Brown & Gambill

Nearly 70 years in the continuous practice of law

The firm of Law, Snakard, Brown & Gambill began with Morgan Bryan, a sole practitioner, who started his career in Fort Worth on July 15, 1892, in a second story, one-room office of a building on Main Street. The building later became Striplings Department Store, for many years a landmark in downtown Fort Worth. Currently that property is the site of a new luxury hotel — the Americana Hotel/Tandy Center.

In 1912 Bryan formed a partnership with B. B. Stone, a young man from Ballinger, Texas who had just completed a term as county judge of Runnels County. Stone continued as an active partner in the firm for 57 years until his death in 1969 at the age of 93.

By 1915 the firm was known as Bryan, Stone & Wade, and in that year it moved to the then Fort Worth National Bank Building at Fifth and Main streets; in the same year, that bank became a client of the young firm, a representation that has continued uninterrupted to the present date.

The next change in the firm name occurred in 1919 when Baylor Agerton returned from World War I and joined the practice. Thereafter the partnership of Bryan, Stone, Wade & Agerton continued for 33 years.

Death and retirement resulted in the addition of new names and the deletion of old ones, but one or more members of the original four partners remained in the firm name until the death of B. B. Stone. The present name of Law, Snakard, Brown & Gambill evolved as a result of the merger of the Stone group with the firm of Tilley, Hyder & Law.

The firm and its clientele have enjoyed a consistent and solid growth through the years. It presently consists of 19 partners, 11 associates, and 33 support personnel.

The firm's practice has been for the most part business oriented, with emphasis on corporate law, banking, security regulations, oil and gas, real estate, taxation, communications, probate matters, and litigation.

While the practice of law has been the dominant concern of Law, Snakard, Brown & Gambill, the firm has also recognized a civic commitment to support community affairs. For example, it has furnished — two presidents of the Fort Worth Chamber of Commerce, a regent of the University of Texas System, two recipients of the Blackstone Award, a district judge, four presidents of the Fort Worth-Tarrant County Bar Association, numerous officers and directors of United Way and a large number of other civic and cultural organizations. Eleven members of the present firm have served in the Armed Forces of the United States.

If the past is in truth a reflection of the future, the firm will for another 68 years maintain its enviable professional stature as well as continue its keen awareness of its role in community affairs.

View of Tarrant County Courthouse and downtown Fort Worth circa 1912 when the Law, Snakard, Brown & Gambill firm was founded.

Lennox Industries Inc.

Innovation fostered expansion from small firm to worldwide operations

Since its beginning in the 1890s in Marshalltown, Iowa, Lennox has grown from a locally owned and operated furnace company to an international corporation ranking among the top three producers of sophisticated heating and air conditioning equipment. In the United States, Lennox operations are geographically divided among five divisions. Lennox Southwest Division manufacturing and sales headquarters, on Highway 121 at Maxine in Fort Worth, was established in 1948 to accommodate Lennox's growing southwestern markets.

The historical development of Lennox began unfolding in 1904. D. W. Norris, a young newspaper editor and publisher, then purchased the Lennox Furnace Company from David Lennox, a mechanical genius who felt uncomfortable in the furnace business and wanted to sell out. As president of the new firm, Norris was instrumental in developing technology that moved Lennox from simple, coal-burning gravity furnaces to sophisticated forced-air gas and oil furnaces. As a result, Lennox expanded into Southwest markets.

The Southwest Division's intitial plant was located in a leased, 40,000 square foot warehouse on South Main Street in Fort Worth. From these humble beginnings, Lennox-Fort Worth has become a major Lennox manufacturing center with over one million square feet (15 acres under one roof) and a work force of some 1,200 employees.

Although growth and change have highlighted Lennox's long history, the company remains a family-owned corporation and retains its direct-to-dealer method of merchandising which has played an important part in the company's success.

Succeeding D. W. Norris in 1949 was his son, John Norris Sr., who added residential air conditioning to the growing Lennox product line in 1952. Following Norris's retirement in 1971, Ray C. Robbins, the first nonfamily member chief executive officer, ushered Lennox into the exciting new age of solar energy. Lennox solar collectors are among the most efficient produced today. It was during Robbins' administration that Lennox corporate headquarters and its research and development laboratory were relo-

The Lennox Southwest Division factory at Highway 121 and Maxine as it looked in 1949.

Today, the same location is the site of more than 1,000,000 square feet of manufacturing and office areas.

cated to the Dallas area from Marshalltown. Today, John Norris Jr., the third generation of Norris leadership, is at the helm as Lennox continues to develop products that make best use of the world's scarce energy supplies.

The pioneering spirit of the early days at Lennox-Fort Worth was exemplified by Jack Melcher and Bill Dirk, foresighted men who recognized potential marketing and manufacturing opportunities for Lennox products in the Southwest.

Melcher was the division's first general manager and was succeeded upon his retirement in 1970 by Dirk. Under their guidance, local facilities were expanded and Lennox became highly visible on the Fort Worth scene.

As vice president and general manager, Dirk now oversees the complete Lennox-Fort Worth manufacturing and sales operation. Lennox high-efficiency commercial and residential air conditioning equipment is produced here for shipment throughout the United States, Canada and overseas.

A revolutionary two-speed compressor, the first in the industry, was designed and produced here in 1972. This two-speed breakthrough is rapidly becoming a standard for high efficiency comfort throughout the industry.

As Lennox continues to develop heating and air conditioning products of the highest quality and efficiency, experience gained since the turn of the century will help provide the technology to do so. As one of the largest Lennox factory/sales headquarters, Lennox-Fort Worth remains a conscientious organization dedicated to the future of the city of Fort Worth.

John Marvin Leonard and Obie Paul Leonard

Ingenuity, determination and $600 built a business empire

When the doors of a small store across the street from the Tarrant County courthouse opened in 1918, no one could have predicted that those counters made of boards on barrels and washtub display cases would grow into a business empire that would have a monumental community-wide impact.

But this is the story of Leonards and Fort Worth.

With little more than $600 and a great deal of foresight, John Marvin Leonard began business in a 1,500-square-foot store. He was joined by younger brother Obie Paul, two years later.

Together, Marvin and Obie Leonard, filled with frontier spirit and optimistic vision, created far more than a mercantile center on the north end of the central business district. As the city grew and prospered, the Leonard brothers grew and prospered. And — good citizens that they were — as they prospered, they gave financial support and help to their adopted city.

Ironically, the business they created expanded most during periods of economic adversity. During the dark, early days of the Great Depression, they moved their store into its own block-long building, thereby creating new jobs and generating activity in the downtown area.

This kind of growth cannot be entirely attributed to the fact that the Leonard Brothers Store (as it was known early on) carried merchandise as varied as stove bolts and fashions, saddles and pastries. More, it was a feeling Marvin and Obie Leonard were able to convey in their personal actions and through their thousands of employees: treat every customer as you would want to be treated.

This spirit of genuine concern for their customers led to innovations in merchandising. The store was one of the first to offer baby strollers so that mothers could shop in a less harried fashion. The installation of one of the first escalators

Left to Right: Obie Paul Leonard, left, and John Marvin Leonard, in 1965.

south of the Mason-Dixon line drew 40,000 enthusiastic riders and sightseers during the first day of operation. A refreshment stand perked up many a weary shopper. Perhaps the most spectacular creation was the store's own subway system. The M&O Subway express carried passengers from a fourteen-acre parking lot into the store ... for free. This creative approach brought people in throngs to the store and into the downtown area to conduct other business, to their jobs, and even to other stores. What Leonard Brothers had done, in effect, was to create a highly successful, even though small-scale, mass transit system that benefited their business, to be sure, but also the entire downtown business community. And the remarkable thing is, it didn't cost the taxpayer a cent!

Mr. Marvin and Mr. Obie (as they were affectionately known) may have been two farm boys from Cass County, but the business empire they began in Fort Worth carried their name across the nation as retailers of an extraordinary kind.

Neither was content to confine his life to that of being a shopkeeper even on such a large scale, but instead took on new challenges in other areas, both as businessmen and citizens.

Marvin Leonard, who died in 1970, expanded his business holdings to include oil, ranching, banking and real estate developments. Besides the philanthropic activities which consumed much of his energy, he had a "hobby" that embraced his recreational activities, his giving nature, and his business acumen: Marvin Leonard built country clubs and extraordinary golf courses.

It is thanks to his desire for perfection that Colonial Country Club and Shady Oaks Country Club have courses recognized as being among the finest in the world.

His major sports contribution, however, focused the attention of the world on Fort Worth. It was Marvin Leonard's convincing nature that brought the U.S. Open to Colonial in 1941 and the Colonial National Invitation in 1946.

Obie Leonard also had divergent business interests. He has devoted a great deal of energy to ranching, pecan farming, oil, savings and loan associations, insurance, and holdings in commercial and industrial property.

Boy Scouting has claimed Obie Leonard's interest for more than 40 years. He served as president of the Longhorn Council for thirteen years and continues to serve as a member of the regional board of the Boy Scouts of America. As a leader in scouting, he has been presented the highest BSA Council honor, the Silver Beaver. He was also presented the Antelope, the highest BSA Regional award. A ranch he donated to the council has been named Camp Leonard in his honor.

Individually and together, Marvin and Obie Leonard created a retail empire of international fame and a record of civic contributions.

Lone Star Gas Company

Despite rough times progressive pace never slowed

Near what is now Meacham Field, a crowd — complete with a brass band and booming dignitaries — gathered to watch a nine-year-old boy hold a Roman candle to a torch, signaling the beginning of natural gas service to Fort Worth. At that precise moment in March 1909, as flames shot into the sky and the crowd broke out in cheers and tears, Lone Star Gas Co. officially opened for business.

Within a year, the company was organized, chartered and set a record by completing the 126-mile pipeline from Petrolia field, near Wichita Falls, to Fort Worth. The first long-distance natural gas pipeline in the Southwest, the line was extended 20 more miles within two months to begin serving Dallas as well. Lone Star was off to a running start. From his office in the First National Bank building, company President H. C. Edrington — a former Confederate captain turned banker — believed the trick would be to keep that fast pace from slowing.

Edrington was right. By 1910 Texas had 14,719 domestic customers, most of them served by Lone Star, and the demand was steadily increasing, gradually outstrip-

The first major natural gas pipeline built by Lone Star Gas was a 126-mile, 16-inch line from Petrolia Field to Fort Worth.

ping the available gas supply. In 1914 Lone Star built its first compressor station to boost the supply, but that wasn't enough. The company had to begin expanding its pipeline system outside the Fort Worth-Dallas area, and the going was even rougher than Edrington had predicted.

New lines were extended to new fields only to find the supply exhausted. The company lacked money and credit, and with the advent of World War I, it also lacked manpower and materials. A 100-mile line was extended into West Texas, but for the first five years, the line did not pay operating expenses.

But help was on the way, and for Lone Star the rescue came in the shape of a compressor unit specially designed by company engineers to draw gas out of small, low-pressure fields. By 1919, as a result of this development, Lone Star eased the supply problem. By the 1920s, Lone Star engineers developed a process for utilizing casinghead gas. Since then thousands of cubic feet of gas have been used instead of wasted.

Back on its feet once more, the firm began to expand. Organized in the beginning as a pipeline company, it had sold gas wholesale at city gates to unaffiliated distribution companies like Fort Worth Gas

Co. In 1924 plans were made to combine both transmission and distribution facilities. The company launched a major, town plant construction program. Within five years, Lone Star built 200 town plants of its own in Texas and Oklahoma. Five construction crews worked on the project — considered the greatest mass-construction program in the history of the gas industry. Lone Star then purchased the properties of its two largest distribution customers, Fort Worth Gas Co. and Dallas Gas.

Lone Star's newly expanded system proved a real lifesaver for the U.S. government when World War II broke out. More than 50 military centers, government housing projects and airplane factories were built, almost overnight, along Lone Star's lines. This building boom was miniscule compared to postwar construction. A 79-mile line in East Texas, a 70-mile line in Oklahoma, and 190 miles

One of Lone Star's largest distribution customers, Fort Worth Gas, was bought by Lone Star in the early 1930s.

of line connecting Katy Field near Houston to the Fort Worth-Dallas area were just a few of the new additions to the system during the two decades following the war.

The LSG pipeline network today stretches from mid-Oklahoma to offshore Houston, from way out west in the Lone Star state of Texas almost to the Louisiana border, and serves 1.1 million customers and 579 towns. In sales volume, annual revenue, number of customers and miles of pipeline, the company ranks as one of the four largest integrated utilities in the country. Its gas supply program adds gas reserves at a rate that assures customers adequate natural gas for the decades ahead.

And what of Lone Star's first line, the one from Petrolia Field to Fort Worth? After decades of service, it lies unused, intact for the most part — a tribute to the day when Lone Star Gas and Fort Worth got their start in a new century together.

Though legwork and "mule power" kept Lone Star going in the early days, horsepower did come to the aid of weary employees by 1917.

Miller Brewing Company

Continuous growth based on traditions of pride and dedication

Aerial view of Miller's Fort Worth brewery, 7001 South Freeway.

In 1855, a German brewmaster named Frederic Miller arrived in this country in search of the ideal place to establish a new brewery. Considering his origin, it's not too surprising that Frederic Miller chose the very young, but growing city of Milwaukee.

He bought a small brewery in a picturesque river valley to the west of the town and began production, which reached 300 barrels in the first year. From the beginning, Frederic Miller insisted that his beer meet the highest standards of "Quality: Uncompromising and Unchanging."

Miller's Plank-Road brewery continued to grow and prosper and what was once a small family-owned business developed over the years into a company with national sales distribution — the Miller Brewing Company.

A milestone occurred in 1966 when the Miller Brewing Company purchased the 300,000 barrel Carling Brewing Company facility located on a 50 acre site south of downtown Fort Worth.

Miller invested an initial $12 million to increase the plant's output to one million barrels.

Miller High Life beer was brewed and packaged in Texas for the first time in September 1969.

In 1970, Miller Brewing became a wholly-owned operating company of Philip Morris Incorporated. The Fort Worth brewery expansions which soon followed were some of the first steps in a decade of corporate growth unparalleled in the brewing industry.

A new management team was assembled which included executives of Philip Morris, brewing veterans from Miller and other professionals from related industries. The new management group set in motion a tide of events that moved Miller from seventh place in the brewing industry in 1972, to second place by 1977. Beer shipments increased 566 percent, from 5.4 million barrels in 1972, to 35.8 million barrels by the end of the decade.

Miller now operates six breweries and five container manufacturing facilities in six states and employs more than 12,000 persons.

Frederic Miller established his Plank Road Brewery in Milwaukee in 1855.

currently has the capacity to produce 500 million containers annually, meeting a major portion of the brewery's container needs.

Today, the Fort Worth brewery is the largest brewery in Texas. It produces eight million barrels annually including Miller's principal brands — Miller High Life, Lite and Lowenbrau.

Approximately 1,500 hourly and salaried workers are employed at the brewery and the container plant. Miller's annual economic impact on the state of Texas is more than $148 million in terms of salaries, wages and material purchases.

Miller contributes a great deal to the Metroplex area from an economic standpoint. Miller also strives to be a good corporate citizen. The company actively participates in activities such as sponsorship of symphony concerts, involvement with an auction for public television, art exhibits and many other events. At Miller, such involvement is a way of life.

Miller's facilities in Texas continue to contribute significantly to the overall growth of the company and to the Fort Worth community as a whole. It is a growth based on a Texas-style tradition of enduring pride and a dedication to uncompromising quality.

In Fort Worth, the Miller brewery significantly increased production and employment during the '70s. An expansion program to increase capacity to six million barrels a year was completed in 1975. The expansion added 400,000 square feet to the plant.

Further expansion increased production to seven million barrels by 1977 and eight million by 1979. Since acquisition by Philip Morris, expansion and modernization projects in Fort Worth have totaled $114 million.

A container manufacturing plant was built by Miller in 1976, northeast of the brewery. This 162,000 square foot facility

Rādy and Associates, Inc.

Dedicated to municipal progress — a 56-year-old engineering tradition

Typical paving job by Rady in the 1920s.

Following the advice of Horace Greeley to "Go West," Joe J. Rady, a Cornell University graduate, arrived in West Texas in 1922. Before the young civil engineer lay a mammoth state whose typhoid rate was among the highest in the nation. The deadly disease, a result of shallow water wells and no sewage facilities, could be eliminated only through the construction of sanitary water and sewer systems — systems Rady had come to create.

Today, 56 years after starting his own firm, the 81-year-old Rady remains active in Rady and Associates, Inc., the second oldest engineering firm in Texas. The firm, established in 1924, was incorporated in 1952 as Joe J. Rady and Company. In 1961 it was organized as Rady and Associates, Inc. For more than a half century it has provided a wide range of civil engineering services to Texas cities. The firm's commitment to high standards of

Another Rady project, the Belknap Street Bridge, 1970.

performance and personal attention to each client's project is the foundation upon which Rady and Associates is built.

Both the civil engineering field and the state of Texas have changed dramatically since the pre-depression era when Rady drove hundreds of miles on unpaved roads to meet the needs of his municipal clients. In those days, only Fort Worth, Dallas and Austin had sewage treatment plants. As a result, one Texan in every 100 contracted typhoid. But thanks to scores of water and wastewater treatment plants designed by Rady and others, typhoid in Texas was virtually eliminated.

The Great Depression of the '30s slowed but did not cease the firm's operations. After moving the company's home office to Fort Worth from Waco in 1934 Rady assisted his clients in planning future engineering needs. Then, when federal funds were available for construction of public works improvements, these clients were ready to build. More than a

hundred water and sewer systems were designed by Rady and his associates during the next ten years.

During World War II, Rady's efforts were primarily directed toward defense-oriented projects. In joint-venture with a group of recognized Fort Worth architect/engineers, Rady designed and supervised the construction of several large defense facilities such as airfields, hospitals and housing projects in Texas.

With the ending of international hostilities, Rady and his firm returned to their primary field of municipal public works improvements. In 1945 a branch office was opened in Galveston. In the next fifteen years, the firm designed and supervised the installation of water and sewer facilities in scores of cities in the Texas Gulf Coast and in the Piney Woods of East Texas.

During this same period of time and to the present, Rady and Associates has focused its efforts in the design of diverse public works projects for the City of Fort Worth and surrounding metroplex cities.

Due in part to Rady's planning and design of uncountable miles of streets, thoroughfares and associated bridges, a transportation network links Fort Worth and its neighboring cities. The numerous water and sewer systems which the company designed for these cities have aided significantly in providing sanitary drinking water and eliminating pollution in area streams. To minimize the hazardous effects of flooding, the firm has also designed a variety of major drainage projects in the metroplex. Each has had a positive and lasting effect upon the orderly and dynamic growth of the Fort Worth area.

Another indication of Rady's commitment to the future of Fort Worth can be measured by community-wide benefits resulting from its projects. In 1946, in joint-venture, Rady prepared the plans for one of the first "limited access" highways constructed in the Southwest, now a part of Interstate Highway 30. Later in 1955 Rady joined with three other engineering firms in the design and construction of the $57 million Dallas-Fort Worth Turnpike. Again in joint-venture, Rady participated in the design of major segments of the Dallas/Fort Worth Regional Airport in 1970. These efforts were recognized by the National Society of Professional Engineers as one of the outstanding engineering achievements in the United States.

During the past five and a half decades, Rady and Associates, Inc. has dedicated its broad spectrum of engineering capabilities to the betterment of hundreds of Texas cities and other public and private entities. Rare indeed is the Texas city that does not possess some public improvement project conceived and designed by Rady and Associates, Inc.

Southland Royalty Company

Origin lies in concern for employees

Ernest Marland and Will McFadden joined forces as one of America's great oil-finding teams from 1910 to the mid-1920s. During that time, they discovered and helped to establish the great midcontinent producing area of Oklahoma. They built Marland Oil Company, which became Conoco; and as a benefit to employees, they also founded royalty companies which would be combined to form one of the country's largest independents over 50 years later — Southland Royalty Company.

Marland and McFadden were men of contrasting styles. Marland, of stout stature, was a dreamer who had made and lost a fortune before coming to Oklahoma. McFadden, tall and lean — a consummate businessman — was a builder of steel mills. Marland's dreams were to lead him to great wealth, then to bankruptcy, then to be the governor of Oklahoma. McFadden's business skills enabled him to combine the royalty companies formed for Marland employees into a flourishing independent oil company.

In 1909, Marland, George Miller and Lew Wentz approached McFadden about financing the drilling for oil on the 101 Ranch near Ponca City, Oklahoma. After four dry holes, they hit a gusher that opened the South Ponca Field. It was followed by other discoveries: Newkirk, Blackwell, Garber, Tonkawa and the giant Burbank Field.

The two men felt strongly about the welfare of Marland employees. They financed employees' homes and loaned them money below the prime rate.

Clinics for free dental and medical care were opened. Most importantly, employee royalty companies were set up to enable employees to share in oil and gas discoveries. These were to later become Southland Royalty Company.

In 1923 Marland's dreams led him to J. P. Morgan, the country's most famous banker. Marland wanted to expand to California and Texas, and Morgan offered to finance this expansion. During the next four years however, Morgan gained more and more control, and in 1928 Marland was forced to resign. In 1929 Continental Oil Company, a refiner and retailer, was merged into Marland Oil Company. Although Marland Oil was the remaining corporation, its name was changed to Continental Oil Company — known today as Conoco.

When Marland left the company, McFadden also resigned and combined the employee royalty companies — Southland Royalty, New Royalty, Crescent Royalty, and Marland Employees Royalty — into one entity, Southland Royalty Company. He served as chairman of the board of Southland Royalty until 1956. Marland, aided by McFadden, became a congressman and then governor of Oklahoma.

From its start in 1924 until World War II, Southland Royalty Company acquired royalty and mineral interests in prospective oil and gas areas. Most of its income was paid as dividends to its shareholders, who were still, to a large degree, former Marland employees and their descendants. Subsequent to World War II, the company turned its efforts to acquiring working interests in oil and gas prospects.

In 1975, a major event in Southland's history spurred the company's rapid growth. Southland had acquired mineral interests in the Waddell Ranch of West Texas in 1926, which were under lease to Gulf Oil Company for 50 years. When the lease expired, Southland and the other mineral interest owners started reaping the full benefits of the mineral interests in these properties. During 1979 the Waddell Ranch produced $51 million in revenues for Southland.

The cash flow from the reversion of the Waddell Ranch enabled the company to acquire Aztec Oil & Gas Company in 1976 for $185 million. The heart of Aztec was properties in the San Juan Basin of New Mexico which contained reserves of nearly one trillion cubic feet of natural gas.

Cash flows from the Waddell Ranch and the San Juan Basin enabled the company to accelerate its exploration program. It currently has successful explora-

P. B. Lowrance, E. W. Marland, W. H. McFadden and G. L. Miller pictured around 1920. McFadden headed Southland Royalty until his death in 1956.

tion programs in most geologic basins in the United States.

During 1979, Southland acquired producing oil and gas properties for $153 million. The largest of these was the Permian Basin properties of Shenandoah Oil Corporation, purchased for $126 million. In 1980, Southland acquired P&O Oil Corporation and its substantial oil reserves in West Texas for $129 million.

From Southland's beginning as an employee royalty company, it has grown to become one of the largest independent oil and gas producers in the United States. During 1979 revenues totaled $256 million, oil production was 9.3 million barrels and gas production was 86 billion cubic feet. By 1980 the company's proved reserves totaled 142 million barrels of oil and 1.3 trillion cubic feet of gas, valued at more than $3 billion.

Southwestern Baptist Theological Seminary

Pioneer spirit developed world leader in theological education

Southwestern Baptist Theological Seminary began as a dream in the heart of B. H. Carroll, its first president. He visualized a graduate institution providing trained ministers for the churches of America's spiritual frontiers.

On March 14, 1908 his dream became a reality, and Southwestern is now the largest seminary in the world.

Southwestern was an outgrowth of the theological department of Baylor University in Waco, Texas, established in 1901.

In 1905 the department became Baylor Theological Seminary with five professors. The Baptist General Convention of Texas authorized the separation of the seminary from Baylor University in 1907, gave it a new name — The Southwestern

Baptist Theological Seminary — and a separate board of trustees.

The seminary was chartered on March 14, 1908, and functioned on the Waco campus until the summer of 1910. Several Texas cities made strong bids for the site of the new institution, but Fort Worth citizens provided a campus site and enough money to build the first building, named Fort Worth Hall in honor of its new location. Much of the original 200-acre campus was donated by Mr. and Mrs. J. K. Winston.

In 1925 control of the seminary passed from the Baptist General Convention of Texas to the Southern Baptist Convention.

Today the campus includes ten major buildings located on the highest point in Tarrant County. A children's center, which has served as a model for day-care centers, opened in 1973. A Recreation/Aerobics Center, providing physical fitness and recreational opportunities, was opened in 1979. Both serve as clinical facilities for students. Fleming Library, with more than 500,000 volumes and items, is the largest theological library in the United States.

Southwestern is accredited by the As-

The campus of Southwestern Baptist Theological Seminary, circa 1920. Fort Worth Hall, the original building, is in the foreground. Cowden Hall, the School of Church Music building, is in the background.

sociation of Theological Schools, the Southern Association of Colleges and Schools and the National Association of Schools of Music.

Today the seminary's graduates serve in the multiple Christian ministries of the churches, primarily in the Southern Baptist denomination. Many denominations are represented among the 36,000 former students.

In 1915 two new departments were created — religious education and church music. Both became schools in 1925 and have been pioneers in innovative training of Christian ministers.

During the 1970s Southwestern expanded to four off-campus centers that provide seminary training for men and women living on church fields away from the main campus. Centers are located in Houston and San Antonio, Texas; Shawnee, Oklahoma; and Nashville, Tennessee.

The seminary has had six presidents since 1908: B. H. Carroll, 1908-1914; Lee Rutland Scarborough, 1914-1942; E. D. Head, 1942-1953; J. Howard Williams, 1953-1958; Robert E. Naylor, 1958-1978; and Russell H. Dilday Jr., who became president in 1978.

Each president has carried the vision of the seminary's founder to fuller reality. During the 1970s the seminary's enrollment increased 107 percent, from 2,096 in 1970 to 4,336 in 1980. Former students

The Memorial Building, Southwestern Baptist Theological Seminary, stands as a symbol of the world's largest seminary.

serve in ministries in every state of the union and on the six major continents of the world. Students represent each of the 50 states and more than 30 foreign countries, as well as 480 under-graduate colleges, universities and conservatories.

Southwestern Seminary has a deep concern for the people of the world and an openness to new strategies, teaching techniques and ministries that will continue to carry it forward in the future as a strong force in theological education.

Southwestern Bell Telephone Company

Fort Worth: A leader in telecommunications

On March 10, 1876, Alexander Graham Bell spoke his historic words — "Mr. Watson, come here I want you." His words marked the invention of the telephone and within months of their speaking, Fort Worth became a leader in communications. Fourteen months after Bell unveiled his incredible invention, Fort Worth had telephones.

An unknown Southwestern Bell lineman poses with lineman J. O. Jones, right.

An early day switchboard.

Bell developed the first commercial phone in 1877. It was a square wooden box with a round opening that served as both transmitter and receiver. You talked into the opening, then placed your ear to it and listened. There was no bell. To get attention at the other end of the line the caller thumped the box, tapped it with a pencil or small wooden mallet.

Two such telephones were installed in Fort Worth in May 1877. One connected the home of W. B. Brooks at Weatherford and Pecan with his drug store at Second and Houston. The other linked the *Fort Worth Democrat's* newsroom with the Club Room, a saloon on Main Street, about 200 feet away.

Banks, hotels, City Hall and livery stables were quick to add the new gadgets. Then, in September 1881, only five years after Bell uttered his famous words, the first telephone exchange or switching center was opened in Fort Worth. The late Dr. J. R. Field had phone number one in that exchange established by Southwestern Telegraph and Telephone Company. The system had 40 customers.

During the early 1900s Fort Worth proved attractive to telephone companies and at one time the city had as many as three competing companies. Customers soon found it impractical to be served by two or three telephone companies in a town. Customers of one firm were unable to call customers of a competing firm. The trend to centralize began and by 1920 Southwestern Bell Telephone Company had taken over the properties and has operated the city's communications system since.

During those days it often took hours to make a call to a distant city. Today, the people of Fort Worth call throughout the nation with a few flicks of the finger in a matter of seconds. International Direct Distance Dialing is available to several of the world's foreign countries, making calls of thousands of miles quicker and easier than telephoning across the street a few years ago.

Six years after Southwestern Bell took over the city's telephone service, a new building was erected at Eleventh and Throckmorton. Part of this space is now occupied by the company's sixteen-story, blocklong building which serves as the major long distance switching center for the area.

Fort Worth was among the first of the major cities in Texas to receive modern dial telephones — in May 1932.

Fort Worth marked another communications milestone in 1960 when it became the first major city in the Southwest to install a system which permitted customers to dial virtually all their own long distance calls.

Fort Worth customers can call direct on a local basis to all telephones in Tarrant County as well as parts of Johnson, Parker and Dallas counties. An optional metro service allows customers to call and be called by all telephones in the Dallas area without a message charge.

Each section of the metropolitan area is served by modern switching centers. More than 60 percent of Fort Worth's telephone customers are now served by the very latest in electronic switching equipment. Plans are to convert the entire area to electronic switching systems within the next few years. This modern switching equipment gives customers the availability of a wide variety of special custom calling features, such as call transfer, call waiting, conference calling and speed calling.

Fort Worth and Southwestern Bell have been linked since their formative stages, growing together, both making sure its business and residential communities receive the best possible service.

Southwestern Exposition and Fat Stock Show

Show is nation's oldest continuously held annual livestock exposition

Home of Southwestern Exposition and Fat Stock Show on Amon Carter Square.

Show cattle in the early 1900s.

Progress in the livestock industry is synonymous with the growth of the Southwestern Exposition and Fat Stock Show and the city of Fort Worth. In 1896, the initial year of the exposition, purebred livestock was becoming serious business and the community was beginning to flourish as a major trade center.

Early day ranchers Captain W. S. Ikard of Henrietta, I. J. Kimberlin of Sherman, Colonel J. W. Burgess of Fort Worth and Colonel B. C. Rhome of Denton County originated a one-day livestock show in March in open-air facilities in North Fort Worth, adjacent to the Fort Worth Stock Yards. The founders believed the show would offer a central meeting place where animals could be judged for quality and stockmen could compare breeding and feeding practices.

The show became known as the Texas Fat Stock Show, then Fort Worth Stock Show, and later National Feeders and Breeders Show. Its present name was adopted in 1918. Sam Burk Burnett, founder of the famous 6666 Ranch, was the first president.

New impetus to the show's growth came in 1908 when the North Side Col-

iseum was erected as an indoor judging arena. Stockyard pens continued to be used as stalls. In 1918, directors staged a rodeo contest, and The World's Original Indoor Rodeo was presented twice daily in the coliseum. The Fort Worth rodeo has consistently been the leader in innovations that have upgraded the sport. Today more than 121,000 spectators annually attend 22 performances, and some 800 cowboys compete for more than $189,000 in prize money.

The show's only silent year was 1943 when all buildings were used for the World War II effort. That year the show moved to the Will Rogers Memorial Center on Fort Worth's West Side, opening there in March 1944.

Permanent facilities at its new home included a coliseum, tower, auditorium and one exhibit barn which the show's late board chairman, Amon G. Carter, had been instrumental in achieving for the city as part of the 1936 Texas Centennial observance. No other man had as great a part in the progress of the show as Carter, who was initially named chairman in 1946 and served until his death in 1955.

The show, a non-profit, educational organization, turned its profits into improvements which were deeded to the city, then leased back at showtime. Under

direction of the late W. R. Watt, president from 1946 until his death in 1977, the show expanded on the 100-acre Will Rogers site. Today the plant has more than 39 acres under roof, making the area the largest municipally-owned complex of its kind in the nation.

In traditions established by their fathers, the show today is directed by Amon G. Carter Jr. as chairman and W. R. Watt Jr. as president-manager.

The Stock Show and Rodeo now begins its annual twelve-day run on Wednesday preceding the final Friday of January. Thousands view the World's Longest All-Western Parade (over two hours and some 1,400 horses), made up of riding clubs, bands, and animal-drawn wagons and floats.

More than 15,000 head of livestock compete for premiums in excess of $165,000. It's the festive exhibition and entertainment of the year for some 600,000 visitors. The show has drawn competitors and visitors from over 40 nations. Local economy is boasted by an estimated $100 million in new dollars annually from show visitors.

An educational avenue, aside from livestock entries, is participation by students from junior and senior agricultural colleges throughout the nation, and Texas 4-H Club and Future Farmers of America members in a variety of judging team competition that provides actual practice of classroom theory.

Looking forward, the Southwestern Exposition and Fat Stock Show marks progress based on experience. Management constantly improves facilities and offers top premiums as incentive in all show divisions to keep Fort Worth in the forefront as one of the nation's major livestock exhibitions.

Tandy Corporation

Family business grew into world's largest chain of consumer electronics stores

Fort Worth had become a key distribution center, serving the growing markets of West and Southwest Texas, when two young men started a modest shoe shop supply business here in 1918. Norton W. Hinckley and David L. Tandy nurtured the Hinckley-Tandy Leather Company through the Roaring Twenties, the Depression Thirties and the Wartime Forties, building a sales force which called on boot and shoe manufacturers and repairers throughout the state. In 1947 annual sales of the company were almost $1 million.

In that year, the 29-year-old son of D. L. Tandy returned to Fort Worth and the family business after a degree at Texas Christian University, graduate studies at Harvard Business School and six years active duty as a naval officer. Charles D. Tandy obtained permission to develop a leathercraft division, having observed

David L. Tandy was co-founder of Hinckley-Tandy Leather Company in 1918.

Charles D. Tandy was primarily responsible for transforming family shoe shop supply business into an international corporation.

during his navy travels the growing use of leather and leather-working materials in therapy and hobby programs of army and navy hospitals, recreation centers and schools. The division would also cater to the postwar civilian interest in do-it-yourself projects.

In 1950, after two years of experimenting with mail-order sales and developing pilot leathercraft stores in El Paso and San Antonio, D. L. and Charles Tandy formed the Tandy Leather Company and removed themselves from the shoe shop supply business. The new venture prospered so that by 1955 sales were $8 million, earnings exceeded $500,000 and several manufacturing facilities had been added. There were then 75 Tandy Leather stores throughout the United States, each with a manager who had been invited to own 25 percent of the investment in his store, which was separately incorporated.

To provide liquidity for the founding Tandys and for their scores of employee-investors, and to provide a single corporate structure in which the business could be operated, all the interests in Tandy Leather Company were sold to the American Hide and Leather Company of Boston in late 1955. By 1959, after the liquidation of two leather tanneries in New England, Tandy Leather Company became the principal business of the company, and Charles Tandy was named chairman and chief executive officer. In 1960 the name of the company was changed to Tandy Corporation, and the headquarters were moved to Fort Worth.

Under Charles Tandy's leadership, the company grew through expansion and acquisition during the 1960s until it encompassed a total of 37 different companies by 1970, including Fort Worth's Leonard's, Mitchell's and Meacham's department stores, the Stafford-Lowdon Printing Company, the Royal Tile Company, the Woody Taylor Vending Company, the Tandy Leather Company, and the American Handicrafts/Merribee Company.

By 1971 it was quite clear that the Radio Shack consumer electronics company, which had been acquired in Boston in 1963 and headquartered in Fort Worth in 1968, had become the dominant business of Tandy Corporation. Accordingly,

Still under development in downtown Fort Worth is the eight-block Tandy Center, headquarters of Tandy Corporation and its Radio Shack Division.

from 1971 through 1975 — by sale, liquidation, and spin-off to shareholders — Tandy Corporation disposed of all activities other than the Radio Shack consumer electronics business.

Radio Shack continued to expand, developing into the world's largest chain of consumer electronics stores. By 1980 it had more than 7,500 retail outlets in this country and abroad, 25 factories, more than 24,000 employees, and sales of nearly $1.4 billion.

The last project of Charles Tandy was the creation of the eight-block Tandy Center complex in downtown Fort Worth in the late 1970s. For the first time in his business career, he occupied a permanent headquarters office, enjoying it for one year until his untimely death in 1978 at age 60.

Fort Worth was home to two gifted merchants, D. L. and Charles Tandy. During their lifetimes they gave of their abilities and their substance to the people and the organizations of Fort Worth, and the corporation which bears their name and imprint continues to do so.

Texas Christian University

Pioneering spirit a measure of the future

The school that became Texas Christian University had roots in Fort Worth, but was 37 years old before it found a permanent home in the city.

In 1869 a group of Fort Worth citizens invited Addision and Randolph Clark to set up a private school in the village. The Clark brothers quickly accepted. They were in their middle 20s, had gone to Carlton College after service with the Confederate Army. Addison was newly married, and they sought a new life in a new land. The young preacher-teachers came and taught classes in the first church built in the raw cattle town. With their father's help, they planned a permanent, higher-level academy and bought a plot of land for it.

All seemed well. But the boomtown atmosphere that came with the railroad led them to question their choice of a home. A disreputable area known as Hell's Half Acre arose next to their building site, and the brothers sensed some discrimination because of their part in a still-new, non-creedal religious movement. A land developer 40 miles away — needing a good school to attract people to what he forecast would become a thriving community — made an attractive offer to the enterprising young men.

Thus in 1873 AddRan Male and Female College opened its doors — not in Fort Worth but at a spot called Thorp Spring. The institution was situated in a quiet valley with a spring-fed stream not far from Comanche Peak. This was the very edge of the settled land. To this frontier the Clarks brought studies in "Ancient Languages, English Language, Mathematics, Physical Sciences, Mental and Moral Sciences, and Social and Civil History." The year began with thirteen students; it ended with 117, many from Fort Worth.

The inclusion of women in the title may have been the first such emphasis on coeducation in the Southwest.

Though students came, income was low. Thorp Spring did not grow. The land developer threatened eviction. The Clark brothers and their wives sold their personal possessions and inheritances and built their own campus nearby. In 1889 the school formally affiliated with the Christian Churches of Texas and became AddRan Christian College.

But soon it became obvious that a site far from major transportation routes was a hindrance. Waco churchmen offered fi-

In about 1923, its twelfth year in Fort Worth, TCU's six-building campus still stood amid grazing land on the edge of the city.

In 1980, work on the 46th major building on campus was nearing completion. This is a sketch of the courtyard entrance to the J. M. Mondy Communication and Visual Arts Building.

nancial help to relocate to an abandoned college campus there. The school moved on Christmas Day 1895, with students, faculty and families getting to Waco on one of those railroads from which the Clarks had tried to escape when leaving Fort Worth.

Waco years were lean ones. The name was changed to Texas Christian University in 1902, when it counted 302 students — fewer than in most of the years in Thorp Spring. After a fire destroyed the main building in March 1910, the trustees accepted an offer to move to Fort Worth. After a year occupying buildings near the County Courthouse, the school moved into three buildings about three miles southwest of downtown. TCU has been an integral part of the city and the Southwest ever since.

It adopted the struggling Fort Worth Medical College in 1912, then dropped it

in 1918 due to costs. It began a law school in 1915, closing it in 1920. But the Brite College of the Bible founded in 1914 became one of the most respected graduate seminaries in the country, educating more ministers for the 850,000-member Christian Church (Disciples of Christ) than any other. In 1922 the University won high academic recognition by election to the Southern Association of Colleges and Schools, the regional accrediting agency. That same year it was also elected a member of the Southwest Athletic Conference.

In 1923 its future was assured by a large gift from Mrs. Mary Couts Burnett.

The School of Business was organized in 1938 and Harris College of Nursing in 1946. Both have gained honors nationally. The School of Fine Arts is recognized widely, especially for music and ballet, and the School of Education is known for its programs with the learning disabled.

During the decade beginning in the mid 1930s, TCU played five bowl games in ten years. The 1938 team outscored opponents 269 to 60, was never behind except in the Sugar Bowl game — which it won — and was named the national championship team.

In the late 1940s and the 1950s, TCU expanded facilities to accommodate increased enrollment. In the 1950s and 1960s it carried out a major thrust in upgrading academic quality. By 1970 it was ranked among the country's true university-level institutions, based on doctorates awarded. It was also awarded a chapter of Phi Beta Kappa, the most prestigious and selective of undergraduate honor societies. By 1980 TCU was one of only fourteen church-related institutions that could point to both achievements. By 1980 TCU students, about 5,800 each semester, were coming from all states and many countries, with more than half the freshmen from outside Texas. Its faculty was highly reputable. Its budget was balanced. One major building was under construction and another planned, filling the last major facility need of the 243-acre, 60-building campus.

With a comparatively low student-faculty ratio, TCU continues to insist that yes, it can provide both the university-level challenges of major institutions and the person-centered concerns of smaller colleges — in a value-centered environment.

It's a different kind of pioneering now, but Addison and Randolph Clark and the Fort Worth citizens who first called them to it would understand. And they'd go for it.

Texas Electric Service Company

Old reliable now energizes a growing metropolis

The first electric lamps began glowing in Fort Worth in 1886, marking the beginning of a new era. The first electric system in Fort Worth was built about three years after Thomas A. Edison's central station was installed in New York City.

While gas lighting predated electric lamps in Fort Worth by almost ten years, growing sentiment favored replacing gas lights with electric lights. Conflicts arose between the city's electric company and gas company. In 1889 Fort Worth Electric Light and Power Co. and Fort Worth Gaslight Co. merged. The new company was named Fort Worth Light & Power Co.

A competing electric company was established in early 1893 when the city council granted a franchise to Standard Light & Power Co. Citizens Light & Power was formed in early 1900, with another electric company, Consumers Lighting & Heating, coming in 1905.

An important factor in the electric industry in Fort Worth was the development of the electric street railways. The first trolley lines were installed in the city only three years after Fort Worth's first electric plant went into service.

As the streetcar systems and power companies developed in Fort Worth, a group of financiers headed by J. R. Nutt, a prominent Cleveland banker, began acquiring and consolidating electric properties in Fort Worth under the name of

This two-story brick building, shown decorated with flags and bunting to welcome Stock Show visitors, was located at Ninth and Commerce streets. The building was headquarters for the company until 1929.

North Main Power Plant in the late 1920s after several additions had been made to the original plant. The spray pond across the Trinity River from the plant is now the location of Dillard's parking lot.

Citizens Railway & Light Co. Citizens Light & Power was acquired in 1906, followed by Consumers and Fort Worth Light & Power in 1910.

Then in 1911, Citizens Railway & Light Co., which had encountered financial difficulties, was liquidated. A court-ordered auction of all the company's properties resulted in a major break-through toward orderly development of utilities. For the first time, different interests owned electric, gas and transportation properties; with Fort Worth Power & Light (organized by Nutt & Associates) owning the electric facilities; Fort Worth Gas Co., all gas properties; and Northern Texas Traction Co. (which operated city streetcars and interurbans to Dallas and Waco), all street railways.

The mid-1920s brought sweeping changes to the Fort Worth area. Cars, buses and better highways led to a gradual decline in electric streetcar traffic. Eventually the electric railways were shut down and their electric properties sold.

As population in North Central and West Texas grew, independent power and light companies began springing up. The demand for electricity continued to increase rapidly, and soon many small electric companies were unable to meet the demand. So in 1926, several companies combined to form one large company. This company consolidated with the Fort Worth Power & Light Co. three years later, on December 19, 1929, and formed the present Texas Electric Service Company.

North Main Power Plant, located on the Trinity River north of the Tarrant County Courthouse, was the largest power plant operated by Texas Electric until 1948 when Handley Power Plant was also expanded.

As Fort Worth grew, the population served by the company in West Texas also continued to grow. Eventually, six division offices were established in Fort Worth, Wichita Falls, Eastland, Sweetwater, Big Spring and Midland.

In 1945, Texas Electric, along with Dallas Power & Light and Texas Power & Light, became part of the Texas Utilities Company System.

Through the years, Texas Electric has grown along with Fort Worth, helping establish the city as a center of industrial, economic and cultural expansion.

Texas Refinery Corp.

Business by the Golden Rule is key to company's growth

The eye-catching red, white and blue drums of Texas Refinery Corp. can be found from Zanzibar to Oslo and from Tokyo to St. Lucia. What was just a gleam in the eyes of two ambitious young Texans in 1922 has grown into a multi-million dollar international organization doing business in more than one hundred countries of the free world.

One of these founding fathers was A. M. Pate, Sr., a successful salesman for an oil company in Dallas. He teamed up with Carl Wollner, whose keen business mind complimented Pate's sales ability.

Together they came to Fort Worth to form their new company, Panther Oil & Grease Mfg. Co. — now Texas Refinery Corp.

The Panther Grease Manufacturing Company original building, 1922.

When the doors were opened on September 9, 1922, the company consisted of "Mr. Outside" — A. M. Pate Sr. and "Mr. Inside" — Carl Wollner.

The two founding fathers set the Golden Rule as a guiding policy, a business tenet that is still the basis of the company's operation. This conscientious regard for the welfare of customers, employees and stockholders has been complimented by products that have become by-words for quality among discriminating buyers.

A modest barn housed the office and manufacturing operations until 1928. Pate and Wollner at that time acquired a tract of land in the 800 block of North Main Street. When they moved to new headquarters at this address, there were 30 salesmen operating in 35 states.

The Great Depression was a difficult time for all businesses. But Texas Refinery did more than survive. Pate and Wollner kept the company growing and expanding. Not one employee was discharged because of the Depression. The post-Depression years saw a continuation of the growth pattern. New sales records were set only to be dwarfed by even more impressive volume feats.

The company officials decided to develop a new product line in 1934. In addition to the established specialty oil and grease products, the manufacture of protective coatings and related building maintenance items was begun.

About 1939 the company began exploring the world market. First the Export Department began shipments to our North and Central American neighbors. Then came orders from South America, and Europe and the rest of the world.

The first foreign corporation — Texas Refinery Corp. of Canada Limited — was established in 1948. Office and factory facilities were opened in Toronto. A. M. Pate, Jr. was elected president of the new company. Under his enthusiastic leader-

A. M. Pate, Sr. (left) and Carl Wollner (right), founders of Texas Refinery Corp.

ship the familiar growth pattern was established in Canada. In 1960 Texas Refinery Corp. of Mexico, S. A. was formed with offices and factory in Mexico City.

The European market continued to grow. So, in 1962, Texas Refinery Corp. Inter-Continental, S. A. was incorporated with offices and factory in Luxembourg. From this base, shipments go to many countries of the free world.

A. M. Pate, Jr. was elected president of Texas Refinery Corp. and its international affiliates in 1965. Under his diligent guidance, the company has enjoyed its greatest growth. Now the Texas Refinery industrial empire boasts eighteen affiliated companies with products ranging from photo albums to roof coatings.

The company and its officers are in the forefront of virtually every civic undertaking, providing leadership as well as financial support. A. M. Pate, Jr. is known as

one of the city's leading philanthropists. He was general chairman of the Fort Worth Centennial Celebration, has received honorary Doctor of Law degrees from two universities, and the Order of Merit from the Grand Duchy of Luxembourg.

The future looks equally bright. In 1980 Wesley Sears became president and chief operating officer and A. M. Pate, Jr. became chairman of the board and chief executive officer. Their plans include a new modern multi-million dollar manufacturing facility.

Born in the Roaring '20s, destined to endure depression, wartimes, boom, bust, inflation and deflation, Texas Refinery has become one of the city's most respected industries. Its worldwide acceptance is further evidence that "business by the Golden Rule" is good business for everyone involved.

Texas Wesleyan College

A vision of excellence

Texas Wesleyan College, from its founding to its present dynamic growth, has built positive change on a strong foundation of tradition. The tradition is one of concern for individuals, linked with intense dedication to a dream.

In 1890 Bishop Joseph S. Key dreamed of a college which would be committed to the professional and ethical develop-

ment of students in both liberal arts and the trades. In September 1891, Bishop Key's dream was fulfilled with the establishment of Polytechnic College, "polytechnic" meaning literally "many arts and sciences." The college was located in a pastoral setting on a hill overlooking Fort Worth. The large tract of land was donated by prominent area citi-

zens who shared the dream.

But in the financial panic of 1893, much of the generous land endowment — used as collateral for loans — was forfeited as the notes became due. However, unwavering belief in the dream by the board of trustees, area financial supporters and the president, helped the college to survive and to build a tradition for academic ex-

The campus of Texas Wesleyan College was enchanced in 1917 with the building of Dan Waggoner Hall. After standing vacant for sixteen years, however, it was restored in 1979 (inset).

cellence that continues to this day.

In 1911 a decision was made to establish a major Methodist university in Texas. When Southern Methodist University was founded in Dallas, Polytechnic College became the first Methodist women's college in Texas. On September 14, 1914, it was renamed Texas Women's College. The tradition of concern for the professional and ethical development of every student continued without dimming through all the years of the Depression — a time when many students enrolled on credit and faculty received their salaries in room and board. Though the

financial difficulties nearly brought an end to the college, the dream survived in the hearts of students and faculty who demanded that the doors remain open.

Then in September 1934, men were again admitted to the college to provide enrollment increases and a wider financial base. And once more the name was changed — this time to Texas Wesleyan College.

Under the able and resourceful direction of President Law Sone, who served Wesleyan for more than 30 years, the college's debts were cleared and an endowment was established. The dream was preserved.

Dr. Jon H. Fleming, who became president of Wesleyan in 1978, has built mightily on that dream. The Wesleyan tradition of dedication to the professional and

ethical development of individuals is foremost in the vision he holds for the college's present and future. That vision is nurtured through a "master plan" which includes renovation of historical buildings, construction of new structures and the continual development and improvement of programs to further increase the professional preparation of students.

As President Fleming states, "We have a vision of the future — and a people or an institution, or even an individual without a yearning such as this, cannot prosper. We know very well where we've been, are aware of where we are, and now we have more than just a notion of where we are going." On such a belief and with such a vision are the dreams of excellence built.

United Way of Metropolitan Tarrant County

Improving Fort Worth's quality of life through six decades

The year was 1922. Woodrow Wilson was president, "Tea for Two" was everyone's musical favorite and a four-piece suit cost $25. In Fort Worth, a group of concerned community leaders convened to attempt a consolidation of the many fund-raising drives conducted by local voluntary health, welfare and social development organizations.

Among the organizations included in the first Fort Worth Community Chest, forerunner of United Way of Metropolitan Tarrant County, was the First Texas Council of Camp Fire Inc. Dressed in the bloomer uniform of the day, a 1930 Camp Fire girl takes aim during an archery session at Camp Civitan, the early Camp Fire resident camp situated on Lake Worth.

The goal was to eliminate the waste and frustration which resulted from competing and overlapping demands for volunteer time and effort. The Fort Worth Community Chest — first Chest in the Southwest and forerunner of today's United Way of Metropolitan Tarrant County — evolved from their efforts.

In all, seventeen agencies ranging from the Boy Scouts to the Salvation Army benefited from the Community Chest's first year in Fort Worth. The 1923 campaign goal was $188,000, a far economic cry from the 1979 figure of $9.4 million which surpassed all previous campaign goals.

In 1931 several new organizations joined the Chest. The addition of the Mexican Presbyterian Mission and Council of Negro Charities reflected the city's diverse ethnic mixture and the emphasis by the Chest on efficient use of contributors' money and continuing responsiveness to changing community needs.

For example, United Way's 1933 budget of $285,800 included emergency grants for unemployment relief and lunches for underprivileged school children during the Depression. Funds also were allocated for distribution of government flour. As World War II raged in Europe, United Way assumed responsibility for raising War Chest funds here at home and disbursed more than $131,000 to ten different national appeals in 1943.

The year 1952 saw the beginning of a major change in Fort Worth fund raising. The Community Chest had raised $13.8 million during its 30-year history but de-

cided to delegate its fund-raising responsibilities to a new organization, Tarrant County United Fund and Community Services. Two years later, satisfied that United Fund had proven itself to be a successful operation, the Chest dissolved and relinquished its remaining allocation duties to United Fund. Community Chest's 33 agencies consolidated with the nine supported by United Fund.

United Fund grew beyond its fund-raising and allocation responsibilities between 1954 and 1973. Complex community needs demanded the creation of new human services, more intensive evaluation of services being delivered already and implementation of short- and long-range planning. In 1973 United Fund adopted its current name to promote a common identity with similar organizations across the country — which had been operating under 134 different names.

Though the titles and times have changed, United Way's basic philosophy of stewardship has not. It remains a locally-owned, private corporation administered by a cross-section of volunteers whose goal is to raise the most money possible to benefit the most people possible at the least possible cost. In accomplishing this mission, it spends only 7.5 cents of every dollar on campaign and year-round administration costs.

Through United Way's research, plan-

YMCA "Gospel Wagon" in 1920s, in front of St. Patrick's Cathedral.

ning and allocation functions, duplication of community services is eliminated and efficient and appropriate agency spending is promoted. The entire process, including establishment of service priorities and fund disbursement, is accomplished by county residents who donate their time. Aided by a relative handful of professionals, more than 18,000 volunteers from all walks of life participate in the local United Way process.

The fruit of their labor can be seen in the work of 126 United Way-supported service centers which benefit people throughout Tarrant County and northeast Johnson County. The spirit of their concern is indicated by the 20 consecutive years that organization has achieved its fund-raising goal on time. One of 2,300 United Ways in America, United Way of Metropolitan Tarrant County ranks among the top 28 — those which raise $9 million or more annually.

Tarrant County continues to grow, and new needs are constantly emerging which must be addressed. In preparing to meet these changing conditions, United Way began a long-range planning process in December 1977. The eighteen-month project made recommendations for 1980 to 1984 and provided a procedure by which the organization can remain vital and responsive during the rest of the century. In this way, the diligent community concern embodied in nearly 60 years of successful United Way operation will continue to improve the quality of life in Tarrant County.

The Waples-Platter Companies

From frontier commissary
to food industry conglomerate

This turn-of-the-century salesman's buggy is emblazoned with two of the Waples-Platter brand names originated during the company's earliest years.

In 1872 big business in Denison, Texas was Katy railroad construction and the Hanna-Owens Company, a commissary supplying provisions for the crews and settlers. Andrew Fox Platter arrived on the scene in 1878. Impressed by the area's potential, he went to work for the commissary and purchased an interest four years later in 1882.

Young and enthusiastic over the future of the food distribution business, Platter persuaded fellow Missourian E. B. Waples to join him in 1885. Waples, his sons Paul and John, and a daughter who would become Mrs. A. F. Platter, arrived when the population of Texas had doubled in a decade to reach two million.

Over the next decade the company kept pace with the burgeoning Southwest, introducing its White Swan line of food products in 1886, incorporating as the Waples-Platter Grocery Company in 1891, and opening branches in three other towns. As cattle became the ranking industry, shifting growth toward Fort Worth, the company purchased a wholesale grocery there in 1893.

Early in this century the Waples-Platter Companies expanded territory and entered new fields, opening the Dallas warehouse in 1902, then three more branches in Texas and Oklahoma. Coffee roasting plants opened in 1906 and 1914. In Fort Worth, on a 27-acre tract acquired in 1912, would evolve one of the nation's most modern food-processing plants. There the food processing division known as Great Western Foods opened in 1913, the label manufacturing division began production in 1915, and the container manufacturing division started in 1917.

Waples-Platter's solid, steady growth can be credited to its insistence on top product quality. When federal food and drug standards were enacted in 1906 — an event predicted by A. F. Platter in 1886 — White Swan products proved to equal or surpass federal levels.

Great Western Foods and its most famous product, Ranch Style Beans, were the brainchildren of Lloyd W. McKee, who headed the company from its founding until his death in 1934. Beans, condiments, rice and tea were processed, but McKee envisioned a unique product to distinguish the company. He introduced Ranch Style Beans in 1934 after three years of research. His vivid black and red packaging design has made Ranch Style products standouts on grocery shelves.

Related by marriage to the Waples family, McKee became the third generation to lead the Waples-Platter Companies, succeeding A. F. Platter on his retirement in 1929. That same year the corporate headquarters relocated to Fort Worth.

During the '30s the company initiated its refrigeration division and branched out into sponsorship of Clover Farm stores. In the '40s the service area was extended westward into New Mexico and southward in Texas.

From 1956 through 1976 under the leadership of Thomas M. Ryan, McKee's son-in-law, company growth accelerated with the aggressive management techniques and problem-solving orientation he brought from Ryan Mortgage Company, one of the oldest and largest mortgage banking firms in the Southwest. With the advent of the interstate highway system, branches were closed and consolidated into urban warehouses.

When the Dallas house closed to consolidate with a new Fort Worth facility, there was no room for the handful of institutional food salesmen handling this ancillary business. The separate foodservice division was born when the Dallas warehouse opened as the first White Swan distribution center in 1958. By 1960 the Lubbock and Austin centers were in operation.

Acquiring Ireland Foods in 1967, the processing division expanded its roster to include Ireland canned meats and then barbequed chili under the Ranch Style label. In 1971 the new bean processing plant opened with its seven-story hydrostatic cooker. Largest of its type in the world, the cooker has a 35,000 cans-per-hour capacity.

Today Waples-Platter is still a privately held corporation in its fifth generation of

Since the 1930s, a period of diversification and expansion for the company, fleets of trucks lined up at shipping docks have been a familiar daily scene.

family management, headed by John P. Ryan, chairman since 1976. Ryan is the great, great grandson of E. B. Waples and the grandson of Lloyd W. McKee. With a yearly growth rate of 20-25 percent, the company's annual sales exceeding the $600-million mark are generated by its divisions and subsidiaries. Retail distribu- tion is from two divisions, Waples North in Fort Worth and Waples West in Lubbock. Full-line foodservice distribution of the autonomous White Swan, Inc. subsidiary is from centers in Dallas, Austin, Lubbock and Houston. Other subsidiaries are Ranch Style, Inc., which continues to expand its product line, and Graphic Arts, Inc., now the Southwest's largest printer of labels for food products. An additional division, Waples-Platter Systems, was created in 1978 to handle the massive administrative and management tasks for the Southwest's leading distributor of retail and institutional foods.

Williamson-Dickie Manufacturing Company

Diversified international enterprise grew from modest start

Williamson-Dickie Manufacturing Company has grown steadily since its founding in 1918 as a small manufacturer of overalls. In that 62-year period, three generations of Williamsons have directed the growth as the company has diversified into hundreds of products that move to customers from worldwide plants, sales offices and warehouses.

C. N. Williamson and his partner and cousin, E. E. Dickie, initially organized U. S. Overall Corporation in Fort Worth in 1918 with other investors. By 1922, when annual sales were only $70,000, the two founders bought out the other investors and installed C. Donovan Williamson as general manager. The corporate name became Williamson-Dickie Manufacturing Company, and at that time the factory was a small building on Boaz Street with 35 workers.

During the ensuing years the company enjoyed steady growth, slowed only by the Great Depression. Expansion accelerated during World War II, however, as the company produced millions of uniforms for the nation's armed forces.

In converting to civilian production after the war, C. Don Williamson began a strategy of geographical extension, establishing new production facilities, warehouses and sales territories throughout the United States.

Highly specialized training programs, streamlined engineering methods and innovative machinery kept the company competitive in the increasingly demanding garment industry. At the same time, customer-oriented marketing programs were installed to ensure that consumer tastes would be satisfied by new fashions, styles and fabrics.

By 1950 matched work garments and jeans were augmented by casual clothes, and the "Dickies" label was advertised nationally via television, radio, and magazines. Total sales reached $15 million that year.

Diversification continued, with Dickies Work Clothes Rental Service starting up in 1954. This subsidiary's mission was to rent and launder work garments and other products for thousands of industrial workers in the Sunbelt.

Sales had climbed to about $20 million by the time of President C. Don Williamson's death in 1961.

After their father's death, C. Dickie Williamson became president and J. Donovan Williamson became executive vice president. The brothers continued the strategy of diversified growth into international markets.

Dick Williamson became chairman and chief executive officer in 1972, while Don Williamson became president. In 1977 the company acquired controlling interest of Blessings Corporation, New York City, along with M. Hoffman Company of Boston three years later. By 1980 the associated Williamson-Dickie companies (employing more than 7,000 people in the continental United States, Puerto Rico, Mexico, Belize, England, and West Germany) included more than 60 operating locations. Added to the product line were plastics manufacturing and the largest diaper service company in the nation.

Skilled and energetic management was a key element in the company's continued profitable growth. A partial list of the top management team includes W. T. Prowitt as president of the apparel manufacturing division; William G. Bush as vice president-finance; Charles M. Crane as vice president-sales; Clifton A. Whatley as vice president-manufacturing; David Lewis as president of Blessings Corporation; James Mason as president and Fleming Jones as executive vice president of Dickie's Industrial Services, and Harry Werst, consultant. Together this executive group led to consolidated sales of over $200 million in 1980.

"We've grown, but bigness alone has never been our major goal," says Dick Williamson. "We've pursued goals of profitability, sound financial condition, and personal management that make Williamson-Dickie a good place to work for all its employees."

"We are confident of continued growth," Don Williamson says, "but this company's roots will still be planted in Fort Worth, its historic home."

Williamson-Dickie's main plant — late 1940s

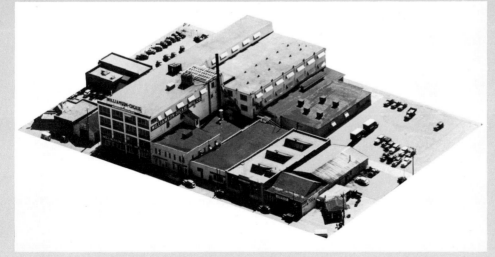

Woodbine Development Corporation

Achieving excellence in real estate development

In the fall of 1972, Ray L. Hunt set out to form a company for the development of his family's real estate holdings located in the prime growth areas of Tarrant and Dallas Counties. He began by assembling a group of three young businessmen to lead the new venture, and together they planned for an exciting future. Their goal for the company was simple — to strive for and achieve excellence in real estate development.

Hunt's father was the legendary oil figure, H. L. Hunt, whose fortune was established in 1921 with the discovery of oil in the Woodbine sands of East Texas. Thus, to give credit to its heritage, the new firm was founded as Woodbine Development Corporation in October of 1973.

Success came early. During the same month of its incorporation, Woodbine became a household word in north Texas with the public announcement of a project of grand proportions. The development, named Reunion, was built upon a forgotten 50-acre tract on the western fringe of downtown Dallas. By the spring of 1980, the development included Reunion Tower — a 50-story landmark, the Hyatt Regency Dallas — a 1,000-room luxury convention hotel, the restored Union Station, and Reunion Arena — a 19,500-seat special events center. Already an internationally-recognized model for revitalization efforts, Reunion will include office buildings, hotels and retail activities in the years ahead.

Continental Plaza at Seventh and Main Streets.

The Hyatt Regency Fort Worth at 815 Main Street.

With Reunion underway, Woodbine began work on its 1,500-acre Fossil Creek development in northeast Fort Worth. Officials of Motorola, Inc., were introduced to the project and liked its natural beauty and fine freeway location. In 1976 Motorola completed its 362,000-square-foot communications facility in Fossil Creek and became one of the largest industries in Fort Worth. It will soon be joined by Coca-Cola, Inc., whose installation will contain 305,000 square feet. Fossil Creek's future calls for a variety of uses — including research and development and light manufacturing facilities, offices, hotels, shopping and housing.

On the very day that Woodbine and Hyatt opened the Dallas property, officials of the two companies toured Fort Worth, giving serious consideration to the establishment of the Hyatt Regency Fort Worth. Long in need of luxury accommodations, the city had already been targeted by Hyatt as a key expansion site. When the historic Hotel Texas was offered for sale, they agreed that the right opportunity had presented itself. Woodbine purchased the dilapidated building in July of 1979.

The Hotel Texas, which opened in 1921, was for decades the social center of Fort Worth. Hyatt and Woodbine were able to look beyond its existing condition to see several advantages — immediate proximity to the Tarrant County Conven-

tion Center, the fondness Fort Worth citizens felt for the old hotel, and the unique opportunity to combine the history of the building with Hyatt's futuristic style. It was determined that the hotel's facade should remain unchanged, and the building was named to the National Register of Historic Places.

In contrast to its exterior, the hotel's interior was completely restored in a style which is both contemporary and western in flavor. Consisting of 530 guestrooms, the Hyatt Regency is Fort Worth's largest hotel, featuring an atrium rising six stories from the heart of the lobby to a sloping skylight, with a waterfall, pools and hanging gardens below. Other features include the 14,000-square-foot Grand Crystal Ballroom and the Crystal Cactus, an elegant specialty restaurant and cocktail lounge. The Hyatt Regency was the first completed element in a revitalization movement underway in downtown Fort Worth since the mid 1970s.

With the hotel nearing completion, Woodbine saw additional opportunity only one block north of the hotel site. There the company envisioned Continental Plaza, a 40-story office tower sheathed in emerald green reflective glass. Sitting diagonally on the site, with its front doors facing the historic corner of Seventh and Main, the building soon will be the home of Continental National Bank, a major Fort Worth financial institution since 1903. Construction began in the summer of 1980, with completion set for 1982.

In its brief history, Woodbine has already altered the skylines of two of the nation's leading cities. Additionally, the firm's suburban developments in Fort Worth, at Dallas-Fort Worth Airport and in north Dallas County, have made a significant impact upon the Metroplex. With a strong belief in Fort Worth and Dallas, Woodbine eagerly moves toward the future.

World Service Life Insurance Company

Diverse history, background gives depth to successful insurance operation

To many people in Fort Worth, this is the insurance company with the skyline weather forecaster.

Yet, the World Service Life Insurance Company of the 1980s is much more. A dynamic, growing organization with a future as bright as Fort Worth today, its roots extend into three decades and three states.

Its formal corporate history reaches back to a company established in Colorado in 1936. "World Service Life" as a Fort Worth company first appeared in 1967 when the merger of a two-year-old Tennessee company — World Heritage Life — and an established Texas company — the Service Life Insurance Company — was finalized. WSL's home office was Fort Worth, Texas, where Service Life had been in operation since its incorporation in 1947.

Established as a limited capital company selling insurance to servicemen, Service Life was purchased by Fred B. Dickey, who became president and board chairman in 1949 just before the Korean War.

A young company with aggressive leadership, Service Life flourished. Represented by agents based throughout the U.S. and the world, and backed by a reputation for excellent service and prompt claim payment, Service Life became one of the most widely respected companies in the service insurance field. In less than three years, its business had skyrocketed 1700 percent to more than $35 million in force.

With such intense activity, Service Life quickly outgrew its original offices at Ninth and Houston. To accommodate the rapidly expanding business, the company purchased the Federal Center at 400 West Vickery in 1953.

When growth forced another move in 1964, Service Life acquired the Fair Building, the Oil and Gas Building, and the Fair parking garage in what was then the largest real estate transaction in downtown Fort Worth's history. Following extensive renovation, the Seventh and Throckmorton buildings, renamed the

Executive and administrative offices are in the Service Life Center complex, Seventh and Throckmorton. Atop the building, World Service Life's rotating weather sign gives National Weather Service forecasts 24 hours a day.

Service Life Center, became one of the most prestigious office facilities in the city.

Initially, the company housed entirely on two floors. Today, however, more than 600 employees occupy eleven floors of the complex, plus another downtown building.

Following the 1967 merger, World Service Life began an aggressive diversification program. While continuing its successful military operations, WSL extended its major lines of business to include credit insurance for farmers, ranchers, automobile dealerships, banks and credit unions, and group insurance for members of professional associations, such as the Southern Medical Association, American College of Surgeons, American Society of Clinical Pathologists and State Bar of Texas.

In addition, four casualty subsidiaries joined the corporation in 1973. These operations, including Early American Insurance Company and Tri-State General Agency, were moved from Louisiana to Fort Worth, where they presently occupy the 900 Monroe Street building.

Results of this expansion program were immediate and impressive. By 1969, WSL had become the first Fort Worth-based life company to pass the $1 billion insurance-in-force mark. Today, WSL has more than $4.5 billion in force, ranking in the top 8 percent of more than 1,750 life companies in the United States.

The groundwork for the World Service Life Insurance Company of today began in 1977. When WSL became part of the Western Preferred Corporation, an insurance holding company based in Denver, Colorado, it heralded the arrival of a new, progressive management team.

Led by Larry Tunnell, WSL's new president, the company continued expanding its established lines, placed new emphasis on involvement in ordinary protection in nonmilitary markets, and implemented new administrative controls, consolidations and automation designed to increase customer service and cost-effectiveness.

In 1978, WSL merged into another subsidiary of Western Preferred, United American Life Insurance. United American, incorporated in Colorado in 1936, changed its corporate title to World Service Life when the merger was finalized. Since that time, the new World Service Life has maintained corporate headquarters in Colorado, while administrative and executive operations remain in Fort Worth.

Tunnell, who is also president and chairman of the board of Western Preferred Corporation, states that long range goals for World Service Life and its parent include remaining an active and vital participant in the local business community. Although home offices will remain in Colorado, plans include the consolidation of many Western Preferred companies into the Fort Worth area.

The Civilized West

There are really two Fort Worths—
the Fort Worth beloved of so many,
of Cowtown and cowboy, saddles and stockyards.

And there is the new Fort Worth,
the civilized city which has sprung from the western roots—
the art museums and opera,
the skyscrapers and big businesses.

Sometimes they appear to be opposites and unrelated.
And yet, they are two sides of the same coin.
For they are both the heritage of yesterday,
nurtured by the spirit of a hungry people—
a people who dreamed large dreams,
a people whose children—
tomorrow's city citizens—
will carry in their bones
the same dreams of limitless possibilities of new life
and new empires,
carved from the Texas prairie
and the sturdy backbone of hide and horn.

Bibliography

Pioneer Fort Worth Texas. Lila Bunch Race, Taylor Publishing Co., Dallas, 1976.

Fort Worth: Outpost on the Trinity. Oliver Knight, University of Oklahoma Press, Norman, Oklahoma, 1953.

Early Days in Fort Worth. Unpublished manuscript of Charles Fred Laue.

The Indians of Texas: From Prehistoric to Modern Times. W.W. Newcomb, Jr., University of Texas Press, Austin, Texas, 1961.

Texas: Its Geography, Natural History and Topography. William Kennedy, esquire, Benjamin & Young, New York, 1844.

The Great Plains. Walter Prescott Webb, Ginn & Company, Boston, 1931.

The Indian Papers of Texas & The Southwest—1825-1916. Edited by Dorman H. Winfrey & James M. Day, Pemberton Press, Austin, Texas, 1966, Volume 1.

Fort Worth Star-Telegram. Historical Issue, February 25, 1973.

Fort Worth, Official Publication of the Chamber of Commerce. Centennial Issue, June, 1949.

The Story of Old Fort Worth. Howard Peak, The Naylor Co., San Antonio, 1936.

A Bank and a Shoal of Time. Published by the First National Bank.

A Guide to Historic Sites in Fort Worth & Tarrant County. Tarrant County Historical Society, Fort Worth, 1969.

Cowtown U.S.A. Gary L. Havard & Don A. Ryan, Fort Worth, Identity Arts, 1976.

Camp Bowie. Bernice B. Maxfield, Thomason & Morrow, 1975.

Fort Worth in the Civil War. James Farber, as published in the Star-Telegram, Peter Hansbrough Bell Press, Belton, 1960.

Fort Worth: A Frontier Triumph. Julia Kathryn Garrett, The Encino Press, Austin, 1972.

How Fort Worth Became the Texasmost City. Leonard Sanders, Amon Carter Museum of Western Art, Fort Worth, 1973.

The Longhorns. J. Frank Dobie, Little, Brown & Co., Boston, 1941.

The Chisholm Trail. Wayne Gard, University of Oklahoma Press, Norman, 1954.

The Wild Bunch. James E. Horan, New American Library, New York, 1970.

The Trail Drivers of Texas. J. Marvin Hunter, Cokesbury Press, Nashville, 1925.

The Raven: A Biography of Sam Houston. James Marquis, Bobbs-Merrill, New York, 1929.

Force Without Fanfare: The Autobiography of K.M. Van Zandt. Texas Christian University Press, Fort Worth, 1968.

A Twentieth Century History and Biographical Record of North and West Texas. B. B. Paddock, Lewis Publishing Company, Chicago and New York, 1906.

Early Days in Fort Worth, Much of Which I Saw and Part of Which I Was. B.B. Paddock, Fort Worth, privately published, n.d.

Longhair Jim Courtright, Two Gun Marshal of Fort Worth. Stanley Francis and Louis Crocchiola. World Press, Denver, 1957.

Reminiscences of the Early Days of Fort Worth. J. C. Terrell, Texas Printing Co., Fort Worth, 1906.

Indian Depredations in Texas. J.W. Wilbarger, The Pemberton Press, Austin, 1967, reprint of the 1889 edition.

In Old Fort Worth. Mack H. Williams, as published in the News-Tribune, 1976 and 1977.

Amon, the Life of Amon Carter, Sr. Jerry Flemmons, Jenkins Publishing Co., Austin, 1978.

The Story of the Frontier. Everett Dick, Tudor Publishing Co., New York, 1941.

Cow People. J. Frank Dobie, Little Brown & Co, Toronto & Boston, 1964.

Tread of the Longhorns. Walter Gann, The Naylor Co., San Antonio, 1949.

Cowboys and Cattleland. H.H. Holsell, The Parthenon Press, Nashville, 1937.

Texas Traditions. Ross Phores, Henry Holt and Company, New York, 1954.

The Cattleman. Mari Sandoz, Hastings House, New York, 1958.

Great Roundup. Lewis Nordyke, William Morrow & Co., New York, 1955.

Norfleet. J. Frank Norfleet, White Publishing Co., Fort Worth, 1924.

Pro Football's All-Time Greats. George Sullivan, G. P. Putnam's Sons, New York, 1968.

Great Quarterbacks of the NFL. Dave Anderson, Random House, New York, 1965.

College Football U.S.A.—1869-1971. Charles H. Pearson, editor-in-chief, Hall of Fame Publishing Co. in cooperation with McGraw-Hill, New York, 1972.

Hogan: The Man Who Played for Glory. Gene Gregston, Prentice-Hall, Inc., Englewood Cliffs, New Jersey, 1978.

"The Little Symphony That Could," W.L. Taitte, Texas Monthly, June, 1980, Austin, Texas.

Index

Acknowledgements

Fort Worth is a fascinating city with a history that's filled with the stuff fiction writers dream about. And so much of that storied past has been chronicled for the ages by writers and historians who care as much about yesterday as they do tomorrow.

A special debt of gratitude goes to Jerry Flemmons, whose writings of the Amon Carter era capture the lusty soul of Fort Worth, the way a lusty city wants to be remembered; to Leonard Sanders, who took the time and effort to put Fort Worth in its proper perspective; to Mack Williams, who dug up and published old eye-witness accounts of the early days in his *News-Tribune* of '76 and '77 and to Julia Kathryn Garrett and Oliver Knight whose works detailed the total picture of a growing frontier city perched on the banks of the unpredictable Trinity River.

Historical research for the book was aided greatly by the insight and cooperation of Ron C. Tyler, curator of history for the Amon Carter Museum of Western Art; Nancy G. Wynne, librarian for the Amon Carter Museum and Amy Simon, her assistant.

The files of the *Fort Worth Star-Telegram*—the columns of countless reporters, present and past— the Chamber of Commerce's *Fort Worth* magazine, the Fort Worth Public Library and the Mary Couts Burnett Library at Texas Christian University were also invaluable.

In addition, it was good to have access to so many words of B.B. Paddock, the frontier editor of the *Fort Worth Democrat* whose title of one book explains it all—*Early Days in Fort Worth, Much of Which I Saw and Part of Which I Lived.*

Delbert Bailey kept us informed on the Fat Stock Show and Rodeo. Mitchell A. Wilder, director of the Amon Carter Museum, graphically summarized its beginnings. Shirley Spieckerman tracked down the important story of the founding of the Kimbell Art Museum. Jerry Flemmons first pieced together the Cultural Acropolis of the Southwest. Norwood P. Dixon who researched and prepared vital information on the Van Cliburn Competition, the Fort Worth Symphony, the Fort Worth Opera Association, and the Texas Boys Choir. And the *Star-Telegram's* Jim Trinkle spilled the ironies of the Colonial National Invitational Tournament.

Fort Worth Public Library
   Patricia Chadwell
   Paul Campbell
Amon Carter Museum
   Marni Sandweiss   Peggy Booher
   Ginger Garrison   Beth Muskat
   Linda Lorenz
   Nancy Wynne
Texas State Historical Association, Austin
   Dr. L. Tuffly Ellis, Director
Special Collections, University of Texas at Arlington Library
   Robert B. Martin, Director
Tarrant County Historical Society
   Frank Goss, President
Fort Worth Museum of Science and History
   Don Otto, Director
Fort Worth Star-Telegram
W.D. Smith Photo
   Gordon Smith
Lee Angle Photography
   Mark Angle

The editors and publishers of *FORT WORTH: THE CIVILIZED WEST* wish to thank the special people who, by their interest and commitments, have contributed to this historical profile of this great Texas city. Our special thanks to author Caleb Pirtle whose humor, cooperation and dedication brought the book to life. Thanks to the staff and volunteer leadership of the Fort Worth Chamber of Commerce for their continuing support and assistance, including James R. Nichols, chairman of the board; Bill D. Serrault, vice chairman; Robert W. Gerrard, immediate past chairman; Bill R. Shelton, president; Neal Hall, communications vice chairman, without whom we might never have gotten started; Barbara Winkle, vice president, who handled the project with sensitivity for the chamber; her staff Linda, Spray, Patty and Barbara, who were all a great help; and to other staff members Susan, Peggy, Mary and Mary, Betty, Jeannie, Mike, Alva, Linda, Brenda and David; to the history book committee of the chamber which was headed by Neal Hall and included William E. Jary, Norwood Dixon and Jerry Gladysz and to Diane Thornton, who helped with great direction. And Gerald Crawford for his photographic contributions.

Others who contributed to the success of *FORT WORTH: THE CIVILIZED WEST* include Mark Angle, Marie Flagg, Sabrina Hong, Paula Sullivan, Dr. and Mrs. Gerald Marks, Cynthia Rainey, Connie Vann, Barbara Jameson, Doug Reese, who kept us on track, Frank Goss, Margaret Tingley, Sharon Garrick, Barbara Ellen, Carolyn Schenkler and special thanks to Leigh Flowe, Betty, Bob, Erich, Ger, Karres, Victoria, and of course to Myrtle.

Credits

Sources of photographs, maps and art appearing in this book are noted here in alphabetical order and by page number (location on the page is noted). Those photographs appearing in the chapter *Partners in Progress*, pages 177 through 231, were provided by the represented firms.

Amon Carter Museum: 4–5, 15, 23, 39, 53, 54 bottom, 55 middle and bottom, 61, 66, 80, 86 bottom left, 87 top, 93 bottom left, 95 bottom, 102, 106 top, 134 bottom, 136 bottom left, 139, 142 bottom, 146 top, 151 bottom left, 172 top inset, 175.
Bexar Archives: 26.
Bradford, Norman: 79.
Burkburnett Chamber of Commerce: 101.
Cantley, Sam B. III: 58, 104 top & bottom, 110 bottom, 114 top, 120–121.
Community Theater: 166 top left.
Crawford, Gerald: 8, 124 left, 140, 141 top, inset, 144 all, 145 all, 148 top & bottom, 152 all, 153 left & right, 156, 157 top & bottom, 160 top & bottom, 161 all, 164 top left, middle, right, 165 bottom right, 168 top & inset, 169 all, 171, 172 top, bottom, bottom inset, 173 all, 174.
Daughters of Republic of Texas Library: 16.
Deckey, Mrs. Bill: 85 left.
Dow, Greg: 63, 71, 73, 114.
Edwin and Bewley: 153 top left.
First National Bank: 88 middle.
Ft. Worth, City of: 170.
Ft. Worth Public Library: 2–3, 6–7, 22 top, 25, 31, 50, 54 bottom, 57 top & bottom, 59 right, 64, 67, 68, 75, 81, 83 top right, 84 top & bottom, 86 top middle, 87 bottom left, 96 top & bottom, 97 all, 98 all, 99 all, 100 all, 103 top right, 107 top left, bottom left, 110 top, 111, 112, 116, 120 inset, 122 top and bottom, 128 bottom, 130 bottom, 132 all, 133 top & bottom, 136 top, 141 bottom & inset, 143, 147, 149 top, 165 bottom left, 166 top right, 232.
Ft. Worth Museum of Science & History: 20, 59 left, 83 top left, 93 bottom left, 175, 240.
Ft. Worth Star Telegram: 46, 47, 51, 103 left, 105, 106, 115, 119, 137, 155 top & bottom, 166 bottom left.
Ft. Worth Ballet Association: 165 top.
Ft. Worth Art Museum: 167 top and bottom.
Ft. Worth Symphony Orchestra: 163 top & bottom.
Ft. Worth National Bank: 60 top & bottom.
Gilcrease Museum: 9, 11 top & bottom, 12 top & bottom, 13 top & bottom, 14 top & bottom, 21, 22, 24, 27, 29, 33, 35, 40, 41, 45, 55 top left, 76 bottom.
Gregory's Old Master Gallery: 38.
Hackney, John W.: 151 top left.
Hackney, Mrs. T.E.D.: 95 top.
Hudson, Mrs. Edward: 30, 88 bottom.
Huguely Hospital: 164 bottom.
Houston Public Library: 43.
Hutchison, Mrs. C.W.: 56 middle, 83 top middle.
Hutchison, Mrs. Virgile Pitner and Mrs. Martha Pitner: 83 top, 94 bottom right.
Jary, William E.: 130 top, 131.
King, Walter: 17, 48.
Library of Congress: 124, 127 all, 128, 134, 146.
Lone Star Gas: 118.

McCartney, Mrs. Catherine Terrell: 85 top.
McClean, Hunter: 88 top.
McClean, Dr. and Mrs. Malcolm: 37.
McPeak, Howard: 107 top right.
Martin Growald Architects: 158.
Minton, Joseph J.: 70, 85 middle right, 94 middle right.
National Archives: 19, 109 top & bottom.
Nunn, Dr. W. Curtis: 44.
Panhandle-Plains Historical Museum: 65.
Portwood, Mrs. Laura H.: 82.
Portwood, Mrs. W.H.: 85 middle.
Sandler Collection: 46 bottom.
Smith, W.D.: 49, 69, 76 top, 87 middle.
Tahmahkera, Benjamin: 77.
Texas Christian University: 150 left.
Texas Christian University, Sports Information: 136 bottom right, 138 all.
Texas & Pacific Railroad: 56 top.
Texas Rangers Baseball Club: 149 bottom left, bottom right.
Texas Refinery: 117.
Texas State Historical Association: 86 bottom right, 108 top and bottom, 109 inset, 121, 142 top, 150 bottom right, 151 top right, bottom right.
Turner, J.C.: 28.
Van Cliburn International Piano Competition: 162 top right & left.
Zeigler Collection: 126 all.

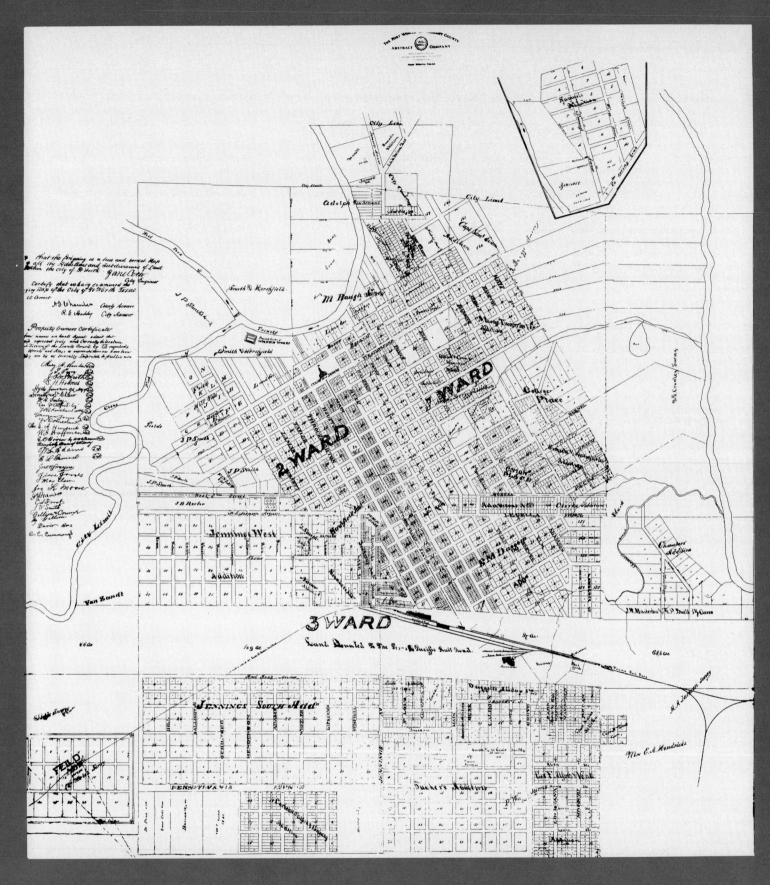

Concept and design: Continental Heritage Press, Inc., Tulsa, Oklahoma.
Printing and binding: Kingsport Press, Kingsport, Tennessee.
Type: Garamond.
Text sheets: Mead Offset Enamel.
Endleaves: Multicolor Textured/Chino.
Cover: Kingston Natural Linen by Holliston Mills.